Words with Music

Creating the Broadway Musical Libretto

Other books by Lehman Engel

Three Centuries of Choral Music: Renaissance to Baroque (1939)
The American Musical Theater: A Consideration (1967)
Planning and Producing the Musical Show (1966)
Getting Started in the Theater (1973)
This Bright Day: An Autobiography (1974)
Their Words Are Music: The Great Theatre Lyricists and Their Lyrics (1975)
The Critics (1976)
The Making of a Musical (1977)
Getting the Show On: The Complete Guidebook for Producing a Musical in
    Your Theatre (1983)

Other books by Howard Kissel

David Merrick: The Abominable Showman (1993)
Stella Adler: The Art of Acting (2000)

Words with Music

CREATING THE BROADWAY MUSICAL LIBRETTO

Lehman Engel

updated and revised by **Howard Kissel**

Applause Theatre & Cinema Books ■ New York

Words with Music: Creating the Broadway Musical Libretto
by Lehman Engel, updated and revised by Howard Kissel

The author gratefully acknowledges permission to reprint the following:
"Early Autumn." Words by Johnny Mercer, music by Ralph Burns and Woody Herman. ©1949 (Renewed) 1952 (Renewed) Cromwell Music, Inc., New York and Warner Chappell Music, Inc., Los Angeles, CA. Used by permission.
"The Elephant Song," from 70, GIRLS, 70. Words by Fred Ebb, Music by John Kander. ©1971 (Renewed) Trio Music Company, Inc. and Alley Music Corp. All rights reserved.
"Guilty Conscience." Words and music by Ronald Stein, Andre Young, and Marshal Mathers. ©1999 Colgems-EMI Music, Inc. All rights reserved. International copyright secured. Used by permission—contains elements of "Pigs Go Home" (Stein) ©1970 Colgems-EMI Music, Inc.
"Hello, Young Lovers," ©1951 by Richard Rodgers and Oscar Hammerstein II. Copyright renewed. Williamson Music owner of publication and allied rights throughout the world. International copyright secured. All rights reserved. Used by permission.

Book design by Mark Lerner

Library of Congress Cataloging-in-Publication Data

Engel, Lehman, 1910-
 Words with music : creating the Broadway musical libretto / by Lehman Engel ; updated and revised by Howard Kissel
     p. cm.
 Includes bibliographical references (p.   ) and index.
 ISBN-13: 978-1-55783-554-3 (pbk. original)
 ISBN-10: 1-55783-554-3 (pbk. original)
 1. Libretto. 2. Musicals—United States. 3. Broadway (New York, N.Y.)—History. I. Kissel, Howard. II. Title.

 ML2110.E6 2005
 782.1'40268—dc22

                          2005023666

Applause Theatre & Cinema Books
19 West 21st St.
New York, NY 10010
Phone: (212) 575-9265
Fax: (212) 575-9270
Email: info@applausepub.com
Internet: www.applausepub.com
Applause books are available through your local bookstore, or you may order at www.applausepub.com or call Music Dispatch at 800-637-2852

SALES & DISTRIBUTION
North America: Europe:
Hal Leonard Corp.   Roundhouse Publishing Ltd.
7777 West Bluemound Road   Millstone, Limers Lane
P. O. Box 13819   Northam, North Devon EX 39 2RG
Milwaukee, WI 53213   Phone: (0) 1237-474-474
Phone: (414) 774-3630   Fax: (0) 1237-474-774
Fax: (414) 774-3259   Email: roundhouse.group@ukgateway.net
Email: halinfo@halleonard.com
Internet: www.halleonard.com

To all participants past, present, and future in my
musical theatre workshops sponsored by Broadcast
Music, Inc. in New York, Los Angeles, Nashville, and
Toronto

L.E

ACKNOWLEDGMENTS

I would like to express my gratitude to Jeremiah Kaplan, whose initial interest in this book encouraged me to write it, to James Neyland for his editorial stimulation in developing it, to Margaret Webster for many stimulating discussions about Shakespeare, to Robert Meyer for his copy editing, and not least of all to Robert Bishop for his invaluable help in preparing the manuscript.

L.E.

ACKNOWLEDGMENTS TO THE REVISED EDITION

The first debt I must acknowledge—yet again—is to Glenn Young, who honored me by inviting me to update Lehman Engel's masterly text. Given what a tiny world the musical theater is, it does strike me as odd that Engel's path and mine never crossed. Knowing him, however, might have intimidated me further. I can only hope that he would approve of my observations.

Over the years I have learned an enormous amount every time I have entered Chartwell Booksellers, whose proprietor, Barry Singer, has turned his tiny space into one of the most astonishing bookstores anywhere in the world and one of the most civilized oases in Manhattan. It was Singer who created the cover image of this book for his own illuminating work about musicals, *Ever After*. For complicated reasons I inherited the photograph, which was taken in the studio of Adam Guettel and shows his grandfather's piano alongside his own electronic keyboard, a perfect image of the traditional and the contemporary.

As always, I owe more than I can express to the musician I married, with whom I first experienced many of the shows I have written about and whose insights added immensely to my understanding of them.

I would like to dedicate my portion of this book to the memory of my father, Leo Kissel, who died shortly before it was scheduled to come out. Had he been able to read it, I hope he would have seen how deeply he influenced my life by imparting to me from a very early age a love of all kinds of music.

H.K.

CONTENTS

1

Introduction

"I'm not really clever," said the parrot honestly. "But I hope to make the most of the brains I have. Have you ever thought of trying that?"

Eudora Welty
The Shoe Bird

Storytelling has, of course, assumed many forms: short story, novel, play, operetta, opera, musical show, and film, among many others. In presentation, the first two are non-theatrical; the last has not assumed a single form and has drawn principally on the first three for its material. On the other hand, plays, operettas, operas, and musical shows are all written specifically for the theatre. It is my intention to contrast plays and musicals in the light of what I believe to be their basic differences, and I contend that these are conditioned by their métiers, styles, forms, and—not in a derogatory sense—limitations. Perhaps their limitations (especially in the musical theatre) control their creation and, when they work well, contribute most conspicuously to their success. Talent or genius are certainly not to be discounted, but neither of these can be acquired. What can be learned is a set of viable principles that govern the working machinery. Talent without awareness of these principles is valueless.

In painting, the size and shape of the Sistine Chapel, together with the fact that the subject matter was limited to Biblical themes, caused Michelangelo to conceive his murals in a certain specific way. In my opinion these circumscriptions helped rather than frustrated the artist. I believe that there is nothing more frustrating for any artist than unlimited opportunity for expression.[1] Where does he begin and end? In music, Wagner is a good example of unrestricted meandering. He wrote longer operas than had been previously dreamed of in any nightmare, requiring a greatly expanded orchestra, and super voices that had been little known previously. Musically, he exploited the chromatic scale to hitherto undreamed-of wandering infinity.

J. S. Bach's greatest music is his church cantatas (more than two hundred), written specifically for the religious services that he was employed to complement. The orchestral size, the kind and number of soloists were limited to the available performers. Often they were numerous. Just as often they were few. But the quality of creativity never varied. The accomplishment of the job was—with a large or a small performing group—apt, resourceful, and, in the end, great.

The freedom enjoyed today in the arts has both good and bad effects. When artistic liberation consists of a gradual laying aside of out-of-date practices that the artist has previously and truly assimilated, his work will be at least interesting and meaningful because it will be disciplined in its own way. It will possess the rationale that will give evidence of an understandable structural foundation that has been inherited and found still to be basic and strong. Where our new experimental art may lead might very well be only the equivalent of a door-opener; it may not represent within itself an artistic milestone. But it will, if it has any comprehensible logic, serve a major purpose in envisaging the future and pointing clearly toward it.

The principal trouble today with music of a currently popular and quasi-theatrical nature is that, in spite of its wide and even frantic acceptance, it has retrogressed. Its harmonic spectrum, melodic profile, and rhythmic patterns are as limited as the music of Protestant hymnology a century ago, and its dynamic range is from loud to loudest.

The public for today's popular music is a demanding and fickle one (despite its fanatical show of devotion), but most of the music and its performers that succeed spectacularly and immediately have a way of vanishing just as quickly and forever. What is best about some of the songs in the contemporary pop genre are the lyrics, which are often fresh and meaningful. The music seems only to negate the immediate past, providing nothing of itself of any particular stature. It is small, repetitious, and, although earsplittingly raucous, ephemeral.

Most of the finest art has been made for a designated space, an occasion, a time, a place, a person, or a purpose. For centuries the best artists earned their livelihoods not by yearning, threatening suicide or feigning epilepsy in an effort to obtain next to impossible materials but by fulfilling precise assignments while utilizing readily available means.

In earlier times the taste of the aristocratic minority which provided the financing seems also to have satisfied the majority—the people themselves. This was certainly true of the Greek tragedies, the works of da Vinci and Michelangelo, the cantatas of Bach, the "operas" of Monteverdi and the later ones of Mozart, Rossini, Donizetti, and many more. Shakespeare and the madrigal lyricists and composers in all countries appealed to people everywhere.

Today it is different. In the theatre alone we have traditionalists among playwrights and composers. We have off-Broadway, which often experiments, and off-off-Broadway, which does little else. The traditional theatre satisfies the larger audience groups despite the fact that the most important writers are themselves undergoing an evolutionary period. Evolutionary or no, they have their formal roots in the past although their subject matter and style face toward the future.

Although there are numerous theatres both off-Broadway and off-off-Broadway, they seldom seat more than two hundred—many under one hundred—so that a well-off Broadway show accommodates six to eight times as many customers as the lesser theatres may at every single performance.

A few of the non-Broadway *new* shows are representative of talent, genuine new ideas, and skill, but these are in the minority. Many try to make a go of their productions on a sensational or shock basis, but sensation and shock for their own sake, wherever they occur, possess the sharpness of gums without teeth.

The average audience to be found in each of these three theatres is by no means representative of a single group despite occasional overlaps. The majority of *Company*-goers (forward-looking semi-establishment musical) is seldom found in the outer-area theatre. On the other hand people who enjoy musicals might be disposed to *Company* (on Broadway) and *The Last Sweet Days of Isaac* (off), and even possibly something with music at Café La Mama. But it is the "with" music that tells the tale, or is the rue with a difference, and indicates to a great extent why *Fiddler on the Roof* plays simultaneously in New York, Los Angeles, London, Tokyo, Amsterdam, and Vienna.

Until about twenty years ago it was unthinkable that American musicals might have any appeal abroad. Increasingly, the best ones are now being reproduced throughout the world to great acclaim. In terms of musicals by Richard Rodgers alone, there have been Japanese productions of *South Pacific*, *Oklahoma!*, *The King and I*, *The Sound of Music*, and *No Strings*; Australian productions of *The Boys from Syracuse*, *Carousel*, *The King and I*, and *The Sound of Music*; and a successful Israeli run of *The King and I*. The hot-ticket items today in many countries of Europe and Asia are *My Fair Lady*, *Fiddler on the Roof*, and *Man of La Mancha*.

When one thinks of *My Fair Lady* in Turkish, *Man of La Mancha* in French, and *Fiddler* in Japanese, a number of important questions arise: How do a Cockney flower girl and her snobbish speech-teacher friend find empathy in a poor country like Turkey? How does a musically very American version of a Spanish classic find favor with supercritical French audiences? How does a Spanish classic find favor with supercritical French audiences? How does a show about Russian Jews at the turn of the century relate to Japan?

The answers to these questions are to be found in two considerations: the universality of the original material, a quality of which we have only lately become aware, and the excellence of the transformation based on a profound knowledge and understanding of local people and customs. This "transformation" process is a far more complex one than the word "translation" would indicate, because the adapter has the problem of preserving the spirit of the original while making no effort to achieve a word-for-word rendering. In my opinion, the successful outcome of a transformation can be accomplished only when the original material is indeed universal and the adapter is sufficiently creative to see it through the eyes of his local audience.

At an earlier time impresarios were concerned exclusively with the importation of grand opera. Although opera is generally sung in the language of the country in which it is performed (America is a notable exception), the libretto language is usually broad and the musical score is what matters chiefly. A translation that manages to convey the plot isn't expected to have literary distinction or special local nuances as well.

When operetta began traveling during the last quarter of the nineteenth century it was the music that furnished the principal attraction. The librettos of Viennese and Parisian hits frequently made little sense in their original tongues, so why should the translations or "adaptations" be expected to be any better? These operettas were great successes, but their lyrics represent a manner of speaking that never existed, either here or in England. The French versions were no better, nor were the German versions of importations from other countries. The operettas found responsive audiences everywhere solely because of the opulence of the music. Since the librettos were inconsequential both in the original and in translations, there came into being a kind of never-never-land verbal style that was found serviceable and was even expected.

The Viennese operettas were the best ones, and at the turn of the present century they exerted enormous influence on the barely beginning American musical comedy. Even the synthetic translations of text and lyrics set the style in our native writing for the musical stage.

In the Thirties and especially in the Forties and afterward, things began to change in America. We graduated into a more highly sophisticated state. We produced lyricists such as Oscar Hammerstein II, Cole Porter, Ira Gershwin, Irving Berlin, Lorenz Hart, Howard Dietz, and, later, Dorothy Fields, Harold Rome, Alan Jay Lerner, E.Y. Harburg, Stephen Sondheim, and Sheldon Harnick. And there are others like them—native, talented, original, stylish, and literate. They allow their characters to sing as three-dimensional human beings.

It should be noted that many of our best shows have been based on plays, novels, or motion pictures that had already succeeded without the help of music and lyrics. Thus Molnár's celebrated *Liliom* became *Carousel*, Shakespeare's *Romeo and Juliet* was popularized as West Side Story, Shaw's *Pygmalion* sang as *My Fair Lady*, Cervantes' Don Quixote formed the basis for *Man of La Mancha*. Writers and composers in other countries have made serious attempts to rival the creative spirits in the American musical theatre. There seems to be no reason why they should not succeed. However, workable, exportable shows have only occasionally come to light in London, and none has emerged anywhere else.

While I am certain that the songs in the best American musicals have provided the bait for foreign markets, it is above all our sensible books and the identifiable characters who inhabit them that are the basic reasons for both local and international success in this field. In the books of our very best musicals, neither the situations nor the characters require explanation or footnote.

Fiddler on the Roof—one of our triumphs—would seem at a cursory glance to be strictly about Jews in Russia around the turn of the century. Such a subject should have a limited appeal and would, if this were the true subject matter, be best suited to production in New York, where indeed it originated. However, *Fiddler on the Roof*, still being performed in the United States, is a success throughout Europe and an enormous hit in Tokyo.

When one considers this phenomenon, it becomes obvious that the show is not primarily about Jews in Poland. The unqualified success of *Fiddler* in places such as Amsterdam and Tokyo requires a deeper examination of the subject matter, and an attempt must be made to see in it something broader and more universal. Of course this is easily found when one is, so to speak, on the right scent. For *Fiddler* is about the "generation gap." It is about the tradition-clinging older generation in conflict with a younger one far less concerned with the perpetuation of customs and mores than with today's living. Once this is understood, the transplanting of this or any other show to a foreign land becomes not so much a matter of translation as a reconciliation of basic ideas to the new local scene with its own peculiar and particular environment.

Certainly forms change, content changes, and resources differ. These occur naturally with changing times and societies because the artist in each period is part of his own time and place, but inescapably—if he is a great artist—he fills out the forms he inherits better than anyone else working in his genre. He possesses *every-*

thing that millions of unnamed microcosms before him have tested and developed. On the other hand, the experimenters perform essential evolutionary functions but in the end succeed in doing only the "exercises," preparing the way, exploring, and testing new materials, but they themselves are never able to achieve the highest goals. They resemble Moses, who led the children of Israel through the wilderness of forty years but was himself forced by God to stand aside and watch his own people, under young Joshua's leadership, enter the Promised Land. Without Moses there would have been no Joshua and no crossing, but Moses himself could not complete the task.

Today, because of what was evolved during more than forty years in the American musical theatre, we have at last achieved successful models of workable musical shows. The best of these have much in common with one another, although not one of them is outwardly similar to another. During these forty years of new musicals in this country, men of enormous and fresh talent composed some of their best music and/or lyrics but, lacking models, what they accomplished, though successful for a time, is unfortunately unreproduceable today. Our dowry consists only of the miraculous songs by George and Ira Gershwin, Richard Rodgers and Lorenz Hart, Cole Porter, Vincent Youmans, Jerome Kern (who was the first big visionary), Rudolf Friml, Sigmund Romberg, and many more. Their shows, with two exceptions, are dead.

The model which they lacked as a guide (because it had not yet existed) was a satisfactory dramatic form: a workable book or libretto. It is this deficiency which renders a vast block of shows—as shows, not catalogues of standard songs—forever useless.

Now, however, we have model musical shows which can be studied. Their librettos are necessarily different in form from the plays on which many of them are based. This form is not only a different one from *these* plays but from nearly all plays. This libretto form is different from operetta libretto (its chief precursor) and from opera libretto. And the books of opera and operetta are also basically unlike one another. An awareness of them and the ability to deal with them properly determine success (popular as well as artistic) or failure, a continued after-life or a complete if sometimes gradual termination.

I am not trying to say that any rigid rules exist, nor am I going to grasp a crystal ball and look into the future. There have always been changes, but these have been brought about by people working *within* an already established movement. Many would-be writers think it is swifter and more comfortable (though in the end it is necessarily unsuccessful) not to study, practice, and learn. These people in all ages come from and go nowhere.

All I can point out is what is. If at the outset this seems limiting, I would remind you again that past artists with the greatest talents have flourished because of existing limitations. We in the theatre must contend with our own peculiar restrictive elements: audiences, trade unions, theatre capacity, acoustical problems, and, not least of all, production costs. And yet withal *My Fair Lady*, *Carousel*, *West Side Story*, and *Fiddler on the Roof* (to name a few) are workable and successful. And because they are also made with artistry, they will continue to function indefinitely. Each of these shows in style, time and place is different from the others, yet all of them function because they apply basic principles they have in common. These are what I would like to point out.

HOWARD KISSEL COMMENTS ON INTRODUCTION

When Lehman Engel wrote *Words with Music* in 1971 it stood out from most books on musical theatre because of its far broader perspective.

The standard approach to musicals then (and, too often, alas, now) was that the form was invented almost by accident in 1866, when a New York theatre burned down. Two impresarios who'd rented the theatre to present a French ballet company negotiated with the owner of another theatre to incorporate the stranded dancers into the play *The Black Crook*, which was a treatment of the same theme Carl Maria von Weber had used in his best-known opera *Der Freischutz*.

The combination of dance, song and drama was an unexpected hit, and *The Black Crook* continued to be revived right down to the Great Depression. Its extraordinary popularity for over half a century certainly made it influential, but it's entirely possible the American musical would have developed exactly as it did without it. Interestingly, Engel mentions it only in passing late in *Words with Music*.

As is apparent from his very first chapter, when he makes casual reference to Debussy's *Pelléas and Mélisande*, the correspondence of Richard Strauss and Hugo von Hoffmansthal and the operas of Mozart, Engel considered musical theatre the descendant of a far more complex and rich tradition than the one that grew from *The Black Crook*.

Certainly the composers who worked during the Golden Age of the American musical didn't see themselves as heirs to *The Black Crook*. George Gershwin, the most ambitious and, despite his perceived cockiness, the most insecure of the Golden Age composers, wanted to study with Ravel (who, when he learned how much his prospective student earned in a year, thought it might be a better idea for him to study with Gershwin). As further proof of his seriousness, the composer of *Of Thee I Sing* subsidized the American premiere of Alban Berg's *Wozzeck*.

One historical progenitor the Golden Age composers would have been proud to acknowledge was Gilbert and Sullivan. *The Pirates of Penzance*, which had its world premiere in New York in 1879 (courtesy of the absence of international copyright protection), was a far more successful and influential show than *The Black Crook*. It continues to be performed because its lyrics still dazzle and its music remains both entertaining and affecting.

No one who listens to the Gershwins' 1927 *Strike Up the Band* can doubt the influence of Gilbert and Sullivan on the brothers. Gilbert and Sullivan were conscious of their kinship with the grand opera of their day, which they parodied mercilessly. They were themselves the heirs of John Gay, who, more than anyone, created the "modern" musical theatre with his 1728 London smash hit *The Beggar's Opera*, an amalgam of music, drama and dance that long predated *The Black Crook* and has long outlasted it. (That Gay's work was also the progenitor of one of the most powerful pieces of musical theatre of the 20th century, *The Threepenny Opera*, makes its influence seem even more formidable.)

Many of the qualities that we celebrate in musical theatre today were present in Gay's remarkably durable work. Unlike the grand opera that became chic in London in the early 18th century, which was often in Italian and concerned mythological characters, Gay wrote about contemporary characters—criminals, in fact, the tabloid heroes of his time. He wrote in a vernacular rather than a highfalutin' English.

Most important, the tunes he filled the show with were also in the vernacular. They were ones the audience could have hummed on their way in, but he rewrote the lyrics to suit his own purposes, often relying on the audience's knowledge of the original lyrics to make his satirical points.

The Beggar's Opera continued to be revived throughout the 18th century. (Its production history also provides striking counterparts to contemporary musical theatre —one of its revivals, for example, featured an all-female cast, an early example of nontraditional casting.)

However, even Gay couldn't replicate the success of his greatest work, and the spirit of English comic opera lay dormant for nearly 150 years until Gilbert and Sullivan revitalized it. The reason *The Beggar's Opera* continues to be performed is not only the wit and social satire of the dramatic scenes but the enduring appeal of the music, much of which is drawn from folk tunes.

It's possible to draw a clear line from Gay to the present because the music he chose remains comprehensible. The tunes in *The Beggar's Opera* are in a musical idiom akin to that of, say, "Danny Boy," a melody of the utmost simplicity, but one which conveys the emotional depth of an equally limpid but powerful text. That idiom remained viable for centuries. It was the musical language that Gershwin and Porter, Kern and Rodgers, Berlin and Loewe employed.

It's still viable, although when Engel wrote *Words With Music* it was being displaced by other popular traditions, which, as we shall see, have grown in importance in the last thirty years.

When Engel wrote this book, in the late Sixties and early Seventies, the theatre was in a much more hazardous state than today. It was standard for two-thirds of the theatres on Broadway to be dark, and much that filled them would not have delighted him. In a sense, *Words with Music* was an act of faith. It grew out of a conviction that the principles that had animated the musical theatre in its golden years—which we might define roughly as the period from *Show Boat* in 1927 to *Cabaret* in 1966—were still valid, that they could continue to yield musical works of great substance.

That conviction remains true. Much has changed, but Engel's discussion seems worth revisiting because so much of what he said continues to be useful. What seems especially important is that he put the American musical theatre into a broad framework. He measured its achievements not against the ultimately marginal standards of *The Black Crook* but against those of the musical theatre that had been born in Italy around the time of Shakespeare and remains alive in the world's opera houses, institutions that exist to perpetuate the highest standards.

Interestingly, the opera houses of Europe, which presumably are more protective of their heritage than we, had already accepted the idea that American musical theatre carried on their traditions when it became common, in Germany in the Fifties, to perform *Porgy and Bess* with white singers in blackface. The Gershwin estate forbids such productions in this country, but there were other, more complex and political reasons that *Porgy,* one of the most powerful operas written in the 20th century, did not enter the repertory of American opera houses until the last quarter of that century.

Starting in the mid-Fifties, as the Civil Rights movement gained momentum, African-American performers refused to do it because they considered its characters negative stereotypes. (Earlier in that decade, however, Leontyne Price had scored one of the early triumphs of her career in a production of *Porgy* that toured Europe, whose chorus also included a young singer named Maya Angelou.)

In the Seventies, as racial relations grew calmer, there was a new perspective on the characters. Crown, for example, a braggart, a bully, a conscienceless womanizer, could also be seen as an image of masculinity uncowed by a white world eager to emasculate him. Black performers were now receptive to exploring the characters and the music. By the time the Metropolitan Opera mounted a 50th anniversary production in 1985, *Porgy*'s place in the standard repertory was uncontested.

It does seem noteworthy that Germany, hardly a slouch when it comes to upholding musical standards, recognized the greatness of *Porgy* well before most Americans did, though not before Engel. His role in bringing the riches of *Porgy* to light was signal—he conducted the first complete recording of the score in 1951, reminding listeners that it was a work of considerable musical complexity, not

just the source of so many tunes that, in the slightly more than fifteen years since the original Broadway production, had become
"standards."

Engel was in some sense an evangelist, spreading the "good
news" about musical theatre both in other archival recordings he did
in the early Fifties (like the never before recorded complete score
of Rodgers and Hart's *The Boys From Syracuse*) and in books like *Words
With Music*.

The thirty-odd years since its publication have seen enormous
experimentation, but Engel's book still has the quality of Gospel, a
standard text that may require reinterpretation but whose basic
ideas endure. Moreover, Engel's conviction that American musical
theatre is an achievement of universal cultural significance is no
longer a voice crying in the wilderness.

More than once Sir Laurence Olivier, renowned for his interpretations of the great Shakespearean roles, declared his great regret at
never getting a chance to play Nathan Detroit in *Guys and Dolls*.
Long before Britain's two great companies, the National Theatre
and the Royal Shakespeare Company, saw the production of musicals (such as *Cats* and *Les Misérables*) as a way of generating needed
revenue, the National, known for its distinguished productions of
the English classics or for inviting Ingmar Bergman to direct *Hedda
Gabler* with Maggie Smith, did a celebrated revival of *Guys and Dolls*.

As in many things, Americans have been slower to accept the
implications of their cultural achievement, positive and negative,
than outsiders. Engel recognized that achievement early on, and his
perceptions remain worth our consideration.

2
Characters

**Two people in a room, agreeing or not agreeing, are
to me truly dramatic. The edges of their being can
never be in accord; psychically as well as physically,
they are assailed by an opposing radiation.**

Lynn Riggs
Preface to *Green Grow the Lilacs*

A play is a composition in verse or prose arranged for enactment (as
by actors on a stage) and intended to portray life or characters or to
tell a story though the actions and usually dialogue of the enactors.

A play with music is one that employs and often requires music
as a secondary element to connect scenes, to underscore dialogue
(usually of an emotional nature). Sometimes there are one or two
songs and perhaps a dance or two. While music is sometimes called
for in this general form, it is usually of such minor importance that
it has come to be referred to as "incidental."

The play without music developed after the play with music. The
Greeks and Romans and probably even earlier civilizations produced plays all of which utilized music. We know that the Greek
plays (comedies as well as tragedies) employed orchestra, chorus,
dancing, and singing or chanting. During the Middle Ages musicalized morality plays using all of the theatre elements were written for
and performed in cathedrals. During the early sixteenth century in
Florence an attempt made to revive Greek tragedy resulted in the
"invention" of opera, which was immediately successful, spread
over all of Europe, and has continued to flourish everywhere, with-

out any hiatus, to our own time. Meanwhile, during this movement and for at least four centuries prior to it in all countries there were various kinds of "folk" operas (called by many different names), most of which employed folk songs or borrowed—as in the case of *The Beggar's Opera* (1729), said to be the first "musical comedy"—from more "serious" music which had already become "popular." More than a century before *The Beggar's Opera*, Shakespeare's plays contained much music: songs, dances, incidental music, ensemble singing, etc. Even in the United States in the eighteenth century theatre did not exist without music. There were songs, dances, olios between the acts—probably to entertain while cumbersome scenery was being shifted and also undoubtedly to satisfy the audiences' normal theatre expectations. The play without any music was unheard of until about the last quarter of the nineteenth century, when musicless drama began to make its own way.

The new "intellectual" dramatists of that period began to write plays with a social point of view. The movement was away from entertainment as such and toward a theatre of ideas. We remember Wedekind, Ibsen, and Chekhov, whose plays were cornerstones of the non-musical theatre. Their line continued uninterruptedly through Shaw, Pirandello, Molnár, Andreyev, and many others to the present time. In America, plays were produced by S. N. Behrman, Maxwell Anderson, Robert Sherwood, Elmer Rice, and Sidney Howard, while the new tradition continued to thrive in Europe and especially in England.

Today's best plays in all countries, of course, stand by themselves, but the point here is that their form is intrinsically different in a variety of respects from what was found to be workable in the musical theatre. By their nature most of these plays—like those of their distinguished precursors—are "filled out." They are whole, complete. They deal in intellectual and philosophical debate. In the best of them, it is essential that every word be heard. A musical libretto, on the other hand, needs to be skeletal to reserve "space" for singing and dancing. Libretto ideas must be so simple that the characters need to appear at the outset to be who and what they are.[2]

We have grown accustomed, especially in musical shows, to having our leading characters in pairs: for every hero a heroine, for every soprano a tenor or baritone. However, this has not been a general practice employed by playwrights for approximately a century, and the effect on musicals is by now beginning to be felt.

Instead of the taken-for-granted pair, writers have employed the single-character heroine. Usually she is a woman of middle age who is in no way typical of any kind of average woman. Sometimes she is larger in stature and perhaps symbolizes a kind of woman who is representative of many others. In any case, she is a fact of drama who occurs, disappears, perhaps for centuries, reappears, and again vanishes. What is most pertinent here is that she has at last invaded the American musical theatre.

Certainly in Greek tragedy she was abundantly present. (I speak of heroines only.) There were Electra, Medea, Jocasta, and Andromache. As far as I am able to find out, this single female ceased to exist for a long time. The medieval mystery plays caused drama's next major eruption, and there was no place for her there. Shakespeare had no use for her except in fun, when he used two middle-aged ladies—Mistress Ford and Mistress Page—in *The Merry Wives of Windsor*.

Again the type took a long nap, but she became a serious threat in Restoration comedy. The real heroine of Sheridan's *The Rivals* is Mrs. Malaprop. Young love was ever present, but the older lady held the stage and attracted the stars. A century or so later Oscar Wilde created Lady Bracknell in his most successful comedy, *The Importance of Being Earnest*. Still there was young love, but…

On a soberer side, Chekhov's heroines were Madame Ranevsky in *The Cherry Orchard* and Madame Arkadina in *The Sea Gull*, while Ibsen made *Ghosts* starring Mrs. Alving, mother of a grown son, and Ellida in *The Lady from the Sea*.

By the 1940s, in the United States, the same thing was happening in plays—especially serious ones. Tennessee Williams' heroine in *A Streetcar Named Desire* was Blanche—not a young woman. There is no young woman in Arthur Miller's *Death of a Salesman*—only the older Linda, the wife of Willy Loman. William Inge wrote *Come Back, Little Sheba* for a middle-aged lady, as did Arthur Laurents in *The Time of the Cuckoo*. And there are more. One not to be overlooked is Countess Aurelia in Jean Giraudoux's *The Madwoman of Chaillot*—not middle-aged, but old; and in opera Richard Strauss and Hugo von Hofmannsthal created the Marschallin in *Der Rosenkavalier*.

The single principal character is not a prototype but someone rather "special." Blanche DuBois is not everybody's older sister, nor is she to be found even in every community. Williams wrote of her:

> She is a blend of infinite gentility, self-deception, strength and vulnerability. She has a numbing need to forget…what? A young husband driven to suicide by sensibilities and desires he could not live with; a wisteria-scented past glittering with youth, beauty and hope, all finally shattered by blows loud and painful enough to crack the spirit and mind. And so, Blanche DuBois becomes the most poetic whore ever invented. An angel, fallen into the quagmire of hopeless delusions, bringing a counterfeit poetry and luminosity into a household that contains their antithesis—the lustful, violent Stanley Kowalski. When he brutally unmasks her, Blanche crumbles and fades into a world of permanent delusion. But she leaves behind her a disquieting music—dissonant, faintly nostalgic—and always seductive.

Willy Loman is no ordinary unsuccessful traveling salesman, nor is Martha, in *Who's Afraid of Virginia Woolf?*, the average daughter of a college president and the wife of one of his professors. Also unusual are Lola in *Come Back, Little Sheba*, Mrs. Alving, *Hedda Gabler*, Nora (*A Doll's House*), Electra, the Clytemnestra of *Electra*, Oedipus, and many, many more who are larger than life. All of them require explanation, and their creators take up the better part of an evening to prove their point. For an atypical character to involve an audience the author must define him carefully, let him develop slowly and in detail, allowing much time to clarify whatever points he intends to make.

I am not complaining about this fact but about its inevitable effect on the musical theatre. And it bothers me because it is an about-face—I think an unhealthy one for which I can find only one possible reason. Perhaps two. The first is that stars, except in the movies, are not young, and perhaps writers in all periods have had difficulties in finding young stars. The second and more uncertain reason is that most theatregoers are themselves past middle age, and perhaps—just *perhaps*—writers are subconsciously writing for them.

But now look at the musical theatre. The character spectrum in musicals is and always has been a narrow one. Part of this is due to time-space limitations and acoustical hindrance to understanding. *All* of the characters in musicals are simple, as recognizable and definable on being seen as on being heard or commented on by others. This was as true in the shows of Herbert, Romberg, Friml as in those of Rodgers, Loewe, Schwartz, Styne, Rome, Bernstein, and Sondheim.

From the latter part of the last century every "musical comedy" was about young love, and in thumbing through the reviews of the period we find that all the leading girls and boys were admirably young, pretty, and handsome. Also please bear in mind that there were *two* leads. The use of a pair of young lovebirds was standard as our theatre began to grow.

By the time we got to *South Pacific* we had two not very young stars. Tevye, the hero of *Fiddler on the Roof* (although there were three young daughters and their young men), was middle-aged. *Fiorello* and *Jimmy* were about two of New York's former mayors. Mame and Dolly were hardly sophomores; they were also *one*. The pair in *I Do! I Do!* were about fifty. Romance in *The Sound of Music* was not young. The heroine of *Gypsy* was not young. The lady in *Pal Joey* was middle-aged.

This condition bothers me because it is special and bizarre. One of the causes of song—romance—is absent. The love ballad has no *raison d'être*, and the love ballad, always in newer and fresher guise, is one of the chief hallmarks of musical theatre. History is not to be shunned so cavalierly.

The characters in play and musical are introduced quite differently. In the musical, they appear at or near the beginning, are defined specifically as the principals, and simultaneously a schism arises between them, while the audience is made to want to see it removed or resolved. In a play, the principals are often not introduced at once and are very often not defined in the beginning as principals. Often their true identity is not revealed until the very end, and in the case of a play by an author such as Harold Pinter not even with the final curtain are we certain about the who, the what and the why of the characters. In many plays of the recent past the entire length of the piece is spent in developing the characters, unfolding them, often changing them drastically and through many complications until the end, when we are allowed to see them whole for what it is they really are. Role is clear but not identity.

Tennessee Williams, in the stage directions to *Cat on a Hot Tin Roof,* wrote:

> Some mystery should be left in the revelation of char-
> acters in a play, just as a great deal of mystery is always
> left in the revelation of characters in life, even in one's
> own character to himself.

These are, on the other hand, curious similarities between Shakespeare's character information and the book of a modern musical, whereas other similarities are shared by modern drama, the classical Greek tragedy, and the Restoration comedy. We know Macbeth and his lady when we first encounter them; also Iago, Romeo, Juliet, Petruchio, and Kate. Williams' Blanche is not totally clear until the end, nor is Miller's Willy Loman. Neither is Ibsen's Mrs. Alving, Jocasta, Iphigenia, or Clytemnestra.

Sometimes characters are made clear in the songs they sing just as Shakespeare clarifies them in their soliloquies. Take *Oklahoma!*, for example. The lyrics of "Oh, What a Beautiful Mornin'" give us a clear picture of Curly and one we must believe instantly. He is a clean-cut young man who exults in nature and in the well-being of his crops in particular. The music serves to make him even more lik-able. Jud, the psychotic farm hand, becomes human because of his one song, "Lonely Room," in which he is able to express his normal romantic cravings. Ado Annie in "I Cain't Say No" makes it quite clear that she is an impossible though thoroughly likable flirt.

At the very beginning of *Pal Joey* the title character is doing a song-and-dance audition and we know he is an untalented phony. Mrs. Anna (*The King and I*) assures us that she feels no self-pity and that she understands what it is to have had love in "Hello, Young Lovers," and Tevye, who opens *Fiddler on the Roof*, reveals himself through his introduction of all of the other characters plus the state-ment of his own position in relation to tradition.

Since the Shakespearean soliloquy is closely akin to the musical's song and the opera's aria, the Bard used this device in every play to reveal character, what the character plans to do, and what he is like. In the nineteenth-century melodrama, the "aside" was a crude way of establishing the who of the characters. The Greek and Restoration plays accomplished somewhat the same thing in their particular and somewhat related methods through the comments of the chorus in the former or single characters in the latter who functioned similarly. This technique was also employed by the primary operetta composers. In these, the chorus or a minor principal described the characters, their histories, problems, and desires. There was no fooling around here!

Audiences need something—a person or an idea—to polarize around at the play's outset. People need to be "grabbed" in the theatre, and much of the force with which this is accomplished will determine how the entire play will make out.

The importance of introducing characters as early as possible in a musical cannot be stressed too strongly. For the audience, immediately after meeting them, begins to see things—whatever—through their eyes and to care that they get whatever it is that they want. There is a very important psychological reason why your interest is captured at once by Julie and Billy (*Carousel*), Curly and Laurey (*Oklahoma!*), Mrs. Anna (*The King and I*), Higgins and Eliza (*My Fair Lady*), Emile and Nellie (*South Pacific*), Tony and Maria (*West Side Story*), Tevye (*Fiddler on the Roof*), and Finch (*How to Succeed in Business Without Really Trying*), and this works against the wealthy English gentleman who wins your sympathy and interest as soon as the curtain rises on *House of Flowers* because you were not intended to be interested. Your reaction was normal. The construction of the book was faulty and misleading.

I was thinking of this recently while walking on a beach in St. Croix. Overhead I saw a pelican soaring seemingly lifeless in the sky. I knew it was searching the sea for a fish, and I wanted to see it succeed. Hardly had the thought crossed my mind when I saw the pelican swoop down like an arrow into the sea. It emerged swallowing a fish. There was no doubt that I was on its side because I had met the pelican first, knew what it was after and wanted it to get it. Then I thought: Suppose I had been snorkeling underwater and had seen a beautiful iridescent blue fish swimming aimlessly, and this fish had got my attention and interest. Then I saw an underwater turbulence, and the pelican had suddenly grabbed the fish! My feelings would have been opposite. I would have been horrified by the incident.

These are two versions of the same thing, yet both are possible. The only difference—and a most important one—was my own point of view. And this, I believe, is what a writer has to be aware of in introducing his chief characters. We hang on to what we meet first unless something more interesting and purposeful is subsequently introduced. And if this happens we are confused because we must surrender one for the other and we may do so grudgingly or be unable to do it all. Obviously if we don't like Number One person, if he is dull and stereotyped, if we cannot go along with what he wants, we will reject him, and in that case there is no show.

So much for the introduction of characters in a musical. One of the chief differences between most plays and most musicals (in this respect) is that characters in plays are often not what they seem; in musicals, they invariably must be. But even among various styles and periods of playwriting, the introduction of characters has been gone about differently. While Shakespeare's method has much in common with today's musicals, I would like to offer examples of character introduction and definition from a Restoration comedy and one from a Greek tragedy. Their similarities—one to the other—are apparent.

The following passage is from Sheridan's *The Rivals*. It is an exchange between Lydia Languish, the romantic heroine, and her friend Julia. In it we are given a considerable amount of information about Lydia herself, her *amour* and her formidable aunt (the principal character), Mrs. Malaprop.

> LYDIA: Then before we are interrupted, let me impart to you some of my distress! I know your gentle nature will sympathize with me, though your prudence may condemn me! My letters have informed you of my whole connection with Beverly: but I have lost him, Julia! My aunt has discovered our intercourse by a note she intercepted, and has confined me ever since! Yet, would you believe it? She has absolutely fallen in love with a tall

Irish baronet she met one night since she has been here, at Lady Macshuffle's rout.

JULIA: You jest, Lydia!....

LYDIA: Quite the contrary. Since she has discovered her own frailty, she is become more suspicious of mine....

LYDIA: ...Unfortunately I had quarreled with my poor Beverly, just before my aunt made the discovery, and I have not seen him since to make it up.

JULIA: What was his offence?

LYDIA: 'Twas the next day my aunt found the matter out. I intended only to have teased him three days and a half, and now I've lost him forever.

JULIA: If he is as deserving and sincere as you have represented him to me, he will never give you up. Yet, consider, Lydia, you tell me he is but an ensign, and you have thirty thousand pounds.

LYDIA: But you know I lose most of my fortune if I marry without my aunt's consent, till of age; and that is what I have determined to do, ever since I knew the penalty. Nor could I love the man who would wish to wait a day for the alternative.

Lydia is "young love" and Julia is her best friend. However, already the single middle-aged character has usurped the position of the young romantic one as the leading lady. Ibsen, Chekhov, Williams, Inge, and many more were to use this model.

More than two thousand years ago Euripides' *Medea* began with a monologue given by the Nurse (replacing here the role of chorus). In it, background, past history, present situation, and future (the action of the play itself) are exposed.

NURSE: Ah! Would to Heaven the good ship Argo ne'er had sped its course to the Colchian land through the misty blue Sympleglades, nor ever in the glens of Pelion the pine been felled to furnish with oars the chieftain's hands, who went to fetch the golden fleece for Pelias; for then would my own mistress Medea never have sailed to the turrets of Iolcos, her soul with love for

Jason smitten, nor would she have beguiled the daughters of Pelias to slay their father and come and live here
in the land of Corinth with her husband and children,
where her exile found favour with the citizens to whose
land she had come, and in all things of her own accord
was she at one with Jason, the greatest safeguard this
when wife and husband do agree but now their love is all
turned to hate, and tenderest ties are weak....Lo! where
her sons come hither from their childish sports; little
they reck of their mother's woes, for the soul of the
young is no friend to sorrow.

* * *

An essential point should be made here. The systems to which
Julia, Lydia, and the Nurse belonged sentenced them to establish
other characters—the most important characters in the two plays. In
Shakespeare, the characters reveal what they themselves are about.

So much for character introductions, their differing methods
among playwrights of diverse periods as well as their sometime
oppositeness in musical-theatre practices.

COMMENTS ON CHARACTERS

Engel begins his discussion of musical theatre with an essay on neither words nor music but on character, which is how one might
begin any discussion of theatre, musical or otherwise. If one had to
focus on one element that distinguishes the musical theatre of the
present from the one Engel was describing, it might well be the element of character.

Engel describes the critical role character has played in theatre
from the Greeks to the golden age of American theatre. The distinguished producer Robert Whitehead used to say that the decline in
American musicals paralleled a decline in the nonmusical theatre—
he was convinced that without a grounding in theatre based on
character, musicals lack a spine.

The kind of play that was taken for granted in the American theatre fifty years ago—Engel devotes considerable space to one of the
greats, *A Streetcar Named Desire*—is a rarity today. Worse, it's

regarded as old-fashioned. Interestingly enough, the play that hinged on the unfolding of a character's past developed during the decades in which Freud played an increasingly important role in American life: now both are regarded with comparable skepticism.

Implicit in such plays, which begin with Ibsen, is a sense of inevitability, of fatality. As we learn more and more about, say, Blanche DuBois or Mrs. Alving, we have a sense of doors clanging shut behind them, forcing them toward the destinies we watch them confront.

The idea of an irreversible fate has never been congenial to Americans. F. Scott Fitzgerald was simply wrong about there being no second acts in American life; it was a rueful observation on his own life but inaccurate about the population at large. It seems even less applicable to post-Sixties America, where self-reinvention, or at least the illusion thereof, is an essential part of the tabloid mythos. Jane Fonda goes from sex kitten (the wife of Roger Vadim and star of *Barbarella*) to leftist radical (assuring Americans that their prisoners of war were being very well cared for at the Hanoi Hilton) to fitness expert to born-again Christian. The Force of Destiny doesn't apply.

Within such a world the idea that the audience will be drawn helplessly into the character's harrowing journey of self-understanding seems less compelling than it once did. When Betty Comden and Adolph Green, under the direction of Harold Prince, wrote the 1982 *A Doll's Life*, a sequel to Ibsen's *A Doll's House*, their Nora, however many vicissitudes she underwent, was eventually reconciled with her family. Her adventures had a picaresque quality. Nothing about her life after slamming the door on Torvald had the inevitable, potentially tragic quality of Ibsen's Nora.

Ibsen, it should be remembered, was by no means a proto-feminist. Years after he wrote the play he and a friend were walking in an Oslo park. "Whatever happened to Nora?" the friend asked him. Ibsen pointed to what we would call a bag lady sitting on a bench. "There she is," he said.

In a character like Mama Rose in *Gypsy* the musical theatre approached that kind of inevitability. Rose's hunger for success through her daughters is so desperate, so unyielding that she forces Louise into burlesque, a huge and humiliating step down from vaudeville.

"Rose's Turn," her aria of self-realization, arouses sadness, pity and a kind of shock. The show ends with the muted, tentative reconciliation of Rose with her daughter Gypsy, but the power of the big number, rather than the quasi-happy ending, is what the audience remembers.

In his 2000 *Marie Christine*, Michael John LaChiusa's quasi-operatic version of *Medea* set in Creole New Orleans, the plot of the original is mimicked—an outraged mother murders her children and feeds them to their father—but it doesn't have the force of the original. This Medea is not a mythological evocation of Woman in all Man's fear of her dark powers. She's merely an exotic, a Creole in an Anglo culture. Although the music is sometimes very powerful, the character lacks the same force. Nothing she does has about it the sense of inevitability.

Engel was troubled by how many musicals had focal characters who were middle-aged, which he thought diminished the possibility of romantic ballads, "one of the chief hallmarks of musical theatre." In retrospect, his concern seems unaccountable and oddly misplaced. If anything, the cultural trend in recent decades has been to place more and more stress on younger and younger characters, more so in television and movies than the theatre.

Nevertheless this emphasis on the youth culture has not expanded significantly the repertory of great romantic ballads. The young composer in Jonathan Larson's 1996 *Rent* speaks of wanting to write a tune like Musetta's aria, the "hit song" from Puccini's *La Boheme*, on which *Rent* is loosely based. In fact the most powerful song in Larson's score isn't a ballad or a love song but a choral number, "Seasons of Love," which was recorded by Stevie Wonder. In the age of AIDS, love was too full of unimaginable risks to give rise to unfettered lyricism.

The first example of this trend that Engel mentions, *South Pacific*, had two stars who were indeed middle-aged, Ezio Pinza and Mary Martin. (She, by the way, was only 35, which, by our standards, is young—it wasn't in 1949, or in Engel's estimation twenty years later.) The songs that were created for the two of them, however—"Some Enchanted Evening," for example, or "I'm In Love With a Wonderful Guy"—are hardly less vital than the song created for the more conventional, younger lovers, "Younger Than Springtime." The latter, in fact, both in its highly poetic lyrics and its elevated melody, almost has more the quality of operetta than the vernacular one of musicals.

The unconventionality of many of the characters Engel mentions in his discussion of the middle-aged orientation of the musical (Tevye in *Fiddler on the Roof*, Mayor LaGuardia in *Fiorello*, Vera in *Pal Joey*, let alone Mama Rose) contributes enormously to their enduring interest. Their age mattered far less than the depths to which they were explored. Nor did their age mitigate the force with which they "grabbed" the audience.

An equally forceful middle-aged character is Bea Asher, the widow in a made-for-TV movie, *Queen of the Stardust Ballroom*, subsequently made into the 1978 musical *Ballroom*, with lyrics by Alan and Marilyn Bergman, music by Billy Goldenberg and book by Jerome Kass. It was directed and choreographed by Michael Bennett, his first Broadway production after *A Chorus Line*. Despite its largely unsympathetic critical reception, *Ballroom* was remarkable for several reasons, one of which was that its entire cast was middle-aged.

Bennett saw the material as an opportunity to do a show with a lot of the dancers with whom he'd come of age. For most of them their dancing days were just about over. He created the show to give them one last chance to strut their stuff. The choreography he devised was not the virtuoso moves they might have done a dozen years earlier. Much of the action took place in a Bronx version of Roseland, and the dancing was standard ballroom genres—a tango, a cha-cha, a waltz. Except for an exuberant disco number, Bennett gave each of his dancers not just steps, but a character. One hopes his choreography was Laban-notated, for it was a truly irreplaceable effort.

Middle-aged characters also demand a kind of maturity in the writing. One of the richest numbers in musical theatre in the last few decades is "One More Walk Around the Garden," a trio from Alan Jay Lerner and Burton Lane's 1979 *Carmelina*. The three middle-aged men singing it are all American veterans of World War II, having a reunion in the tiny Italian village where they served. They all had brief affairs with Carmelina, now a mature woman. Seeing her, their memories of young love are rekindled, but from a perspective not of life beginning but life drawing to a close. The music and lyrics are deeply evocative.

By 1979, when *Carmelina* had its brief Broadway run, America was already dominated by a culture that worshipped youth. It was easy to see why such a culture should slight the achievement of "One More Walk." It's still hard to see why Engel was so dismissive of the perspective of middle age.

Whereas many of the musicals Engel discussed focused on a single character whose actions had consequences for many people around them, many musicals of the last few decades have focused on collectives rather than individuals.

The most successful (with lyrics by Ed Kleban, a member of Engel's BMI Workshop) was *A Chorus Line*, in which no single character was central. A series of Broadway "gypsies" tell individual stories about their lives, or, in the brilliant sequence, "Hello, Twelve," describe the experiences they had in common during adolescence that propelled them into the theatre.

The genius of Michael Bennett, who conceived *A Chorus Line,* managed to weave these disparate strands into a coherent, compelling narrative. The huge success of *A Chorus Line* had many repercussions in the musical theatre over the years. Because *A Chorus Line* began its life at the Public Theatre, a not-for-profit institution, its early stages of development could proceed at very nominal costs. The period of experimentation had performers virtually donating their services, sometimes but not always in exchange for a percentage of profits, should the work ever be performed commercially.

The term given to this process was "workshop." Suddenly all embryo musicals were developed in workshop. (The noun even became a verb—writers talked about musicals being "workshopped.") Unlike *Chorus Line*, however, in which the material was being developed from the experiences of the performers rather than the conceptions of the writers, most of the subsequent workshops were really little more than extended rehearsal periods for backers' auditions.

One musical genuinely workshopped was *Working*. In 1978, three years after *A Chorus Line*, Stephen Schwartz, who'd enjoyed triumphs with his Off-Broadway *Godspell* and his Broadway *Pippin*, tackled a musical based on Studs Terkel's oral history *Working*. Schwartz developed the musical in Chicago, where it enjoyed a successful run before moving to Broadway.

In a sense *Working* was a revue, though one with greater seriousness than, say, *New Faces of 1952*. Because it was built around individual numbers rather than a narrative that required a unified tone, Schwartz could invite other composers to contribute. Among them was pop icon James Taylor, a rare instance of a pop composer entering the Broadway landscape. (When a pop figure of comparable importance tried to write a Broadway score two decades later—Paul Simon with *Capeman*—it was a disaster. Elton John's two scores, *The Lion King* and *Aida*, owe their success as much to the visual productions as to the music.)

Working's main parallel with *A Chorus Line* was that characters sang about their lives directly to the audience (in *Chorus Line*, they're theoretically singing to the director at the back of the theatre.) *Working*, however, had no through-line that gives these "monologues" an overarching shape or even a connection to one another. Each of the songs was about character. Some were remarkably insightful about the relationship between character and profession.

Often the people singing were believably self-effacing, though what they did was clearly far more important than they acknowledged. "I'm just a housewife" was the refrain of one of Craig Carnelia's songs. "What I do is kind of boring. All I am is someone's mother/someone's wife./Drop the kids off, pick the shirts up." This was a touching irony, but the understanding of character did not build into a story larger than the individual ones.

Moreover, none of the monologues had any internal drama, comparable, for example, to that in Murray Grand and Elisse Boyd's "Guess Who I Saw Today, My Dear" in the admittedly frivolous *New Faces of 1952*. Interestingly, the most effective numbers in *Working* were "Joe," by Carnelia, and "Fathers and Sons," by Schwartz. In both cases the songs aren't, strictly speaking, about working. "Joe" is about a man coping, bravely, with retirement; "Fathers and Sons" is about a son taking stock of his changing understanding of his father, which he can only do because he's come to understand what it means to have a son. Though occasionally moving (as in these songs), the overall effect of *Working* was diffuse.

In 1997 Maury Yeston, also an alumnus of Engel's workshop and later Engel's successor as its artistic director, created *Titanic*, a musical based on the famous disaster, with a libretto by Peter Stone.

Here too there were characters aplenty—the crew, the wealthy, often famous passengers—but the portrayal of character was not deep enough to make us care about their fate. Nor did the treatment enliven or freshen the well-trod tale. (The same might be said of the 1998 movie, despite its boffo box office.) The strongest moments were the choral pieces at the beginning and the end, but that strength was entirely musical. It had to do with the glorious choral writing rather than the revelation of character.

Although hardly a mainstay of musical theatre of late, character remains the link between musicals and their elder progenitors, non-musical theatre and opera. In recent years many shows have been successful without sophisticated understanding of character. Conversely, shows that did understand character, such as *Ballroom*, were not successful. Engel wasn't dishing out formulas for success in *WordsWith Music*. He was trying to understand what makes a good musical work. Character, it need not be argued, is indispensable.

3

Subject Matter

A comic opera, on its dramatic side, has come to mean mostly an inane and occasionally indecorous play, performed by self-satisfied bunglers who have all the amateur's ineptitude without his disinterestedness, one or two experienced and popular comedians being thrown in to help the rest out by such fun as they can improvise.

George Bernard Shaw

Subject matter as employed typically in plays and musicals should be considered because although they are frequently similar—Eve having been made from Adam's rib—there are points at which their physical limitations (particularly in musicals) eschew precise and identical transformations. The distinguishing and all-important difference between a play and a musical is that in the latter, music is a concomitant of the spoken word. It is integrated so as to share an equal importance with the other principal elements. When it is sung, the music (with lyrics) can become functional as a plot element, an emotional heightener (for both humor and pathos), and a foundation for dancing. A well-made integrated musical show cannot be performed without music, whereas it is barely conceivable that play with music might.

For example, in the *Carousel* "Soliloquy" the hero, on learning of his wife's pregnancy, recognizes for the only time in the show a sense of responsibility. A development takes place in this song, and at its conclusion the hero has reversed his earlier decision and now agrees to cooperate in a hold-up which will result in his death. Also in *Carousel* there is a beach ballet in Act Two in which the anti-hero father (and the audience) sees Billy's daughter and witnesses in music, dance, and pantomime the humiliation which Billy's notorious life has caused.

These two examples in one musical are not singular among all musicals, and they demonstrate clearly the comprehensive position of the music: Without these two musical numbers, the plot and the character motivations would be incomplete.

Since the characters in dramas of our time are more complex and nearly continuously in the process of evolution, it follows that subject matter in plays which have little time limit and no musical interference can be more varied, more complex, and less restricted. *A Streetcar Named Desire* centers around a woman whose disintegration we observe. Everything about her past (before the play begins) and her fluctuating present contributes to her tragic denouement.

Death of a Salesman is a poetic play of compassion that revolves about an unsuccessful "little" man who frequently takes refuge in a fantasy world which helps him to create some illusion of self-importance. At the end, hopeless—except for an insurance policy which could benefit his family—he commits suicide.

Who's Afraid of Virginia Woolf? is an ever-changing, kaleidoscopic, philosophical game of four-ball billiards. Its four characters appear perpetually in new, complex, and developing relationships with one another. It "feels" like a set of horrific variations on "man's life is a cheat and a disappointment." [3]

Come Back, Little Sheba concerns a dreary, talkative housewife who is despondent over her lost youth. The play deals with her life, that of her husband (who had to marry her hurriedly years before, at the expense of a career), a female art student who lives in their house, and the latter's friend, a college athlete.

In none of these plays is romance an important element. In *Rhinoceros, The Homecoming, Rosencrantz and Guildenstern Are Dead, The Birthday Party, The Zoo Story, Hadrian VII, The Royal Hunt of the Sun*, and dozens of others, romance as we have known it is nonexistent. Those plays are based in part on other emotions, and ideas sing along well enough on their words without romance. It is not necessary to make this point with mid-twentieth-century plays only, for while romance exists in the plays of Ibsen and Chekhov, it is of secondary importance. This is also true of contemporary American comedies: *The Odd Couple*, *Barefoot in the Park*, *Plaza Suite* (all by Neil Simon), and Robert Anderson's *I Never Sang for My Father*.

In Shakespeare's *Romeo and Juliet*, *Othello*, *Antony and Cleopata*, *The Comedy of Errors*, romance was the central topic, whereas in *The Merchant of Venice*, *Hamlet*, *Macbeth*, *King Lear*, *The Tempest*, and others, it existed as a subordinate element. Likewise in *Electra*, *Iphigenia in Aulis*, and *Oedipus*, the incidence of love was far less than primary. Shaw also seldom brought his couples together in blissful resolution. However, in musicals (in opera and operetta as well) romance is at the center. This does not mean that its treatment is a single-track affair. Nevertheless, love is at the core. This is a fact, and its need or reason seems also quite clear. Another fact emerges. In all of the plays listed above, the plots can be told quite simply in a single sentence. While plot is a necessary cohesive element, one which binds the interest together with references to past, present and future, it is nevertheless slight. Theme, argument, discussion, philosophy in all of these plays exceed the plot in importance and size. In the librettos of musicals, the plot is just as slight, but the other facets are treated minimally—sometimes to the point of nonexistence.

Throughout the ages when we have sung, we have done so only about emotional things. There is happy love, unrequited or sad love, misery, victory, defeat (Jeremiah), celebration (marriage, anniversary, coronation), and other key demonstrative, sensuous, sentimental, pathetic, ecstatic causes which have found expression in song. In religious celebration and ceremony there has always been music.

The first major opera was *Orfeo* (Monteverdi's, not Gluck's). Here was romance with a twist. That same subject served countless composers for the musical theatre for several centuries. Don Juan provided grist for the mill. A toreador is not a far cry from a football player. Radames' vocal with cornet reception after his victory follows in a real-life tradition. Its high theatricality is obvious. Then there are many other emotions that have been treated theatro-musically: fear, misery, madness, jealousy, and not least of all, love.

Pinter and Shaw succeeded in writing anti-romantic theses. Nearly all of the others I have listed could be (in some cases have been) adapted to musical theatre. Just exactly what form the adaptation may take depends largely on the "weight" of the material. *Romeo and Juliet* provided an opera for Gounod and a musical *(West Side Story)* for Leonard Bernstein, Stephen Sondheim, and Arthur Laurents. But this is probably an exception. Because of the emotional qualities implicit in *Death of a Salesman, A Streetcar Named Desire, The Royal Hunt of the Sun*, and *Madwoman of Chaillot* (for example), I can find no logical reason in their not being musicalized, but I think they could best become operas because of their weightiness, essential seriousness, and the stature and quality of their heroes.

On the other hand, none of the Neil Simon comedies present us with characters. They are monologues. And they give us nothing to sing about. The Pinter plays especially *seem* to be emotionally antithetical. Albee's *Who's Afraid of Virginia Woolf?* is basically a dramatic diatribe and many of the comedies of Molière and the dramas of Ibsen and Chekhov are discussions, despite the lyricism present to a large degree in the works of the latter.

In the ancient Greek tragedy prior to the start of the play (which was in a single act) all of the action had occurred except for the denouement. Oedipus had already slain his father and married Jocasta, his mother, although he was as yet unaware of his parents' identities. The kingdom was in trouble. Oedipus, bit by bit, learns the truth, and the play itself is concerned with this and the tragic expiation of his sins.

This was the shape of all Greek tragedy. It worked so well not only because of the scope and grandeur of its poetry but also because its subject matter was so well known historically or mythologically that it was intimately familiar to everyone in the land. Electra and Iphigenia were known to all Greeks more intimately than Washington and Betsy Ross are to Americans.

In fewer than a thousand years this form had changed drastically. Characters were no longer drawn from the recorded past but were the creations of writers who indeed most frequently borrowed from earlier writers or "fictionalized" the people and situations they personally knew. In either case, the characters required definition and exposition, and this was achieved by a variety of means, mostly conditioned by the style current at the writer's time. It is my belief that this latter-day practice led to the beginning-middle-end play form, or, if you like, exposition-development-denouement that we have come to regard as *the* form of a play.

Neither characters nor subject matter has changed greatly from the beginning; only the form has undergone an evolution, and there are changes of style. The subject matter involved in musical theatre as opposed to its non-musical sister has, in my opinion, only three basic differences—simplicity, pinpoint clarity, and operation on an emotional basis—which, whether comic or dramatic, employs music in a legitimate and desirable manner—*The Wild Duck* versus *Otello*.

A large and significant change occurred during the latter part of the nineteenth century. Everything that happens in Ibsen's *Ghosts* is due to Mrs. Alving's pre-play history, which emerges little by little during three acts. If Mrs. Alving's life were clearly exposed at the start, *Ghosts* would be no more than a one-act play. Madame Ranevsky in Chekhov's *The Cherry Orchard* likewise is fully known only by the end of the play when the audience has had the opportunity of piecing together her history with what we have *seen* of her unrealistic living.

This method has continued to be employed in plays in our own time. Blanche DuBois, Willy Loman, the family in Pinter's *The Homecoming*, the characters in Anouilh's *The Rehearsal* are never set up. Blanche simply enters quietly. She has never been mentioned. We know nothing about her. Willy enters unannounced at the beginning of *Death of a Salesman* and begins a dialogue with his wife—an innocuous one at the start—about fatigue. Father and son play a scene of irritability at the start of *The Homecoming*, and more than two pages of interchange are spoken before there is even a hint that they are father and son. It is the slow emergence of the past which explains itself and propels present and future action.

What is important is that we be carried along to that often predictable finish in a manner that interests, entertains, and engages us. Toward this end in our lyric theatre we have not only the plot but also the songs, and when it is pertinent, the choreography. The existence of defined characters carries with it as much promise of a plot as a desert palm tree assures an oasis.

As exposition and character development are inseparable, it is unimaginable that one could occur without the other. In fact, plot progress and even nonplot plays go hopelessly nowhere without the existence, definition, and at least *some* movement within, for, or against characters who achieve immediate or gradual audience empathy and interest. Exposition by definition infers plot. It creates audience interest and participation through particularization. We hear or witness accounts of specific people caught up in specific actions, situations, and conflicts. If exposition exists at all, it must involve characters (and vice versa), and it functions as the force which propels action as well as emotion. It also binds action and emotion together into a single entity which becomes the show itself.

The guises, shapes, and methods in which exposition is used are varied. Sometimes it defines characters in relation to a single plot or story line. Sometimes it introduces an explicit situation requiring development and resolution, and the characters—while still the doers or the done to—seem buffeted about by the story which propels, guides, or destroys them.

Shakespeare alone among playwrights worked in the "libretto style," which is to say that he usually announced a theme (through a character and frequently by means of his introductory soliloquy), and what followed enhanced and proved the theme by way of a plot (a series of actions, interactions, and reactions).

Restoration comedy's method of introducing and describing characters and situations through secondary characters is for us today clumsy and too obvious. Once this introduction was accomplished, the announced and usually planned future action was completed with desirable if predictable results. In contemporary plays, exposition as such has taken a longer time, been less direct, more complex, and frequently at the end has been left unresolved.

In the "message" plays from Strindberg through Chekhov to Williams and Miller, exposition as such is slight, and the chief interest lies in character development, which, in turn, forms the substance of the entire play. Take, for example, *The Three Sisters*, or *The Sea Gull*, or *The Wild Duck*. Their plots are slim. Their characters are strong and so are their themes. The plays are filled with incidents large and small, people speaking without connecting with one another and therefore to little purpose. In *The Cherry Orchard* the theme, I believe, is the folly of unreality or the attempts of an aristocratic family to retain status-quo values in a bourgeois world. The protagonist is Madame Ranevsky. The plot, which is the Q.E.D. of the theme, is simple although it is thickened with many people and happenings that add color, some comedy, and much theatricality to the whole. In two simple sentences, the plot concerns a dear unrealistic lady who, because of financial problems, is advised to sell her enormous cherry orchard as sites for houses. She fails to take the problem or the suggestion seriously and loses everything. The exposition—the set-up of the situation—is scattered like so many seeds throughout the first of four acts. The lady, at one point only, tries lamely to prevent the nearly inevitable catastrophe. Otherwise the development proceeds in a straight line through four acts, the final one being the coda.

To skip more than half a century to Tennessee Williams' *A Streetcar Named Desire*: It is well-nigh impossible to separate character exposition from development. The first seeps out drop by drop along with the development. It is the exposition of Blanche's life and her pathetic development which occur side by side from the beginning of the play to the very end. The same pattern exists in Miller, Pinter, Anouilh, Ionesco, and others. It is a satisfying pattern that keeps audiences attentive and absorbed with the import of the play's meaning long after the theatre has been darkened.

Comedic plays seem to employ plans identical to one another today as well as to those in time past. The people and the situation are exposed soon after the curtain rises. Long before the end of Act One in a usually three-act play, everything is set up. We also know how it will end. It seldom surprises.

In the superb farces of Feydeau, the exposition is defined almost at first. Sometimes it is only hinted at so that we are playing a delightful guessing game in which we normally go to the head of the class. What we cannot begin to guess are the devious bypaths the development will take. There are speedy surprises. The rate of speed is incalculable and so are the surprises. Not nearly everything that works well in either play or musical, of course, needs to be surprising.

In musicals, exposition among the best of them goes along as a concomitant to the introduction and definition of the principal characters. Since the saving of time in a libretto is a vital consideration, this method seems most reasonable. It is antithetical to what happens today in spoken drama.

The following are terse accounts of expositions in musicals as to position in the libretto.

My Fair Lady In Act One, Scene 1, both protagonists are introduced and defined. We see (and hear) their impossible schisms. We (and Eliza) hear Professor Higgins give his address to Colonel Pickering. Eliza will be there sooner or later. We will await developments.

Wonderful Town The locale (Greenwich Village), the house in which the two girls from Columbus will live, and nearly all secondary characters are introduced in the opening number. On the entrance of the girls we learn that they have come to New York in order to build careers, Ruth a writer and Eileen an actress. Their lives now will be entangled with those of the people we have met. And more.

West Side Story In the opening pantomime, the two opposing factions are fighting. These are the destructive forces that will hang over all future action.

Carousel The opening pantomime scene at an amusement park introduces Billy, Julie, Carrie, and Mrs. Mullin. We note the attraction between Billy and Julie. In the following scene Carrie tells of her own engagement and Julie contrives to win Billy, which is the beginning of the action.

The King and I The first scene is on the deck of a ship within sight of Bangkok. The captain warns Mrs. Anna of her danger if she insists on landing in Siam (1860s), where she has been engaged to teach. What will happen?

A Funny Thing Happened on the Way to the Forum Prologus tells us we are to see a comedy. In the opening song he tells us what will happen in Rome "around and about these three houses" and he fills us in on the occupants' backgrounds.

These are typical examples of the expository method employed in the best musicals. The principal difference between these and exposition in today's non-musical theatre is the compactness, precision, and immediacy of it in musicals.

The libretto style, akin as it is to Shakespeare's, is at best not something to be looked down on as on an idiot child. The fact that the libretto necessarily lacks character complexities which are inseparable hallmarks of the plays of Ibsen, Chekhov, Williams, Miller, and many others should not denigrate it. At its best the libretto is a skeletal play dressed with inseparable songs. One can admire Chekhov and Miller but also Rodgers and Hammerstein and Frank Loesser. The taste for caviar should not put down a craving for chocolate ice cream.

Actually the selection of subject matter in play and musical must frequently be quite different, and this difference is dictated solely by the problems raised by music inclusion. Subject matter in a play can cover a wider gamut than in a musical because of the greater time allowance in drama plus the non-interference of music. Not only can the subject matter itself be more complex but also the characters can be more changeable—less fixed. Because of time allotted to spoken dialogue in a musical, which is limited by the necessity of song and dance inclusion, it follows quite naturally that subject matter must be less complex—easier and more quickly exposed, developed, and resolved—and the characters who seem to bring these about must be correspondingly simple, direct, and non-complex. The librettist of a musical must be certain that plot and character machinations are clear in spite of time limitations and musical interference. Otherwise, subject matter per se in these two principal theatre divisions need not be especially different.

COMMENTS ON SUBJECT MATTER

Although he addresses many issues in "Subject Matter," Engel here raises what may be the single most important question about a musical: What is there to sing about?

The years since *Words With Music* have, in fact, increased our understanding of what a musical can sing about. Interestingly, several of the plays Engel imagined might be musicalized have been— Giraudoux's *The Madwoman of Chaillot* had already been made into *DearWorld*, a Broadway musical by Jerry Herman. (Engel discusses it in later chapters.) Many years after Engel proposed it, *A Streetcar Named Desire* was adapted into an opera by Andre Previn.

In comparing the subject matter of musicals to that of dramatic literature, even such unconventional plays as Edward Albee's *Who's Afraid of Virginia Woolf?* or Harold Pinter's *The Homecoming*, Engel reiterates points he made in his chapter on character, especially the way subject matter governs what happens and the need to clarify the way it does so.

He stresses that musicals are more limited in what they can cover and how subtly they can do so. Time may have proved him wrong. One of the breathtaking things about musicals in the thirty years since Engel wrote *Words with Music* is how fearless they are. We've had, for example, a rock version of *Hamlet* (the 1976 *Rockabye Hamlet*), admittedly a debacle, but a work displaying incredible chutzpah. We've had several musical treatments of the Vietnam war, one a huge success (*Miss Saigon*), another a rock treatment of Michael Herr's award-winning book, *Dispatches*, long and deservedly forgotten.

We've had a musical about American presidential assassins (named, appropriately enough, *Assassins*), and a musical based on the science fiction premise that extended drought has forced the population to use overpriced pay toilets (named, appropriately enough, *Urinetown*).

It would probably not have occurred to Engel to suggest that a musical could be based on the aesthetic theories of the French pointillist painter Georges Seurat, as Stephen Sondheim did in his 1984 *Sunday in the Park with George*. There can be differences of opinion on the success of what Sondheim achieved, but there can only be admiration for the audacity of the attempt.

In *Sunday*, the structure of the musical was based only in part on character and plot. The musical numbers took on a life of their own using the aesthetic principles rather than the personal idiosyncrasies of the main character.

Although the painter himself is the figure who ties everything together, *Sunday*, like the shows mentioned in the previous chapter, was a "collective" musical. It had numbers about all the main characters in Seurat's celebrated painting, *Sunday Afternoon on the Island of La Grand Jatte*.

If the musical *Sunday*'s understanding of character rarely went very deep, it might have been by design. One might say the characters were deliberately (painterly) flat, two-dimensional constructs, as if to conform to the reigning theories in 20th century painting, of which Seurat was a significant precursor.

What gave them depth was the power of Sondheim's music. It imitated Seurat's use of daubs of paint as building blocks, using simple musical motifs but combining them with extraordinary force in the finales to both acts, when the characters come together to "create" the painting.

The originality of *Sunday*, however, doesn't necessarily refute the general points Engel makes, especially the need for clarity, compactness and simplicity. Sondheim's experiment is almost the exception that proves the rule. It also suggests that, to use Engel's phrase, musical theatre can be caviar as well as chocolate ice cream.

The romantic element, which Engel considers integral to the musical, plays almost no role in *Sunday*, unless one counts as romance George's overriding passion for his art. It would be easy to list some extraordinarily successful musicals over the last thirty years, starting with *Cats*, in which romance was a side issue.

It would also be useful to list shows in which the idea of romance goes beyond the conventions Engel discusses, like a show that opened the same season as *Sunday*, Jerry Herman's 1983 *La Cage aux Folles*. A standard young couple in love did provide a necessary spur to *Cage*'s action, but the real focus was on two middle-aged gay lovers.

Gay subject matter had been the subtext of musical theatre long before either *La Cage* or the 1980 *March of the Falsettos*. In *Company*, back in 1970, there was some question about whether Bobby, whom all the other characters want to marry off, is gay. In a mid-Nineties London production Sondheim and the book writer, George Furth, permitted a suggestion that Bobby might have had flirtations with men but that he wasn't necessarily gay. In 1970, of course, even the idea that Bobby might be a closeted gay would have thrown the whole show out of whack.

The year before, 1969, there'd been an Off-Broadway show, *The Boys in the Band*, which had broached the issue of gay life, but many felt it did so in a caricatured way. Well before that there were the plays of Tennessee Williams, which dealt with gay characters often in cruel ways. In *A Streetcar Named Desire*, Blanche DuBois's offstage husband, when she discovers him with an older man, commits suicide. Brick in *Cat on a Hot Tin Roof* is undone by the rumor he's had a sexual relationship with a man who killed himself. In *Suddenly Last Summer* the homosexual man is assaulted and destroyed by a gang of adolescents. But all these situations were regarded as figments of Williams' fevered, poetic imagination. If anything, the subject seemed too radioactive to deal with. The idea of treating it in a musical seemed especially odd.

The show that really brought gay subject matter into the open was the 1975 *A Chorus Line*, the brainchild of Michael Bennett, who'd choreographed both *Company* and *Follies*. Ostensibly, *A Chorus Line* is about an audition for the chorus of a splashy musical. That is, it's about all the ciphers who go through years of training and agony in order to do time steps behind The Star. But if show business is the stated topic of *A Chorus Line*, the subject that occupies much of its attention is homosexuality. Throughout "Hello, Twelve, Hello, Thirteen, Hello, Love," the long number about adolescence, several of the male dancers recall the moment they realized they were gay.

Ultimately, the emotional high point of the show is the long monologue in which a dancer recalls the moment when he could no longer conceal from his father that he was gay. The response he expected—anger, disavowal—isn't what his father displays. Instead he asks one of the other dancers to show a fatherly concern for the boy. Interestingly, this dramatic high point is not sung. In a show that moves seamlessly between song, dance and very terse dialogue, this crucial scene is entirely spoken. "Coming out" was not yet something to be done in music.

The most dramatic statement along these lines came eight years later in Jerry Herman's *La Cage Aux Folles*. At the end of the first act Albin, the female impersonator, angry about his longtime partner's nervousness about acknowledging his identity before prospective in-laws, sings the defiant, "I Am What I Am."

Hugh Southern, an Englishman, fell in love with Broadway in 1954 when he saw *Damn Yankees*. Southern, who ran Theatre Development Fund, the National Endowment for the Arts and the Metropolitan Opera, once theorized that the great arc of Broadway musicals, most of which were written by Jews, began in 1943 with *Oklahoma!*, when Richard Rodgers and Oscar Hammerstein II, two assimilated Jews, wrote a show celebrating being American. The arc reached its peak twenty-one years later in *Fiddler on the Roof*, when another set of assimilated Jews, composer Jerry Bock, lyricist Sheldon Harnick, bookwriter Joseph Stein, and, above all, director-choreographer Jerome Robbins, were comfortable enough in America to celebrate being Jewish.

Something similar crested in *La Cage Aux Folles* with its unabashed assertion of gay pride, even in as silly a manifestation as a night club devoted to drag entertainment. By 1983, when *La Cage* opened, AIDS had made enough of an impact that there was no point in being coy.

Nor was it possible to treat gay issues without acknowledging tragic possibilities. In 1980 William Finn and James Lapine's *March of the Falsettos*, which began with a quartet entitled "Four Jews in a Room Bitching" told the story of a bisexual who leaves his wife and child for another man but, amazingly, does so without creating any bitterness. This might have been construed as wish-fulfillment rather than drama, since all the conflicts the plot raised were resolved amicably.

But in only a few years AIDS transformed the landscape. Gay subject matter seemed less conducive to happy-ever-after endings. Finn and Lapine revisited their characters in the 1990 *Falsettoland*. What began as unconventional romantic love had grown into something stronger—communal love, which enabled the community to look beyond the tragedy that had befallen it. In 2003 Finn wrote *Elegies*, a concert piece based in part on the friends he'd lost to AIDS. The tone of some of the numbers had a sombreness unimaginable from the composer of "Four Jews in a Room Bitching." Reality, which the musical theatre had generally kept at bay, was now darkening, even deepening its perspective.

Gay themes and concerns began to predominate the musical theatre. When *Cabaret* was revived in 1998 in a production directed by the English director Sam Mendes, it was no longer a proscenium show. It was set in the Berlin night club where Sally Bowles performs. The audience became patrons of the club, whose "regulars" are unusually decadent.

When Hal Prince began rehearsals for the original 1966 production he showed the cast a photograph taken in Chicago that year of a group of white supremacists threatening civil rights marchers. The subtext of *Cabaret*—heightened by the use of a mirror that reflected the audience—was that we were all potentially racists, like the citizens of Thirties Germany in which the show is set.

But thirty-odd years later the focus has shifted considerably. Now we're all decadents, hedonists. We're no longer potential Nazis. We're potential victims. Whereas Joel Grey, the original host of the cabaret, acknowledged he based his mesmerizing interpretation on Hitler, the spellbinder who held stadiums full of people in his thrall, his successor, Alan Cumming, played the emcee as a sexual provocateur. In the final image of Mendes' version we see him wearing a pink triangle in a concentration camp (somewhat confusing given that at the end of the first act he bared his rear end, which had a swastika tattooed on it). The thirty years had wrought a huge change in interpretations. Interestingly, Prince, who defined the political subtext of the original production, complimented the revival for raising gay issues, suggesting that was not possible the first time around, as if homosexual concerns would have taken precedence over the social issues implicit in the original.

If *Sunday in the Park with George* seemed an unlikely answer to the question of why a given subject necessitated song, so did an earlier Sondheim show, the 1979 *Sweeney Todd*, about a vengeful barber who slits his customers' throats, then sends the bodies down to his neighbor, who bakes them into pies. Would Rodgers and Hammerstein have considered this a theme for a musical? Lerner and Loewe? Probably not. It's hard to imagine any other practitioner of musical theatre eager to deal with so dark a theme, but Sondheim tackled it triumphantly, again because of the depth of his musical and verbal resources.

However extreme a situation *Sweeney* represents, it does deal with a fundamental human concern, revenge. Revenge resonates with a larger part of the population than, say, the call for tolerance that underlies *South Pacific*. Revenge is, among other things, at the heart of Elizabethan tragedy. *Sweeney* depicts vengeance on a comparable scale while relying on the same means, a mastery of the English language.

When we look at successful shows, it strikes us as entirely natural that they should have been turned into great musicals, but inevitability is often a product of retrospection. It wasn't inevitable that someone who optioned James Michener's collection of short stories, *Tales of the South Pacific*, would have turned it into the masterpiece we know. Several songwriting teams rejected the idea of turning Shaw's *Pygmalion* into a musical. It was hardly inevitable that the supremely elegant *My Fair Lady* would result.

In both cases the success of the show depended on the skills— let's use a more precise word, genius—of the creators. In recent years there has been no limit to ideas for musicals. However, few have attained the classic status of those we've been discussing. Very often these shows have, so to speak, "followed the rules." They meet the criteria Engel enunciated in this book and in his workshop at BMI. But they never took off, because they lacked that spark of inspiration that goes beyond "the rules."

Conversely, a show written well before *Words With Music,* but largely neglected because of its "book problems," was the Kurt Weill-Ira Gershwin *Lady in the Dark*, based on Moss Hart's experience with psychoanalysis. In 1943 this was considered radical territory, and the results are admittedly uneven. Whether or not Sigmund Freud's ideas were worth singing about, whether or not Hart treated them validly in his story about a successful magazine editor trying to solve the riddle of her unhappy childhood, Weill's score retains its luster simply because he was a composer of genius.

The choice of the right material to sing about, of course, is by no means a guarantee a show will work. Certain subjects seem logical for musical treatment. What, for example, could be more natural to sing about than the birth of a baby? Richard Maltby, Jr., and David Shire looked at the subject from several perspectives in their beautiful 1983 score for *Baby*. They rose to the level of the subject matter in their impassioned songs, but the plot seemed rather petty, almost like a TV sitcom, not of sufficient stature for the subject.

In a similar vein, given that a large percentage of the people who've written great musicals have been Jews, it's curious there have been no major musicals about the immigrant experience. Not surprisingly, Irving Berlin, himself an infant immigrant, made a powerful statement on the subject in his choral setting of "The New Colossus," the Emma Lazarus poem on the base of the Statue of Liberty, but the seriousness of this chorus stands out from the convoluted, not very convincing plot of the musical in which it appeared, *Miss Liberty*, a whimsical treatment of how the great symbol came to its place in New York Harbor. The chorus also resides in a different musical universe than the rest of the generally light-hearted score.

In 1986 Charles Strouse, Stephen Schwartz and Joseph Stein set out to tackle this colossal theme in their musical *Rags*, based on an original story by Stein that encompassed early 20th century New York politics, the Triangle Factory fire and the difficult subject of assimilation.

What should have contributed to making this a landmark musical was the Broadway debut of the great dramatic soprano Teresa Stratas, the child of Greek immigrants to Canada. It also had a remarkable score, including a bravura aria for Stratas, "Blame It On the Summer Night," some powerful choruses and a beautifully ironic number for Larry Kert expressing a "greenhorn's" yearning to be an American, sung with a dignified but unmistakable Yiddish inflection, "I Want to Be a Yankee Boy."

Despite its talented team and cast, the musical endured a troubled tryout in Boston, where its inexperienced director, Joan Micklin Silver, best known for her 1975 film *Hester Street*, was fired. She had directed for the theatre (the modest revue *A . . . My Name Is Alice*) but never on this scale. (It was to the credit of the creative team that they recognized there were problems with the show in spite of the fact that the Boston audience was extremely receptive. If they'd gauged the need for change on the enthusiastic audience response the night I saw it in Boston, they wouldn't have altered a line.)

Virtually every major director was flown to Boston, including Jerome Robbins, who urged the creators to leave it alone. Gene Saks, who eventually accepted the assignment, looked back on Robbins' advice ruefully, when the show closed after a week on Broadway. "We took out the things that camouflaged its deficiencies," he observed.

The problems, in fact, were far more fundamental. Among those asked to take over the show was the South African director Louis Burke, who pointed out that the approach underlying *Rags* was totally wrongheaded. The plot, he said, implied that coming to America had been a mistake. Given the fate of the Jews who'd remained in Eastern Europe, such thinking made no sense. Here was a case where the choice of subject couldn't have been richer, the score full of treasures, but the overall execution was undermined by philosophical myopia.

Many musicals have taken their subject matter from other forms, especially films. One of Cole Porter's wittiest works was *Silk Stockings*, based on the equally witty Ernst Lubitsch film *Ninotchka*. Jerry Bock, Sheldon Harnick and Joe Masteroff created an enchanting musical, *She Loves Me*, from another enchanting Lubitsch film, *The Little Shop Around the Corner*. One of the most novel of these transformations was John Kander and Fred Ebb's *Chicago*, a musical version of the film *Roxie Hart*. Long after its initial 1975 Broadway run, *Chicago* made a glorious return to its Hollywood roots in the 2002 Oscar-winning film.

English classics have not always worked as musicals. Lionel Bart's *Oliver* remains popular. *Pickwick* enjoyed popularity in London, not New York. One of the most innovative adaptations of Dickens was Rupert Holmes' 1984 *The Mystery of Edwin Drood*, which Dickens left unfinished. Holmes allowed the audience to vote on the ending. (On the original cast recording you can hear all the endings; in performance you would only hear the one you'd voted on.) Among other beloved English books, the 1985 *Wind in the Willows*, with book by Jane Iredale, lyrics by Roger McGough and William Perry, and score by William Perry, is an endearing version of the story, misproduced on Broadway in 1985. *The Secret Garden* was given a lush, quasi-operatic treatment by Lucy Simon in 1991 that failed to convey the simple verities of the book. A few years earlier TheatreWorks USA presented a 90-minute musical version of *The Secret Garden* by Kim Oler and Alison Hubbard that conveyed the book's themes much more powerfully.

Interestingly, fiction hasn't always been a productive source for musicals. One of Rodgers and Hammerstein's few outright failures was *Pipe Dream*, based on John Steinbeck's *Sweet Thursday*, though they achieved moderate success with *Flower Drum Song*, based on C.Y. Lee's novel, and, of course, a triumph with Hammerstein and Joshua Logan's adaptation of *Tales of the South Pacific*. Lerner and Loewe struggled, not always successfully, to bring T.H. White's *Once and Future King* to the stage in *Camelot*.

Fictional Americana has sometimes translated successfully to the stage, as in one of the most remarkable of all musicals, Oscar

Hammerstein and Jerome Kern's *Show Boat*, based on an Edna Ferber novel. Howard Dietz and Arthur Schwartz made a lovely adaptation of the Betty Field novel *A Tree Grows in Brooklyn*. For my taste, *Big River* lacks a score to capture the depths of Twain's *Huckleberry Finn*.

Richard Adler and Jerry Ross made a rousing musical, *The Pajama Game* from Richard Bissell's bestseller about labor relations, *Seven and a Half Cents*. A year later they repeated their success with *Damn Yankees*, based on Douglass Wallop's *The Year the Yankees Lost the Pennant*. Both these shows appeared within a few years of the novels' runs on the best-seller lists. A musical version of Marjorie Kinnan Rawlings' beloved novel *The Yearling*, however, was just a one-night stand in the Sixties, decades after the book had achieved classic status. Harold Rome's musical version of Margaret Mitchell's *Gone With the Wind* had a long run in Tokyo but has never been mounted close to home.

The most recent attempt to transfer fictional success to the stage is *Ragtime*, based on E.L. Doctorow's bestseller about America in the presumably tranquil, innocent years before World War I. With an adaptation by Terrence McNally and score by Lynn Ahrens and Stephen Flaherty, *Ragtime* carefully replicated the characters and story of Doctorow's book. The musical has several powerful numbers, especially "On the Wheels of a Dream," as sung by Brian Stokes Mitchell. What made the novel distinctive, however, was the author's detached, ironic voice, which the musical did not capture.

Most of the musicals we've been considering have been conceived for Broadway, where they must please a large and diverse audience in order to stay afloat. In recent years many musicals have begun their lives Off-Broadway, where they need not attract as large an audience, though they won't succeed if they don't appeal to diverse tastes.

The first and most successful musical to begin life Off-Broadway (where it ran for nearly 42 years) was Tom Jones and Harvey Schmidt's *The Fantasticks*, based on a late 19th century French play about parents, who, contrary to convention, want their children to marry and thus set out creating obstacles so their wish might come to pass. *The Fantasticks*, turning the tables as it does on the conventions of romance, might not have seemed an obvious choice for a musical.

That Jones and Schmidt had to audition their piece for more than fifty potential producers suggests how odd their choice of material seemed. Jones's whimsical book and lyrics and Schmidt's literally enchanting score, however, turned what might have been a cerebral conceit into an emotionally powerful experience.

My hunch is that if Engel had been presented with a premise for a musical based on a young man's memory of an immigrant woman who babysat for him while turning tricks in a trailer, he'd have blanched. Nor, as we shall see, would he have been enchanted by the prospect of a rock score, though he would have acknowledged that it was the only appropriate musical idiom for John Cameron Mitchell and Stephen Trask's *Hedwig and the Angry Inch*, an enormously seductive show about an East German immigrant whose sex change operation has been botched and who is searching for his "other half."

If anything, the last thirty years have taught us that no subject matter can be dismissed outright. All depends on the execution.

Engel devotes considerable space in this chapter to the first scenes of musicals, which let the audience know at once what the evening is about. This is one area where the musicals' structure is importantly different from that of nonmusical plays. There can't be guessing games. In part this difference has to do with the audience. People coming to a musical, though nowadays prepared for things far from conventional, aren't necessarily willing to exert great intellectual effort to understand the terrain. This may explain why there has yet to be an effort to musicalize *The Caretaker*.

Even with a musical intended to be unabashedly entertaining, the opening apparently made all the difference. Sondheim's 1962 *A Funny Thing Happened on the Way to the Forum* was floundering in its tryout in Washington, D.C. Knowing the score and the plot, we may find it hard to understand why the audience failed to respond to its charms instantly, but they didn't. Only with the insertion, late in the Washington run, of "Comedy Tonight" as the opening number— to tell the audience unmistakably that they were about to see a farce, long an out-of-fashion genre —did the rest of the show click.

Forum is a useful reminder that even with subject matter that seems basic and surefire, the exposition has to be solid, which is why Engel next addressed the issue of structure.

4

The Outer Shape

Still glides the stream, and shall forever glide;
The form remains, the function never dies.

William Wordsworth
The River Duddon

The single stage setting is frequently an expression of production economy. Not only did the play cost much less to mount but there was always an eye on later reproductions in stock, little theatres, amateur presentations, etc., and such considerations were not to be ignored. But sometimes the single set defines a style or manner.

In the American musical in the beginning (nineteenth century) shows ran into as many as five acts and few were done with fewer than three sets. It is my suspicion that from the outset, musicals were considered "frivolous," and the spectacle aspect was therefore regarded with pleasurable anticipation. At first each act was a single scene with a single setting. This was undoubtedly due to underdeveloped stage machinery, which caused long delays in scene shifting. By the time we reached the Twenties and Thirties of this century, we had "improved" the mechanics of production; the book musical, then evolving, was in competition with the lavish and, at first, popular revues and movies which abounded in scenic spectacle. The competing musical show authors, producers, and directors began to "open up the proscenium" because, in the first place, frequent scene changes had become possible. Secondly, the aspect of seeing the action instead of having it described was theatrically more desirable, and finally this multi-scene practice automatically provided the opportunity for spectacle.

For example, the play *My Sister Eileen*, in three acts, transpired in the Greenwich Village basement apartment of two career-seeking sisters from Ohio. Jerome Chodorov and Joseph Fields, who had written the original play, adapted it as the libretto for *Wonderful Town* and opened it up into thirteen scenes (two acts), which included the street in front of the apartment, the apartment, the "garden" court-yard behind their apartment, the editor's office (which included three fanciful vignettes), a subway, a producer's office, the Brooklyn Navy Yard, a police station, a street, and a Village night club! (The apartment itself was reused several times.)

In order to keep the action in a state of nearly perpetual motion, the "crossover" was invented, and this immediately became a musi-cal-comedy must. (A "crossover" is usually a brief scene which takes place in front of a "traveler"—a curtain that moves from side to side insead of up and down.) This short scene—often assigned a specific locale, a street, a park, etc.—was sometimes a song, a reprise of a song for chorus, a dialogue, a parade or, as often as not, anything that followed immediately after the conclusion of a "full-stage" scene and carried the characters into the then reset new "full-stage" scene without a break in the action. For at least two decades this practice inhabited every musical show. Although it prevented any "wait" it was also too obvious that it was employed as a device to bridge change of scenery and it very often served no other function.

I have tabulated the plays in the "Best American Plays" series edited by John Gassner (six volumes) in relation to the factors I have mentioned above and I find that out of a total of 113 successful and occasionally distinguished plays in this period (1916–1963), fifty-three employ a single set; seventy-six are in three acts; twenty-four are written without divided acts—i.e., there are no separate scenes; thirty-seven have large interior passages of time (between acts and/or scenes); forty (only) were comedies (perishability?). Out of those 113 "best plays" covering a span of approximately fifty years, a number of the serious plays survives in production, while only eight of the comedies still receive any major attention. Eleven have been adapted as librettos for musicals, and of those only four were box-office successes. Four were converted into operas and two others were great successes.

The dividing of plays into three acts has not nearly always been a theatre practice. While the Greek dramatists employed a single-act form they pointed ahead to another greatly expanded outer shape in their trilogies, such as Aeschylus' *Oresteia*—actually three long one-act plays, *Agamemnon, The Choephori*, and *The Eumenides*, which occupied three separate performances and scenery was usually employed (fifth century B.C.).

Scenery in the theatre has been discarded from time to time, reintroduced, elaborately expanded in the Renaissance and Baroque periods, and again today, especially with "theatre in the round," it is often not employed although every kind of complex stage machinery exists and theatrical lighting has become a fine art. There was no scenery in the theatre of Shakespeare, who in his plays invariably (most scholars agree) employed five acts. Each act was further divided into two, three, or as many as nine scenes. While insofar as we know Shakespeare gave no indication of place in his sceneryless plays, he frequently began the dialogue with precise signs.

In *Macbeth*, Act One, Scene 6, Duncan, the king, begins: "This castle hath a pleasant seat," etc. In *Othello*, Act Two, Scene 1: MONTANO: "What from the cape can you discern at sea?" In *Hamlet*, Act One, Scene 5 begins: HAMLET (to the Ghost): "Whither wilt thou lead me? Speak; I'll go no further"—indicating that they have arrived at another place.

Shakespeare never indicated time between scenes either, but the necessary information was supplied in the dialogue in an earlier scene which pointed ahead, as for example in *The Comedy of Errors*: "I'll go to the Centaur, to go seek this slave; I greatly fear my money is not safe."

Because in Shakespeare's theatre there was no scenery, the playwright had every opportunity to proceed from place to place without pause—a practice which also allowed the audience to use its own not inconsiderable imagination to the fullest.

In the theatre of Richard Brinsley Sheridan, which followed Shakespeare's by more than a century and a half, both *The Rivals* and *The School for Scandal* were in five acts, with each act further divided two, three, or four times. The settings are indicated in the scripts, and scenery was used.

In the seventeenth-century French theatre (taking its inspiration from the Greeks) the plays of Corneille, Racine, and Molière also follow the five-act formula, but with a difference. In these plays a single setting applicable to the entire act (sometimes to an entire play) is listed, although the acts themselves are divided into scenes. These latter, however, are not "scenes" according to our understanding of the term, nor, for that matter, Shakespeare's. As employed in the French theatre, they repeat a practice used in opera. The term "scene" indicates merely a section of an act involving one or any number of characters who have either just made an entrance or who have been left onstage when others have exited. The onstage players then play a "scene," which, as indicated before, corresponds to similar terms in, for example, the operas of Mozart. It is as if in *Hamlet*, after the departure of the court in Act One, Scene 1—leaving Hamlet alone for the "Oh, that this too, too solid flesh" soliloquy—Shakespeare had given that aria a scene number.

In Spain, half a century before Corneille, the great Lope de Vega, who wrote many verse plays, divided them into only three acts, each of which was in turn divided into numerous small scenes, all designating changes of place. In the early nineteenth century the German genius Georg Büchner, operating outside the mainstream, wrote thoroughly original fragmentary expressionistic plays. His *Danton's Death* is set down as four acts, each act divided (and each with a change of locate) into six, seven, ten, and nine scenes respectively. *Woyzeck*, even more episodic, has no act division but is set in twenty-nine scenes.

The later nineteenth-century dramatists, who eschewed music entirely, set out directly for realism and comment (stated or strongly implied) on contemporary social problems. Chekhov wrote his plays in four acts with set changes, while Strindberg wrote his in three, nearly all contained in a single set. In the plays of both writers, time or passage of time is stated explicitly in the text. Until the middle of the nineteenth century time indications had not been traditional, but they have become so again today.

The act-scene practices of Shakespeare versus Sheridan versus Molière versus Lope de Vega versus Büchner versus Chekhov versus Strindberg only demonstrate the wide differences among these distinguished playwrights through three centuries and in many places. Only each "school" seems to have established its own particular outer shape, and we today can only observe and accept as fact what was, without assigning any special reason to any one practice.

On the other hand, in musicals today the crossover has become old-fashioned and we have some new things going for us. Both *Man of La Mancha* and *1776* are given in a single act without intermission, although there are scene changes in both. And *Company* has a single set throughout which *seems* to change, owing to varied lighting and the employment of different playing areas. *Company* is in two acts with many *suggested* place changes.

Before leaving this cataloguing of act-scene divisions practiced by leading playwrights through several centuries, it seems appropriate to make a comment about act-scene lengths. In a majority of cases the plays' lengths are quite evenly divided by the number of acts. The five-act play is divided into five more or less equal segments. A three-act play trisects. The scenes which in turn divide the acts into smaller cells, however, are in no way equal in length to one another. Take, for example, Act Five of *Julius Caesar*, which is not "special." Act Five contains five scenes. In print, Scene 1 occupies nearly three columns; Scene 2 is six *lines* long; Scene 3 fills two columns; Scene 4 less than one; and Scene 5 is nearly two columns long. This same general asymmetry is to be noted among the scene divisions of all plays.

Let us now examine briefly the musical theatre only from this one point of view, the outer shape. Monteverdi, a contemporary of Shakespeare, wrote his opera *Orfeo* in a prologue and five acts. The sets are not stated but, as in Shakespeare, they are nevertheless clearly implied by the characters, their lyrics, and the situations. Jean-Philippe Rameau, one and a half centuries later when opera at the court of Louis XIV was truly spectacular, wrote usually in five acts, each of which was divided, as in the plays of Corneille and Racine, into many "scenes" which similarly did not constitute set changes. Gluck's *Orfeo*, first produced in Vienna (1762), two years before Rameau's death, had four acts. Mozart's *Don Giovanni* (1787) had two acts but ten scenes, all clearly indicating change of place. Rossini's *Il Barbiere di Siviglia* (1816) had only two acts, Wagner's *Die Meistersinger* (1868) had three acts with four scene changes, and Verdi's *Aïda* (1871) and Bizet's *Carmen* (1875) had four acts. Again in opera, as in the plays recounted above, there was no uniformity of outer shape.

On the operetta side, the works of the Viennese Johann Strauss were usually in three acts, the Parisian Offenbach's in four, and London's Gilbert and Sullivan wrote invariably in two acts. The Strauss works stemmed clearly (musically and libretto-wise) from opera. Offenbach also followed his own native opera models, but he satirized what they did, unabashedly and seriously. Gilbert and Sullivan created their own style and form. The two-act shape they more or less invented in many ways parallels our current musical-comedy form. It is curious that coming at the same period, Strauss, Offenbach, and Sullivan wrote so differently from one another, but it is true that they sprang out of (or away from) opera and all lampooned their common mother.

Victor Herbert, an Irish émigré who had studied in Vienna, made a conscious effort to reproduce Viennese operetta in the United States, but what he wrote was no more Viennese than the early Florentine operas were revivals of Greek tragedy which they purported to be. What Herbert actually did (and the Florentine Monodists as well) was to start something new. Whereas the Viennese operettas never actually took root here (nor did those of Gilbert and Sullivan or Offenbach), what Herbert wrote, being simpler musically, lyrically, and bookwise, became a jumping-off place for American musical theatre as we now know it. It *connected* with the American audience because this audience fully understood and empathized with it. The early Herbert shows were strongly local in feeling, plot, and song, and these qualities were essential bases for anything that could have taken root here. What he wrote was not an importation; it was, by default, something new. Serendipity at work!

Today's American musical has followed almost exclusively the outer shape evolved here by Herbert and used exclusively, at a somewhat earlier time, by Gilbert and Sullivan, though this latter fact played no part whatsoever in the American musical evolution. With the notable exception of the Stephen Sondheim-Arthur Laurents recent three-act *Anyone Can Whistle* and Frank Loesser's *The Most Happy Fella*, all contemporary musicals are multi-scene shows divided into two acts. The why of this must be largely a matter of conjecture. It is not obligatory. That this outer shape works well, when it works at all, is true. It is also an easier one to work in since an act break—especially in a musical—poses precarious problems. The end of Act One must beg a question that will involve the audience sufficiently to *necessitate* its return to the theatre even if it knows how the question will ultimately be answered. When the show is in *three* acts, the same problem has to be faced twice!

It is relevant here to mention again two recent musicals—big successes—which contained no act divisions at all: *Man of La Mancha* and *1776*. While this is the safest way of keeping an audience—suspense or no—in both cases the shows work better without interruptions.

In our two-act form, the first act is usually the longest and strongest—the best foot forward—and Act Two is generally only two thirds as long, containing the resolution of the multiple situation set-ups and often a number of musical reprises. There is invariably less *new* musical material in Act Two, partly because there is little time to establish or develop it. It is not impossible that our usual three-act play—if it is a good one—works without the requirement of the sharp act break-off that seems so essential to the musical because we (audiences) are creatures of habit. Perhaps we are all Pavlov dogs. We have grown accustomed to one practice and easily accept the tenseless act breaks in plays, whereas in musicals we have been conditioned differently.

It is curious to conjecture that the musical theatre may have begun in various ways to influence contemporary drama. Many new plays—and for the first time—have adopted the two-act form and a few others have abandoned the intermission altogether. This business of mutual influence is common practice. Classical music leaves its imprint on popular music usually about thirty years later. Contrary-wise, Aaron Copland employs rhythmic ideas which were in common usage in popular music three decades before Copland. Picasso has been greatly influenced by centuries-old African primitive art. The general style and purpose of Debussy's *Pelléas et Mélisande* (1902) were inspired by opera's earliest beginnings in the sixteenth century. And so it goes.

In stimulating plays we do not have these same needs. We witness a more complex intellectual problem—a game of chess—in which every speech (or move) makes enough of a contribution in itself to stimulate and hold our interest. From this point of view, let us examine *A Streetcar Named Desire*. Although Williams wrote *Streetcar* in eleven scenes, it was performed at its first production with two intermissions. There is no question that it worked well with the act breaks, but it is my feeling that it would have been even better had it been given as written—with no intermissions. I think that 1947 was just too early for anyone to have had the courage to try it without a break.

There are, however, differences between this play, which is not unique *(Death of a Salesman, A Thousand Clowns, Come Back, Little Sheba,* and others possess similar qualities), and musicals—differences in the "cell" or scene structure. These "cells" are not so much defined by their physical limits as by what they achieve singly and their relationship to the entire scheme of things. *A Streetcar Named Desire* in "cell" structure is not vastly different from other best contemporary plays. *West Side Story* is similar in its structure to *My Fair Lady, Fiddler on the Roof,* and others of its kind. But in this respect there are basic differences between plays and musicals. These differences constitute a basic interior formal difference between all best plays and all best musicals.

In *Streetcar*, the action is not thrust forward; the principal character is gradually, painfully developed from her first entrance to her final exit. (The outer action is minuscule.) The action is not what is most essential to the play. What is essential is the unfolding, reacting, desperate character of Blanche DuBois and (mentioned earlier) the sensitive poetic writing that Williams infuses it with.

In *Death of a Salesman*, also, the *action* is slight. The principal (also single) character evolution and the sometimes fanciful dramatic style of Miller's writing are the important elements. *The Member of the Wedding, Who's Afraid of Virginia Woolf?, They Knew What They Wanted, Desire Under the Elms*, and many others might be termed "character development" plays. The action is secondary and exists as a kind of cohesive framework for the more important element of character development. This is neither new nor peculiarly American. It was a method practiced by Chekhov, Ibsen, and Strindberg and more recently by Pinter, Albee, Sartre, Anouilh, and Ionesco.

Because the action (plot movement) in most of these plays is so secondary in importance, designated time spaces separate many scenes or many acts. There is no sense of urgency. In *Streetcar*, Scene

1 is early May; Scene 2, the following evening; Scene 5 is not indicated as to time and could be weeks later; Scene 6, later the same evening; Scene 7 is mid-September (four months later than Scene 1); Scene 8, three quarters of an hour later; Scene 9, later that evening; Scene 10, a few hours later, Scene 11, some weeks later. In much of Chekhov and Ibsen, although lapse of time is not indicated between acts, a director could easily place them months apart.

Let me return to the "thrust," or forward propulsion, which is by no means new to some plays and very important to most musicals. Certainly in *West Side Story* it is most obvious. Tony's meeting with Maria must result in still more meetings. His promise to her to halt the scheduled rumble cannot possibly be carried out. After the killing of Bernardo, Tony is doomed. How, when, or where will it happen? The audience is thrust ahead of the action itself, knowing that it must happen, and waits breathless to see how, when, and where.

In the farces of Feydeau, the thrust is incessantly shoving the audience ahead. We see disaster forming, we wonder when a door will open, revealing to an irate husband his wife in bed with another man. We see people tiptoeing up a staircase in an effort to avoid being seen by someone. It seems inevitable that the avoidance will fail. We sit on the edges of our seats stifling a scream. Sometimes helplessly the scream slips out. Sometimes we simply hold our breaths, then breathe again when the threat of recognition has disappeared.

Shakespeare, centuries earlier, used the same devices with similar effects in *Twelfth Night* and *The Comedy of Errors*. He also used the thrust in *every* play. We know that Hamlet will go to confront the ghost of his father, that he will endeavor to use the players to show the king's guilt, etc. (These things we anticipate and more like them.) We know that Macbeth and his lady will murder the king, since the first of the witches' prophecies has materialized and their ambition will not allow them patience in the face of opportunity. We know that Iago's evil plot to torture Othello will succeed, and we are always one step ahead of him as he proceeds with his destructiveness.

It is because of the thrust in musicals that the best of them (the tightest and most effective) occupy in their entirety very short spans of time: one day, two days, or three. In the best musicals usually it is the action, the plot, and subplot that take precedence over character development. Because the action must proceed at a rapid pace (the songs and dances consume so much time that everything else needs to be paced especially quickly) there is normally little or no opportunity for character development, and there is no need for it since the time span in most is constricted and interior character revelation occupies many of the songs. *West Side Story*—action-packed—is in two acts with fifteen scenes. It commences at 5 P.M. and concludes at midnight the next night. Most of the fifteen scenes follow in time immediately after or simultaneously with each succeeding one. *My Fair Lady*, in two acts with eighteen scenes, is slightly different. The first five scenes span four days; the next three (several months later, allowing Eliza Doolittle to improve her speech) and the last three of Act One six weeks later to demonstrate her complete speech mastery. All seven scenes of Act Two follow the end of Act One by only a few hours. The eight scenes which constitute Act One of *Wonderful Town* follow one another almost immediately and the five scenes of Act Two continue on at once. The *Oklahoma!* scenes are consecutive in time. In *Carousel* there is a one-month pause in Act One to show the effects of Billy's marriage to Julie and a fifteen-year lapse in Act Two to show Billy's daughter's growth. This latter lapse, however, is accomplished in the "heaven" scene in three lines:

> STARKEEPER: …SHE's fifteen years old.
> BILLY: …How could that be? I just came from there.
> STARKEEPER: …A year on earth is just a minute up here.

I think it must be clear that the outer shapes of both plays and musicals run a wide gamut. It must be equally clear that no rules govern the writer's choice of shape appropriate to his ideas and style. While there are some basic similarities between the outer shapes of some plays and some librettos, the factor that must receive primary consideration is tempo. If the playwright is dealing with characters rather than events, philosophy and argument as opposed to plot and movement, he can linger and savor every small dynamic, provided, of course, his material is rich enough to sustain the audience's attention. The outer shapes can be broad. Ionesco's *Rhinoceros*, Sartre's *No Exit*, Pinter's *Caretaker*, and Chekhov's *The Sea Gull* are notable examples. The physical requirements are small, the emotional and inner conflicting churnings enormous.

On the directly opposite end of the spectrum—not less, not more, but differently conceived—are those plays that explode with happenings, bristle to say what they mean, erupt restlessly through many small units that often leave audiences gasping. *Macbeth, Hamlet*, and *Woyzeck* amply illustrate plays in this group, and I think *Fiddler on the Roof, West Side Story*, and *Guys and Dolls* are models of musicals similarly conceived. But the "cells" (scenes) in all of the best musicals have these two things in common: Each ends simultaneously with an exclamation point (figuratively) and an index finger that points ahead to future action.

The outer shape contains, like bookends, one quality that is too often misunderstood. This is predictability. It occurs in the minds of audiences at a musical show especially soon after the initial set-up, continues throughout, and leads to an "I knew it all along" at the end. While it is strongly related to the outer shape, in reality it "lines" its insides and, if used wisely, can contribute enormously to the workability of the whole show.

Predictability, whether in a play or a libretto, can be a most useful and compelling force, or it can destroy everything by making it devastatingly dull. Somehow there has arisen a totally untrue idea that predictability in a plot is something that should be avoided. The only possible excuse for this, to me, is in the case of a detective story, which I think—because of complications and red herrings—should necessarily be eschewed by composers and librettists for musicals.

Sometimes what we experience consists only of a feeling that something will go amiss. In *Carousel*, when Billy and Jigger leave the clambake to perpetrate a hold-up, we are uneasy, but in this case, that is the extent of predictability. At other times, as in *West Side Story*, when the two romantic strangers from violently opposing groups meet and fall carelessly in love, we can predict the direst of results. (I say "carelessly" because had they been capable of realizing the precariousness of their positions, they might have exercised more caution and perhaps run away.) But this Romeo and Juliet plot knows no caution and can see no danger. The latter view is given to the audience.

Predictability can take on many different workable guises. In *Fiddler on the Roof* we know bit by bit that Tevye, out of love for his daughters, will break with tradition just as far as he is able to. But over the whole show hangs the threat of a pogrom. It is so intrinsically important that the strongest manifestation of the threat closes Act One. Act Two—the end of the show—is the *real* thing, and Tevye and what remains of his family will have to go on. We knew it at the start.

When the curtain rises on *My Fair Lady* and we hear the wailing and we see the filthy Eliza trying to sell her flowers, we know at once that we are watching Cinderella. We say, "Wait till she gets cleaned up, learns to speak properly, and wears a lovely gown! What a moment that will be!" That takes care of Act One. In Act Two, Scene 1, when Eliza states her position ("Now that you've made me a lady, what am I to do?"), we know how it will come out. Furthermore, we care a great deal about its coming out our way.

1776 is the clearest example of all because we know by the title, the setting (the Continental Congress in Philadelphia), the progressively changing calendar on the wall what must inevitably happen, but we are nervously concerned until the very end—when the Declaration of Independence is actually signed. In Frank Loesser's two fables, *Guys and Dolls* and *How to Succeed in Business Without Really Trying*, the people are not intended to be more than cardboard. Both shows are morality plays and farces. We know that everything will turn out well, but we need to see how.

Certainly with classical plays the same is true. Iago will avenge himself on the gullible Othello, who will finally destroy himself. Macbeth's overambitiousness will lead to his own ruin. Romeo and Juliet's total disregard of danger will destroy them. Portia will best Shylock. All will end well in the comedies of Shakespeare, and this pleases and interests us from the start.

The Restoration comedies hold no surprises. Nor does Chekhov. It cannot truly be said that the major contemporary playwrights surprise us. Often they leave us guessing *after* the play.

When predictability works against a stage work—that is, when we are bored *because* we know how it will all come out—something is drastically wrong. After all, in the other arts we go again and again to see El Greco's "View of Toledo" or "Burial of Count Orgaz" or Praxiteles' Hermes or Michelangelo's David, provided that we are deeply involved with them, that each experience is a new one and we see *all* of them in every detail that we saw before and perhaps find new details we did not notice earlier. We see ballets again and again (sometimes, to be sure, because of different stars). We go to revivals of plays and to operas and musicals not because we have seen and heard them before and know how they will "turn out" but because we enjoy them.

There is the crux and the crux is due to the weaving throughout of characters, dialogue, songs, dances, verses, and every imaginable fresh kind of development. Knowing the end in advance becomes one of the smallest elements of our going again and again but one which can elate us. We say "Now wait," "Now watch this," "Now this song," etc. The air of predictability has turned to one of joyous expectancy. This is a large part of the value of predictability.

On the other side of the coin, it can destroy, and when it does it is the fault of the creative people who have conceived a start and a finish and let the devil work out what lies between. (This makes for an endless evening!)

Look at *The Music Man*. The hero is a charming con man who gets the girl (ho-hum), and we neither care nor wonder why. However, this man is a phony and deserves nothing. Billy Bigelow (*Carousel*) is not a good man, Joey (*Pal*) is stupid and talentless—but neither is really bad and determinedly crooked. The music man is a self-made phony. Even the young man who is going to succeed without even trying wins his point but improves the position of the man he unseats. These characters are likable and even sometimes pitiable, but they are not dishonest.

Skyscraper was a flop that everybody in the world could have foreseen could not be made to work *because* of its predictability and the dullsville which surrounded a nothing triangle. Based on Elmer Rice's play *Dream Girl*, it did not have enough matter for a play or a musical. There was a kookie heroine (senseless), and her problem in the musical was boiled down to a subtle choice between a queen who runs her antique shop and a smart, handsome, muscular male who really had the only problem in the show: how to make the dizzy dame agree to sell her small property which he badly needed for the completion of the skyscraper he is involved in building.

Purlie is obvious and thoroughly foreseeable. Harold C. Schönberg, *music* critic of *The New York Times*, has written (*Harper's*, July 1970):

> ...The plot concerns Purlie's efforts to steal $500 from a local redneck. In this case it's okay to steal, because the redneck talks about Nigras and is a louse, and you know how we Northerners feel about *that* kind.

Furthermore it began and ended with the same white man's funeral, so we had nothing much to worry or care about: It would all come out right in the end. And besides this flashback method did allow the Nigras to sing good and loud and with the rhythm that only *they* have, and it was the same music I heard at Nigra baptisms in Mississippi when I was a child. I hope that today's blacks hated *Purlie* because it portrayed them as shiftless, lazy, lying, and conniving. It also showed that you could see through them all like glass and that their music hadn't changed in at least a century.

I hope also that by now it is abundantly clear that predictability helps to pile boredom upon boredom when nothing stimulating happens every step along the way from beginning to end to help keep things moving, and this is one reason I lay so much stock by the subplot (discussed later), which helps to carry some of the total burden; or without it the writers should supply something that they are conscious of that satisfactorily replaces what they are purposely omitting. And the music must be interesting and made so by the situations and by the characters which evoke it. And the dances must help and the humor and the quality of the idea as well as the writing itself. With this kind of fulsomeness all along the way predictability becomes a lovable guide to the inevitable.

While predictability may apply occasionally without causing a major catastrophe to the unfolding of a situation *within* a show, its proper and knowing use concerns only the end—the wrap-up. The end, however, is not necessarily what takes place when the final curtain falls or even when the audience is well outside the theatre. If a show works very well—especially a musical—there will remain with the homeward-bound audience some memory of a musical phrase, in some kinds of plays, some as yet unresolved character who was intended to go on for perhaps even a long time after the theatre has gone dark.

Having established the play-libretto variance which is basically the most primitive difference between words used by themselves for their own sounds and meanings and words imbedded in other and sometimes more overpowering sounds, I should like to consider for each what may be left with the audience after each performance and what may be left after the passage of time—weeks, months, and especially years. The first might be called an "after-image" and the second—after passage of time—"after-life."

I think it is necessary and in no way spurious to cast aside those elements which might intrude on and becloud the principal issues here, such as star performances, scenery, costumes, and other accessories to the play and libretto themselves.

The play first. In each epoch, the after-image must vary considerably. Since the Greeks (in the case of their tragedies) knew so intimately *ahead* of time the plots as well as the characters (predictability), it would be my guess that audiences were left in awe of the poetry, which is what the playwright created. They might also have pondered the "moral."

In Shakespeare's case, although most of the plots were familiar to the audiences, the original manner of approach, the development, the predictable denouements, and the poetic achievements must have been matters for discussion. However, I should find it difficult to believe that the quality of entertainment was not the main point of related conversation and after-image. In *Macbeth* there are the tenseness of the murder scene, the drollery of the drunken gatekeeper, those nightmarish witches, the correct materialization of the prophecies, including the end twist concerning "no man of woman born." Also the moral: The foolishness of ambition and the ending which promises a better world, etc.

After the Shakespearean comedies audiences must have laughed themselves sick at the mistaken identity that was so much used. "That moment when they almost…" The good feeling that everything would work itself out in just the way the audience would want it to.

In Ibsen I would guess there was more empathy with the stage. "How terrible for poor Mrs. Alving!" "That poor child and her duck and that idiot of a father." Chekhov really left his audiences with the unsolved problems—threw them straight out over the footlights into their laps. In almost every case, the characters developed, the plot usually moved from A to B, but a powerful traumatic situation ended each play without really ending anything. This was the audiences' problem. What would you do? Something must be done. This was Chekhov's very special after-image that must have haunted his spectators for a long time after witnessing a performance. At the very least they said after *The Cherry Orchard*, "What a stupid waste!" After *The Three Sisters*, "What is to be done about it?"

Contemporary playwrights go still further but in the same direction. Often now the identity of the characters can only be guessed at. The situation is intentionally not made clear, and the play ends long after the curtain falls. In some of Albee's plays it is my feeling that the end is the beginning. Pinter in *The Birthday Party* and *The Homecoming*, Sartre in *Huis Clos*, the plays of Doris Lessing and of Ionesco have a haunting, continuing progress. I need personally to discuss them and think for a long time afterward (not being able to toss them out of my mind). For me, this is *their* after-image.

In a batch of distinguished plays immediately preceding the present time—those of Tennessee Williams, Arthur Miller, Lillian Hellman, William Inge—there is a clear conclusion, but the mind is concerned about the fate of the characters for a long time afterward.

Now for musicals. To date there has been, to my knowledge, no inconclusive finish, nobody and nothing left unresolved.[4] In the more "serious" (that is to say, the sadder ones), with the invaluable aid of music there is a strong emotional effect which forms part of the after-image, but it is my belief that the *music*, that element in the best musical shows that can become so integral as to go unnoticed, forms the largest part of its after-image. People whistle tunes. They hear them on the radio, TV, Muzak, and jukeboxes. They buy the cast album and continue playing it long after it has been memorized. And in trying to explain a song enthusiastically to a friend who has not been lucky enough to see the show, they become a mass of hysterical confusion trying to describe who the character is and why she says in the song what she says.

Before laying aside this topic I should like to answer an accusation that has doubtless arisen in many readers' minds. Why have I mentioned so much about "serious" plays and musicals and so little about comedy? It's a legitimate gripe and one that is difficult to answer, but I shall try. First of all, what the average audience sees in a comedy is the performance, which we are deliberately not discussing here. Spectators, time and time again, attribute every laugh they have to the skill of the player. I'm deaf from hearing "Isn't *she* funny?" Never the poor author who has trouble hiring enough vehicles to take his money to the bank.

I would like to quote a few things at random from Walter Kerr's brilliant book *Tragedy and Comedy* (Simon and Schuster). It is Mr. Kerr's thesis that "Comedy...derives from what we normally regard as tragic." And later: "The term comedy came into being to describe a performing art..." In my opinion that is not only correct but well proven. This being the case—and Mr. Kerr's book as regards comedy concerns itself more with the visual than with the written—it is next to impossible to divorce the comic performer from his material. On the other hand, the written material exists. It is my thought that its sole after-image is a feeling that you had a good time (if you did). Most of the characters are not real, the situations fabricated, and there are lots and lots of jokes on which the success of the show depends. The chances are ten to one that even on opening night you've heard some version or other of every joke before. If the performer is special, he may make you believe you are hearing it for the first time. Good when true. But after this show no dodo is likely to indulge in a further repetition of the jokes. The "after-image" of comedy is almost entirely attached to the memory of a performance and not to the product itself. Which brings me to the business of after-life. I had never been aware of, until this moment, the close relationship that exists between after-image and after-life.

Plays first. The Greek tragedies have continued living now for some 2,500 years because they are of heroic proportions, affecting all people who are able to give themselves to a performance of one. They are moving and they are universal. The comedies of Aristophanes—written only slightly later—have not survived (certainly not as comedies, with the exception of *Lysistrata*, which deals with a timeless humorous situation. The others need explaining and are not either self-sufficient or timeless; in fact, they are *imbedded* in their own day.

The plays of Shakespeare are universal. The poetry that they contain would, by itself, be enough to keep the plays alive. They are all about recognizable human beings living at any time. The tragedies have implicit morals. They contain every kind of contrast a playwright could dream of. They are about all things. In *The Merchant of Venice*, the garden scene, this line occurs: "There's not the smallest orb which thou behold'st/But in his motion like an angel sings…" What the hell. This was written in the seventeenth century by a non-scientist and we didn't know until three centuries later that the planets actually give off a musical sound as they spin in space!

And Shakespeare wrote about a black man whose problem became even more serious because he was black; about a Jew who was in every way wrong and then the writer lets you pity him; about freedom, treachery, ambition, love, jealousy, and all the other qualities indigenous to every age. After-life?

I believe in the historic importance of Ibsen but feel that he is dated today. Nevertheless, he has been around for along time because he kicked the human race in the solar plexus, where it hadn't been kicked before.

Chekhov, I believe, is timeless because the problems he presents (and masterfully) are the same that we experience today and unfortunately always will. His pertinence is enough without his superb skill as a definer of characters and a creator of nearly unbearable tension.

Much of what Noël Coward, Lillian Hellman, Tennessee Williams, and Arthur Miller have written is enjoying an "after-life" that augurs well for their future.

Music of the theatre. The operas of Mozart, Gluck, Rossini, and Verdi will live chiefly because of their music. Also Debussy and Berg. For Donizetti, Meyerbeer, Massenet, Gounod, Saint-Saëns, Bellini, and Wagner, they've had more than their share of after-life due entirely to music. Time's up except as vehicles in museums for a golden high D which this and that soprano can deliver. The librettos are ghastly and often motiveless.

In operetta, I believe Gilbert and Sullivan are deathless. Although they laugh directly at the mores of Victoria's day, they made words, music, and plots for all people in all times. Johann Strauss's music will go on and on; productions, less and less. Offenbach is caviar to the general, and at the moment nobody seems to understand this special style well enough to perform him. We'll see.

From the American musical there is a vast quantity of songs that are now over age forty and still going strong. I think that the "best" musicals (1940–1965) will go on because of the books as well as the music. As for most of what is presently happening in the musical, it is my feeling that it is shabby, repetitious, and a bore. Most of it is still-born. It has a big life in its mother's womb and is dead on arrival.

But this is a time of transition. The dust of revolt must settle before anyone will be able to see clearly in any direction—new or old. It will eventually be all right because what already exists that is good will still exist, and the best of the next and the next and the next generations will understand what has been good and they will be nurtured by their roots buried in and nurtured by the past, their eyes and eagerness stretching out for the new that has not broken ranks with the past. It will all work itself out, and we will once again know the joys of new and exciting after-images and the nostalgia that can only be explicit in an after-life.

COMMENTS ON THE OUTER SHAPE

In this chapter Engel betrays an almost cabbalistic concern with how plays and musicals are divided. (Chekhov wrote in four acts, most American plays now take place in two, *Wozzeck* is segmented into 27 scenes, etc.) Behind this seemingly obsessive fascination lies a deeper interest in how you structure a narrative.

As he points out, one reason it has become increasingly common to divide plays in two is that you need only one "cliffhanger," that is, a single act where you leave the audience curious enough about what will happen that they'll return after the intermission.

In the thirty years since he wrote *Words with Music* nonmusical plays tend to run 90 minutes without intermission. Musicals them-selves have now become fairly standardized in two acts. When *1776* was first performed, in 1969, it was one long act. In recent years it has become standard to perform it in two. *A Chorus Line* and *Man of La Mancha* remain long one-acts.

What all this is about is simply the most effective way of telling a story. Many of the great 19th century novels first appeared serially in magazines. The writers were forced to fill a certain number of pages and had to end each chapter in a startling enough manner that the reader would buy next month's issue. Sometimes, as in even Dostoyevsky's richest novels, this structure seems forced. You understand the pressure he was under and marvel that the often awkward structure coexists with such profundity.

In the postwar period traditional narrative came under assault by Absurdist works whose essential impulse was to challenge the conventions of storytelling, to thwart the audience's conventional expectations. An example is Arthur Kopit's *Oh, Dad, Poor Dad, Mama's Hung You in the Closet And I'm Feeling So Sad*. A more recent case is *Urinetown*, in which the characters speak self-consciously about the conventions of the forms they're satirizing.

A more powerful assault on traditional narrative was commercial television, in which stories were broken up every few minutes by a commercial. Television accustomed its audiences to stories that have no great arch, not even any sense of momentum. They're episodic. This may not be compelling storytelling, but it is a kind of narrative audiences readily accept, substantially reducing the demands it makes on their attention. (Equally appealing—though probably not for Engel—it reduces the demands on the authors in structuring the plot.)

An equally powerful blow to conventional narrative, which Engel couldn't have foreseen, was the music video. By the mid-Eighties it wasn't enough for a song to be heard. It also had to be seen, and the structure and content of music videos owe less to novels or plays than to commercials.

People often feel that the volume is louder during the commercials than during the programs surrounding them. We're constantly reassured this is not the case.

Whether it is or isn't, one reason it's easy to assume the volume has been increased is that the *visual* volume has undoubtedly been cranked up. Every second of a commercial counts. It must be at a high level of visual intensity. It must convey something with much greater force than the story it interrupts. This is the case even when the story's style seems disjointed or illogical.

If the influence of Madison Avenue techniques on music videos is incalculable, so is the effect of music videos on our understanding of dramatic structure. Often perfectly serviceable books now strike us as plodding because we've become so accustomed to absorbing great amounts of information in flashing images. This has placed a burden on musical book-writers that the theatre has not fully come to terms with.

Engel makes a useful comparison with Greek plays. The audience in ancient Athens knew the plot well in advance. What kept their interest was the quality of the verse. And it was the verse that haunted them afterward. With musicals the plot may not be known, but in the shows Engel focused on, the plot wasn't hard to follow. The characters defined themselves through the plot. What gave these shows an after-life was their tunes.

Engel saw the structure and the music in a healthy balance, which was what he stressed in the BMI Workshop. In recent years, however, that balance matters less and less. Does the plot of *The Lion King* matter? For that matter, does the score? For most of the audience, both are known quantities before they see the show. What they take away is Julie Taymor's visual magic.

Musicals from the Fifties onward were often sumptuous spectacles, but the idea that a musical would succeed largely because of its visual imagination would have struck Engel as strange.

A cynical person might point out that selling a musical on the basis of its visual effects makes the performers' work easier. If they have to project the material eight times a week there will likely be performances where they're not up to it. If, however, it simply depends on the computers moving the scenery with precision, the performers are off the hook.

Audiences are more willing to forgive mechanical mishaps than a lukewarm actor. During the run of *Miss Saigon*, a stagehand once told me, there were times when the helicopter effect malfunctioned. Now this moment—a simulation of the tragic, chaotic scene in 1975 when a helicopter tried to rescue the last detachment of Americans and South Vietnamese from the American Embassy in Saigon before the Communist takeover—was in many ways the chief selling point of the show. For a while seats in the first few rows of the mezzanine, where the effect could be seen to best advantage, were sold at a premium.

There were times, however, when it didn't take place. When that happened, the stagehand said, they simply intensified the swirling lights and the already high-decibel sound effect. Never, he said, did they receive complaints. The audience was so primed to experience the moment they did so even when they hadn't.

Engel begins his chapter with a discussion of how scenic limitations affect the structure of plays and musicals. He couldn't have imagined that technology would create a theatre in which, for all intents and purposes, there are no such things as scenic limitations.

The weakening of dramatic conventions helped create another success of recent years that might have baffled Engel, *Rent*. Here the plot is extremely episodic, often not plausible. A character dies, for example, then is handily resurrected. A nasty landlord suddenly and inexplicably turns generous. Some of the songs grow out of the plot. Others do not. It doesn't matter.

The show has an improvisatory tone, suggesting that what matters is the author's sense of invention, his mercurial imagination, which supersedes the need for verisimilitude. Under other circumstances this whimsicality might have been treated dismissively. In the case of *Rent*, however, the material blends with the haunting backstage story of the promising author, Jonathan Larson, who died after the final dress rehearsal. That tragic event gave the show a subtext more powerful than any structural advice from Engel might have done.

The hopes he expresses at the end of the chapter are based on the assumption that the theatre, like the surrounding culture, was going through a bad spell but would soon come to its senses. By coming to its senses, of course, he meant coming to embrace his rather traditional values. What this optimism reveals is the extent to which someone making his living in the world of musical theatre could be unaware of the convulsions in the outside world and how those convulsions would eventually affect his world.

5

The Needs of the Musical

Some plays depend almost wholly upon mere bustle and rapidly shifting movement, much of it wholly unnecessary to the plot. Large portions of many recent musical comedies illustrate this.

George Pierce Baker
Dramatic Technique

Both spoken drama and its musical-theatre relative have contained plot (movement or action) and appropriate characters who unfold the plot. The outer shape or form likewise has been taken into account as regards its special applicability to both musical and non-musical theatre.

There are now six elements to be discussed.

> Feeling—one way or another at the core of all art.
> Subplot and
> Romance—intrinsically important to the workability
> of musical theatre;
> Lyrics and Particularization, which help to focus
> feeling, give meaning to lyrics, character, and plot.
> Music and
> Comedy, not the least essential element of all theatre.

Romance is nearly always present directly or obliquely in all theatre. Particularization is essential in helping writers to focus ideas in general and lyrics specifically. Without feeling, music and lyrics become weightless, characters and situations are of no consequence to anyone. Theatre ceases to exist. Without comedy the fabric of theatre lacks contrast. Everything sits on a flat plane; characters lack an important dimension. There are no real shadows because there is no light. Of all these elements, music is the only one which for about a century has been discarded from the non-lyric theatre, although the subplot is also often absent too.

Let me attempt to clarify the foregoing, which is little more than a list. First of all, each of these elements is interdependent on the others. They are, in a good show, the components of a machine. They work together.

First let us consider the relationship of feeling and romance. A good part of a romantic play or musical might generate its feeling from romance. That is, of course, primitive. But there are kinds of feelings other than romantic ones. In *Fiddler on the Roof* the most emotional moments are those between father and each of three daughters, and each is different from the other. There are also three romances which count for a lesser part of the feeling.

But since feeling also includes comedy, its separation from romance also occurs frequently. The humor derived from Adelaide's troubles (*Guys and Dolls*), while they are the *results* of romantic problems, have little to do with love. Her "lament" is a soliloquy of frustration. We laugh at this, and it is unromantic laughter. Some of the feeling in *West Side Story* is directly generated by two romances; another aspect (to me the keenest) is engendered by the ballet when we see the very boys and girls who fight one another in real life holding hands, happily dancing in the open yellow fields—something that we know they are impotent ever to be able to do. We feel pride (another of the many components of sentiment) for her when we see Eliza Doolittle passed off as a "real" lady at the Embassy Ball in *My Fair Lady*. We feel suspense in the radio-shack scenes of *South Pacific* when Emile de Becque's voice is heard and we are concerned about the danger he is in. We feel considerable warmth for Mrs. Anna (*The King and I*) when she recalls her happiness with her husband, now dead. We feel embarrassment at the coarseness and one-directional methods that Gypsy's mother lives by.

In drama, feeling for Oedipus comes from his act of expiation of sins which he committed in innocence, in Iphigenia because of her impending self-sacrifice, in Othello from his having become a prey to duplicity.

Particularizaton—another of the elements—is essential to the well-being of feeling. The more specific the acquaintance we have with characters, the more we become involved in their problems, whether these seem funny or melancholy to us. We are incapable of having any feeling for or against any character or any situation which is vague. It is also unthinkable that a romance could be generalized. All romance concerns particular people in a particular situation under particular conditions.

Comedy is equally impossible without particularization. (Perhaps that's why "jokes"—good or bad—begin with "This priest and this rabbi were walking down the street," etc.) Tevye in his humorous song addressed to God, "If I Were a Rich Man," finds himself in a clearly defined specific situation and he spells out precisely what he desires. Meg Brockie in *Brigadoon* is humorous in "The Love of My Life," only because she relates four very distinctly personal events. Nothing in this song is a generality.

Music (and lyrics) in a first-rate show must at least *appear* to be generated by characters in situations. The songs must express feeling of one kind or another (this is the essence of lyric theatre). Otherwise why employ music at all? Much of the music will be expressive of romance. Lyrics that are not particularized are too general to create humor or, for that matter, any interest.

Comedy—another element—is a part of feeling. Its dependence on particularization was pointed out above. It can serve as an invaluable contrast to sadness or as relief, as does "Office Krupke" (*West Side Story*). It is romance's foil.

Only subplot, in my opinion, has no specific relationship to the other elements. In the early days of American musical comedy the subplot—usually a loose and obvious device for relieving the audience as well as the romantic performers—was given the task of supplying comedy which in turn usually bore little if any relationship to anything else going on. The subplot is needed largely for division of the burden of filling out a show and sustaining the audience's interest; a single plot line is usually too thin, too quickly told, especially in a musical, to be able to take on the responsibility of sustaining an audience's interest for a full evening.

While all six elements briefly discussed in this section are of enormous importance, I would say that especially in any kind of musical, feeling is first. Music with appropriate lyrics takes second place and will help invaluably to project feeling. Romance or love is needed, but this may not necessarily be between a man and a woman. (In *Fiddler on the Roof* it is between a man and an ideal.) Particularization must pinpoint the characters, the situations and the lyrics if the effect and supremacy of feeling is to be present. Comedy in varying degrees must help as entertainment and as contrast. A real subplot, as the name implies, must help to sustain the interest and enrich the fabric of the whole.

My exposition of the uses of these six elements in both musical and non-musical theatre comes from an observation of what works in both media. Their careful consideration is suggested.

FEELING

since feeling is first
who pays any attention
to the syntax of things
will never wholly kiss you;

e. e. cummings

There is an impression that feeling and sadness are inseparable. This is of course nonsense. To feel is to laugh as well as to cry, to be charmed as well as repulsed. To feel is to experience, and in order to experience any kind of emotion from a play or musical one has to care about the characters and the situations.

It is possible, just possible, that in certain kinds of plays there can be a substitute for feeling which would assume the intentional form of an intellectual or philosophical discussion. In a musical, any attempt in this direction would be disastrous because it would be anti-lyrical.

Who's Afraid of Virginia Woolf? does not involve my emotions. It neither amuses nor saddens me. I care no more for one character than for another, and therefore I do not care what happens to any of them or who wins or who loses any of the innumerable and somewhat complex bouts. This does not mean that I find it dull. I am interested but not otherwise affected. Often *Who's Afraid of Virginia Woolf?* creates a sort of kinetic tension. I am momentarily breathless, but I believe that this involvement is intellectual rather than emotional. What Albee has done is to fascinate his audience with a sort of game. What will the next move result in? Who will carry off the honors and by what means? And by the way, what's his name? Harold Pinter seems to have tried to engage in a similar exercise in *The Homecoming*. Each of the characters tries desperately to tell us that he does not care: the father for his visiting son, the latter for his wife, the brothers for each other, the wife for her husband and her children, etc. There is an endless chain of these *apparent* protestations. However, what the characters say and do in a sense resembles classical choreography. What we hear and see moves in a preordained design—the author's concept—but out of all this clearly arranged negativism there emerges in us in this pavane something much deeper than what we actually perceive outwardly. This, for me, is an oblique and original treatment of feeling. But feeling it is, because we care very much about these people, and when we leave the theatre and for a long time after the play has ended it continues to live with us, to haunt, puzzle, and perhaps depress us.

It is my belief that both Albee and Pinter intend this non-feeling method but that Albee means it for real and succeeeds in arriving where he means to go. I think that Pinter does not eschew emotion or feeling in his plays but rather he *pretends* that his characters don't care and that this non-feelingness will put the audience off as well. What he has actually done, I believe, is to avoid what he might think of as "old-fashioned," and perhaps it is. However, the effect in *The Homecoming* is to horrify the audience—this lack of feeling among the characters—and we wait tensely until later—perhaps much later. But at some point it is we who feel just because it has been predetermined and deftly planned that we will. In a way it's like seeing a child crying very hard and having someone say, "Oh, pay no attention to her. It doesn't matter. She'll get over it." From then on your attention is riveted on the child and I think it is because you have been instructed not to care.

But Pinter in *The Birthday Party* creates a mystery and terror employing similar methods to those he used in *The Homecoming*. After it is all over you may not yet understand much, but you feel a very great deal. This feeling will make you care enough to go on trying to unravel its meaning in your own mind.

Ionesco's *Rhinoceros* came to me as though I were sitting precariously on the edge of a precipice. I had this experience because I was made to care about the hero and to become more and more concerned about his fate and the preservation of his own identity while one by one all of the other characters deserted him: one man against the whole frightening, stampeding animal world. I recall a mounting feeling of tension during the play and deep anguish for a long time after it was finished.

These four plays I have used as examples, rather different from one another, nevertheless have one thing in common: All of them set out primarily to engage the mind. I believe that *Who's Afraid of Virginia Woolf?* does this to the exclusion of everything else; that *The Homecoming* and *The Birthday Party*, despite their overt attempts to avoid feeling, engage the emotions as well as the mind; that *Rhinoceros* absorbs the attention and only beginning with the very end of the play *releases* the emotions.

No musical show could even attempt to accomplish any of these things. There is not enough libretto "time" for such extensive statement and development, and in melodic cadence syllabic elongations could too easily jeopardize comprehension. But above all other considerations, in *Who's Afraid of Virginia Woolf?* there is seldom anything to sing about. And the complexities of *The Homecoming*, *The Birthday Party*, and *Rhinoceros* suggest to me grand opera in the traditional sense. The single-character crescendo of *Rhinoceros* recalls an effect similar in Büchner's *Woyzeck*. *The Homecoming* suggests perhaps a new kind of opera in which what the people sing is antithetical to the orchestral comment *about* them: anti-lyricism versus lyricism. In a way this might result in the kind of music drama that Wagner espoused but never actually practiced, carried away as he was by the interminable dramatic vocal line as well as by the turgid commenting orchestra. I see no reason why the pure Wagnerian dream inherent in *The Homecoming* might not become a reality.

At the start of this section, I made the point that feeling was not limited to sadness, but until now I have dealt only with unhappy emotions. There is the other side, but any consideration of comedy is fraught with complexities due to its own ephemeral nature. Among successful "modern" plays in this category let us list *Born*

Yesterday, *You Can't Take It with You*, *The Odd Couple*, *The Moon is Blue*, *Black Comedy*, and *You Know I Can't Hear You When the Water's Running*. All of them were funny (not merely amusing) to immense audiences. This fun is an important aspect of feeling.[5]

The Odd Couple is to me related in one way to *Who's Afraid of Virginia Woolf?* in that both are exercises in wit expressed solely in badinage. The rapier-like dialogue in both always makes its points—comedic in *The Odd Couple*—but do we care about these people? We are in varying degrees amused and entertained, but I do not think we ever become involved. On the other hand we are entertained and amused by all the other plays in the foregoing list, and additionally in each case we want something to eventuate *for*, in behalf of, at least one central character. The girl in *Born Yesterday* must triumph. Papa in *You Can't Take It with You* must bring the whole world around to his point of view, outrageous as this is. The girl in *The Moon Is Blue* must learn her lesson but also must get her boy. The boy and the girl of *Black Comedy* must and will be united despite the complications which would seem to make this an impossibility. In each of the short plays comprising *You Know I Can't Hear You When the Water's Running* we are given a central character to root for. The nearly constant laughter provided by the author importantly embellishes the slight situations, but at rock bottom a common human element also provides a stout thread for tying the play together and for giving the audience a need which must be satisfied in the end.

The most enduring plays from the past—comedies and tragedies alike—have been built around a magnetic central feeling. The Greek tragedies, performed behind masks, commemorated their poetic anguish—built solidly upon a single character—through the sounds of words and complex intonations. The principals had long virtuoso "arias." There were also dances and choruses. However, the most remarkable part about the Hellenic tragedy is that it is timeless and universal. The comedies of Aristophanes and the later Roman playwrights have fared less well. Most of the humor today is in dire need of footnotes. It has to be explained in order to be understood, and no explained joke is a funny one. Most of these plays are not universal because they are tied tightly around their own time and to people long dead whose every mannerism, thought, and nuance were popularly recognized. *Lysistrata* (noted previously) is the grand exception because its premise is timeless, and its title character is known in every age, every girl's school, every beauty parlor, and every marriage. We see her (in each passing age) as our own; we love her and perhaps in spite of ourselves want her to win her fight.

The Birds, The Frogs, June Moon, Brother Rat, Three Men on a Horse, and thousands of others like them were buried just after the initial laughter had died away. They were time-bound. But comedy and satire have always been of a more perishable genus than tragedy or problem plays. The best of Shakespeare's comedies work well today but the less good ones seem hardly possible as compositions by the author of *Hamlet* and *Romeo and Juliet*. And in those funny ones that do work today, there is again the hard central core of people whom we know and care about. There is scarcely a single character in *A Midsummer Night's Dream* or *Twelfth Night* or *The Comedy of Errors* with whom we are not in love. Yet these are funny plays with complex plots, music, magic, poetry, farce, incredulity—but because of the characters they are credible and adored. Puck is not far removed from Huckleberry Finn; the Dromios were friends of Carroll's Alice and later went to college as the Bobbsey twins.

The evocation of feeling seems to be a many-sided thing because it seems to happen differently in so many different plays.

Madame Ranevsky (*The Cherry Orchard*), Mrs. Alving (*Ghosts*) and Blanche DuBois (*Streetcar*) are helpless, foolish, and try to be brave. Nothing can save them, but we are made to care because they themselves are the victims and they ask for no pity.

A Streetcar Named Desire has one quality which all distinguished plays have in common with distinguished musicals: *feeling*. The very terse plot line indicates little of this all-important aspect, but it is feeling more than anything else that propels the plot and the characters. Blanche at first appears fuzzy and indistinct. Little by little her sham and pretense become clearly recognizable and make her an object of compassion. She is wriggling desperately to persuade everyone that she is more than she is or ever was. Our feeling for her grows and finally—at the play's end—when the doctor and the cruel, businesslike nurse arrive to remove her from life forever, we are deeply moved.

We feel empathy also for Blanche's sister, Stella, who *wants* to help but is torn between love and pity for her sister and a stronger, more realistic love for her husband. We feel surprisingly for Stanley, the crude, insensitive man who, by sometimes easy stages, is shoved about ruthlessly if daintily by his invading sister-in-law, who threatens his home and his happiness and nearly succeeds in destroying his freedom of spirit. It is this abundance of feeling and the lyricism of Williams' writing that moves the audience to feel, to care, to be immobilized for the duration of the play and perhaps for a long time afterward. This feeling is literally *thrust* upon us. It does not reach us by accident, and I think that this is a major point: The author created it knowingly and required us to accept it. This is a primary cause of the success of any theatrical work.

Doesn't one simple factor emerge? The character (or plural) is caught up in a conflict and we care *because* he is unable to escape. (We abhor the sight of a wounded bird. We care.) In comedies it is also the conflict which imprisons the characters. We would like to free them. In every case it is the situations in which the characters find themselves that elicit our empathy.

Musical stage works, I would say categorically, cannot exist without feeling as the most basic element. I am aware that Stravinsky disclaims emotion in his music, and some years ago the great Arnold Schönberg told me that his music also was devoid of it. Both of these gentlemen said what they believed to be true, but their attitude is further proof only that no creative artist is fully aware of his own work and that what he says is interesting only from a psychological rather than a factual point of view. Nevertheless any serious listener would be hard put to deny feelings of terror in *Pierrot Lunaire* or *Erwartung*, awesome majesty in The *Symphony of Psalms*, or celebrative exuberance in *Le Sacre du Printemps*.

Opera is a hemorrhage of feeling to the exclusion of almost everything else; operetta in general pokes fun at this when it isn't itself falling into the same trap; musical theatre in recent times in America has tried to make an adjustment toward a more even balance between heart and mind. When this balance has succeeded and feeling has not been discarded in favor of elaborate production, divertismental choreography, comedy for its own sake or for some other unconnected reason, we have musical theatre at its best. This is the theatre of *Fiddler on the Roof, The King and I, Carousel, Annie Get Your Gun, South Pacific, My Fair Lady, Pal Joey, Brigadoon, West Side Story,* and a few others. These were shows during our Golden Age between 1940 and 1965.

Certainly the growing know-how that led up to this Golden Age proclaimed feeling to an almost insufferable degree. But the best of the American operettas—*The Student Prince, Rose-Marie, The Desert Song, Show Boat*—are more than forty-five years old and still going strong everywhere but on Broadway. They had their roots in the European past but nevertheless could have been created only in America. They were simultaneously the high point and the end of musical theatre in this genre. Today although they are a thick miasma of feeling and a bookless folio of often memorable songs, they are constantly revived as shows in our hinterlands.

On the other hand, the "new" experimental shows of Gershwin, Porter, Berlin, Rodgers and Hart, Youmans, and Schwartz were also filled with feeling if with a difference. The mawkishness of the operettas was replaced with a more modern "citified" kind of expression, but the results nonetheless exuded feeling.

Porgy and Bess illustrates well the idea that although "romance" and "feeling" are closely related, they are not synonymous. While there is a great deal of feeling in this work, in size alone, romance takes a secondary place. In the entire work there are two romantic duets only: "Bess, You Is My Woman Now" and "I Want to Stay Here." However, in addition there are "Summer-Time"—a ballad (not connected with love); "Gone, Gone, Gone"—a funeral chorus; "My Man's Gone Now"—an aria of lament; "It Takes a Long Pull to Get There"—a spiritual; "Oh, I Got Plenty o' Nuttin'"—a song of celebration; "Buzzard Song"—a dramatic aria; "Oh, I Can't Sit Down"—a picnic song; "It Ain't Necessarily So"—a comedy song; "What You Want Wid Bess?"—a duet of protest; "Oh, Doctor Jesus"—a spiritual; "There's a Boat Dat's Leavin' Soon for New York"—a ballad; "Bess, Oh Where's My Bess"—a trio for distress; "Oh Lawd, I'm on My Way"—a spiritual; plus many other choruses, recitatives, etc.

In *Porgy and Bess* there is an immense amount of feeling but only two songs expressing romance, and the music is continuous for about three hours.

It has been suggested to me and quite correctly that romance without feeling gives us Vincent Youmans and feeling without romance gives us Harold Pinter. But feeling is the first and most important element.

Today there is something else, and this has come about either as a conscious attempt at an evasion of feeling or an unawareness of its necessity as an inescapable concomitant of lyric theatre. Since contemporary writers now have a dozen or so exemplary models, they have little excuse for failures. Nevertheless, too often the important quality has gone out, and the results are far less than desirable. About "caring," a fairly recent example from life will help prove this all-important point. The day that the three men in the Apollo moon landing returned safely to earth was one of relief for nearly every human being everywhere. On that same day I read in the morning (Turkish) papers that twenty people had died in an earthquake, twelve had been killed in a bus accident, hundreds were dying of Hong Kong flu in the United States, etc. etc. To this news I clucked my tongue. Too bad. But the safe return of the three astronauts was an occasion for rejoicing. I do not believe that we rejoiced because of their magnificent accomplishment which we actually know little about or because their historic flight marked an enormous advance in man's efforts to "conquer" space. I do believe that these three human beings had been so carefully introduced to all people everywhere through press, TV, radio and all other news media that everyone knew what they looked like, knew the members of their families, and understood so many of the hazards of their journey that all of us saw *ourselves* in their identical predicament—and we were made to care. We did not care about the dead in the earthquake, the bus accident, or the victims of Hong Kong flu—mere lists—just as we did not care about the characters in many shows (mostly ignominious failures) which never provided this all-important essential *setup*.

In well-made shows, after the characters are identified, they are placed in a situation—a precarious one—and we care to see them safely out of it. The question of how we get to know characters in musicals is relevant, and then there are many elements which change from show to show and often from style to style. One of the most complicated shows to draw conclusions about, and one of the earliest and best, is *Pal Joey*. Once the audience recognizes Joey's lack of talent, his brashness, his basis naïveté and his contorted innocence, they understand him. He thinks he is God's gift to all females and he is helplessly stupid. He has a certain charm. We like him even as we laugh at this gaucherie. Later we know that he is providing pleasurable services to Mrs. Simpson, who can well afford them. When Joey becomes a threat because of subplot crooks, he must be got rid of, and Mrs. Simpson, who has already paid for her peccadillo, must not have to pay again. We are satisfied when Joey finds himself as he was at the start (after all, he was given a club, a wardrobe, and a bank account—more than he had ever know before), and Mrs. Simpson gets away unscathed, charmingly, without undue concern. Incidentally we know Mrs. Simpson because she is discussed and identified when we first see her (Scene 3), and in two early-on songs (soliloquies) she reveals all: "What Is a Man?" and "Bewitched, Bothered and Bewildered." She is canny, experienced, sophisticated, and charming. She can be counted on to get what she wants, to pay for it, and to dispose of it easily when she can no longer hold onto it safely.

Getting to know characters in musicals is generally less complicated than this, and I would remind the reader that most of them are exactly what they look like. They are not gradually or suddenly going to become someone else. Laurey in *Oklahoma!* is a sweet, simple girl—no complications, just a bit too coy for her own good. Ado Annie in the same show is a flirt. She will (one day) settle down with her lifelong friend Will Parker, but at the moment she wants to see New York or Siam before she marries, has kids and is chained to Oklahoma Territory for the rest of her life. And as the peddler Ali Hakim who is present on his occasional rounds, represents the outside world and to her too young mind and inexperience, for the moment she is taken with the fake romance which he represents, and she puts off Will.

Mrs. Anna (*The King and I*) is established in the first scene as brave (she is coming unprotected to a then "savage" country to teach the king's children and wives), dignified, charming, one who will stand up to tyrants, will insist on the fulfillment of the king's contract, and she is warm. We admire and love her.

At the opening of *Fiddler on the Roof* Tevye sings the thematic song "Tradition," and one by one he introduces *all* of the characters in the show. He himself has great charm and wit. His attitude toward his family is loving, and he tells us this with a kind of wry lightness—never with sentimentality. He lets us know how he feels about everyone else. It's a good feeling but—simple man that he is—he is not taken in by the rabbi, a kind of waspish idiot, the marriage broker, a greedy and self-centered parasitic woman, the chief of the town police, who is a real threat but Tevye helplessly regards him as a friend, etc. Tevye is never heavy-handed, is rational without being solemn, full of problems with legitimate complaints that are sufficiently outrageous to be amusing. He is religious without being canonical. He is a full, lovable human being—part clown and at once a recognizable victim of life today as well as in the past.

There are very basic differences between feeling as such in a play and the same play well musicalized. The reason is quite obvious and seems to me to point to the proper use of music as an aid to the production of a superior end product. First of all there is an historic practice in the combining of words and music for intense effect—particularly mournful ones. In the nineteenth century in both England and America, dramas were inevitably employing background music for the intensification of emotional scenes. (This was for the audience.) In the early days of silent movie-making similar music was used while the scenes were being photographed in order to stimulate the actors' emotional performance.

Othello's last speech as he has realized his tragic stupidity in having killed Desdemona is: "I kiss'd thee ere I kill'd thee; no way but this." Within Shakespeare's play this speech is appropriate and effective. However, compare it, for example, with its musicalized version (Verdi), in which the love theme associated with a kiss is soaring and tugs at our emotions. First, we feel sadness (the woefulness of the situation), then the lyricism of the music, which is romantic rather than tragic. This fact tends to make *us* rather than the actors feel—an accurately computed device on the composer's part. This scene is effective as it was originally written, but with the added music it is nearly unbearably so.

The same devices can often cause the effect of comedy *because* of the music. In today's theatre we cannot have actors—particularly comedians—recite verses. An artificial and stilted effect would not make an audience laugh—particularly if the whole were not a verse play—but would produce a feeling of self-conscious, contrived artifice. Yet a *lyric* set to music and coming within a scene that is otherwise made of naturalistic prose has long ago become a convention, which we never—in performance—stop to examine.

In *Guys and Dolls*, how possibly could the humorously pathetic Miss Adelaide herself say (in recounting her continuing frustration):

> When they get on the train for Niagra and she can hear
> church bells chime
> The compartment is air-conditioned and the mood
> sublime—
> Then they get off at Saratoga for the fourteenth time,
> A person can develop La grippe, etc.

Not only does the music make this possible, but it gives the lyrics a framework which, especially in a comedy song, makes the *place* of the joke or "pay-off" predictable, and if it is a workable "payoff" the audience will wait for it expectantly, hopefully, and then will respond to it in the spot when the music allows "space" for such a reaction. These words provide a time for reactive laughter during which the audience feels free to respond. The following words will *not* contain another "payoff," and we *know* this even while it is happening because the shape of the music goes along evenly, rhythmically, without imparting any sense of further progression.

All of this lies squarely in the province of feeling. It is the most important of the musical-theatre elements.

COMMENTS ON FEELING

It is in the subject of feeling that we begin to see the huge gulf between Engel's world and ours.

Even today, of course, no one who has created a play or musical would be happy to declare it (or hear it declared) devoid of feeling. Everyone would agree that feeling is at the heart of a dramatic work, especially a musical one. This does not mean everyone would agree on what feeling means.

Perhaps a good starting point for understanding the different meanings feeling can have is simply to ascertain what Engel meant by using the word. He makes it very clear that certain characters inspire it, others do not.

All of the characters in Edward Albee's *Who's Afraid of Virginia Woolf?*, he says, leave him cold. Blanche DuBois, on the other hand, in Tennessee Williams's *A Streetcar Named Desire*, is a character with whom he has deep empathy.

Is this because Blanche is a more sympathetic character than Martha? In terms of their capacity for destructiveness, the two women are almost equal, though Blanche achieves more destruction than Martha.

To begin with, Blanche is hardly the innocent she presents herself as being—this we know from the gossip Stanley hears from a fellow salesman who explains the real reason she had to leave the little Mississippi town she has so romanticized, not to mention her onstage seduction of the newspaper boy. Knowing this, we can see her attitude toward her brother-in-law as deliberately seductive. By the end of the play she has achieved her goal. Stanley has taken her. It's generally perceived as a kind of rape, but she's hardly an unwilling victim.

Martha, on the other hand, however difficult, retains a loyalty to George. One of the most poetic moments in the play comes when Martha, alone and drunk, sings her husband's praises. By rights we should find her marginally more sympathetic than Blanche.

That we don't confirms that Engel is right. Few of Albee's characters create an emotional hold on us the way all of Williams' do. Engel cites declarations by both Albee and Harold Pinter that they don't want to create emotional identification. He uses the term "clearly arranged negativism" to describe this off-putting dramaturgy.

When Engel wrote *Words With Music*, Pinter's work was still surrounded by an aura of hocus-pocus that puzzled sophisticated theatregoers, making them eager to penetrate a mystery they assumed was profound.

With the passage of time it's harder to pretend that Pinter's negative paradigms truly reflect the human condition. At the end of *The Homecoming*, for example, the wife of the college professor who has met her husband's father, uncle and brothers for the first time, agrees to remain behind in London when her husband returns to America. Without any protest, she agrees not only to have sex with them but to work a certain number of hours a week as a prostitute to pay her room and board. Is this truly the answer to Freud's question: "What Does Woman Want?"

Engel defines both Albee's and Pinter's intentions as intellectual rather than emotional, though he suggests that, despite himself, Albee did create an emotional resonance in his plays.

It might be said of both that they were in rebellion against the notion of playwriting advanced by a leading writer of the previous generation, Terrence Rattigan, who described himself as working to please Aunt Edna, a middle-aged, unpretentious woman who probably munched chocolates while she sat in the theatre. She just wanted to become emotionally involved in and amused by the story.

Albee and Pinter, on the other hand, were more concerned with, let us say, Cousin Jason, who has been to university, works as a lawyer or an architect and wants to put his costly and impressive education to use even when he goes to the theatre. Nor does he seek fellow feeling with Aunt Edna.

Correctly, Engel asserts that while you can have plays that are intellectual guessing games you can't have a musical that only engages the mind, not the heart. Which is to say, that you can have plays for Cousin Jason, but probably not musicals. Even *Sunday in the Park With George*, though Cousin Jason doubtless admired it, had a surprisingly powerful emotional undercurrent that might have delighted Aunt Edna. She might, in fact, have a much greater intuitive understanding of a song like "Children and Art."

The theatre had antipathetic characters at the center of plays well before Albee and Pinter. Even musicals had astringent leads, most notably *Pal Joey* in the 1940 Rodgers and Hart musical, but also the leading man in Rodgers and Hammerstein's 1947 *Allegro*, who was the subject of one of its most elegant (and Hart-like) songs, "The Gentleman Is a Dope," a number as much about the woman who sings it as the man she's foolishly been in love with.

These brittle characters, however, operated within worlds that counterbalanced their coldness. The same score that has "The Gentleman Is a Dope" has the sentimental "A Fella Needs a Girl" and the haunting "So Far." The limits to antipathy may have been established in Sondheim's 1981 *Merrily We Roll Along*, based on an unsuccessful 1936 "comedy" by Kaufman and Hart of the same name, whose novelty was that it was a story told backward. In both cases the human landscapes were icy.

Engel devotes a considerable amount of space to Albee and

Pinter, though neither had a direct influence on musicals. (Interestingly, Albee was brought in by David Merrick to rewrite the book of the musical version of *Breakfast at Tiffany's*, which closed in previews at a loss of $1 million—a lot of money in 1966. The debacle was hardly attributable to him, but it did bring to an end his contributions to the musical theatre.)

Engel may have considered it important to discuss these playwrights because they represented a new sensibility gaining ground in the theatre. Both reflected the changing understanding of the role of feeling in dramatic works. Both wanted to avoid the conventional dynamics that had driven the theatre for centuries—the audience identifies with a character and experiences an emotional catharsis as the character undergoes some crisis.

The internationally renowned ceramicist Eva Zeisel once wrote about how harmful it was to much of 20th century art that the governing principle was negative. Artists defined their work not by what it was but by what it was *not*, by which they generally meant the principles that had informed art of the previous century. Zeisel, whose own work began in the Twenties and whose designs are still being sought by manufacturers in the early years of the 21st century, felt that the emphasis on what art was *not* had limited the creativity of many of her fellow artists.

In the theatre, too, the reaction against the venerable formulae of the past yielded interesting, challenging works, but often these iconoclastic plays offered little to interest audiences once the main argument, the need for theatre forms to be more flexible, was won.

Just as the Absurdists made their attack on conventional structures but were aided by the thoroughly un-intellectual force of television, the playwrights Engel cites overturned the emotional mechanisms that were standard practice in the theatre, but their impact was far less crucial than an equally un-intellectual movement of the time.

Around the time Engel was writing *Words with Music* two young Englishmen were writing *Jesus Christ Superstar*. It was not originally conceived as something for the theatre, though Andrew Lloyd Webber and Tim Rice had already enjoyed great success with their school theatre piece, *Joseph and His Amazing Technicolor Dreamcoat*.

Superstar made its first appearance as a record album, which suggested several things, the most important of which was that they aspired to fame in the world of pop music rather than, strictly speaking, as composer and lyricist. In some ways a concert was the perfect format to present the material. *Superstar* isn't really structured as a narrative, though it roughly follows the final events in the life of Christ. Rather, it's a series of star turns, most of which have a similar level of intensity. The songs aren't really written for characters to sing to one another. As in a rock concert, they're intended to be sung straight to the audience.

Only after a successful concert tour did producers present *Superstar* in a proscenium theatre. In New York, Tom O'Horgan, who'd directed the Broadway version of *Hair*, was hired to translate *Superstar* into a theatre piece. He did so in his characteristically overblown way. The show had a short run.

There was no shortage of feeling in *Superstar*, but it was an understanding of feeling that came from the world of rock rather than the traditional theatre. Most of the characters fairly erupted in emotion. Many of the numbers were designed as emotional fireworks, but the intent is to let the actors vent, not necessarily to create emotional identification with the audience. Moreover, a lot of the lyrics are satiric and self-satiric, which further limits emotional identification.

The exception is Mary Magdalene, whose "I Don't Know How to Love Him" is a traditional theatre ballad, a character explaining an emotional dilemma and inviting the audience to share her frustration. Most of the numbers in *Superstar*, however, fall under the heading of declamation.

Declamation can be quite intense but is seldom nuanced. Toward the end of the chapter Engel describes the different kinds of feelings different musicals evoke. What is interesting is that all the shows he discusses—from *Fiddler* to *Pal Joey* to *Guys and Dolls*—are written in a musical idiom that is straightforward, simple, but emotionally varied in its effects.

Rock, the dominant musical style of the last few decades, is also straightforward and simple, but essentially it can only convey a particular historical moment, the late 20th century. Rhythmically, lyrically, and in its melodic simplemindedness, it is the music of adolescence. In our culture adolescence can be prolonged virtually until old age. (Mick Jagger, for example, is nearly eligible for social security.) The music of American adolescence, however, is not suitable for other times and cultures. It would seem out of place in *Fiddler*, even more so in *Pal Joey*, not to mention *Guys and Dolls* or *The King and I*.

Rock offers feeling in abundance, but whether it has emotional range remains a question. When Engel wrote *Words With Music* rock seemed a side show, but with every passing year it became increasingly more important and, as we shall see, had greater bearing on all the other topics he discusses.

SUBPLOT

> **The contrapuntal secondary plot belongs almost exclusively to the musical theatre and came about at its very inception. It is almost unknown in the nonmusical theatre.**
>
> **Lehman Engel**

It ought to go without saying that if a play or musical has no plot, there clearly cannot be a subplot. However, this condition can exist only in plays and musicals of the future in which plot is done away with. Even so, it is far from impossible or unlikely that the lines of development might not be stated in primary and secondary order, in which case the relationship between the two would parallel the standard relationship between plot and subplot.

Due to many kinds of confusion relating to the nature of subplot, it might be clarifying to say what a subplot is *not*! It is almost an impossibility to write a play or a libretto in which all of the characters are not in some way related. They are friends, schoolmates, family, opponents, a group of people thrown together in a common situation, or almost anybody imaginable. This fact, however, does not constitute a subplot in any sense. Unless one group of people is organized to play one plot and another group—through related— is organized in a concurrent one, there is neither plot nor subplot. A subplot—if it is one—should be precisely what the name implies. It is in itself a complete plot and it is subordinate to another.

The characters involved in both are related to one another. But the secondary plot is complete. It can be told by itself without reference to Plot One. The characters are fully drawn, have their own conflicts and interests and situations. They run parallel to or contrapuntally alongside the principal characters in *their* plot. They do not form a separate "block" so that Characters 1 do a part of their stint, then Characters 2 do a part of theirs (this did happen in early musical comedies), but all of them weave in and out of the other camp's doings, each still preserving and pursuing his own plot's integrity.

The uses of a subplot are numerous, especially in a musical. Since—due to restricted length of a libretto and desirable simplicity because of musical use and unavoidable interference—the principal plot must be succinct and as uncomplex as possible, still maintaining substantial interest and conflict, the addition of another concurrent plot involving other characters is advantageous. Besides, it relieves the performers by not making them always necessarily present, and the audience is refreshed by changes of people and interest in another dramatic line.

In nonmusical plays, employment of a subplot is an exception. In the plays of Shakespeare they appear infrequently. In *Hamlet*, *Othello*, *King Lear, Romeo and Juliet*, *Julius Caesar*, and most others all of the characters relate strongly to the principal character but generate no separate and complete plots of their own. For example, in *Hamlet*, the King and Queen, Ophelia, her father Polonius and brother Laertes, Rosencrantz and Guildenstern exist only in relation to the central Hamlet. However, in *The Taming of the Shrew*, while most of the dramatis personae owe their lives to Katharina and Petruchio, there is also the related couple Bianca and Lucentio, who provide a slight subplot which even so is dependent on Katharina. The lovers in *The Merchant of Venice* add only a different color. *The Tempest* contains subplot elements.

Later in the comedies of Sheridan there is a set of lovers who, while related to the dominant principals, also have a slight life of their own. In still later plays, this occasional dual interdependence has almost totally disappeared. In Ibsen's *Ghosts* the small cast proceeds in one single line led by Mrs. Alving. In Chekhov's *The Cherry Orchard* it is Mme. Ranevsky who dominates and is dominated by everything and everybody. The characters in *The Sea Gull* are hopelessly intertwined, and even the "young love" duo does not emerge as an independent entity because of the girl's additional involvement with the older playwright, who in turn is also involved with the boy's mother. The whole is a single complex mechanism.

The same is true of later plays such as *Pygmalion*, *Man and Superman*, *The Madwoman of Chaillot*, *The Enchanted*, *Rhinoceros*, *A Streetcar Named Desire*, *Death of a Salesman*, *The Price*, and *The Birthday Party*, all of which are representative of common practice in recent best dramas.

The absence of subplot is undoubtedly appropriate since the writers have set out to make only a single point. All of the characters contribute in varying measures to the making of that point. The argument is launched and kept alive by differing points of view which negatively or positively add up to a "presentation of the case," the author's specific argument. In *Macbeth* the "case" is the inevitable and disastrous result of ruthless ambition. In *Rhinoceros* the author shows us the single tragedy of the single non-conformist. In these plays the denouement is reached through an intellectual and sometimes emotional *contretemps* between the forces at work on both sides of the argument, and the audience becomes involved in watching and/or hearing the dramatic development and its conclusion.

Genuine subplot is a rarity in grand opera, and, in the main, operas follow closely the shapes of plays they are based on. Because of the emotional weight of the music and the time it consumes in performance, there is generally no need to find an engaging complement for the basic plot. If this argument has any merit, it should be instantly clear that this "emotional weight of the music and the time it consumes in performance" form the basic differences, especially in libretto-need, between opera and musical show. Opera and play are two manifestations of the same thing (drama), but the musical show makes its own special requirements of the librettist.

Operetta also seems to have required something different of its librettists. In the highly successful Viennese variety there are two elements consistently employed in unwavering juxtaposition: romance and farce. Each of the best-liked operettas employed both, independently but together. Thus a romantic couple working against some divisive opposition carried that one assignment alone. On the other hand, a second couple—sometimes more than two people—were given the farcical assignment. The characters belonging to each group were somehow related to those in the other, but this relationship was never important.

In *Rose-Marie* (1924), the principals were the title character and Jim Kenyon, her romantic opposite who has been falsely accused of murder. Rose-Marie helps Kenyon to escape and offers herself to Ed Hawley, who is loved by Wanda, an Indian girl who actually committed the murder. Lady Jane and Hard-Boiled Herman are the comedians and the subplot. Lady Jane is a friend of Rose-Marie.

In *The Desert Song* (1926; originally called *My Fair Lady*) Margot and The Red Shadow are the leads. Ben, a society correspondent, and Susan, ward of General Birabeau, form the subplot. Margot is the general's guest, and The Red Shadow (actually Pierre) is the general's son.

These are but two examples of the relationships of the two sets of operetta characters. The members of the lower echelon were generally connected as friends, servants, or relatives of at least one of the principals. All of the plots and subplots were extremely complex.

In England Gilbert and Sullivan had developed their own style, and all of their librettos are so similar to one another in structure that it would be ruthful to say that Gilbert and Sullivan developed a formula. All of their operettas are in two acts. The characters in all are so parallel that a single cast can play corresponding roles in all. In broad lines, the whole is presided over by a character-comedian (the Lord High Executioner, the Ruler of the Queen's Navee, etc.) who has an opposite number in a character-comedienne (Katisha, Buttercup). Below these there is the romantic couple: young, wholesome, and foolish.

The shape of the music also has a recurrent plan. There is a male chorus at the start. After the introduction of several characters who separately or together have several songs, the female ensemble enters and warbles alone. More complications develop before the Act One finale, which is in every case an enormous operalike musical scene in which all the characters participate and for the first time the choral sexes are fused. Act Two begins in reverse with a female chorus, travels along through plot and song to male chorus, and with the conclusion everyone is again combined. While shape is formula, the content of each is a treasure trove.

In Gilbert and Sullivan operettas the character duo are the principals and the romantic pair form the subplot. However, the plot-subplot line is not so simple and clear-cut. For example, in *The Mikado* Nanki-Poo (son of the Emperor) is disguised as a Wandering Minstrel. He is running away from an elderly lady of the Court, Katisha, who expects to marry him. He, in turn, is in love with a young girl, Yum-Yum, the ward of Ko-Ko, an elderly man, the Lord High Executioner, who plans on marrying his ward that very day. The plot thickens, but in the end, of course, Nanki-Poo is united with Yum-Yum, and Ko-Ko must marry Katisha.

The shape of this type of libretto has the elements of subplot as defined at the outset. However, the events which pass between start and finish become incredibly involved not only (in this particular case) with the two couples but two friends of Ko-Ko's, two friends of Yum-Yum's, and the Mikado himself.

Whereas the Viennese principals were usually young (both couples), in Gilbert and Sullivan the main pair were sixtyish and comic while the romantic pair were dutifully young. Neither the Austrian nor the English school are related in their librettos to the precepts of the contemporary non-musical dramatists. The biggest difference is to be found in the form and in the inevitable division between comedy and romance—both ever-present in operetta and each represented by a different set of characters.

When the American school was beginning, early in the twentieth century, the influence from Vienna was strongest, although the music created here was far more modest. The American writers came up with romantic American melodrama. There was always young love, and this was usually thwarted by a villain until just before the very end.

Some words about *Show Boat* (1927) would seem appropriate here, because this one long-lasting work of Jerome Kern's is unique in many ways and it came just after the end of the Americana operetta period. Because of its subject matter and the quality of its music it is part operetta and part musical, part old and part new, more humanized than the Friml and Romberg statues and vastly more American. Its combination of plot and subplot pointed the way to the next generation of writer-composers and succeeded far better than anything that came after it for more than thirteen years.

It ought to be pointed out that in *Show Boat* there are five couples threaded throughout. Nothing as rich as this had happened before it in any other libretto, nothing as courageous in subject matter and nothing in America as opulent musically.

The romantic leads are Ravenal, a gambler, and Magnolia, daughter of the owners of a riverboat, the *Cotton Blossom*. Near the beginning there is an actress (older than Magnolia, but still young and attractive) who works on the show boat. Julie is Magnolia's closest friend. She is married to an actor in the troupe and she resists advances made by a scurrilous character who is so vengeful that he calls the local sheriff (Mississippi) and reports that Julie is a Negress married to a white man. As this is against the law, the two are ordered away. The husband never again appears, and Julie with one great song, "Bill," appears once more only many years later in Chicago. Her husband has long been dead. She is ill, an alcoholic, and doesn't want to rehearse a new song for that evening's opening of the nightclub she works in. Her job is threatened and she does sing the song. A couple of young dancers, Frank and Ellie, also work on the show boat. Then there are Magnolia's parents, a lovable Captain Andy and his straight-laced wife, and a Negro couple, Joe and Queenie. Neither of these "teams" has a plot. They simply relate to the others. There are literally only a single plot (romantic) and a brief subplot (Julie and her husband). The other three couples are embarrassingly full of coincidences. *Show Boat*, despite any limitations, was indeed a unique link between everything preceding it and every good thing that followed, and its presentation of Negroes and their problems put it nearly half a century ahead of its time.

In the Thirties the young native writers of book shows (musicals as opposed to the then popular and lavish revues) were eschewing the old Graustark tales, mistaken identity, villains, as well as royalty, in favor of life and people as they saw it and them here at home. The one thing they did not fly away from at once was the old idea of the coexistent romantic and comedic couples. These persisted until the Forties, when at last they were gradually merged.

Nevertheless, out of all of this the form of the American musical became crystallized and nearly all of the best shows that were to emerge between 1940 and 1950 were to employ the plot-plus-subplot shape. The subplot, which had once been only a flimsy "entertainment" that went nowhere independently, was now to have become a real plot of its own. The best writers obviously felt this was essential to the well-being of a musical show. Before questioning the *why* of it, let us establish clearly the fact of its existence.

When Richard Rodgers and Oscar Hammerstein II came up with their first collaboration, *Oklahoma!* (1943), the libretto was fashioned from Lynn Riggs's not so successful folk play *Green Grow the Lilacs*. No subplot existed in the play, but Rodgers and Hammerstein upgraded a dull ragamuffin named Ado Annie to a bright, sexy, and humorous tease. They retained a peddler who had always beguiled her imagination, and invented a qualified opposite for her whose name, Will Parker, had been mentioned only once in Riggs's play. This trio was endowed with a genuinely humorous and independent existence. The same team converted Ferenc Molnárs's *Liliom* to *Carousel* (1945). In this they changed completely the drab characters of Mr. and Mrs. Beifeld and made them the amusing Carrie and Mr. Snow, who also have a complete life of their own.

When Frank Loesser adapted Sidney Howard's *They Knew What They Wanted* for *The Most Happy Fella* (1956), he gave the heroine, Rosabella, a girl friend, Cleo—a fact which allowed the heroine to "open up," to be clearly defined and sympathetic to the audience at the very outset of the musical. Then in order to give Cleo a more independent life, Loesser further created a farm worker, Herman, with whom Cleo falls in love. Cleo's character is a most outgoing one. Her chief interest in going to the Napa Valley farm at Tony's invitation is to be with her old friend Rosabella. Her romance with Herman is on a comedy level and this comes as an essential relief. Their natures are quite contrasting. Cleo is aggressive, while Herman accepts life as it comes along without complaint or comment.

In *Guys and Dolls* (1950), Frank Loesser, working with Abe Burrows from Damon Runyon's stories, balanced the musical with two sets of characters, each member as well as each couple telling his own tale. Furthermore, the couples are divided so that the male member (Sky Masterson) of one couple is the male star of the show, and Miss Adelaide, who belongs to the second couple, is the female star. This is a unique accomplishment and one which prevents the audience from feeling that it is dealing with a secondary plot at any time. There is no secondary or subplot—only two coexistent and

closely related ones. *Guys and Dolls* is a morality play, concerned
with professional gamblers versus reformers. It is also, according to
the title page, "a fable."

In most good musicals plot and subplot are complementary to
each other. One supplies in style, quality, mood, contrasting kinds
of characters, and perhaps many other things what is not integral to
the other. When it is this way, the combination forms one complete
unit.

Although in the Jerome Chodorov-Joseph Fields *Wonderful Town*
(1953) the older of the two sisters, Ruth, is always played by a star,
again, as in *Guys and Dolls*, each of the two sisters generates equal
interest. What *seems* to give more importance to the older one is the
fact that her romantic opposite is defined, whereas the younger sister, Eileen (by the end of the show), has not as yet committed herself to anyone. As a matter of fact, among the string of men
attracted to her, none would completely satisfy either Eileen or the
audience, and the show ends without the necessity of a decision.

Alan Jay Lerner and Frederick Loewe followed the traditional
pattern in *Brigadoon* (1947) but with three sets of characters—two
romantic and one comedic. In 1949 (with Joshua Logan) Rodgers'
and Hammerstein's *South Pacific* had *three* pairs. The middle one was
pure romance, the older was romantic-dramatic-comedic, and the
third (Luther Billis and Bloody Mary) was almost pure comedy. In
1951 Rodgers and Hammerstein gave us *The King and I*, in which the
reverse of the usual was done. The principal two were dramatic and
humorous with only a faint suggestion of romance which never
materialized. The young and less important couple were the lovers.
Frank Loesser in *The Most Happy Fella* used the older formula but
with one important difference: the principal man was older, fatter,
less physically attractive than had ever existed among earlier heroes.
In 1964 *Fiddler on the Roof* used the courtships and marriages of
three daughters for subplots (in tandem) and an over-all threat of a
developing pogrom as a grand finale.

Hair (1968) has neither plot nor subplot—only a little talk to
connect twenty-six songs. *Applause* (1970) has no subplot—only a
number of characters who relate in various ways to the star. The
show works because there are so many distinctive characters (the
star, the girl who has ambitions, the star's boyfriend, her dresser,

producer, playwright and his wife, and a flock of lesser ones who are kept busy moving about very smoothly).

Company (1970), the most important of today's newer shows, has five couples and there single girls versus one unmarried young man. Each of the couples is engaged in at least one vignette (with the young man) with somewhat similar results; the three girls each play a scene with the boy with differing results.

There has to be some logic for the subplot *need* beyond the mere observance of a tradition. Besides, in more modern times, romance and comedy, once divided, have been joined together. The romantic principals such as Mrs. Anna, Ensign Nellie Forbush, Ruth McKinney, Eliza Doolittle, the King of Siam, Henry Higgins, and many others serve double purposes without themselves becoming in the least bit tarnished.

The question still is why the employment of two (sometimes three) sets of characters and why the feeling of the need for a subplot? My own answers will have to be purely conjectural, but I think it is important to consider the possible reasons since this practice has been so generally employed in the best of shows, and the absence of subplot has faulted other less than best ones.

Although no subplot exists in Shakespeare's *Romeo and Juliet*, Arthur Laurents, working with the "concept" of Jerome Robbins, invented (he must have felt the need to) in *West Side Story* (1957) a brother for their Maria (Juliet). In Shakespeare's play, Juliet has a cousin, Tybalt, who killed Romeo's friend in a duel and was in turn slain by Romeo. But Tybalt (Bernardo in *West Side Story*) was not involved in a subplot. He related solely to Juliet and her Romeo. In *West Side Story*, however, Laurents created Anita (sometimes the nurse in Romeo), the romantic opposite to Bernardo, and this pair is given a life line of its own.

I believe that *West Side Story* would have been too thin to involve an audience for two and a half hours without its subplot. Shakespeare succeeded in *Romeo and Juliet*, but even with poetry of the highest order and without music Shakespeare complemented his tale of the two lovers with lengthy related scenes involving Juliet with her nurse, her mother, the nurse with her mother, her father, Romeo with his friends (especially Mercutio), with Tybalt, with Friar Laurence, who appears prominently in seven scenes, Paris, etc., etc. Certainly Shakespeare felt the need for spreading his story around and of enlarging it by involving many others in its unfolding. As a matter of fact, after the first brief meeting between Romeo and Juliet they have only one single lengthy love scene (Capulet's orchard), a brief scene prior to the marriage in Friar Laurence's cell, and a brief scene in Juliet's chamber. These four are the sum total of their dialogues in a play containing five acts with twenty-four scenes and two prologues! Nevertheless, these two unquestionably dominate the play, and they do so chiefly through their separate actions with the others.

This demonstrates exceptional resourcefulness in apportioning the elements of a single plot among many different characters. In this way the rather too simple bones of a plot were spread apart in order to involve a large number of people in its working-out. Such a method certainly—if nothing else—lessens the danger of monotony and heightens the interest. In the four scenes in which the lovers meet, they can and do speak of nothing but love. In the remaining scenes Romeo is arranging their secret marriage, Paris is also arranging *his* projected marriage to Juliet, Friar Laurence prepares Juliet for the potion which will make her appear dead, Tybalt, who has killed Mercutio, is himself killed by Romeo, Juliet's supposed death is discovered and her funeral arranged. Romeo kills Paris and, thinking that Juliet is dead, kills himself at her tomb. And finally Juliet awakens, sees her lover's dead body and stabs herself. In and around all of these events there are domestic scenes in the house of the Capulets, a clear statement of the animosity between the Capulets and the Montagues, plus a sort of epilogue (not indicated as such) in which the rival houses are united.

The responses of the characters (other than Romeo and Juliet) to the events and to the central theme provide the audience with a greater sense of credibility. Then, too, the background of the social life and schism between the two rival families must be understood if the predicament of the lovers is to be comprehended properly.

It is the contrapuntal tale of Maria and Tony in *West Side Story* versus Bernardo and Anita that creates a single whole fabric. Tybalt (Bernardo) had no truly strong emotional attachment to anyone. The Anita-Bernardo romance is in sharp contrast to the Maria-Tony one. Another color is introduced. Also by making Bernardo (Tybalt)

Maria's (Juliet's) brother (her cousin in Shakespeare), his death brought about by her beloved seems more meaningful. Also the personalities of the two couples are as opposite as possible. Maria is innocent and inexperienced; Anita is "fancy," worldly, and physical. Tony is a clean-cut kid who from the start has lost interest and belief in his "gang" or its necessity. Bernardo is morose, sullen, romantic in a Latin sense, a firm believer in the necessity of his gang (both gangs unknowingly are the victims of society) and the unquestionable caretaker of his sister. The balances and contrasts provided by the two couples are incalculably valuable to the whole of *West Side Story*.

Since a musical show is necessarily lyrical and since romance is one of the chief breeders of lyricism, it follows that the essential core of musicals has always been and is romance. This in the best librettists' experience has seemed to be an insufficiency when unaccompanied by other contrasting elements; hence the usual existence of a subplot.

A second probably reason for the dual-plot arrangement—mentioned earlier—is the need to give singing actors some respite and the audience some relief from the same performers operating in a too narrow mold. In this connection it should be noted that in most of the best musicals, as in most multi-scene plays, actors are not required to follow themselves in succeeding scenes. Such practice is better served when the intervening scenes consist neither of padding (merely to allow for a costume change) nor water-treadings. In many popular small-cast American plays of the Twenties and Thirties there were invariably scenes with a maid or a butler answering a telephone (perhaps several times in the same play) while the star was making a costume change, or in order to give the audience necessary information in the most unvarnished, primitive way. This childish device mercifully seems to have vanished.

As all principles seem to have exceptions, the libretto of *My Fair Lady* (Shaw's *Pygmalion* faithfully followed) is the only notable one that comes to mind. In *My Fair Lady* there is the merest suggestion of a subplot: Alfred P. Doolittle, his beginnings, rise, and malcontent with success, but this is by no means a complete one. What is special and remarkable in this play, as in *Romeo and Juliet*, is the importance and singularity and fullness of every character. All of them revolve about Eliza *and* Higgins: the housekeeper Mrs. Pearce,

Higgins' mother, Colonel Pickering, A. P. Doolittle, Freddie, and even the only once seen Hungarian Professor Karpathy, to whom is given the all-important spot of providing a period for the end of Act One in the musical.

Every character serves many important functions, which collectively replaces the need for a subplot. In terms of mechanics alone, Higgins and Pickering together relieve the need of Eliza's constant presence. Either man, with the housekeeper, relieves the other. Mrs. Higgins with Eliza excuses Higgins. Doolittle with Eliza and/or his pals gets rid of Higgins and Pickering. Freddie's olio gives everyone else a breather. All of the players are important enough so that the combination of any two or three in a scene serves the stage's needs amply.

This is unique. If you tried to do *Oklahoma!*, for example, minus the subplot (Ado, Will and the Peddler) the remainder (Laurey, Curly, Judd, and thin old Aunt Eller) would not work. There would be too little substance and no relief for audience or performers.

Of course it is unfair to contrast *Pygmalion* with *Green Grow the Lilacs* since the first is a masterpiece and the second would have been forgotten long ago but for the musical dressing it came to wear twelve years after its failure.

In the 1966 revival of Irving Berlin's *Annie Get Your Gun,* the subplot that existed in the original (1946) was eliminated and the show worked perhaps better than ever. I have searched for the reasons and believe that there may be at least two accountable possibilities. First of all, the original secondary pair were pasteboard. They were throwbacks to early musical comedy—unreal, two-dimensional excuses for "relief." The job of removing them amounted to little more than a simple erasure, and what remained was the core of the show. The remarkable remainder is an unpretentious plot to which everyone can relate and a fantastic set of songs—eleven blockbusters, all of which are judiciously reprised (many of them more than once)—to which in the 1966 production Berlin added a new duet which also scored an immediate bull's-eye: "An Old-Fashioned Wedding."

Perhaps *Annie Get Your Gun* succeeds without a subplot because of its simplicity, its unsurpassed wealth of songs, its good-natured humor, and, not least, its many excellent and extensive production numbers. In any case, it adds up to a full evening which works as it is, and the two principals are given just enough time out through appearances in alternate scenes for their own and the audience's relief.

Among fairly recent failures (discussed more extensively later) where the librettos had no subplot are *Candide, The Happy Time, Maggie Flynn, Skyscraper, Darling of the Day, Her First Roman, Ben Franklin in Paris, Billy, Dear World*, etc.

I cannot help feeling that the absence of a subplot in a musical is seriously detrimental. The fabric is too thin, the carrying responsibility piled on two or there people is too heavy, and the range of possible action is too limited, with an end result too quickly arrived at. Inversely, this is not meant to imply that a libretto containing a secondary plot is well on its way to success, but I believe that any writer who attempts to create a single-track musical is asking for trouble.

The relationships of plot, subplot, and theme in a show finally is as varied as there are shows. As was pointed out earlier, the relationship of plot to subplot is usually a matter of the one complementing the other. Now as to the relationship of each or both to the theme: in *South Pacific*, bigotry rears its ugly head. It figures in both romantic tales. In the main plot the bigot (Ensign Nellie Forbush), separated perhaps forever from the lover whom she was formerly unwilling to accept, has grown, revised her thinking, and conquered her feelings. In the subplot Lieutenant Cable is in love with Bloody Mary's lovely daughter Liat, but he declines marriage because he feels he cannot take this Eurasian bride home to his Main Line society family in Philadelphia. Lieutenant Cable's death resolves the problem.

In *Brigadoon*, the main plot, which concludes that "love is stronger than death," is tormented by the idea of death and separation. In *The Most Happy Fella*, the theme is personal insecurity. Because of this most dangerous absence of self-worth in the main plot Tony begins by confusing his bride-to-be by sending her a photograph of his handsome foreman, who is supposed to go away. The photograph purports to be Tony himself. This is the explosion that sets everything off in a mess. The gradual unraveling of this and the gradual belief given him that he is indeed lovable despite his middle age, fatness, baldness, and broken English unfold from beginning to end of the show.

The question as to whether or not the use of a subplot in a musical is essential can only be answered as a matter of opinion. To me, the reasons for its uses are manifold, and, almost invariably, past uses of subplot seem to validate strong arguments in its favor. If it is to be eschewed, there had better be something else equally functional—what, I do not exactly know—to replace it. (It would depend upon the specific plot and the quality of the characters.) But failure to employ a secondary plot in a musical, I think, must be considered an omission, and without strong positive action in some other equally effective direction the omission must be responsible for serious consequences.

In all truth, I should mention four separate deviations that did work, or in one case might have been made to. As pointed out before, the many three-dimensional characters each of whom was richly defined in *My Fair Lady* allowed for scenes written for and played by a combination of any two or three without either of the two principals.

In *Sweet Charity* (1966), which I think might have been made to work had it been given any heart, there is a series of three separate tales—in tandem—joined together by a single principal, all relating to the main theme: Charity in search of love.

In *The Mikado* there is a sizable group of principals relating to two sets of characters, all of whom together work out satisfying denouements.

In *Annie Get Your Gun* the extraordinary richness of the songs plus the extensive production numbers and the simplicity of the characters seem to leave us lacking nothing.

These indeed are four examples of subplots-to-the-contrary, but in each case a would-be vacuum (or could have been) is satisfactorily otherwise filled. And it is that vacuum which under normal conditions is more safely filled by a good workable subplot.

COMMENTS ON SUBPLOTS

The importance Engel gives to subplots seems curious, since it's easy to think of many successful musicals that have none.

Gypsy comes immediately to mind. So do *Porgy and Bess*, *Fiorello*, *She Loves Me* and *Funny Girl*, to cite shows written before *Words With*

Music. Afterward, as we've seen, structures become looser. As Engel himself notes, the concern for a subplot becomes less important when there may no main plot.

Still, although his concern for subplots seems formulaic, he's certainly correct that a well-developed subplot can add immeasurably to the texture of a musical. He dismisses the subplot of *My Fair Lady*, which, of course, comes directly from its source, *Pygmalion*. His judgment may be hasty, given that the author of *Pygmalion* generally knew what he was doing.

Alfred Doolittle is not merely, as Engel puts it, "malcontent with success." Unlike his daughter, who's striving for respectability, he has a healthy disrespect for it and resists it with all his strength. His attitude represents a witty counterpoint to hers. The two numbers in which he appears, "A Little Bit of Luck" and "Get Me to the Church on Time," add a wonderful Cockney earthiness to an otherwise high-toned, elegant score.

In this chapter Engel discusses the lineage of the musical, both its Anglo-Saxon antecedents (Gilbert and Sullivan, whose importance cannot be underestimated but will be discussed later) and its Viennese forebears.

An often overlooked model for American musical theatre is German operetta, particularly the enormously popular Oscar Straus operetta *The Chocolate Soldier*, an adaptation of *Arms and the Man*, which Shaw hated because he felt it trivialized his play (a hatred no doubt intensified by his principled nonparticipation in its profits, which were substantial).

It's often forgotten how German New York was in the late 19th and early 20th centuries—at least musically and culinarily. This may account for the operetta-like style of musicals until World War I, when Jerome Kern's Princess Theatre shows began introducing a lighter, Anglo-Saxon vernacular style that gained ground in the Twenties.

One way of looking at the plots and subplots of musicals in the classical period—Engel cites *Oklahoma!* and *The Most Happy Fella*, both of which make excellent examples—is the peaceful coexistence of two musical styles, one based on the romantic music that had its roots in Central Europe, the other based on the snappy, urban rhythms of America or, more specifically, New York.

Although the sassy style of New York is unmistakable in the lyrics of, say, Lorenz Hart, who was in every way a child of the city, it's useful to remember that emphasis on the verbal started with Gilbert and Sullivan. Ira Gershwin said he became interested in the art of lyric writing when, as a teenager in 1911, he read the obituaries for Gilbert, which quoted generously from his brilliant oeuvre. Before he embarked on a career as a controversial publisher, Lyle Stuart edited and published a trade paper for songwriters. At one point he requested an interview with Cole Porter, who wrote back that everything he knew about lyric writing he learned from Gilbert.

The early musicals of Ira Gershwin and his brother George, especially the 1927 *Strike Up the Band*, show how profoundly Ira was influenced by Gilbert, not just the extraordinary cleverness, but the ability to use this verbal facility and archness to advance the plot. Just as Gilbert and Sullivan balanced brittle numbers with eloquent ballads, the Gershwins balanced their patter numbers in *Of Thee I Sing* with such tender songs as "Who Cares?" and "Love Is Sweeping the Country," not to mention the title song.

The tunes Richard Rodgers wrote for Laurey and Curly—like the music Frank Loesser wrote for Tony and Rosabella—have a melodic sweep that could just as easily have been written in an earlier time. What the two composers wrote for Ado Annie and Will Parker or Cleo and Herman owes more to the bouncy rhythms and snappy lyrics of pop music than it does to any of the Strausses.

It is Jerome Kern who dramatizes this contrast—perhaps unwittingly—in his monumental 1927 *Show Boat*. The love songs for Gaylord and Magnolia are right out of operetta. By contrast, the songs sung by the black characters, especially "Ol' Man River," with all its political undercurrents, are unthinkable in the Vienna of *Die Fledermaus* or the Paris of Offenbach.

One of the most interesting ideas in *Show Boat* is the use of the song "Can't Help Lovin' Dat Man of Mine." It's a tune drawn from black culture, appropriated by and transformed by the white culture, and this cultural contrast figures in the plot. It's one of the ways Julie reveals her octoroon background. But, quite unconsciously, it's a metaphor for what was happening to American music, which, since the popularity of ragtime at the turn of the century, had been absorbing and modifying black musical idioms.

Something similar takes place in Henry Krieger's 1981 *Dreamgirls*, which begins in the Fifties, when a song by a black group, "Cadillac Car," undergoes a comical transformation into a hit by a white bread group, along the way losing its rough edges and its drive.

Dreamgirls is set in the turbulent world of pop music in the Sixties, when black groups developed their own identities and their own power. By the end of that decade, black music no longer needed the white recording industry to develop and market its product. Nor did it need the white music-buying public to validate its creative output.

These dramatic changes were taking place just around the time Engel was writing *Words With Music*, although their implications for musical theatre were not necessarily clear. In 1975, three years after the book was published, *The Wiz*, an all black version of *The Wizard of Oz*, devised and directed by Geoffrey Holder, opened on Broadway. It brought a welcome vitality to a season in which the only other musical of note was *Shenandoah*, a bland attempt at musicalizing American history à la *1776*.

Shenandoah might have passed unnoticed had it not been the beneficiary of Bob Fosse's heart attack. What was to have been the high point of the 1974–75 season, *Chicago*, had to be postponed until that summer because Fosse was hospitalized. All the theatre parties that had been booked for *Chicago* were transferred to *Shenandoah*, enabling it to remain open despite lackluster reviews. Its relatively long run made it an inadvertent "classic." It's always wise to bear in mind that the history of the theatre sometimes rests on accidents.

The Wiz turned out to be an isolated phenomenon. Although it was succeeded by a number of revues featuring black music and performers (*Eubie*, *Ain't Misbehavin'*, *Bubbling Brown Sugar*) *The Wiz* didn't spawn successful imitations. The closest successor, six years later, was *Dreamgirls*, but that was conceived, written, and directed by white men.

The composers of the Golden Age could handle both the vernacular and the operetta styles comfortably, but by the time Engel wrote *Words With Music* both were old-fashioned. Pop music itself was changing dramatically. What would take a while to perceive was that the gulf between it and show music was increasingly unbridgeable.

In 1967 the producer David Merrick, who was certainly aware of trends and the way to capitalize on them, engaged Hal David and Burt Bacharach, the last exemplars of non-rock-oriented pop music, to write a Broadway score, *Promises, Promises*, based on Billy Wilder's 1960 Oscar-winning film *The Apartment*. His instincts were correct. The show yielded a huge hit, "I'll Never Fall in Love Again."

Bacharach and David had hits all through that decade, culminating in one of their most successful songs, "Raindrops Keep Fallin' On My Head," in the summer of 1970. (It was, curiously enough, the theme song for the movie *Butch Cassidy and the Sundance Kid*.) But shortly after that, the tide turned. When they did the music and lyrics for a bizarre movie musical of *Lost Horizon* (starring, of all people, Liv Ullmann!) in 1973, their work seemed unimaginably dated.

Lyrical melodies and clever lyrics both came to be seen as part of the "establishment" that young people belligerently rejected in the Seventies. The two different musical styles that plot and subplot had once represented were now equally unfashionable.

ROMANCE

> **Romance—a playboy who is born each spring**
> **To teach a nightingale to sing**
> **A very pretty song!**
> **"I love you"**

> From *The Desert Song* (1926),
> Book and lyrics by Otto Harbach, Oscar
> Hammerstein II, and Frank Mandel

For nearly a century the most durable dramas have veered sharply away from romance as their central themes. This, I think, came about largely as a reaction against the treacle which undermined most early nineteenth-century plays so that new drama (Ibsen, Chekhov, etc.) was based on purposeful themes. Drama in this direction has continued to the present time in America and it has been accompanied perhaps unintentionally by yet a second change, mentioned earlier: the single-character principal.[6]

Thus we have developed plays with sociological theses, minus romance as a *modus operandi*, thereby eliminating one half of the classical couple and throwing into strong relief the single remaining principal.

In musicals of all periods, including the present, the avoidance of romance has not occurred, and it is questionable that it ever will or can since music is, by its nature, lyrical. Composers and lyricists must have something to sing about, and these topics—whether comic, tragic, charming, or lyric—are of necessity based on the communication of *feeling*, not of pure ideas—the heart without the brain. Moreover, it is hazardous even to contemplate putting to music a philosophical discussion of any depth or an argument involving an exchange of complex ideas. Most importantly, in musicals and because of music, audience comprehension might be jeopardized.

This is in no way meant to imply that the theme of a musical need be inane. There have already been musicals and operas based on essentially serious subjects, but in those that have succeeded best, the themes have lent themselves to simple statements, developments which can be *seen* and/or *felt* and denouements that may be clearly visible above the sometime din of the orchestra.

In the operetta days of our musical theatre, romance was not only large but saccharine. Despite this fact—and surprisingly enough—romance occupied perhaps only one third of the whole. The romantic songs or ballads, in every case, were the principal features of the score, but they inhabited no majority in time, and comedy songs in those days (circa 1926) had not yet satisfactorily evolved.

Operetta is perfectly exemplified in *Rose-Marie*. Here boy meets girl, girl reluctantly but heroically loses boy but finally, of course, boy gets girl. The other most successful American operetta survival from the same period is *The Desert Song*. This one is even more romantic: Girl loathes boy as a pretended fop. Girl falls in love with masked boy after she has met him (masked) as a dashing hero. Girl finds out in the end that they are one and the same. Curtain.

In both of these classic surviving operettas, after more than forty years although remembered, celebrated, and still performed and recorded, songs were given the romantic pair, yet the larger part of the shows was assigned to the comics and sub-principal characters, and the musical remainder to folderol, including marches, comedy (?) songs, sentimental ditties (unrelated to the principal love birds), and incidental music, which, though in itself was unimportant, nevertheless worked toward bringing about a cohesive whole.

But romance in musical shows can and has assumed many different shapes. In opera, romance was written for two large bovines who (perhaps luckily) never managed to reach each other before death overtook one or the other. Operetta in its Viennese, French, and English forms did a coy turnabout. It was especially coy in Vienna, where the same two large bovines made love and won each other against all pastry-cook pitfalls. In France, this very Viennese formula—derived from Grandma—was made fun of, although in the course of the lampoon hero and heroine continued to win each other.

In England (Gilbert and Sullivan) while boy and girl claimed each other at the end they were less important than some older person with a yen for romance but a less youthful if more interesting claim to it. Ko-Ko is vastly more beguiling than the young pair (*Mikado*); so is the Major-General (*Pirates of Penzance*); so is the Lord Chancellor (*Iolanthe*); so is the Captain of the Queen's Navee (*Pinafore*). The oddest part of this is that the young folks with their dramatic differences are invariably exposed first (as in later American musicals), but the emphasis on "caring" is successfully shifted to the "character," one we ironically care most about! This is a neat accomplishment which obviously suggest contemporary musicless plays, but with this exception: The resolution of Number One Man is always an integral part of the resolution of boy-girl problems.

When operetta reached its high point in the United States in the mid-Twenties romance was first in importance and the best songs were created for it. Familiar guideposts were present: Mistaken Identity (*Desert Song* vs. *Die Fledermaus*, *Gypsy Baron*, and *Il Trovatore*), duty (*Student Prince*, *Eugen Onegin*), villainous relatives (*Rose-Marie*). In these works love or the righteous triumphed in the end. When the Student Prince foreswore love and married for the welfare of his kingdom, the entire family audience cheered as it wept. These pieces in greater or lesser degree owe their survival (Gilbert and Sullivan excepted) to the music. But all of them worked as pieces and because of the romantic quality of the libretto—if sickly, if foolish, if sentimental. In England, Sullivan was more fortunate than all the rest in having the brilliance of Gilbert, with whom he created satiric masterworks for all time, and Gilbert was equally fortunate. If Gilbert and Sullivan operettas were nearly perfect from every point of view, Offenbach sly and stylish, Strauss pieces musically opulent, their American descendants were talented in a new musical way although copy cats in the book department. Something had to be freed if there was indeed to be an American musical theatre. And this did happen.

First off—in the Thirties—there were shows with contemporary local characters and a brave attempt at realism. But there can be no real plots without real characters to germinate them. Jerome Kern with the invaluable collaboration of Guy Bolton and P. G. Wodehouse (both English) conceived the idea of musical-book-lyrical-dance integration, all working together as a unit for the achievement of a single entity. What Kern and his collaborators were able to achieve was perhaps no more important in itself than *Hair* is today. However, what they did initiated a new kind of thinking (too rare lately) which influenced not only everything afterward but captured particularly the attentions of two young men: George Gershwin and Richard Rodgers. To them was given the concept, the chalice, and both of them, plus the other writers of their generation, did everything conceivable to realize this concept.

The Gershwin librettos (*Porgy and Bess* excepted) achieved little beyond the entertaining of their precisely contemporary audience. Although the characters were local everyday people, they were nearly as unreal as the ersatz ones of their operetta forebears. The same can be said of the shows, musically unique, of Vincent Youmans. Nevertheless, both the Gershwin and the Youmans products made contributions to the musical repertory. For future audiences, the failure as *shows* of most of Rodgers and Hart was solely due to book inadequacies. Youmans had not a single after-success— a fact which I attribute to his too faithful reproduction of his own period without the addition of a literary quality that could relate to all boys and girls living even only ten years later.[7]

The Gershwins became immortal with *Porgy and Bess* (1935). The songs are marvelous, but then also are many others in *Girl Crazy*, *Of*

Thee I Sing, Oh, Kay! and *Lady, Be Good!* The difference between Porgy and the others is the difference between reality and romantic wistful dreamland. The songs of Porgy are generated by flesh-people. Together these songs add up to a score. As a piece, there is a core of something to care about. The other Gershwin shows did not have scores, but there were always distinguished songs. These were not produced by substantial characters. Their romantic situations were synthetic. But the Gershwin brothers' talents transcended the typical 1930s librettos they had to choose.

Toward the end of Rodgers and Hart's memorable collaboration came their monument, *Pal Joey* (1940). Here at last were real (at the time, too real) people in a situation with which every honest-thinking person could identify. Here was romance with a decided difference! The female was middle-aged if attractive, wealthy, socially prominent, flirtatiously serious, but not seriously serious. The boy was a young punk with only sexual attraction. The woman–boy combo worked but with what a difference. Here we have "particularization" at work helping to develop romance and feeling. Romance as it is usually conceived (or love) does not exist in Pal Joey. The feeling (to me) is one of nostalgia. You empathize with someone who wants something that reminds her of something else, something better, perhaps lots of different things that happened when she was younger. This Joey Evans will bring back for an invaluable little while the happy days and the careless dreams.

This is all created through specifics. First of all, the doing, the action, the arrangement—all are Vera Simpson's. Joey is simply available. Vera tells us specifically her point of view about men in her first song. (We have a jumping-off point.) Then in "Bewitched, Bothered and Bewildered" she tells us in detail about her own foolishness and how badly she behaves and precisely what she sees in Joey in spite of what she know of his limitations. Then in their one duet—the nearest thing to a love duet between them—"Den of Iniquity"—so very much happens simultaneously. Joey, for his part, remains humorless, loveless, brainless. But Vera concurrently is making fun of him, wallowing in nostalgia, and enjoying Joey and his gaucherie. Every syllable of the lyrics is a gem of particularization. We know why then—if we failed to know earlier.

In Vera's final reprise of "Bewitched," the new lyrics bid an unconscious Joey farewell. Here too there is feeling. Something desirable of necessity is being lost. It is not a sad song. It is realistic and regretful and even funny. Again, particularization at work.

After *Pal Joey* things in the libretto department began to happen. To be sure, all of the best musicals that followed were based on solid plays or books, and all of them contained a hard core of romance. Without the necessity of going into massive detail here, the books of *Oklahoma!*, *Carousel*, *South Pacific*, *Annie Get Your Gun*, *Guys and Dolls*, *The Most Happy Fella*, *Brigadoon*, *Fanny*, *The Pajama Game*, and *The Fantasticks* all fall into the boy-girl meeting, loss and reunion.

But romance is not necessarily limited to boy meets girl, boy loses girl, boy gets girl. This general pattern has worked more often than any other, but there have been satisfying variations and in more recent years these variations have been further explored. However, even in the good shows where this still worked, the devices responsible for their all-important mid-show separation are different in each show, and these differences are in direct accord with the characters and the situations they engender. The contrast between two characters from rural America in approximately the same period will suffice as an example.

Both Annie (*Annie Get Your Gun*) and Laurey (*Oklahoma!*) are American country girls. Annie is ignorant (today she would be termed "underprivileged") and Laurey belongs to the comfortable middle class. Annie wants her man but is his rival in marksmanship—and superior to him. Very late in the second act she loses a contest to him and finally enjoys the fruits of defeat. Laurey is better educated than Annie. She likes her man from the beginning, and we are given the certain feeling that they are intended for each other, but Laurey rather coyly refuses Curly's (the hero's) invitation to a "social" and accepts her psychotic hired hand's bid. This rueful peccadillo leads to the "situation" in *Oklahoma!*

The other shows in this general category—romantically—have their character individualities but all of them follow the same general pattern. Other successful shows set up this pattern but develop it somewhat differently. Some of these differences are worth noting.

In *West Side Story* the romantic pair are united at their first meeting. It is society that plays a hard and tragic tug of war with them, and their short-lived bliss is concluded with his death. In *Gypsy*, as in

Fiddler on the Roof, the "hero" is a single character: Rose and Tevye. Rose forcefully effects her daughter's success at the expense of their mother-and-daughter relationship and the proffered romance in her own life. At the very end Gypsy (daughter) forgives Mama (Rose) and they are reunited. Rose's antagonist is anything that stands in the way of her daughter's success.

Tevye *(Fiddler on the Roof)* also still cares romantically for his wife—if only as a matter of memory—but he also fears her. When he has allowed his first daughter to marry a poor tailor with whom she is in love instead of a rich butcher to whom she had been promised, Tevye creates a wildly humorous and false dream (presented as a ballet) to frighten his wife into actually desiring the less desirable match. All for love.

In *My Fair Lady,* outer signs of romance appear first in the second act although audiences "write them in" (perhaps out of habit?) from the beginning of the show. It is late in Act Two when Eliza (the heroine) tells Professor Higgins that she wouldn't marry him even if he asked her. He hasn't. But in the final tableau it is clear that their relationship will at least continue and the audience will create the denouement according to its own needs. No kisses, no love-making, but *My Fair Lady* is highly romantic nevertheless.

Romance hovers over *The King and I* but never materializes. There are other shows which have enjoyed success in varying degrees but ultimately failed because of romantic inadequacy. *Candide* is a regrettable example and *The Happy Time* a foolish one—both to be discussed later.

Man of La Mancha (1965) pits the doddering, hallucinating Don Quixote against a young whore and spends the entire limits of the show persuading the girl that she is better than she has ever imagined herself to be. This romance is to me jaundiced.

One of the flaws in *Camelot* (1960) was its incredibility as romance. Why was Guenevere disenchanted with Arthur, a kind, loving and attractive husband, and so carried away by Lancelot, a second-rate romantic superman? It is not lack of fidelity that makes for our dissatisfaction but an unmotivated, rather arbitrary choice that seemed to make no sense. (I am referring to the musical and not to the novel on which it was based.) There were no real love scenes between Arthur and Guenevere and many furtive ones between

Guenevere and Lancelot. Romance (in the first case) to work was not given any opportunity. Besides which Guenevere had more costume changes than the mannequins in *Coco,* and so she wasn't around for very long at any time.

On the other hand, the same legend serves as a basis for Wagner's *Tristan und Isolde,* but in this opera the King (Marke) is an elderly man and awfully "talky" in the only scene in which he appears. The Knight is a young man who in the beginning is bringing the captive heroine to wed the King (uncle of the hero). The age difference between the two men and the first love scene between the two young people (engendered by a love potion) occurs in Act One when we have not even met the King. It precedes the forced marriage. We are on the side of the lovers from the start. Debussy's *Pelléas et Mélisande* is closely related, but the young people meet only *after* the marriage. However, the age difference is at work and we are once more on the side of the young romantic pair.

A curious treatment of romance—and a most satisfying one—occurs in Charpentier's *Louise.* The opera opens with a duet between the lovers (Julien and Louise) on their respective balconies, which face each other from opposite buildings. In Act Two, Julien takes Louise away from a dress-making atelier where she works. In Act Three, they are living happily together in Montmartre until Louise's mother asks her to come home because Louise's father is ill. Now to the point. In Act Four, which is the last, the father has recovered. Louise's home is drab. She hears Paris dancing around her. Unable to bear life without Julien and the young joys of the great city, she once again leaves home.

Here is certainly the most romantic of all operas, and it works today, seventy-one years after its premiere, as it did then. However, it is unique that the romantic male to whom Louise is obviously returning does not appear at all in the final act. This is still new.

It should be clear that—to date—no musical without principal romantic involvement has worked. Romance is the fuel that ignited the music and lyrics. But romance has not been a prerequisite of the most significant non-musical plays of almost a century. I think the simplest explanation is to be found in the difference between words (drama) and music (feeling). Shakespeare alone combined both with a grandeur and magnificence that is still unique. And his methods of employing romance are echoed in today's best musicals. Even in *Hair* there is the romance of self-discovery, in *1776* the romance of a high ideal, and in *Company* a comment on the inability to feel romance, all the while needing it. The foregoing serve to help point out several facets of romance that usually go unrecognized. Not all of it is contained in lovemaking.

There have been and are at the present time certain changes and reciprocal influences at work in the non-musical and musical theatre. The matter of romance which I have made so much of is still an indispensable element in musicals. The non-musical has been hammering at this since Ibsen and Chekhov. This century-old trend has not changed. In *Home* and *The Contractor* there is no suggestion of romance—except unimportantly and comedically.

What helps to make *Applause* (1970) appear old-fashioned is its emphasis on romance and youth as the chief points.

There is a curious aspect to all of this. The new generation—so corny by now, in beards, sandals, an abundance of hair wherever it chooses to grow and a generally soiled look—attributes everything that it does as representative of and expressive of "freedom." The world races drastically from one cliché to another. This generation, beginning to grow a little long in the tooth, claims that the use of drugs has helped to free love and sex. Freedom of choice, attraction, common tastes, and many other at least temporarily discarded ideas are for the moment passé.

Now the musical theatre of this current age group and their juniors (Clive Barnes?)—to go back to the point—also does not employ romance as its emphatic prime element. In *Hair, Salvation, Oh! Calcutta!, Promenade*—the ones that come to mind because I've been told how *good* they were—have substituted sex for love. Okay, kiddo, if that's the way you see it and want it, but you can't develop sex. When you've had your orgasm, you've had it. Maybe you sometimes start again. But this is repetition and not development. Love or romance (a phase of love) can be developed so that the writers and the audience have somewhere to go and somewhere they want to go.

I point this out because the absence of romance as a prime element in musical theatre points possibly to a new road, but it is one which can perhaps lead somewhere; the other one—sex as a substitute for love—can go nowhere.

It seems appropriate to note an article by Jan Sjöby with a Copenhagen date line which appeared in the Paris edition of *Herald Tribune (July* 30, 1970), titled "Denmark and the Pitfalls of Pornography." I quote from it the following paragraphs:

> The tide is out, a year after the flood of pornography that hit the Danish capital when Parliament abolished almost all indecency statutes in the law books. Porno publishers, producers of "Danish blue" movies and operators of "live show" sex clubs are looking around for other means of making a fast buck.
>
> The Danes, it appears, have had it. They don't look twice at the picture of a naked girl or a loving couple. If they look once, it is usually with a yawn.
>
> It all went over last fall, while it was still new. But the interest faded fast: "You've seen one and you've seen it all," commented one Dane. "I'm crazy about girls," said another, "but I'm not really interested in gynecology..." "The Danish market is dead," said one of the club operators. "We'll have to depend on the tourists...."
>
> Copenhagen's daily tabloid *Ekstra Bladet* made an extensive survey of the situation on the pornography market. Eighty-five or 90 per cent of the clubs will have to fold when the tourist and convention season closes, was the verdict.

Personally I was greatly relieved when there was no censorship of the nude scene in *Hair* and the dull *Oh! Calcutta!* Had there been, the whole idea might have become a *cause célèbre*. As it is, it has happened as it inevitably would. Now that nudity has been accepted and the minuscule shock has passed over, I believe it will happen again only when there is good reason. Nudity itself will not be the *raison d'être*. And, oh, how we missed the role of Costume Designer in these shows!

These changes are also more than faintly noticeable in films, which perhaps for too long a time have been the spawns of theatre in one way or another. Now the best films defy or eschew adaptation to other media. One of the most memorable recent films is

Midnight Cowboy. It is extraordinarily affecting, and one of its chief elements is love. Not man and woman love. Not man and man sexual love. But love. And this is one of many reasons for its great success. *The Graduate* has a romantic element, but it is minor and in a sense those responsible for introducing it made the least contribution to the film. Romance here is a coda or "tailpiece" (of course, I refer to the young couple). *M*A*S*H* has form as element A, then much flickering sex, no romance, and hooray! It is a film about war which it is obviously anti, and there isn't a single battle scene! Some time ago Spencer Tracy made an excellent film, *Bad Day at Black Rock,* that concerned a plucky one-armed hero representing justice as opposed to lawlessness. One female was a small part of a small cast and she was far removed from romance or even sex.

As the reader knows by this time, the author didn't think highly of *Hair, Salvation, Oh! Calcutta!* or *Promenade.* He thinks they lead to dead ends. These shows lost their genitals before they were born, and, like people who want you to believe that they have just what they totally lack, they are very noisy about it. But for the rest, those that have found a new way of using romance *(Company, Midnight Cowboy,* and others) not only provide their audience with unadulterated joy and admiration, but they very well may—along with others—be pointing in new directions. If this is so—welcome! The shape has not changed, but what a difference the shift in emphasis has made! And what remains first and foremost is feeling, as it always has and always will.

COMMENTS ON ROMANCE

While Engel was writing *Words with Music* something called The Sexual Revolution was in full swing. The rumblings of this event had been heard for several decades in the plays of, among others, Tennessee Williams. But by the early Seventies, the revolution seldom manifested itself onstage beyond the use of nudity and naughty language in such works as *Hair* and *Oh, Calcutta!*, both of which drew withering comments from Engel.

He was sophisticated enough to realize that romance—a word that, thirty years later, has an atmosphere of rosewater about it, like "courting" or "fiancée"—was changing. He's flexible enough to find in *Hair* the romance of self-discovery and in *1776* the romance of a high ideal. He even finds in Mama Rose a lover's ardor in her commitment to see her daughters' success.

Strangely, although he acutely analyzes the brittle romance in *Pal Joey* and the extremely subtle one in *My Fair Lady*, he undervalues the romance in *The King and I*, perhaps because he did not see Donna Murphy and Lou Diamond Phillips in the 1996 production, where all the unexpressed romance between Anna and the King of Siam flowered in their powerful duet, "Shall We Dance?" (Nevertheless, even if the romantic elements of the main story are underplayed, there's romance aplenty in this show's subplot, the doomed affair of the king's concubine and her lover.)

Romance as the essential subject for a musical was once so ingrained that even as iconoclastic a composer as Leonard Bernstein broached to Noël Coward his desire to write a musical based on Coward's arch-romantic film *Brief Encounter*. The subject of romance seems far more tenuous thirty years after *Words with Music*. In the summer of 2001 a study in the *Journal of the American Medical Association* on the dating habits of American teenagers reported that one in five high school students had been physically or sexually abused by a dating partner. The study also reported a lot of casual sexual activity without romantic entanglement.

Another report, limited to high school students in Minnesota, stated that 1 in 10 girls and 1 in 20 boys have been raped or physically abused on dates. Of these, 6 percent reported some sort of violence on dates before they were in the ninth grade.

This is hardly the place to analyze these figures or their repercussions in the society at large, but they help explain why romance in any conventional sense fails to figure in a lot of contemporary musicals.

In the 2000–2001 season, for example, there were four major musicals. One was a retelling of Charlotte Bronte's *Jane Eyre*, in which the score had romantic elements but was unable to sustain the dramatic tension of the narrative. There was nothing romantic (or even mildly entertaining) in the adaptation by Lynn Ahrens and Stephen Flaherty of the children's books of Dr. Seuss into *Seussical*.

A note of romance was added to the adaptation of the modest British film *The Full Monty* when, in a plot development not in the film, two of the unemployed factory workers, who are rehearsing a strip show to raise money, realize they're gay and fall in love.

The major musical of the season was Mel Brooks's adaptation of his 1968 movie *The Producers*. In many ways the show, set in 1959, was a regression to another era. Hence, romance was acceptable.

There's a Gershwin-esque charm to "That Face," the one ostensible love song, between the shy accountant, Leopold Bloom, and Ulla, the bombshell secretary. But the real romantic ballad comes at the end of the show, when Bloom expresses his affection for his unscrupulous business partner, Max Bialystok, in "'Til Him." Both these numbers have, musically and lyrically, a throwback quality, but they were unquestionably imbued with an aura of genuine romance.

Engel ends his chapter on romance on an extremely dour note with his quote from a Danish newspaper about the ultimately anesthetizing effect of pornography on the population of Copenhagen.

The medical journal report cited earlier suggests a somewhat different impact of the Sexual Revolution in this country. Instead of resulting in indifference toward sex, the attitude has become more brutal, more impersonal. Certainly in the lyrics of popular music, where women are often seen as "'ho's and bitches," romance seems entirely beside the point.

Nevertheless if the public were truly satiated with sex, it would not have been possible for a musical like *The Full Monty* to be such a big hit. The show builds on the titillation of seeing its male cast members do a strip tease, which would not create dramatic tension if the public were inured to the shock of frontal nudity. That a whole show could hinge on this issue suggests we have not come all that far since *Hair*.

Romance has been at the heart of literature and theatre for millennia. An early observer noted that the most thumbed pages of the First Folio of Shakespeare in the Oxford Library in the 17th century were those of *Romeo and Juliet*.

Romance remains essential even if the objects of affection may have changed. Even as quintessentially romantic a work as *Tristan und Isolde*, to which Engel devotes considerable space, has been given an unusual interpretation by no less a figure than W. H. Auden. He suggests that the real love in Wagner's conception of the medieval myth is between King Mark and Tristan, which explains, Auden says, why Mark, who might have easily remained offstage, is given a long monologue that Engel, irreverently but accurately, describes as "talky."

If Engel's emphasis on romance strikes us as a little quaint, it is nevertheless true that the libido is never far from center stage. Even in our unromantic times, the most successful musicals—*Phantom of the Opera* and *Les Misérables*, to cite just two examples—are heavy on romance. Tellingly, both are set in 19th century Paris, a place steeped in romantic imagery. The implication is that romance on this level can only happen in some other time and place. In these plots romance hinges on the seemingly unattainable—the Phantom must love from afar lest the object of his affection see his disfigured face; the young swain must scale a fence to woo Jean Valjean's ward. "The unattainable" has little currency in contemporary romance.

In a curious way both these pieces evoke the mood of operetta, the genre American musical theatre theoretically supplanted. There may be elements of rock in both these scores, but the mindset is of the past as something remote and exotic, not exactly in an Ivor Novello mode but hardly in the hard-edged style with which Sondheim treated 19th century romance in *Passion*.

We may be skeptical about traditional notions of romance, but there's something fascinating about the emergence at the end of the seemingly anti-romantic 20th century of one of the quintessential figures of romance in the 19th century, Giacomo Puccini. The composer of *La Boheme* and *Madama Butterfly* was long unfashionable — the British critic who went by the single name Beachcomber once declared, "Wagner is the Puccini of music"—but his work has never diminished in popularity.

Apart from Lloyd Webber's appropriation of a theme from *The Girl of the Golden West* to play a key role in *Phantom*, two of the most successful shows of the Nineties, *Miss Saigon* and *Rent*, were based on *Madama Butterfly* and *La Bohème*, respectively. In the winter of 2002 a version of *La Bohème* itself opened at the Broadway Theatre, directed by the Australian movie director Baz Luhrmann, who'd done a production of the opera for the Sidney Opera House a decade earlier and was now hoping to lure fans of his Oscar-nominated *Moulin Rouge* to a hip version of the opera.

The times may be anti-romantic but in a darkened theatre we can leap beyond the mood of the present moment, toward unabashed yearning.

LYRICS AND PARTICULARIZATION

The poet should seize the Particular, and he should, if there be anything sound in it, thus represent the Universal.

Goethe, quoted in
Johann Peter Eckermann's
Conversations with Goethe,
June 11, 1825

The pinpointing of characters and situations is a theatrical necessity common to both drama and musical because we can relate only to specific individuals. Immediately the question is raised as to whether or not we care about masses, poverty, suppression, want of freedom, etc. I think we become exercised over principles and *ideals* (specifics) but *not* people (general).

In the December 14, 1970, issue of *The New York Times,* Alvin Shuster wrote:

> Quinhon erupted last Monday after an American soldier shot and killed a 12-year old student, Nguyen Van Minh, who was sitting on the fence at his high school waiting for class. American officials said the boy was killed accidentally after the soldier fired warning shots to frighten other boys trying to steal from an army truck parked near the school. The Vietnamese reaction to the incident reflected a growing resentment in this country against the behavior of numerous American soldiers. Worse incidents have occurred. The alleged massacre at Mylai in 1968 caused more excitement outside of Vietnam than in it. But, as one Vietnamese said, "It is easier to galvanize anger over one individual than it is over one hundred."

Particularization is an essential funnel to feeling.

Ibsen might have written a lengthy diatribe on congenital syphilis that could have horrified people in the late nineteenth century, but he succeeded in affecting both his own audiences and today's, emotionally, in *Ghosts* by unfolding a tale of a specific Mrs. Alving, her late husband and her victimized son.

Particularization is not a new idea. It has been employed consciously or not for a variety of purposes by dramatists and librettists. It is most important in the creation of characters, plot, and especially of lyrics.

In drama, Williams' Blanche *(Streetcar)* and Miller's Willy Loman *(Death of a Salesman)* are particular enough to be called "special." They are neither prototypes nor average people. They are fascinatingly apart from average people with whom they are tellingly contrasted. "There but for the grace. . ."

It is the specifics with which all good writers endow their dialogue that captures the audience's attention and empathy. Miller, in the final section of *Salesman,* has Charley at the cemetery explain Willy, the salesman, to Linda (Willy's wife) and to Happy and Biff, their sons. What Miller *might* have written could have been: "He was a salesman. He traveled all the time. When his customers didn't buy, he felt it was the end of the world. If his clothes were dowdy, he was finished."

In essence that *is* what Charley said. However, Miller's incredible use of specifics made this speech not only memorable, but profoundly touching.

> Willy was a salesman. And for a salesman, there is no rock bottom to the life. He don't put a bolt to a nut, he don't tell you the law or give you medicine. He's the man way out there in the blue riding on a smile and a shoeshine. And when they start not smiling back—that's an earthquake. And then you get yourself a couple of spots on your hat, and you're finished....

It is particularization that enables prototypes to transcend the ordinary.[8] Without particularization, they would be stereotypes. In the best musicals, characters are recognizable human beings with whom anyone can empathize, but they will have been endowed through particularization with their own special qualities. This is especially apparent in good songs, which invest them with something uncommon. This is brought about in two ways. The music clothes them in a style or characterization that distinguishes them from all other usual people, and the particularization of lyrics confers a kind of distinction that separates any one from any other one. That is, in a good musical.

It is this very focusing on precisely who they are that fires them into orbit for an entire evening. Laurey (*Oklahoma!*) is any nice clean rural American girl of some means. Julie Jordan (*Carousel*) is any demure but knowing American girl who is prepared to pay any price for what she considers to be her happiness. Nellie Forbush (*South Pacific*) is nearly every Southern girl about the time of World War II (now more than a quarter of a century ago) with charm, graciousness, and unconscionable home-grown bigotry. Joey Evans *(Pal Joey)* is every no-good attractive if ignorant boy who, because he is ignorant and attractive, thinks he can bluff his way into any position. Tevye *(Fiddler)* is any establishment father in conflict with the younger generation. The examples are limitless, but note that they—all of these people and the others who are here unnamed— are specifically defined, recognizable, and therefore understood and empathized with.

While all characters in every stage piece must be brought clearly into focus, some may require considerable explanation, development, change, and unfolding in a play, but in a musical who they are and what happens to them must be immediately understood.

Dramatic developing time in a musical is considerably foreshortened (hence the need for immediate definition), and the music itself can too easily interfere (vocally and orchestrally) with the clear comprehension of a character complex enough to require shifting explanation.

Much of musical character set-up depends not only on the quality and style of the music but even more especially on the lyrics[9] through which the singing characters "speak." For about forty years now American lyricists have, in the main, known what to do in order to produce necessary results. They have not always known.

It is interesting to speculate on the reasons and influences that caused early twentieth-century American lyricists to write as they did. In every case the words to songs were artificial. They did not characterize the "I am" of the singer. (Schubert and Schumann understood this long before.) The words had little if any relationship to the everyday manner of speaking. Considered as poetry—a form of "speech" on a higher, more stylized and perhaps more idyllic plane—these early lyrics were indeed poor. What, then, contributed to their stilted and artificial style?

These turn-of-the-twentieth-century lyricists did not lack excellent models among English poets. Well known here then were Keats, Tennyson, Byron, Wordsworth, Shelley, and many more who were stylishly regarded. In America, there were Emerson, Longfellow, Whittier, Lowell, and a host of others.

It must be true that lyricists are influenced by other lyricists and models could have come only from one of two sources: W. S. Gilbert and *translations* of Viennese operetta. From Gilbert they might have learned sharp satire, but this style was not practiced at all by our earlier lyricists. Then it is possible—just possible—that they were spoon-fed with translations that were invariably artless, awkward as poetry and as English, and remote from any naturalistic kind of expression!

Take, for example, *The Merry Widow* (1905), which was first unfurled here (in English) in 1907, when it enjoyed a then enormous run of 416 performances. *There* was status for you, and status must be good and is therefore inevitably emulated. The lyrics by Adrian Ross (English adaptation) were par for the course. Some of the song first lines will illustrate:

> "We are alone, there's no one here."
> "Gentlemen, I pray! We can't tear ourselves away."
> "My Fatherland, it is for thee."
> "If I could go with you beyond the distant blue."
> "Ladies choice! That's the universal voice."
> "I bid you wait here for a minute."

And this *Merry Widow* was a "naughty" and "risque" little devil. Lest anyone think I have singled out one work to ridicule, allow me to refer to *The Chocolate Soldier,* done here in 1909, also highly successfully, with a run of 296 performances. Here the English songs by Stanislaus Stange began:

> "We are marching through the night."
> "Fight*ing* for du*ty*, Sigh*ing* for beau*ty*."
> "We are searching for the foe."
> "Lonely women watch are keeping."
> "How handsome is this hero mine."

(This is the start of "Come! Come! I love you only, My heart is true.")

> "It is a burden hard to carry" is the verse of "My life is
> sweet, I hold it dear."

Is there any wonder that G. B. Shaw was devastated that his *Arms and the Man* had been *so* badly used?

It is pointless to give other examples since they all match the same artificial, stilted, unreal pattern.

In 1903, Glen MacDonough composed "verses" for Victor Herbert's *Babes in Toyland.*

> See the shadow sway!
> That is nothing dear.
> You must near me stay!
> I am watching here—
> Hark! the fairies call!
> No, that cannot be—
> See the ogre tall!
> 'Tis a cypress tree.

Note especially the awkward word transpositions.

And in 1905 the fecund Henry Blossom wrote the words for Victor Herbert's successful *Mlle. Modiste* containing lines like:

> Ah! When the moon in her splendor is high in the sky,
> And her bright silv'ry light makes radiant the night,

While soft winds sigh:
It is then we forget that the world has a snare or a care,
Life's a dream then,
Love's supreme then etc.

Vague and general.

Victor Herbert in 1913 produced *Sweethearts* with lyrics by Robert B. Smith. Throughout, one will find the vacuous, empty, nonspecific words that accurately represent other lyricists of the period.

If you ask where love is found,
The sort of love that's fond and true,
I will bid you look around;
It may be very near to you.
Sometimes love is very trying,
But you really must not mind it;
If it comes not to your sighing,
There is always one place you may find it:
Seek the dwelling of two happy sweethearts,
You will find it there!

Sweethearts make love their very own,
Sweethearts can live on love alone,
For them the eyes where love-light lies
Open the gates to Paradise!
All other love is doomed to fade,
It is like sunshine veiled in shade,
Such joys of life as love imparts
Are all of them yours, sweethearts!

One contributing factor to this kind of influence may have come as an expression of distaste against the "native" musical theatre which disturbed "serious" writers. These latter regarded successful contemporary American theatre creations as beneath contempt. In New York in the years between 1844 and 1900 the following production statistics seem relevant:

22 European operettas (other than Gilbert and
   Sullivan)
68 American operettas or "musicals"
13 Burlesques
18 Extravaganzas
2 Pantomimes
10 Gilbert and Sullivan operettas
29 Harrigan and/or Hart shows
3 Weber and Fields shows
2 Revues

Our lyricists were not influenced by Gilbert and Sullivan or
Offenbach. I feel certain that they loathed burlesques and extravaganzas, Harrigan and Hart's homespun Irish patter, and Weber and
Fields' German "vulgarisms," but it is certain that they were taken
with Viennese operetta and Austro-German culture in general.
German immigrants, many of whom achieved financial success in
New York, included the aristocracy about the turn of this century,
and they contributed the most money to cultural projects. In 1890
there was a total population in greater New York City of about
1,500,000. Of these, about 250,000 were German—a sizable percentage. The large Irish group had Harrigan and Hart (later George
M. Cohan) to entertain it; the Italians—largely poor—had occasional Italian opera, if they could afford the ticket tariff, but the
Germans represented culture with a capital "K" and the leaders
among them had the money not only to buy tickets but to subsidize
whatever interested them. Part of this giving had its motives in the
high-nosed society, and these onetime immigrants, now financially
powerful, used their resources to support "high-class" enterprises
which were the status symbols of the society of which they longed
to be a part. This is graphically set forth in Stephen Birmingham's
Our Crowd. The names of people we recall most vividly as art spon-
sors include Lewisohn, Warburg, Otto Kahn, August Belmont,
Guggenheim, Wertheim, and many more—all Germans.

Oscar Hammerstein I, himself German, opened an opera house
in New York (the Manhattan) in 1906 where many great singers
were engaged to perform some standard fare, as well as new operas
such as Strauss's *Salome*. The Manhattan was a serious rival of the

Metropolitan, which was twenty-three years old when the Manhattan opened. Subsequently the Met bought out Hammerstein with the understanding that he would not produce opera in New York for at least ten years.

The Metropolitan Opera House had opened its doors in 1883. In its second year Leopold Damrosch (father of Walter and a German by birth as well as indoctrination) took over the leadership. Damrosch engaged many German singers and presented a repertory largely of German operas. Although French and Italian operas were also given, they were sung in German! Conductors and singers as well as repertory-composers were largely German and among the most celebrated people of their era. Even the operas of Wagner were given only one year after the composer's death and at the height of anti-Wagner feeling. By 1890 all of Wagner's operas except *Parsifal* had been sung successfully at the Met, along with many other German operas with little or no distinction. The symphony orchestra repertory and chief conductors were also German. The New York Philharmonic Society, founded in 1842, gave the following program at its initial concert:

Beethoven   Symphony No. 5
Weber   Scene from *Oberon*
Hummel   Quintet in D Minor
Weber   Overture to *Oberon*
Rossini   Duet from *Armida*
Beethoven   Scene from *Fidelio*
Mozart   Aria from *Il Seraglio*
Kalliwoda   Overture in D

Aside from a single Rossini aria and an overture by a then contemporary Czech, the entire program was German. The succession of illustrious conductors during the century following the opening was to be nearly 100 percent German.

Besides the Philharmonic there were four singing societies: the Deutscher Liederkranz (1847), the Männergesangverein (1854–1918), the Mendelssohn Glee Club (1866), and the Oratorio Society (1873) under Leopold Damrosch.

On the popular musical-theatre front I have already pointed

out the high regard for Viennese operetta, which was presented in highfalutin, bastardized English. The founding fathers of the American musical not only greatly admired Viennese operetta but also had studied it lovingly in Europe. Victor Herbert, born in Ireland, studied in Germany and Austria and played cello in an orchestra conducted by Johann Strauss's brother. Rudolf Friml was born in Prague and studied composition with Dvořák, but settled in New York in the early 1900s at the age of twenty-one. Sigmund Romberg was born in Hungary in 1887 and came under the influence of Strauss and Lehár before he too settled in New York early in the 1900s. Although Jerome Kern was born in New York in 1885 he was educated musically as a young student in Europe. Herbert, Friml, Kern, and Romberg may well be listed as "founding fathers."

But the original idea was German. Even the most casual glance at the lyrics of German opera, operetta, and art song will reveal a common-denominator vocabulary which is ever present. *Ewig* (forever), *Liebe* (love), *Tod* (death), *Mond* (moon), *Himmel* (heaven), *Nacht* (night), *leiden* (suffer), *Dämmerung* (twilight), etc. This is all romantic, general, and painful. No particularization, no laughter.

The association of "pain" with "love" is a purely nineteenth-century idea. The poets, painters, composers, and other "artists" of that period died constantly of love. Nobody seemed ever to find it happy or joyous. This sick philosophy permeated everything produced during that period and wreaked havoc with creativity, which at an earlier time had been cooler and less unhappy not to say less hysterical.

One essential difference between German expression in the nineteenth century and creativity in other countries was the presence in the former of a kind of false grandeur, pomposity, and *pseudo-morality*. I think the latter is undreamed of in French or Italian art but one that was carried to a nauseating extreme in German art. It is this false grandeur, pomposity, and pseudo-morality, I think, that colored the writings of our earliest lyricists. With these three gargoyles as guides the gnarled finger has to have pointed in the direction of the unnatural, stilted, and even antihuman style and expression. The American lyrics of this period fall into this category. Their generalizations as opposed to particularizations made them vague. Their style of expression was unreal and artificial. Their vocabulary was nearer a translation than anything native to our country. Their philosophy was imprecise and dissembling. They had an origin in a kind of German never-never land, and they had finally to be ignored by the oncoming, thoroughly native lyricists if these were not to be engulfed and destroyed.

By 1930 American lyricists had succeeded in bypassing their own shabby heritage and had begun creating something important and new in the theatre and in the language.

It has been due to the talents and genius, exploration and development of the men and women in our musical theatre—the lyricists, circa 1930 to the present time—that a very special art has finally come of age. Without this achievement, accomplished in a wide variety of ways and styles, character stereotypes could not have been elevated to a significantly higher level, transcending a general ordinariness to become a unique and individually pinpointed prototype.

This high quality and very personal know-how among lyricists in the theatre should be attributed to Lorenz Hart, Irving Berlin, Oscar Hammerstein II, Frank Loesser, Ira Gershwin, Cole Porter, Nöel Coward, Howard Dietz, Dorothy Fields, E. Y. Harburg, Harold Rome, Robert Sour, Sheldon Harnick, Betty Comden with Adolph Green, Stephen Sondheim, Johnny Mercer, Alan Jay Lerner, Fred Ebb, Hal David, Carolyn Leigh, and a few others. They mastered the ballad, arrived at the comedy song, created the charm song. Looking about themselves—here—they invented fresh new images that had not heretofore existed anywhere in the world.

They, in collaboration with the composers, in many cases their alter egos, made musical theatre possible by raising it up out of the ordinary and general into the particular and specific. They translated into a kind of singable poetry of their own times the "smell of the rain-washed pavement," measured the growing corn to the height of "an elephant's eye," observed with simple profundity that

> a man never trifles
> with gals who carry rifles,

found that a woman can be grateful for being

> vexed again,

perplexed again
[and] Thank God I can be oversexed again,

invented a lazy man who sang

I'm Bidin' My Time,
'Cause that's the kinda guy I'm,

advised a friend quite madly

If you're ever down a well,
Ring my bell,

eschewed ordinary romance with a command to

Sing me a song with social significance
All other tunes are taboo,

warned

Phone rings, door chimes, in comes company!
No strings, good times, just chums, company!,

went back in history to remember

Jubilation T. Cornpone,
Old "Toot Your Own Horn" Pone,

had a girl leaving her family forever to go

Far from the home I love

to marry a man realizing

Yet—there with my love I'm home.
The list of accomplishments is long and the present samples are
of course only just that. It is the qualifying precise descriptive or
modifying word that—in both dialogue and lyric—helps more than

anything else to capture and to hold the audiences' attention and interest. It defines the singing character.

> With kings I've à la carted
> But I can't get started with you.

This girl is neither a nun nor one who at the turn of this century presided over a ranch in the Oklahoma Territory. She belongs to the city and has been around. We know this for sure. In the minuscule examples quoted above, there is not a single generalization in verbiage or style, and the singer who is to deliver them becomes unique.

Sometimes lyrics are quite graphically suggested by the author of the original play, but the lyricizing of the idea plus the musical framework lifts what is fairly small into something larger and more memorable. Two examples of this one-for-the-other treatment can be cited here. In Lynn Riggs's *Green Grow the Lilacs* (1931), in Scene I Curly *says:*

> A bran' new surrey with fringe on the top four inches long—and *yeller*! And two white horses a-rarin' and faunchin' to go! You'd shore ride like a queen settin' up in *that* carriage! Feel like you had a gold crown set on your head, 'th diamonds in it big as goose eggs. . . . And this yere rig has got four fine side-curtains, case of a rain. And isinglass winders to look out of! And a red and green lamp set on the dashboard winkin' like a lightnin' bug! . . . Don't you wish they *was* sich a rig, though? Nen you could go to the party and do a hoe-down till mornin' 'f you was a mind to. Nen drive home 'th the sun a-peekin' at you over the ridge, purty and fine.

What Hammerstein did with these ideas in "The Surrey with the Fringe on Top" in *Oklahoma!* is too well known to be quoted here.

Another example of the same kind of translation is to be found in Sidney Howard's play *They Knew What They Wanted* (1924):

> JOE: ... I only intended to stay a few days. I'm that way, see? I been here goin' on five months now

> AMY: Is *that* all?
> JOE: That's the longest I ever stayed any one place since
> I was old enough to dress myself.
> AMY: You *have* been a rover!
> JOE: I been all over—with the Wobblies, you see.
> Before I come here, that is.
> AMY: What did you used to do?
> JOE: Cherries an' hops—melons down in the Imperial
> an' oranges down south an' the railroad an' the oil-
> fields.... Before I come here. When I come here I just
> stayed. Maybe I was gettin' tired of bummin'. Now I'm
> tired of this....

Compare this exchange with Frank Loesser's lyric for "Joey" in *The Most Happy Fella.* The ideas were originally Howard's, but by comparison with the song version, the former were only a kind of sketch for the latter. It takes a special genius to recognize the latent song in such speeches.

Sometimes a simple but expressive song in a musical replaces a great deal of dialogue from the original play. The song creates in capsule the feeling of a long scene which in turn renders the scene unnecessary. There are many examples of this, but I would like to point out (without quoting) the scene of Liliom's death in Molnár's *Liliom* (1921). There are *six and a half pages* of dialogue *after* the anti-hero's death. Some of it is effective, some is, I think, non-essential and even boring, and none of it can compare with the feeling engendered by the Rodgers and Hammerstein music and lyrics of "You'll Never Walk Alone."

There are many other functions of music and lyrics. Another kind of example is Jud's song "Lonely Room" in *Oklahoma!* Nothing remotely resembling this (pointed out earlier) occurs in *Green Grow the Lilacs,* and as a result Jeeter (as he was called in the play) is an incomplete and non-understood malicious character. In the musical, this one song brings him alive and, without depriving us of the fear which we have of him, Jud is understood and even empathized with.

The immature practices of the 1920s were undoubtedly due to lack of better models as well as to the then general acceptance of lyrical doggerel. They sang, they scanned, they rhymed. What more could anybody want? The continuation today of similar practices in some quarters results, I think, not so much from a lack of talent as from glib non-thinking. In Meredith Willson's *The Unsinkable Molly Brown* (1960) the weaknesses are the basis of a song telling us of the heroine's determination to learn to read and write and to see everything. This is sung by an uneducated girl who wants to be and will become a "lady"—in spite of her vagueness. Compare this lyric with one by Irving Berlin from *Annie Get Your Gun,* written thirteen years earlier, which says you don't have to know how to read and write when you're out with a feller in the pale moonlight. That comes natur'lly.

The latter is also an uneducated girl but one who is razor-sharp precise about life. She is far more interesting than Molly because her naïveté is refreshing and there is neither pretense nor ambition to deal with. Annie is just simple fun and she will get what she wants *particularly* because she doesn't try to get it.

Irving Berlin is surely one of the masters of simple lyrics. His words are usually monosyllabic, the rhythms simple and the rhymes seldom surprising, but they are fresh, develop the subject matter economically, and their images are specific to the extreme.

Richard Rodgers, in his introduction to *The Rodgers and Hart Song Book* (1951), quoted his first collaborator, Larry Hart: "If you wanted to write about New York, you didn't have to be as naive as "East Side, West Side." A couple of years later he (Hart) said, "We'll have Manhattan/The Bronx and Staten/Island, too...." ("Manhattan," 1925).

And certainly Larry Hart was one of the all-time greats because of his wit, craftsmanship, originality, freshness, and particularization. The lyrics he wrote, like Rodgers' music, also characterized the people who were to sing the songs.

Especially writers will be interested in Mr. Rodgers' account of Larry Hart's creative technique:

> If I am trying to write a melodic song hit, I let Richard Rodgers get his tune first. Then I take the most distinctive melodic phrase in his tune and work on that. What I choose is not necessarily the tune or the first line

but the phrase which stands out. Next I try to find the meaning of that phrase and to develop a euphonic set of words to fit it. For example, in one of our songs, the first line runs like this: "Here in my arms, it's adorable." The distinct melodic phrase came on the word *adorable*, and the word *adorable* is the first word that occurred to me, so I used it as my pivotal musical idea. And as the melodic phrase occurs so often in the chorus, it determined my rhyme scheme. Of course, in a song of this sort the melody and the euphonics of the words themselves are really more important than the sense.

It must be remembered that this was a strictly personal creative process, but since it was the method employed by such a distinguished lyricist, it should be known.

Ira Gershwin is another sophisticate in technique as well in rhyme and treatment. In his book *Lyrics on Several Occasions* (Alfred A. Knopf, 1959) Gershwin adds an amusing note: "Since most of the lyrics…were arrived at by fitting words mosaically to music already composed, any resemblance to actual poetry, living or dead, is highly improbable."

Cole Porter employed a technique which has much in common with Ira Gershwin's. The ideas are basic and specific, the rhymes often unusual, the choice of words simple, and the development leads to an inevitable conclusion.

The same Oscar Hammerstein II who served such a long and important apprenticeship with the operetta composers in the Twenties and Thirties—Kern, Friml, and Romberg—emerged in maturity as one of the freshest and simplest lyricists of all time when he began his memorable collaboration with Richard Rodgers.

A new voice among lyricists was heard in 1937 at a revue played by amateurs, produced by the International Ladies' Garment Workers Union, called *Pins and Needles,* which had a run of 264 performances and after a successful cross-country tour ran again in New York for 680 performances. This was the work of composer-lyricist Harold Rome and his first show in New York.

The newness of the lyrics was that those in *Pins and Needles* and in two subsequent shows, *Sing Out the News* (1938) and *Let Freedom Sing*

(1942), had a social point of view and at the same time they were highly amusingly satirical. Withal, they are gay, carefree, and deliciously naive.

Frank Loesser achieved many lyrical feats which are uniquely his own in manner and style. Sometimes sophisticated, sometimes disarmingly plain, always they are precise and tasteful.

In *Bells Are Ringing* (1956) Betty Comden and Adolph Green, whose art is also special (lyricists as well as book writers), wrote a song of disappointment and frustration in the ballad "The Party's Over." Despite the fact that the basic idea is not a new one, the simplicity of both music (Jule Styne) and lyrics makes this song a distinguished one.

One of our youngest and most talented lyricists is Stephen Sondheim, who has already created an enviable library of both words and music. The opening number of *A Funny Thing Happened on the Way to the Forum* is a model beginning for this show. It defines the style, pace, and genre of the whole work. Besides, it sets up time and place, indicates character, and hints at plot. It is totally functional. Sondheim also has written distinguished lyrics for *Gypsy, Anyone Can Whistle, West Side Story,* and is currently represented by the highly original *Company* and *Follies,* for which he also wrote the music.

No list of "best" lyricists would be respectable without a low obeisance to E. Y. Harburg's work. In *Finian's Rainbow* (1947) especially there is a folklike simplicity and unsophisticated wit.

There is also Sheldon Harnick, who is responsible for the sung words in *Fiddler on the Roof* (1964). Harnick is an unusually skilled craftsman. He knows how to characterize, to be folklike (necessary in this show), precise, modest, and guileless.

Since lyrics are sung and must be comprehended aurally (and against the accompanying orchestra) it follows that the simpler, less complex ones are preferable. But simple or complex, they must function as part of the show, represent the innards of the character who delivers them, and they must be fresh and specific. Too often it is obvious that a lyricist simply sticks in any lines that seem adequate in the situation, especially in love ballads. These songs with their stale clichés cannot possibly "hold stage." While they are being performed, the show loses its audience.

One element all best lyrics have in common is directness and precision of idea and image. Any lyric that lacks this quality of sharpness has missed its opportunity to make an important contribution to its show.

The late Oscar Hammerstein II, in his book of lyrics (Simon and Schuster, 1949), remarked: "There are few things in life of which I am certain, but I am sure of this one thing, that the song is the servant of the play, that it is wrong to write first what you think is an attractive song and then try to wedge it into a story."

Alan Jay Lerner wrote a masterpiece of a lyric in *My Fair Lady* (1956) in "Why Can't the English?"—an extension and elaboration of Bernard Shaw's prose idea. The words stuff the song with precise images and become a theme with variations. It begins as a part of the scene, then takes over as a song. It progresses from "An Englishman's way of speaking absolutely classifies him" and progresses through the foibles and vagaries of many other languages.

At the risk of pointing out what may be already too well known, I would like to quote two speeches from G. B. Shaw's *Pygmalion* which also appear in *My Fair Lady*. Each of these illustrates particularization and the effect it can have on emotion and characterization.

When Eliza Doolittle comes to Professor Higgins for speech lessons, she is treated rudely by the professor, and indeed she is to the audience a thoroughly comic character until, in answer to a simple question from Colonel Pickering—"What is it you want, my girl?" —Eliza responds, "I want to be a lady in a flower shop stead of selling at the corner of Tottenham Court Road. But they won't take me unless I can talk more genteel."

This simple speech contains nothing but a fact—a dream, if you like—and it is nothing if not specific. It is my opinion that it is "particularization" which gives this little speech a sudden note of pathos and turns a big corner for the audience in its view of Eliza.

Two scenes later when Eliza's father, Alfred P. Doolittle, the grimey dustman, calls on Professor Higgins in fake protest against Eliza's staying in the professor's house, he asks for five pounds.

PICKERING: "He'll make bad use of it, I'm afraid."
DOOLITTLE: "Not me, so help me, Governor, I won't.
Just one good spree for myself and the missus, givin'

> pleasure to ourselves and employment to others, and satisfaction to you to know that it ain't been throwed away."

Higgins comments, "This is irresistible." And so it is, because it is precise. It is truth, no shilly-shallying, and it is Doolittle and funny.

Shows lacking focus on the particular are always failures (in the true sense), and their sometime box-office success is invariably due to some other quality of entertainment (ersatz fluff) which, for the undiscriminating many, seems to provide sufficient bizaz for an enjoyable if soon forgotten evening. All of these latter have at least one thing in common besides vacuousness: speedy production numbers which help to gloss over weaknesses and omissions. The characters who should matter a great deal to the audience lack definition, development. Human beings and the plots which they should be capable of generating become the olios while the olios become the main (if any) events.

But their theme, plot, choreography, and direction also can, individually or collectively, be as vague, pointless, common, corny, and unconnected as lyrics and music. Agnes de Mille's beach ballet in *Carousel* was none of these things, whereas the hippie ballet in *Georgy* was all of them. The theme in *Billy* was never discovered, while that of *Fiddler on the Roof* was stated at the outset, omnipresent, and developed. The plot of *The Happy Time* was cluttered with embroidery and indistinct, while that of *Pal Joey* was precise. To quote Kurt Vonnegut, Jr.: "And so it goes."

Vagueness, pointlessness, commonness, corniness, plus thinness of characterization and dullness of plot, etc., are the things that contribute most to the making of a failure. In those hysterical pre-opening days "on the road" when things are going badly, when no one is able to pinpoint the precise reasons, when frightened uncontrol creates pandemonium and few of the hierarchy can sit quietly and truly evaluate the errors and weaknesses, the general practice is to switch directors and/or choreographers, sometimes part of the cast, the orchestrator, or just anybody. The real culprit —seldom noticed—is not a product of any of these people but everything *basic,* everything that was approved and bought by the producer in the first place. These are non-fixable by all the new personnel in the whole world. Many a lame show has been made to *seem* fixed and has been somewhat improved, but the fixing and the improving have affected only small things. The major ones in the unworkable shows are so basically inept that the changes, in the end, fool no one. "You can't make a silk purse"—etc.

By the juxtaposition of words not commonly joined together or the use of clever or unexpected rhymes, a writer may come up with something "fresh" or "ingenious" or "unusual." Words which elicit such descriptions, however, are not necessarily new, but each in its way may be—by its usage—original.

The lyrics I have described with such adjectives have been written within the last thirty-five years. But let me quote an English madrigal with music by Thomas Morley (1558–1603) and lyrics of unknown authorship. (This is one of hundreds and no better than most others.)

> April is in my mistress' face,
> And July in her eyes both place;
> Within her bosom is September,
> But in her heart, a cold December.

These lyrics, now nearly four centuries later, are still fresh. Shakespeare, a contemporary of Morley's, wrote a lyric in *Henry VIII:*

> Orpheus with his lute made trees,
> And the mountain tops that freeze,
> Bow themselves, when he did sing;
> To his music plants and flowers
> Ever spring; as sun and showers
> There had made a lasting spring.
>
> Every thing that heard him play,
> Even the billows of the sea,
> Hung their heads, and then lay by
> In sweet music is such art,
> Killing care and grief of heart
> Fall asleep, or hearing, die.

This lyric is likewise fresh, despite its age.

Lyrics, because they are contemporary with us, are necessarily new but not necessarily fresh. Examples of *new* theatre lyrics are abundant, but they cannot nearly always be called "fresh."

From *Hair*—book and lyrics by Gerome Ragni and James Rado (still playing everywhere)—comes a lyric in nine lines, seven of which begin with "I got" and end with "life, mister," "laughs, sister," and end finally with "And bad times too/Like you" for fourteen additional stanzas in this pattern, followed by two other sections in other patterns.

Fresh, anyone? Particular?

In *The Me Nobody Knows*, a current show, there is a prose lyric by "C. M.," age fourteen, which is quoted in the program.

> There was a man waiting under a baby apple tree. He was waiting for an apple to grow on it. He would just sit there and wait and wait but it never grew. He watered it every day but it just didn't grow. No matter what he did, it did not grow. So the man got discouraged and gave up hope for the tree. He wanted to cut it down. So one day he decided to do it. He said he would do it on a Sunday afternoon, rain or snow. So on Sunday there was a fog and he could not see the tree and so he did not cut it down.
>
> The following Sunday a baby apple was hanging on it.

In my own opinion, new *and* fresh and narrative and very specific.

Let us not confuse new and original. Neither has anything to do with any one age or the age of a lyric—but only with the thoughtful, knowing, creative genius of the writer.

I should like finally to call special attention to a few overused words. *June* and *moon* are particularizations. So are *moon* and *stars, clouds* and *hills, spring* and *autumn*. So is *love*. All but the last of these are very, very tired. The last ought to be buried. It's just conceivable that *June* could be somewhat furthered by adding a fresher modifier, such as *wild* or *peaceful*, and that *moon* might be made more interesting with *devil* (already done in 1947) or anything except *yellow, bright or harvest*. Lyricists have surfeited us with *enchanted,* applied to star, various colors with clouds, climbing and sitting upon hills, lovely, warm and bright spring, cruel and dying autumn.

Love is the most abused and re-used of all words in lyrics, and writers who continue to use it except in the direst of crises or in an unimaginably new way ought to be ashamed of themselves. Among theatre love ballads which eschewed the word entirely are:

"On the Street Where You Live"
"I've Grown Accustomed to Her Face" (*My Fair Lady*)
Music by Frederick Loewe, lyrics by Alan Jay Lerner

"To My Wife" (*Fanny*)
Music and lyrics by Harold Rome

"Maria" (*West Side Story*)
Music by Leonard Bernstein, lyrics by Stephen Sondheim

"Miracle of Miracles"
"Sunrise, Sunset"
"Now I Have Everything" (*Fiddler on the Roof*)
Music by Jerry Bock, lyrics by Sheldon Harnick

"If I Were a Bell" (*Guys and Dolls*)
Music and lyrics by Frank Loesser

"September Song" (*Knickerbocker Holiday*)
Music by Kurt Weill, lyrics by Maxwell Anderson

"Come to Me, Bend to Me" (*Brigadoon*)
Music by Frederick Loewe, lyrics by Alan Jay Lerner

"A Foggy Day in London Town" (*A Damsel in Distress*)
Music by George Gershwin, lyrics by Ira Gershwin

"Out of My Dreams" (*Oklahoma!*)
Music by Richard Rodgers, lyrics by Oscar Hammerstein II

COMMENTS ON LYRICS AND PARTICULARIZATION

Reading Engel's chapter on lyrics today is very poignant. It seems so naive that he assumes there's a correlation between quality and success. He didn't live to hear the lyrics of *Les Miz*. Admittedly, they're translated from the French, but they're also, by his—or any—standards, subliterate. This seems not to have prevented the show from translating into big bucks.

It seems surprising that Americans should have achieved far greater mastery in the art of lyric writing than the English, to whom Americans invariably defer when it comes to the use of our common language. With the exception of Noel Coward, none of the British lyricists, theatre or otherwise, has the dexterity or the elegance of, to name a few, Cole Porter, Lorenz Hart, Oscar Hammerstein II, Frank Loesser, Betty Comden and Adolph Green, Dorothy Fields, Sheldon Harnick, E.Y. Harburg or Stephen Sondheim.

The astute reader will immediately wonder why I have omitted the masterly P.G. Wodehouse from the list of British lyricists. It is because he wrote most of his lyrics for American shows. Moreover, after an unfortunate blunder that led him to be perceived as a Nazi propagandist (which he most certainly was not), he spent his last three decades living in America. As a lyricist, he belongs on our side of the Atlantic.

Yet, due to the extraordinary popularity of the British musicals, they now serve as the models for the form.

The period of British hegemony on Broadway began in 1982 with *Cats*, whose lyrics are by an American poet who adopted British citizenship. The bulk of T.S. Eliot's poems in *Old Possum's Book of Practical Cats* have a jauntiness and elegance. The lyric that most mattered in the musical, however, was "Memory," which is in a different style because it was based on a fragment Eliot's widow discovered. As a fragment, it presented the fewest obstacles to the composer.

At least with *Cats* there was a level of verbal musicality and literacy. That cannot be said of the Brit shows that followed or, for that matter, the one that preceded it, *Evita*. What gave the Andrew Lloyd Webber-Tim Rice show its allure, apart from the stunning staging by Harold Prince, was the mesmerizing quality of the historical character on whom it was based, Eva Peron.

She provides the subtext that gives life to ordinary lyrics. In lyrics of classical musicals the words express character in the manner of a dramatic monologue. When Sky Masterson sings, "My time of day is the dark time / A couple of deals before dawn," in *Guys and Dolls*, we learn an enormous amount about him in a concise and poetic way.

When, on the other hand, Evita sings,

> I come from the people.
> They need to adore me.
> So Christian Dior me. . .
> It's my turn to sell me.
> So Machiavel me. . .
> I'm their symbol.
> That's what they call me.
> So Lauren Bacall me. . .

what we learn is how clever Tim Rice can be. It doesn't really seem to emanate from Eva Peron, who would not have been so charismatic if her sense of herself were so ironic.

Evita, like its predecessor, *Jesus Christ Superstar*, is in the tradition of a rock concert, where the numbers must have a certain level of intensity to sustain the momentum, but they lack the shape of a play. *Hamlet* isn't just a series of famous monologues. These set pieces punctuate the dramatic action that precedes them. In the case of *Evita*, the action is ill-defined. The show is essentially a succession of set pieces, which have great theatricality if not dramatic form.

During the Forties and Fifties even lyricists who wrote pop songs had a greater literacy than they do today. Johnny Mercer, who wrote lyrics for movies and Broadway shows, did much of his writing for Tin Pan Alley. This doesn't mean he did second-rate work. He had enough respect for his listeners that he always maintained the same standards. His lyrics have a simplicity, a directness that owe a lot to the straightforward character of American speech. These Spartan virtues co-exist with a sophisticated verve and wit that were inimitably his.

Think of his jocular, "when an irresistible force such as you— meets an old immovable object like me" or the poignant,

When an early autumn walks the land
And chills the breeze
And touches with her hand the summer trees,
Perhaps you'll understand
What memories I own.
There's a dance pavilion in the rain
All shuttered down
A winding country lane
All russet brown . . .

Moreover a lot of the lyrics Mercer wrote for pop songs have the dramatic irony that used to be considered essential for theatre music. An example is "P.S., I Love You," in which a lover separated from her beau pens a letter detailing the uninspiring events that have filled her days but, in the tag line, preceded by P.S., suggesting it's just an afterthought, sings the message that underlies everything else.

Engel always stressed that the diction of a lyric must reflect the character of whoever sings it. Mercer showed he could do that in his sly lyrics for the underrated *Li'l Abner*, based on the Al Capp comic strip.

Even when he wasn't writing for shows, Mercer's lyrics had a clear voice. They were never impersonal. It was the voice of what we might call a mid-century Everyman, whose emotions Mercer understood perfectly. He was a latter-day incarnation of something G.K. Chesterton wrote of Charles Dickens. Dickens, he said, doesn't give the people what they want. Dickens wants what the people want.

Compare Mercer's work with that of a modern master, Eminem:

Yo! This girl's only fifteen years old.
You shouldn't take advantage of her, that's not fair.
Yo, look at her bush, does it got hair? (Uh huh!)
Fuck this bitch right here on the spot bare
'Til she passes out and she forgot how she got there . . .

We are in a different universe.

If the lyrics for more ambitious musicals in recent decades have a sense of artifice, it's because they have to invent their own language. The vernacular has become the province of rebellious adolescents.

It's the language of the gutter, which is only appropriate if you happen to be writing a musical about the gutter.

George Abbott, who directed one of Rodgers and Hammerstein's least successful shows, *Me and Juliet*, attributed its short run to the lyric for its best known song, "No Other Love," which seemed stilted, unrelated to normal speech.

There's a reasonable explanation for the lyric. Rodgers wanted to use the great melody he'd written a few years earlier as background music for a documentary about the Navy in World War II, *Victory at Sea*. In most cases when he worked with Hammerstein, the lyric came first (quite different from what he did with his earlier collaborator, Lorenz Hart). Here, it was the tune that preceded the words, which may account for their highfalutin' tone, an ironic contrast with the highly colloquial title of the show.

A lot of Rodgers and Hammerstein shows had contemporary settings, so it was important for the lyrics to sound natural. There's a comparable naturalness to the lyrics Hammerstein wrote even for shows in exotic settings. Is there anything un-natural about the verse to "Hello, Young Lovers?"

It's sung by an educated mid-19th century Englishwoman. The tone is elevated and formal, but nothing about it seems strained or starchy:

> When I think of Tom,
> I think about an evening
> When the earth smelled of summer
> And the sky was streaked with white,
> When the soft mists of England
> Were sitting on a hill.
> I remember this,
> And I always will.

It's deeply poetic, but we perceive it not merely as beautifully fashioned verse but rather as the memory of a woman sensitive to the world around her, a woman whose experience of love is as intense in memory as it was in actuality. At the same time that it enchants us (in no small part because of Rodgers's simple, eloquent melody), it tells us a great deal about the character.

When Engel speaks of particularization he means details that get beyond clichés. His list of theatre songs that "eschew" the word love altogether is particularly fascinating. What was remarkable about lyrics in the classical period is that they could be so particular but also so universal. That's why they remain so affecting.

Increasingly, in recent years musicals have not been set in the here and now. The lyricists have to devise a vocabulary that seems appropriate to the time and place in which they're set. It's very unlikely that the vocabulary will be in synch with contemporary speech. If you're writing a musical about the sinking of the *Titanic*, after all, you cannot use the vocabulary or syntax of Eminem.

One of Sondheim's most innovative musicals was his *Pacific Overtures* (1976), which was about the decline of a rigid, highly ritualized culture when it comes in contact with the force of the modern world. Set in Japan in the 1850s, around the time Commodore Perry gained entry for American commercial exploitation, *Pacific Overtures* utilized the techniques of traditional Japanese theatre to tell the story of Japan's absorption of Western culture.

In the early part of the show Sondheim made use of very particular rhythms to create the feeling of an intensely hierarchical culture. One number, in fact, had two men improvising haiku as they made a journey. In another, "Chrysanthemum Tea," the lyrics make judicious use of repetition to create a feeling of court formality.

It's a sign of Sondheim's mastery that these numbers never seem like pastiche. They have their own force, but they're also unmistakably Sondheim. Although the number that ends the first act, "Someone in a Tree," has the repetitive quality of "Chrysanthemum Tea," the verbal formality of the haiku and its own striking ideas, its music has a sensuality and propulsion that are very modern.

The very last number in the show, "Next," set in the present, has a drive that is unmistakably characteristic of today. There are no longer any traces of the old, restrained culture with which the musical began. The degree of control in both lyrics and music that Sondheim exhibits throughout *Pacific Overtures* is an extraordinary example of the particularization Engel feels is essential to good musicals.

It is, alas, also an example of the lack of correlation between the highest standards and commercial success. It eked out six months on

Broadway and had a slightly longer run in an Off-Broadway revival a few years later.

Engel begins his discussion of particularization by attributing overly general lyric writing to the influence of the Germans. Certain bad things can be attributed to the Germans (the welfare state, head cheese), but it's not fair to blame them for lazy lyric writing.

The tendency to rely on clichés (rhyming June and Moon) came from a conviction that the words didn't really matter. There was, unfortunately, some truth to this feeling. Engel cites the hackneyed and unmetrical lyric to a song from *The Chocolate Soldier* as an example of particularly bad lyric writing. (Part of the blame may be attributed to the translation from the German.)

More important, however, is that these admittedly dreadful lyrics come from the introduction to "Come! Come! I Love You Only," the beautiful song that's the only reason Straus's operetta is still performed. People may be forgiven for not paying enough attention to the words when they know the hit tune is approaching.

Even Oscar Hammerstein, in the introduction to his collected *Lyrics*, published in 1951, confesses he took a cavalier attitude toward his own craft until, sometime in the early Thirties, he flew over the Statue of Liberty. He was astounded at how much effort the sculptor, Frederick Bartholdi, had lavished on the back of the statue's head. When Bartholdi finished the work in 1886, there was no reason to imagine anyone would ever see it.

The sight made Hammerstein rethink his assumption that writing humdrum lyrics could be excused on the grounds of mere expedience—they fit the pre-existing music. If Bartholdi went to such pains to sculpt something he thought no one would ever see, could Hammerstein be less conscientious in an art form that automatically got great exposure?

Unfortunately, as the British behemoths demonstrated, we have come almost full circle. In the culture at large, words no longer hold the value they once did. In lyrics or in other matters, we have indeed become a visual culture. There are still lyricists who try to maintain the exacting standards Engel sought, but their work is generally done in non-commercial venues, Off-Off Broadway or regional theatres.

The fastidiousness of Edward Kleban, best known as the lyricist for *A Chorus Line*, is directly attributable to the years he spent in Lehman Engel's BMI Musical Theatre Workshop, though Engel refined rather than created that fastidiousness. It already existed, both in Kleban's approach to his work and even his manner of dressing. (The orchestrator Jonathan Tunick, who went to high school with him, remembers him as a very careful dresser, not the careless bohemian he was depicted in the quasi-fictional musical biography of him, *A Class Act*.)

Kleban's concern for the *mot juste* created a huge block for him as a writer, though there's no sense that had he been more prolific he would have found a larger, more appreciative audience. His work on *A Chorus Line* should have brought him enormous recognition, but the lyrics are so impeccably linked to the characters who sing them that Kleban virtually disappears, which might indeed have pleased him.

When the accomplished young songwriter Ricky Ian Gordon selected materials for his album *Bright Eyed Joy*, he turned to poets from several generations prior, Langston Hughes, Edna St. Vincent Millay and Dorothy Parker. All these poets, by the way, especially Hughes, worked in a style entirely derived from the American vernacular. But they showed the power that could be achieved in this presumably mundane language.

Similarly the texts for Adam Guettel's *Myths and Hymns*, as the title implies, are either Guettel's own, which are vernacular, or those of Protestant hymns, which are decidedly not. Guettel's song cycle, as it may be termed, was given a production at the New York Shakespeare Festival of a few weeks' duration. Gordon's album has remained just that, a showcase for his considerable talents. In both these cases there is no correlation between the writer's care for words and what Engel imagined was an inevitable success. In this case only cognoscenti even recognize these names.

The theatre no longer reaches the broad audience it did in the Golden Age. That the theatre continues to attract artists whose standards are so high they need not worry about widespread public acceptance is no doubt to the theatre's credit. However, there was a time when it wasn't necessary to compromise or condescend to receive such acceptance.

MUSIC

'Tis good; though music oft hath such a charm
To make bad good, and good provoke to harm.

William Shakespeare
Measure for Measure, IV, i

I would like at the outset to clarify my point of view regarding two things: 1) Any words at all, including the multiplication table, the alphabet, and the Manhattan telephone directory, can be set to music. 2) There is nothing wrong with the English language used in song if it is used knowledgeably.

The question that arises from the first proposition is simply: What is to be gained by setting the Manhattan telephone directory to music? Composers should ask themselves the same question about the shows they write and the lyrics they set.

The second statement is less important here except as a point of view, since there is a widespread misapprehension that any language other than English is better suited to singing. This attitude has usually been the result of careless translations or bad composers who refuse to take into proper account the rich sounds and special cadences our language has. We have to *think* more about melody, accent, cadence, and especially vowel and consonant effects than Europeans because we are newer in this field and preferable uses of our language have been less explored. George Bernard Shaw wrote:

> ...there is a great deal of feeling, highly poetic and highly dramatic, which cannot be expressed by mere words—because words are the counters of thinking, not of feeling—but which can be supremely expressed by music. The poet tries to make words serve his purpose by arranging them musically, but is hampered by the certainty of becoming absurd if he does not make his musically arranged words mean something to the intellect as well as to the feeling.

What words we should choose to set to song is what we are gradually finding out about. I think it is essential here to consider what music can *suggest* on its own—that is, music without words, accompanying explanation, scenery, movement, or any of the other visual elements.

What it is able to suggest is limitless but imprecise and is a personal experience. It would therefore be foolhardy for a composer to *rely* on any specific audience reaction to whatever sounds he puts together.

To most Western ears, which have become accustomed in a broad sense to certain effects and moods—a military march, a funeral march, a heroic grandioseness, a quiet shimmering, a luscious melodic line, a scherzolike jumping figure, a fast passage which might seem ominous, etc.—these devices are instantly translatable in fairly specific, if personal, terms. It was on the success of these suppositions that silent-film music was based and the interaction of the picture and the music became inseparably united in a deathless embrace, that went on for half a century and still threatens to choke the life out of "dramatic" music. When films began carrying sound tracks, the same musical vocabulary was employed. From there it crossed over without noticeable change to radio drama, thence to TV, where we are still stuck with it.

The "effects" I have reference to are of course clichés, but the largest part of them came lock, stock, and barrel out of serious music. Saint-Saëns' "Swan" (sadness), Rossini's "William Tell Overture" (to the rescue), Wagner's "Ride of the Valkyries" (on to victory), Beethoven's "Funeral March," Strauss's *Till Eulenspiegel* (Puck-in-Germany): how much more illustrative can you get?

However, to uninitiated Eastern ears, these clichés (minus the visual illustrations) produce no such reactions. By the same token, when I was in Turkey recently I listened hard to recordings of native music and I confess that although I recognized considerable technical dissimilarities between this and that record, in the main, they all sounded much "alike." Their moods, to me, were identical. My guide then explained titles and lyrics and showed me that this was a love song, another funereal, another a religious chant, etc. And this brings me to the point: Music alone *may suggest,* but because such suggestions rely on personal background and experience, music *cannot define.* I remember attending an interminable Noh play in London. The music charmed me (nothing more specific than that) for five minutes and bored me to tears for the remaining

three hundred hours. Even in our own culture I remember the tit-
ters of some audience members in earlier performances of Martha
Graham when I, one of her composers, was in the auditorium. I
could not distinguish whether the merriment was caused by the
music, the movement, or both! It had not been our intention to
amuse.

Theatre music (after 1600) was first opera, then sometimes
"spectacle," and then also ballet. But the sung word came first.
Opera branched off into operetta, which has been absent creatively
in the United States for more than forty years. Now and then there
is a revival or putting of lyrics to a dead composer's music, but as a
continuing form, except for parodies such as *Little Mary Sunshine*
and *The Boy Friend,* it does not now exist. However, operetta was a
kind of steppingstone between opera and musical comedy. We used
it like Plymouth Rock, landed where we always meant to go, and the
stone is still there full of inscriptions like all other monuments.
Then we went on our way.

I am a musician, but still and all (as they say) I've never in my life
come out of a theatre humming a tune. On some occasions I have
come into the theatre whistling all of them. The first time I
attended *Fiddler on the Roof* I was completely absorbed in a total
experience. I laughed and cried and applauded. Someone asked me
later that evening what I thought of the musical score. I was
stunned and could only reply that I bad been totally unaware of it.[10]
I believe that this is the highest compliment anyone can pay,
because it indicates that all of the elements worked together so
integrally that I was aware only of the total effect. When I saw
Fiddler a second time, I was less involved (in spite of continued
laughter, tears, and applause), and I heard the music and lyrics,
both of which I greatly admired.

I had a similar response to *My Fair Lady* the first time, but I did
hear "On the Street Where You Live" and I believe this happened for
two reasons. In the first place, nothing else was going on when the
song was sung; the singing character was simply (and intentionally)
stupid—nothing complex about that. But secondly I *heard* the song
because I disliked it intensely. (I love everything else in the score. But
this song, to me, did not fit.) It was the picture that shoved its way
out of the frame with a bang. Suddenly there was a "pop" song that

had strayed into a score otherwise brilliant, integrated, with a great sense of the play's own style and a faithful, uncompromising exposition of characters and situations. I think this experience with this single song in an otherwise great show tells me that when everything is of such special quality and everything works and involves the beholder, something less fitting calls attention to itself, just as a small defect in the glass of a windowpane suddenly calls so much attention to itself that, for the moment, the view outside is obscured.

Because examining musical theatre is an integral part of my own life, I return again and again and the second time in each case I am determined to isolate music and lyrics from the rest, so that I may pay special attention to them. When I am able to divorce them from the whole, I understand them. Perhaps it is because of this kind of rare and wonderful happening in the case of a distinguished show that makes me look with a jaundiced eye at criticism written just after the fall of opening night's curtain. This quick evaluation usually contains consideration and judgment of each of the elements. When I read that the direction was wonderful and the scenery marvelous, I begin to wonder gravely about the *content* of the show, because how can direction be so wonderful—or how can one tell that it was—if there were no book, music, and lyrics to be directed? But then criticisms usually also deal with all of the elements. If I, at least an experienced lifelong musician, fail to attend to music because it belongs so well within the whole, how was the critic able to function so consciously in all these other areas?

It's a great deal like the critic being an umpire at a baseball game. Each ball, strike, run, etc., is judged and immediately tabulated. A very fine musical show is not like that because, if it is so fine, it results in a sum total of the whole, and when I first encounter it I encounter it as a whole. Later I examine its elements.

To the contrary when a show fails to work, it is a simple matter for me—because it is so unabsorbing that I view it detached, as from a great distance, and can see only the separate parts. At such times I hear scores that I recognize as bad, or a single song as fairly good. I can see all of the separate elements as such, and usually I can tell precisely as the show lumbers along why it is not working and what is responsible for its deficiencies. Very often on such occasions I come out of the theatre humming a tune of the somewhat older original version of it, which is the only reason I'm able to hum it at all.

I think that any or all of several things are operating at once when the audience comes out humming a tune. The most important, in my opinion, is the one alluded to above: the similarity it bears to earlier songs. (You come out of *The Desert Song* or *Hamlet* singing or saying something which appeals to you because you have heard them many times before.)

Which brings up the second point. In nearly all musicals, including *Hair* but especially in those of some earlier time, tunes (songs) have been reprised a number of times and when these are simple to begin with, the repetition, of course, helps the audience to remember and to be able to reproduce. In *Annie Get Your Gun,* for example, the "There's No Business Like Show Business" chorus is sung four times, played once to connect scenes. is contained in the overture, and is the "out" music which is heard as the customers scramble from the theatre.

During the next to the final scene in *Brigadoon* when the hero, Jeff, is remembering Fiona, the latter appears again and again behind a scrim and sings a sample of each of four songs introduced earlier, concluding with a choral section from the market-square chorus from Act One—altogether five reprises. (For me this is the only weak part of the show. It seems to have been written by or because of the publishers.) Nevertheless you've *really* heard the songs before you go home, and it is likely that you will hum a number of them. Also these songs—good as they are—are traditional in style, and they somewhat resemble Scottish folk songs, which was undoubtedly Frederick Loewe's intention.

I believe nobody expected *West Side Story* to be a popular hit. It seemed too new in style and it had a tragic ending. I doubt that many members of the audience carried anything away with them after attending one of the early performances. However, *West Side Story,* after a relatively short run in New York, enjoyed a successful tour, returned and played on Broadway much longer than originally. In the meanwhile, the cast album became an enormous seller. Then many artists quickly recorded this song or that, and by the time of the Broadway reopening the jukeboxes in all the bars were repeating "Maria" and "Tonight" endlessly. *Then* when audiences attended the show they knew the songs and quite naturally they came out humming them.

At the opera, the same similarities exist. Who hasn't heard the "Habanera" from *Carmen* a thousand times in a variety of arrangements or as sung by this or that diva? Quite naturally it is remembered before and after, and in many other operas similar situations exist. Recently when I attended a performance of *Cavalleria Rusticana* and *I Pagliacci* my ears were assailed by the humming of a gigantic audience-chorus which went along more or less accurately with the "Intermezzo" from the first and the "Prologue" from the latter.

As I am extremely familiar with both *Wozzeck and Pelléas et Mélisande,* both "far out" to the majority, I am haunted by their scores for days after attending a performance. Recently I spent three endless nights at the Bayreuth Festival, and Wagner took me over for many days afterward.

The real point is that I feel that no one is entitled to be disappointed at not coming out humming the tunes—or even one tune—from a really new show. The main reason for their failure may lie in their total absorption with the show as a whole, or their lack of familiarity with a new style which will not necessarily remind them explicitly of any other style they have ever heard.

It is quite natural for a non-musician to be even *unaware* that a certain musical style is new, and a new style practiced in any of the musical elements (harmony, in particular) will be almost certain to generate a new kind of melody. *Company* has one kind, *Hair* another, *Mlle. Modiste* still another, *Tristan, Pelléas, Wozzeck,* and the operas of Monteverdi still others. All contain memorable melodies. Few of them, including those in *Carmen* and *La Traviata,* which seem so simple and obvious today, were thought to exist at all when they were first performed.

Another explanation for remembering or not remembering a song has to do with the extent of importance that the other elements of the show—those which complement or are concomitant with a specific song—exert at precisely the same time. If the song in question happens to occur during a particularly absorbing dramatic scene, or with especially interesting choreography, etc., the song may be so properly imbedded in the show along with its companion elements that it may pass unnoticed as nothing separate.

It should also be remembered that exposition of a song in a show is very swift, even if it is a slow song. It passes by. It ends. It may be reprised later. This too comes after other songs have been exposed and it too passes quickly. The opposite of this type of experience which operates only in the performing arts, especially opera, symphony, musical theatre, movies, and the others, is that when a spectator faces a new painting or a reader a novel or poem he has the opportunity of examining it without any time limitations whatsoever. He may look or reread for as long as be wishes in order to comprehend the artist or the writer. The music-theatre experience is so fleeting and multiple as to leave only a passing impression. Time is of the essence.

I believe it is wrong to make so many absolute judgments—for or against—a musical show after a single performance, particularly if the score does not automatically fall into an idiom so common that what is glimpsed musically is at once recognized for what it has always been in many, many earlier shows. And I believe it is wrong when an audience feels cheated at being unable to leave the theatre humming a song. In the "good old days" when songs were restatements of many other songs and when the musical style was simple, this habit of remembering tunes was most usual. Now things are different. Styles are new again (I do not include rock here, because it is basically old and simple) and so are the tunes they generate. It will take time for these tunes to create new neural patterns in the brain. This has been the history of classical as well as popular music. After a time, what was good has emerged as comprehensible and simple. What was not good has faded into a general nothingness.

Instead of being disappointed at being unable to remember a tune after a single or double hearing, let's rejoice that perhaps, just perhaps—we have been exposed to something new for a change. Time—not the disappointed hummer—will decide its ultimate worth.

Remembering or not remembering the sound of music is, in the beginning, of least importance. What counts most is the functions of the songs in a show: how well they characterize, charm or amuse, help to propel the action, further the plot, etc. Before the great

period of the musical theatre (prior to 1940) certain musical practices were inevitably a part of nearly every show. For one thing, the
sequence of musical numbers was quite predictable. There was
always an opening chorus that shared the chore of assuring the audience that there actually were young girls and boys in the company
and making a racket—prior to "Here she comes now"—loud
enough to cover the noisy seating of the latecomers. The lovers had
love songs, the comics had unintentionally uncomical songs. There
was a real hullabaloo before the end of Act One when boy and girl
were pried apart never to meet again. Etc. One of the important features of our lyric theatre during those formative decades when the
books were far less than literate was the high level of the songs—
music and lyrics. Although they hardly ever grew out of the characters because the latter usually were truly nonexistent, as songs they
were unique, and when the books were quickly embalmed in amber
the songs sang on indefinitely on the crest of every wave length.

From the Forties on, for twenty-five years, the opening chorus
was either functional or it didn't exist. The opening of *Carousel is*
played in pantomime against a suite of waltzes, and the openings *of
Oklahoma!* and *Fiddler on the Roof* each begin as solos for the leading
man. *The King and I* and *Kiss Me, Kate* are nonvocal at the very start,
and *South Pacific* gets under way with the piping voices of two small
children. (My, how far we had come!)

Comedy songs began to be sung by flesh-and-blood romantic
heroes and heroines with—just because they were also funny—no
skin off their teeth, and the songs were funny too after so much
effort spent at only *trying* to be funny. The only non-changes were
the ballads: They remained the staples.

After the Thirties in the best musicals the songs were an integral
part of the show. They grew from and helped to define the characters who sang them, were a part of the situations, helped to advance
the plots, became a living organism in a score. These changes
marked an important growth. These songs of ours—compared with
the extended ones in nineteenth-century operetta and the even
larger arias in grand opera—are small and compact in form. They
are written for small voices that are echoed again and again after the
theatre by sometimes even smaller voices in recordings and on TV.
The smallness of the form does not denigrate it. A truly good com-

pact song is as difficult to come by as a large, long, freer operatic aria. But the musical-show score is made of only some twelve, fourteen, or at most sixteen *(Hair* has twenty-six) of these complete "cells" which operate among one another as developing motifs, making the whole "a score"—not simply a program of unrelated paeans.

What these songs have to say in their lyrics must provide continuous growth and contrasts. They must speak *from* the characters who sing them, not be imposed on them. Each song must say what only this specific character *can* say, not just loosely what *any* character (for example) in love might say. It is the duty of the lyricist to find material in this particular character in this particular play in this particular scene which has not been said again and again by every character in every previous play. This requires genuine creativity, thought, patience, and invention.

No song for Laurey in *Oklahoma!* can be sung by Mrs. Anna in *The King and I* though both scores are by Rodgers and Hammerstein; no song given Fiona McLauren could suit Eliza Doolittle, both creations of Lerner and Loewe. The very thought of such an interchange is, of course, absurd. By the same token, the Laurey-Curly songs in *Oklahoma!* would not suit—musically or lyrically—Ado Annie or Will Parker in the same show. Why? Because of their character differences. To illustrate, Laurey the prim, romantic girl would be incapable of "I Cain't Say No," which is the expression of a quixotic, gamine, flirtatious child, with fun-loving (wherever she finds it) as her prime motive for living. As different characters will require contrasting songs, these will provide the varied elements essential to a full "score." This sounds simple and it is surely logical, but all too often it is not even considered in the making of a musical score.

It is interesting that "good" songs have survived the dead shows of the Twenties and Thirties and a little later; for example "My Funny Valentine," "A Foggy Day (In London Town)," "Embraceable You," "Tea for Two," "I Get a Kick Out of You," "Body and Soul," "Dancing in the Dark," and countless others are used again in new recordings and by today's latest-style combos as kind of "cantus firmuses" on which newest treatments and styles are superimposed. The new generation making with the new treatment know and/or usually care nothing about those long-ago defunct shows that spawned the tunes. Yet these tunes, very often nearly unrecognizable today, are being continually reused. The larger army of bad and indifferent songs from the same periods are in the discard. The eras change. The basic taste does not.

Today there are new movements, and where they will or if they will go I can no more predict than anybody else. I believe in the inevitability of some kind of new movement, and considering the old-style junk that has lately been unveiled along Broadway, there can be no question that some changes are sorely needed. However, it is my opinion that what has been wrong lately with Broadway is not so much a matter of old age as that what has been "non-created" has been truly bad. The books haven't been well made, the music has been quite unmemorable, and the whole put-together has been redolent of fatigue. Besides, there has grown up a mass of confusion in reference to current activities, and at the risk of calling down all of Jove's thunderbolts, I would like to try to unravel some of it. Most of it is about music, which today attracts more attention than ever before.

Clive Barnes, the English dance and theatre critic now presiding at *The New York Times's* console, has been laying laurel wreaths on nearly every piece of rock-'n'-roll music attached to the theatre that swings his way. Okay. That's his opinion, even if I don't agree with it. But then how in blazes can the same Mr. Barnes suddenly throw identical laurel wreaths at the old, old deadly music of *George M!*? I call that confusing to the highest degree. Then too the same Mr. Barnes celebrates other shows because he considers their songs "new." Among them were *Promenade* (1969) and *Salvation* (1969). Now. *Promenade* ought to be subtitled "Or a Night at Asti's," because nearly all of the songs are aria-like— Italian or French—or they stem from early twentieth-century American "art" songs. In all cases these yodels are vastly inferior to the models they attempt to imitate and on no account are they even slightly new. (Mr. Barnes's gold discovery upset the entire Broadway and musical community to the point where bewilderment and incredulity have given way in some quarters to submission and blind attempts at just any kind of imitation in the hope of pleasing *The New York Times*.)

The night I saw *Promenade* I overheard a conversation between an old and a young man:

> OLD MAN: I think this writer has a hang-up about style. The music comes from all kinds of styles.
> YOUNG MAN: How can you say that! He was on the *Merv Griffin Show*!

Actually Mr. Barnes's rave review of *Promenade* was interlarded with nonpraises and a mass of contradictory epithets.

> "[The book] comes close to being no book."
> "*Candide*-like episodes."
> "Dada zaniness."
> "Topsy-turvy Brechtian morality."
> "It [the music] cascades out of him [Carmines] in all shapes, sizes and *styles*. He is devastatingly eclectic…He can write you a twenties tune or a thirties tune, give a touch of Friml, a dash of Gershwin, a little Puccini even, spiced with Nöel Coward, faced with Kurt Weill and Jacques Brel," etc.

Might I venture to remark that these non-specific qualities describe to perfection the work of all amateurs and immature composition students who are trying—consciously or not—to find themselves and their own style? Yet these varied labels applied to the music of a single show can be framed with "It is a joy from start to finish." "If *Promenade* is a triumph for its authors—and it is…," "…these sweet, happy and inexhaustible pastiches all come out with the Carmines signature."

Where, oh, where? The music of *The Beggar's Opera* was a pastiche, but Dr. Pepusch who *assembled* and arranged the score had the good taste and judgment to steal wholly, to quote literally, and to tie all of the many pieces together with a unifying style harmonically, melodically, and orchestrally. Everything was the real McCoy, and imitations were both unthinkable and eschewed.

But the first paragraph in Mr. Barnes's review of *Promenade* said:

Presumably *Promenade* will be one of the more controversial musicals of the year—it will also presumably be one of the most successful. It is a joy from start to finish. If you want my advice, go to the box office of the new Promenade Theatre.... as soon as practicable, before they start raising the seat prices.

"Presumably" is a large and vague word that can presumably mean nothing. *Promenade,* with the entire weight of Mr. Barnes behind it (considerable weight, but presumably not enough), had a run of 259 performances. Presumably too few people heeded Mr. Barnes's questionable advice.

As for *Salvation* and "newness," I was bred on this music half a century ago in Mississippi. It was played by small black combos on the street corners every Saturday night and sung at Holy Roller services on Sunday (also in the rural Baptist and Methodist churches.). New in *Salvation* it isn't. It is not a discovery because it has existed and been used for a long time. Easy to make it is. It marks no advance in any direction and contributes nothing whatsoever either to the theatre or to the *progress* of theatre music. I do not object to it because it brings back my own childhood. I do object to anybody's naïve proclamation of it as "new" and "contemporary." It ain't.

I would like to quote from *Time's* review of *Salvation*, which quite perfectly expresses my own point of view.

NEW MUSICALS
A GUIDE TO MODCOM

Hair begat *Salvation*, and this new musical is an aesthetically retarded child. However, *Salvation* is instructive because it epitomizes a specific kind of phoniness that began with *Hair* and surfaced again in *Promenade* and the Living Theatre. What knits these shows together is something that might be called Modcom.

Modcom is the commercial exploitation of modernity without regard for dramatic art. Modcom peddles the youth cult as a product. It is replete with cynical counterfeits of innocence, freedom and dissent. Enough evidence has now accumulated about how to put together a Modcom show. The rules:

Be plotless. It saves time. Nothing is quite so easy as not to write a book for a show. If plot insists on cropping up, be opaque....

Be lavish with four-letter words. This is the largesse of an impoverished mind. It is a hair transplant on a would-be manly chest.

Beslime the U.S. Find some degrading way to display the flag....

Mock religion. This should preferably be the Catholic religion, since it is distinctly more theatrical, and not terribly retaliatory these days. Avoid knocking Judaism. After all, the bulk of New York theatregoers are Jewish, and if unduly nettled they might complain to B'nai B'rith. Protestants, like other apathetic majorities, may be savaged at will....

Drug taking is a must. A Modcom producer ought never forget that it is good box office to offer simulated wickedness as an act of liberation. That is what is known as a low high. Many a boy's only contact with opium was Dr. Fu Manchu....

Be blatant about sex. Nudity is optional, but crudity is mandatory. Sex may be fun, but Modcom insists that its main purpose is to end the war in Viet Nam and provide a physically acceptable substitute for violence....

Deafen the audience. Cudgel it severely about the ears with a blunt amplifying instrument. A hard-rock Modcom musical gives a theatre-goer an acoustic third degree. His eardrums are refunded on the sidewalk....

Mingle with the audience. This takes a little effort, but it is well worth the time wasted. . . . It's a good way to smell an actor, too, and the odor isn't always as appealing as ham.

Excoriate Viet Nam. Even hawks, let alone parrots, have learned to deplore Viet Nam by now, so this particular arsenal of invective doesn't stir up a Modcom audience as visibly as it once did....

Apart from its manifold defects, *Salvation*, like all Modcom products, trades on the residual puritanism behind its ostensibly antipuritan outlook. A people at ease with sexuality, and casually and thoroughly iconoclastic, would not pay good money to see an inept affirmation of a puerile paganism.

The success of two rock musicals has created general confusion. *Hair* began off-Broadway (1967), ending up revised in every way on Broadway (1968), and *Your Own Thing* (1968) began off-Broadway, *stayed* off-Broadway and to me, despite weak music, was a legitimate hit.

At the beginning *Hair* had a loose, nothing plot line that added up to nothing. What bothered me most at the time was that it was crudely made and filled with clichés. While about three-quarters of the score was rock, the best of what I heard was not rock. Never mind labels; much of the music was excellent.

Hair closed, was redone with even less plot, with new songs added, a greatly expanded production, and it was resurrected on Broadway. I cannot possibly deny the excitement I felt frequently about this or that number, but I was also irked by the lack of writing and performing discipline and the incessant din.

Your Own Thing was unpretentious, small, resourceful, and witty, did well by Shakespeare, on whose *Twelfth Night* it was based, and was tasteful and enjoyable. The twin mix-up works better with today's long-haired boys than I've known it to work before. The back-and-forth switch between Shakespeare's dialogue and today's was deftly handled. The use sometimes of Shakespeare's lyrics was superb and the music occasionally delightful if not ever memorable.

Hair, I think, is not to be considered as a musical at all since it has no plot, sets out to go and indeed ends up nowhere, has only vaguely defined characters who can best be identified visually on a clear night by the performers themselves. It is a kind of vaudeville without introductory placards. It is a series of nightclub acts and neither it nor *Your Own Thing* makes any appreciable contribution to the repertory of the American musical theatre. What *Hair* especially *tried* to accomplish is far more important than what it succeeded in doing. It tried to break loose from all kinds of traditions, but lacking any technical know-how and eschewing discipline, it ended as it began, as only a kind of self-conscious mawkish "happening."

If anything were truly to be learned from either of these experiments, I think it would come from a realization of what did not happen in the music department. Long years ago Irving Berlin, having succeeded wildly with one song, "Alexander's Ragtime Band," thought he could also succeed with an entire ragtime show. History proved him wrong. Ragtime is a style or vocabulary, not an all-inclusive language. Jazz (a more permanent and longer-developed style) has turned up as "adaptations" in successful theatre scores. Gershwin's jazz in, say, *Porgy and Bess* is by no means the real McCoy. It is one composer's adaptation (integration) of a style into his own personal musical language. Rodgers has employed features of jazz, as have Porter, Schwartz, Styne, and all the others. Duke Ellington's single attempt at a real jazz theatre score *(Beggars' Holiday)* was as much a failure as Berlin's attempt at a rag score. Rock also is only a style—a narrow one—and the spawner of many related styles.

My feeling is that the total adaptation of any of these styles as the firm exclusive basis of a theatre-music score is impossible first because of a fundamental non-theatrical woodenness that each of them—rag, jazz, swing, rock—possesses as its very own hallmark. Furthermore, none of them in its authentic style allows for appreciable variety, a quality that is essential to the musical score of any show.

Putting aside popular styles for the moment, in the lineage of "art music," impressionism gave birth to a single opera which thoroughly succeeded and was totally in that style: Debussy's *Pelléas et Mélisande*. But this too was personal and a dead-end due to the narrowness of the stylistic, technical, and dynamic range.

What I refer to should be fairly obvious to musicians. But to restate it: Whereas Western music for at least five full centuries has been based on twelve tones (the chromatic scale) and arranged in twelve keys, each with two modes (major and minor), Oriental music has progressed far less in its limited five-tone scale with no harmonic or polyphonic excursions at all. Everything is in unison. Its sole difference within itself is to be found in rhythm, which can be complex.

With Debussy and the French Impressionists there was the first conscious break-away toward what was considered "freedom" from the twelve tones, by the discovery of the whole tone scale in which there are only six notes instead of twelve, and there can be only two possible different if identical whole-tone scales as each overlaps with its own beginning. There is no change of mode.

Debussy and Ravel were the two major talents in this school, and it is curious that even in *Pelléas et Mélisande* Debussy had obviously found the whole-tone scale and its harmony—a single augmented triad—so limiting that even this one major monument to impressionism is far from confined to this single technical element. In fact Debussy used anything and everything in music that suited his purpose. The stylistic mode was another thing. This was new in a number of ways and was defined by what was being evolved in impressionism as well as by Debussy's own personal and highly individual, sensitive style. Also in this opera Debussy set out to compose an "anti-opera": The play must come first (just what the Florentine Camerata had set out to accomplish in the beginning). The music was to be secondary. There are no arias. While I believe Debussy *intended* not to write melodies time has found this score soaring with fragmentary ones that are unforgettable.

To digress purposefully, it was Schönberg who next revolted against the Wagnerian use of continuous chromaticism, the too free roaming about without tonal center which he himself had at first also used. In its place he "found" the "twelve-tone row" which involves all the notes of the scale but employs them in the most rigid technical manner yet prescribed by anyone. Schönberg himself wrote two very short operas in this mode, which, by the way, was music's contribution to *Expressionism*. (One shackle cast off again only to be replaced by another, but always with discipline and roots.)

The two Schönberg operas were *Die Glückliche Hand* and the frightening *Erwartung*. Unlike Debussy, who had used *all* materials including those which were the hallmark of his school, Schönberg in these operas and in his subsequent works (I think, in *all* of them) was faithful to his cause, his technique, and his beliefs. Schönberg's most talented pupil was Alban Berg, who composed two operas (the last not quite completed before his death), *Wozzeck* and *Lulu*. *Wozzeck,* like *Pelléas,* is a monument, and Berg, steeped in twelve-tone technique, employed this when it suited his purpose but also used any and everything else when he preferred. He was true to the spirit of his school but was not limited by it.

Now it is absurd on the face of it to compare *Wozzeck, Pelléas* and rock as applied to the theatre, because the first two are mature, thoughtful and talented works. The latter is a harking back to many kinds of past, is most often written by people with no roots, usually has narrow melodic profiles, a very limited, worn-out harmonic palette, and an almost undeviating, insistent rhythm. The composers of the operas mentioned above were involved in art movements they knew inside out, used its methods when it served them, and used everything else when it didn't. In rock—of which there are many kinds and each about as different from the other as A is from B—the writer chooses his own "poison" and is happily stuck with it. In the case of rock, so far, everything is brief and nothing develops. Whatever *is* repeats and repeats. Certainly repetition is not freedom.

I am not against rock as such but only against the fact that it is born of a "freedom" more rigid and limiting than anything that ever before existed in music. Both Debussy and Berg, brought up in antithetical schools and philosophies with great works highly representative of their own schools, were never (within these works) stuck with the limiting technical appurtenances which would have prevented their arrival at the high places in art where they were. Neither of them could have existed without their creators' thorough knowledge of what it had grown out of and the rules of precisely what it was to be opposed to.

When a rock composer of talent (with *roots* in the musical mainstream) comes along, and if he bothers to learn about music theatre workability, he may come up with something significant and new. But he will have to know and he must understand the restrictions of his school so that, when he wants to, he too can wander away in any direction he either chooses or needs.

Although impressionism as such—purely—went no further than *Pelléas* its harmonic coloration is felt in all of the serious music which followed it, and thirty years after *Pelléas* its nuances were easily detectable on Broadway. The name "Gershwin" has appeared as an adaptor of jazz, of French impressionism, and, although not mentioned here before, of blues. How can this be, and what does it mean? I think it does demonstrate that a personal style can be and frequently is made up of many elements which have become successfully synthesized into one new something else. In this case it is called Gershwin.

But hold on! There is something more. Although these are merged as one into "Gershwin"—jazz, blues, and French impressionism—that is not quite all. The finished baked pudding is American. Employed to make the Western *Girl Crazy,* the Southern Negro *Porgy and Bess,* the symphonic *An American in Paris,* the electioneering lampoon *Of Thee I Sing,* it is still all Gershwin that is the sum of all the microcosms synthesized into a single organism.

We all know that *Madama Butterfly* is Puccini and Italian with a *slight* flavor of jasmine. *Salome* is Strauss and German-with-tambourines, which I guess suggested the Bible to its creator. But nobody—nobody—should sound like anything but himself in his own time and place.

Richard Rodgers—one of the musical-theatre "greats" and perhaps the greatest—set shows in the Oklahoma Territory, the New England coast about 1873, the South Pacific of World War II, Siam, San Francisco, Salzburg, and many other places, but the basic melodic, harmonic, and rhythmic style of all are quite recognizably Rodgers. Here and there, there are colorations. The melodic style of *Oklahoma!* is unrelated to that of *Carousel. South Pacific* has its "Orientalisms" ("Bali Hai," for example), Salzburg is here and there slightly more "musical" musically than *Oklahoma!* But, throughout all of it, it is obviously American and Rodgers.

Leonard Bernstein, a younger man with a flavor of his own, began in the theatre with *On the Town* (1944), grew into *Wonderful Town* (1953), matured elegantly in *Candide* (1956), and skyrocketed in *West Side Story* (1957). He grew out of many forces, including Rodgers and Porter, but also Copland and Stravinsky. However, Bernstein's style has always been his very own.

Alas this personal consistency is not always clearly understood and I would like to speak for a moment about the wavering musical style of a very talented theatre composer named John Kander. I do this because I respect him, care a great deal about the danger I think he is in, and I want to see him go as far as I believe he can go provided.... (The temptation on the part of some composers not to be totally themselves seems to come only in the theatre, where alien settings, dialects, strange costumes, and times—more or less remote—beckon to them to "go native.")

Look at three consecutive Broadway scores by John Kander. I cannot understand why so much of *Cabaret* sounded like Kurt Weill. Was it because Weill's widow, Lotte Lenya, was cast as the old lady? Was it because the setting was Berlin? Either explanation, of course, contains a worldful of fuzzy reasoning. The Berlin of Weill was about fifteen years earlier than the period of *Cabaret* and nearly half a century before this production. What has casting to do with the style of a musical score? Why also did the *Zorba* score make a pale attempt at imitating Greek music? In the end, this sort of thing must fail since at best it is only an imitation, as is the "Spanish" music of *Man of La Mancha.* In the case of *Zorba,* the sound more nearly resembled Israeli music. *The Happy Time* sounded like an imitation of French-Canadian folk songs.

It's time that John Kander began to find John Kander, who, it is my belief, is infinitely worth finding. Let's never forget that style should be the property of the copyright owner and said owner should not pretend he is the pianist for a silent-screen performance—changing from cowboys to Indians to Chinese with the greatest of ease and with the same unimportant results that one has in unwinding a roll of toilet tissue. While these elements—personal style, *suggestions* of time and place—may make contributions to all shows, personal style is of greater importance. This is because without a distinctive personality and a special manner of expressing things musically and lyrically, the end product must lack characteristics which differentiate the work of this writer from that of all others now living or long dead.

This personally different and set-apart style must come about as a result of either or both of two things: a special and distinguished talent and/or expressivity propelled by a unique personal feeling. It is the latter that must be sharply conveyed to audiences by composers for the theatre if there is to be any response—sad or happy —to the basic lyrical elements which are the chief characteristics distinguishing musical theatre from its non-musical cousin.

Undoubtedly feeling is an inseparable and significant element of music and poetry, but it cannot be conveyed wholly if the contributing writers are not themselves motivated by it. This is why establishment of a personal style as opposed to vacillation among a variety of styles is so necessary. Vacillation suggests a non-belief or uncertainty in both the writer and what he seeks to convey.

There was a time about two centuries ago when within a single period there was a musical style that was common to *almost* all writers of the same period. Personal style had not yet been dreamed of. Bach and Buxtehude are almost indistinguishable—one from the other. Mozart and Haydn and many others of their day frequently are stylistically inseparable. Mozart's *Don Giovanni* and *Le Nozze di Figaro,* both set in Spain, are as Spanish (nor did their composer even *dream* of their being) as the Schönbrunn Palace in Vienna. A century later composers were filled with the new need for self-expression and personal identity. Chopin cannot be confused with Schumann or Mendelssohn or Wagner or Brahms or any of the others, although all of them lived at approximately the same time and all but Chopin were German. (Poor lonely Pole.)

In any case, things today in the matter of personal musical style have not changed much until perhaps just now. Richard Rodgers, Cole Porter, Frederick Loewe, Harold Arlen, Arthur Schwartz, Jule Styne, Harold Rome, Irving Berlin, Stephen Sondheim, and, lately, Burt Bacharach, the Beatles and a few others are quite distinguishable. What is certainly different again today is the vast numbers of "composers"—many here today and not here tomorrow—who, like those many nameless period composers of every century until the nineteenth, were indistinguishable from one another. These today to whom I have reference are in the main not theatre composers. They make records almost exclusively, and so, strictly speaking, do not concern us here. However, they concern many people all of a sudden and then equally suddenly they concern no one.

While attempting to make the point regarding musical style that composers should write in their own way without reference to time or locale, there is a related practice about which I should like to make a similar point.

The literary style, like the musical one, also should be expressive of the author's own time, or at the very least it should be couched in a style so universal that it calls no attention to itself as being either imitative of any other imagined period or makes no attempt to vulgarize an earlier time through the use of expressions too colloquially today's. The first method would be too patently fabricated and the second too self-consciously "cute."

In his introduction to *Five Comedies of Medieval France,* Oscar Mandel, in speaking of his translations, wrote: "When the original expressed no feeling of strangeness, we too must leave strangeness out. I am referring, of course, to the strangeness of the archaic, the long-ago, the quaint…it was absent from the original…."

What Mandel was trying to clarify was that in his translations he thought it preferable to use present-day "American" rather than a literal version of what was written in the twelfth century, since the original play was written for the popular audience of its own time and it should today be heard in a comparable style. It should not try to evoke a long-ago or "quaint" time.

This also is what I believe and what I have tried to say in relation to music composed today.

Alas, there are pitfalls, and Mandel, while wearing his heart in the right place, is, I believe, guilty of going too far in attempting in his translation of *The Play of Saint Nicholas* (circa 1200) to make it so contemporary that the language suggests that this miracle play is without *any* style.

The shape and subject matter of the play obviously dates it as centuries old while slang—in constant use—is at loggerheads with it, making it appear *inconsistently* contemporary. For example:

> CLICKETT: Say, how about a game right now?
> PINCHDICE: Right! Loser to pay out of the loot we're gonna rake in if we're lucky.
> CLICKETT (To the Innkeeper): Listen, brother, I want you to lend me a tenner. That'll be sixteen I owe you, including interest….

I said "inconsistently contemporary" because there is so much slang that, in the context of these characters and this play, it begins to sound like a group of foreigners who—not really understanding such terms—are trying to impress the reader by employing it endlessly and not always correctly, or in a manner consistent with the characters. At one point *only* the Innkeeper says: "Can I really trust the guy?" and in all other places he speaks like an upper-class educated man, for example: "I'm sure you realize that I'm entitled to solid security."

I think these examples of what in my opinion no writer should do should help to sharpen what it is that I think they *ought* to do.

I believe that composers and authors should write in their own contemporary style no matter whether the show is laid in Shanghai or Fairbanks—and in the fourteenth or twentieth centuries. But their style should not indulge in "tricks" that will appear "cute" and specifically pseudo-contemporary. The language should be universal and timeless. I believe that the use of today's common-denominator English, plain, unvarnished, is what is called for since it will not call attention to itself and will appear usual and natural.

T. S. Eliot begins his verse-play *Murder in the Cathedral,* set in 1170, with a chorus:

> Here let us stand, close by the cathedral, Here let us
> wait.
> Are we drawn by danger? Is it the knowledge of safety,
> that draws our feet
> Toward the cathedral?

Archibald MacLeish, in his verse play *J.B.*, about the Book of Job, has the title character say (selected at random):

> He was wrong.
> It isn't luck when God is good to you.

Tom Stoppard in his contemporary play *Rosencrantz and Guildenstern Are Dead,* set at Denmark's court and in Elizabethan times, has Guildenstern say:

> The law of averages, if I have got this right, means that
> if six monkeys were thrown up in the air for long enough
> they would land on their tails about as often as they
> would land on their—

In medieval pictures, backgrounds of scenes of the Crucifixion usually contain landscapes that include castles of the painter's own time. Rembrandt painted many crucifixions as well as portraits of the Holy Family and in all of them the costumes are of the artist's time. However, the total effect in all of these pictures is somehow timeless and the subject matter emerges believably and as art as seen through other eyes, yet totally acceptable to *all* eyes in any time or place. The anachronisms are obviously honest—not rigged." We understand at once that they are, and we accept them without question. And we know them—the plays, the pictures, and the rest—as expressions of the artist's time and talent, not as half-guessed archaeological reconstructions.

If I seem to belabor this point of writers and composers being themselves alone, it is because, in my opinion, this is one of the most misunderstood of all aspects of art. The error seems to have begun only a decade or two prior to the present century and is today in full flower. The mistake is largely the property of theatre creators and is seldom to be found in painting, sculpture, novels, verse, or even in opera and ballet. In the plays of earlier times, opera and operetta, it did not exist.

In the thirty-seven plays of Shakespeare, the locales include Italy, England, France, Greece, Cyprus, Egypt, Troy, Denmark, Wales, Scotland, and what is today the Middle East. In *Henry V* there is some dialogue in French. These are words, not *colors*. There are special characters who have a great relevance to their plots: a Jew, a Moor, an Egyptian queen, Spanish, Danish and Scottish noblemen, and yet not a single one of them speaks in any dialect. Juliet (Italian), Othello (Moorish), Shylock (Jewish), Macbeth (Scottish), all speak a common language. This is not to imply that Shakespeare failed in any way to *characterize* them as the special individuals that each one is, but he accomplished the characterization in each case through *what* it is that the people speak and think instead of resorting (foolish notion) to tricky inflections. In the end the characters and the plays are universal. The inevitable comment that the author makes appeals to the brain and the heart and not to the effects of caricature.

Although Molière wrote his plays in French, Cervantes his novels in Spanish, Goethe his plays in German, Ibsen in Norwegian,

Chekhov in Russian, these and countless others are translated into nearly all languages. These translations are not written in dialects and the plays are performed in America, for example, in good straightforward English. And yet composers for the theatre are too often misled by the mention of a foreign locale or an earlier period, either or both of which lead them to fabricate a style foreign to themselves. In addition to *Cabaret* and *Zorba* already alluded to, I recall only too well a most unfortunate musical, *First Impressions,* which ran for a brief time in 1959. Perhaps the worst single feature was the musical score, which obviously felt obliged to be faithful to Jane Austen's novel *(Pride and Prejudice)* and tried to occupy its very period. The result was disastrous, since an audience has enough reminder of early nineteenth-century England in the costumes and sets without the additional and in my opinion incorrect tastelessness of music which was ersatz English and early nineteenth-century poorly imitated by American writers of our own time and place.

Actors, directors, and critics have also been muddled on more than one occasion because of these very same red herrings. I have myself been witness to serious discussions among writers, actors, and directors prior to rehearsals of a new play written in English but set in Paris. Some of the people involved have actually argued that the actors ought to effect French *accents!* I personally can find no reasonable defense for such an attitude *unless all* of the characters are French and perhaps *one* is Russian. It seems correct to me that *all* of the French speaking together in Paris (in an American play, or one translated into English) ought to speak perfect English—just as their French would be perfect French, but that the Russian should speak with an accent. Yet when *Fanny* had opened, I recall vividly one critic who attacked Harold Rome's music on the grounds that it was not *French* even though all of the dialogue by S. N. Behrman and Josh Logan was in English. A muddle, anyone?

I believe that the hoopla about rock as the newest saving musical grace in our theatre is unthought-out hogwash. Neither rock—nor any other style as such—is going to save anything. To save, it first has to be. And to be, it has to achieve status as one single phase of some knowledgeable and talented composer's musical alphabet. It can't and won't survive as a mere transplant. It won't work on the stage in its unalloyed form any more than rag or jazz has. It will have its effects but it will not be.

In the Sunday New York *Daily News* (August 31, 1969) Douglas Watt wrote:

> The entire question of the future of the Broadway musical is, naturally, inseparable from the question of the future of contemporary music itself. Is rock, which erupts around us in so many varied forms but always with an electronic drive, an end in itself or is it a peculiarly vital addition to the language that will eventually be absorbed into the mainstream?

What Mr. Watt has written covers precisely the point I have been trying to make. Rock is not an end in itself but *possibly* may become a "peculiarly vital addition to the language" if it is "absorbed into the mainstream," or it could turn out to be a successful passing phase which might influence composers in the theatre and everywhere else. Only time can decide this.

I think a feasible analogy is to be found in our language. One of the glories and a significant part of the richness of English is due to the fact that English has integrated its colors (and is continually adding more) from Anglo-Saxon, Latin, French, German, Greek, Spanish, Italian, Hindu, and practically every known language in the world—past and present. One does not say that English can be saved by a clean switch to Bantu or Chinese.

Music and lyrics in the theatre go together and at best are wedded as one. Each complements the other in creating an entity. But music—separated for purposes of examination—has its own contribution even if that contribution does not include any specifics. Within its own context inside a framework of plot and characters and situations it can and does supply to the audience all kinds of things without which—despite the libretto, which is good or bad, lasting or fleeting—there is no show. If there is a good overture, it will create a mood that will either be good or helpful in settling in the audience for what is to come, it will define a style, or it may make excitement, which after all is an important facet of workable theatre.

The ballads, which are the tunes of the score, will define the composer's style and interpret the characters. Music may be used non-vocally to strengthen the action or vivify the emotions. It can lift the dancers into the air, or tell us that lovers are unhappy, or accompany something humorous which could not otherwise have been said as well in prose. It can impart a sense of well-being or predict serious problems. It can punctuate a moment or connect one scene to another. It can—especially through the discreet use of reprise—make us feel we are seeing once more a dear old friend. It can make us cry when it correctly complements a situation. It can prod the right lyrics into making us laugh through the use of its formal patterns. It can indicate regularly where we may *expect* to laugh. It is the dominant force in the imparting of feeling, which, after all, is of the very first importance in the musical theatre.

To be sure, the incorrect use of music or a score that lacks inventiveness can also in every way prevent the satisfying unfolding of a show. It can remind us of every other score for every other show. In this way it is destructive not only in and of itself, but because it becomes a steady reminder of other things we have known or heard. This particular show unwinds with the audience playing a guessing game as to what song this one *was* or nearly was.

What music has contributed to the theatre or what it has to continue to contribute is an almost endless variety of drama expressed in song, in kinetic springboards for dancing, and in lyrics and dramatic backgrounds for spoken words and pantomime. This is what it has always given, and what, at its best, it will continue to give as one of the least perishable of the theatrical elements.

COMMENTS ON MUSIC

Who was Lehman Engel?

He was born in Jackson, Mississippi, that is to say, in the heart of the Old South, in 1910. When he came to New York during the Great Depression he wrote incidental music, which was then a standard practice, for numerous new plays, including T.S. Eliot's *Murder in the Cathedral*, as well as such revivals as *Hamlet*, *The Trojan Women* and *The Shoemakers' Holiday*.

With Kurt Weill's first major American score, the 1936 *Johnny Johnson*, produced by the Group Theatre, Engel began his career as one of Broadway's most respected musical directors. He conducted such notable musicals as Harold Rome's *Call Me Mister* in 1946; the Leonard Bernstein-Betty Comden-Adolph Green *Wonderful Town* in 1954; Comden, Green and Jule Styne's *Do Re Mi* in 1961; the Johnny Mercer-Norman Panama *Li'l Abner* in 1956; and all of Rome's other Broadway shows—the 1954 *Fanny*, the 1959 *Destry Rides Again*, and the 1961 *I Can Get It for You Wholesale*.

In the early Fifties, Lehman Engel began a parallel career, which may have been equally important, as an archivist. With the visionary record producer Goddard Lieberson, he recorded a series of Broadway musicals from the Thirties that had never had original cast recordings. The custom of recording shows with their original casts only began in 1943 with *Oklahoma!*, which opened during a musicians' strike.

Normally, big recording stars covered a new show's hits, but the strike made that impossible. As an experiment, Decca recorded the score of *Oklahoma!* with members of the cast. It was an unexpected success. Two of the recordings of previously unrecorded scores, for which Engel did both the arrangements and musical direction, were by George Gershwin—his lightheaded, lighthearted *Girl Crazy*, from 1930, and the one American opera that has been accepted into the repertory of opera houses all over the world, the 1935 *Porgy and Bess*.

Engel's version of *Porgy* was in fact the first complete recording of Gershwin's extraordinary score. Excerpts had been recorded when the show, heavily cut, had been revived in the early Forties, with members of the original cast, but that production treated it as if it were simply a musical, not the full-fledged opera Gershwin intended.

As a further service to the musical theatre, in 1963 Engel initiated the BMI Musical Theatre Workshop, to impart the principles of sound theatre music writing to aspiring young people. His experience in the workshop he founded underlies his writing in *Words With Music*. One of his assistants, John Sparks, founded a similar workshop in Chicago, New Tuners. ASCAP has also had a workshop, run by such composers as Charles Strouse, Richard Maltby and Stephen Schwartz. ASCAP's Los Angeles branch is run under the auspices of the Disney Organization. In New York there are comparable workshops at the Elaine Kaufman Cultural Center, the Manhattan School of Music and Musical Theatre Works.

If I mention Engel's credits this late in the game it's only because I fear that younger readers, perusing this chapter, which inveighs so heavily against rock, might be tempted to question his authority. Younger readers, after all, have grown up in a world where rock is everything, which was not the case when Engel wrote these words.

What is interesting is that thirty years later what he says remains true. I, too, remember hearing people say that rock would save the musical theatre. That it certainly has not done. It has had a huge but indirect impact on the musical theatre because it changed everything about the music industry, of which the musical theatre, once an integral part, is now, at best, a side show.

What Engel could not have envisioned was the massive apparatus that accompanies contemporary pop music. In his day there were obviously many efforts to promote music. John Kander, for example, remembers being in Boston for the tryout of his musical *Cabaret* and already hearing the title song on the radio. Every Broadway score was played for important recording artists well before the opening so that some of the songs could be hits the audience would know on its way *into* the theatre. (How brave of Engel to admit that, even though he was an accomplished musician, he wouldn't necessarily leave a new Broadway show humming the tunes!)

These efforts, however, were penny ante compared to what goes into marketing pop music today. As a simple example, magazines in 1971 generally had statesmen or politicians on their covers, seldom figures from the entertainment world. Pop musicians are now better known than heads of state, and their private lives are chronicled relentlessly, as if the public's hunger to know about them is insatiable. The fact that news organizations vie to write about them is a sign of how pervasive they have become, not necessarily in proportion to their talent. (It's also a sign, I'm afraid, of how the media have trivialized themselves.)

I often think of a song that was popular when I was very young, "In the Chapel by the Moonlight," which spent a long time on the Hit Parade in a recording by a former Big Band singer, Kitty Callan. It made its way on the basis of the singer's following as well as the merits of the tune and its sweet lyrics. In the early Fifties, newspapers outside New York had movie critics, sometimes classical music critics who reviewed major artists who made visits there, sometimes theatre critics, almost never critics to review pop records.

They certainly did not have an army of writers, as exist now, to analyze how this song figured in Callan's career, whether it was a breakthrough for the songwriters or whether the record would go platinum. (For that matter, I doubt newspapers fifty years ago gave their readers weekly breakdowns on the weekend box office receipts of movies.) The doings of show business were not considered News.

Rarely is the theatre given a ring in this modern media circus. Its music may be subtler, richer than that of, say, The Spice Girls (remember The Spice Girls?), but it seldom gets the kind of coverage such groups receive as a matter of course. I doubt that at any time in his career Lorenz Hart ever received the kind of serious analysis or lavish praise that most pop "artists" are accorded in their meteoric and happily brief trajectories from the top of the charts to the Betty Ford Clinic.

Whether or not rock made any impact within the theatre, it totally changed the world in which the theatre exists. Forty years ago theatre music and pop music were almost indistinguishable. Now they have virtually nothing in common. Worse, the fact that theatre music bears so little relation to what people hear on the radio or listen to at home makes it seem like a foreign language. For all intents and purposes, it is.

Several years ago a friend asked me to take over a class she was teaching in musical theatre performance. One of the students had prepared the song "Heat Wave" from Irving Berlin's revue *As Thousands Cheer*, and her idea of how to present this witty song was simply to have three male students dancing energetically behind her as she fairly shouted out the words while doing her own busy steps. This understanding of the "dramatic interpretation" of music derives from MTV and the general notion that music exists largely as a background for dancing.

Once we dismissed her backup dancers and began discussing what the song was really about—it's not a weather report—she brought a great understanding to it as well as a wicked sense of humor. The class laughed uproariously as she really interpreted the words. What was disturbing was that in a class about musical theatre performance none of this had occurred to her. The pervasive influence of pop culture overshadowed the theatrical understanding that should have been natural to her.

Similarly, many years ago I used to walk my dogs in Central Park with the great dancer Hugh Laing. He used to prepare young dancers at American Ballet Theatre when they revived the ballets of his lifelong friend Antony Tudor. He said they were technically far better equipped than he ever was. But, he lamented, they had no musicality, no understanding of what was meant by a musical phrase, no emotional response to the music. At the time I was puzzled by what he said. What could account for such a gap?

In retrospect, it is obvious how far the music young dancers have grown up with is from the music Tudor used in his ballets. How could someone whose musical understanding was oriented, as back then it might have been, to Run-DMC grasp the subtleties of a piece like the Chausson *Poème*, which Tudor used for one of his most moving ballets, *The Lilac Garden*? (Even the title has a quaintly faded sound.)

Rock is now a more significant element of the Broadway theatre than it was in Engel's time, but one can only be amused to look at which rock works have made a Broadway impact. In the 2002–03 season one of the important shows was Twyla Tharp's choreographic essay on Vietnam, *Movin' Out*, which utilized Billy Joel songs, largely from the Seventies. Another hit was *Hairspray*, based on the 1989 John Waters spoof film about music as a force for integration in Sixties Baltimore. Its score, by Marc Shaiman and Scott Wittman, parodied early Sixties rock. One of the big hits of the previous season was *Mamma Mia*, which dished up songs by ABBA, again from the Seventies. Yes, rock has made it to Broadway, but mostly retro rock.

The rock we hear on Broadway is for middle-aged people, not the young, for whom rock is old-fashioned. (Interestingly, the British columnist Peter Hitchens, commenting on the Live-8 concert of July 2005, wrote of the hungry children of Africa providing a pretext "to rescue the sagging reputations of that needy and deprived group of balding, clapped-out rock stars who still long for the crowds that once listened to them.") Hip-hop, the music they listen to, is even more limited to a certain age group and an urban mentality that would seem out of place anywhere other than contemporary America.

To go back to Engel's assertion that rock would not "save" the musical theatre, it's interesting how few of the hit musicals of the last thirty years have had rock scores.

One that did was Stephen Schwartz's *Pippin*, which used rock wittily to describe a medieval figure whose experience paralleled that of contemporary kids. Schwartz is conversant with both rock and theatre music. As a result he recognizes the need for literate lyrics in a way that musicians oriented only toward rock do not. There is a similar literacy in his lyrics for the 2003 *Wicked*, based on the Gregory Maguire novel that is a "prequel" to *The Wizard of Oz*. Schwartz's score reflects the stylistic inconsistencies of the novel, which is part melodrama, part pastiche. In the duet "As Long As You're Mine," he achieves an artful blend of theatre music and rock. I have always remembered interviewing Schwartz in 1978 at the time of *Working*. He described himself as a suburban kid, which, in the context of the theatre, is unusual. Few theatre people can resist the allure of Manhattan. By contrast, Schwartz was raising a family in suburbia. (This background of respectability did not prevent his son Scott from becoming a theatre director.) Schwartz's acquaintance with The Real World, which most theatre people prefer keeping at a distance, may account for his success in adapting the music of The Real World listeners to the needs of the theatre.

Even the British shows have only used rock to a limited extent. There's a rock quality to "Master of the House," the song the villainous Thenardins sing in Boublil and Schoenberg's *Les Miz*, but the duet for the young lovers late in the show is straight out of operetta. So is the anthem of the revolutionaries.

As for Lloyd Webber, *Superstar*, *Joseph and His Amazing Technicolor Dreamcoat* and *Evita* are rock-oriented. *Phantom of the Opera*, however, owes a lot to Puccini. By *Sunset Boulevard* he's coming closer to the classic Broadway idiom, which was similar to the Hollywood style appropriate to the material. In the version of Lloyd Webber's *Whistle Down the Wind* I heard in Washington, D.C. in 1996 (it has yet to open in New York), the most interesting part of the score was the religious choral writing akin to his *Requiem*.

Lloyd Webber has been treated as a whipping boy both by the American press and by the Brits, but the chameleon quality of a lot of his work serves to point up one of the dilemmas facing composers of musical theatre today. There's no universal style comparable to the one in which Rodgers and Loewe and Porter worked. If a lot of Lloyd Webber's work has a derivative quality, it's because nowadays every show demands its own idiom. Every score adopts some some style that the audience will recognize as signifying X or Y.

Engel alluded to this problem in 1971 in his strange exhortation to the estimable John Kander and his partner Fred Ebb to find an idiosyncratic style rather than to parody other styles, as they did when they wrote *Chicago*, which may be their most idiosyncratic work. It's pure show biz, and the 1996 revival may have captured its witty energy better than the original. But it's also hard to know why Engel was so peeved by the tone of *Cabaret*, which is appropriately Germanic (and by no means exclusively in the style of Kurt Weill, as he suggests) or that of *Zorba*, which has an entirely apt Greek folk quality.

If Stephen Sondheim seems to have solved the problem of finding the right idiom for the material without losing his own voice more successfully than his contemporaries, it is perhaps because he writes words as well as music.

In *Assassins* he parodies a lot of American music styles, since the subjects themselves span nearly a century. The score gives the work the through-line of Sondheim's disturbing musical intelligence. Nevertheless, there's a lack of consistency about the material that can puzzle even Sondheim fans.

One of the oddest songs in the score, for example, is that of Garfield's assassin Guiteau, who sings about "I Am Going to the Lordy." Audiences can be excused for being puzzled about this primitive lyric, which does not sound like it was written by Sondheim. It wasn't. It was written by Guiteau himself the morning of his execution. Not surprisingly, it eluded the attention of other composers until Sondheim came across it and decided to incorporate it into this unsettling show.

In some ways his most remarkable score is the underrated *Passion*, which alludes to no other style but is rather a distillation of Sondheim's own. It's virtually a series of variations on a very simple theme, but in its permutations it creates a variety of emotional moods of great depth. Unlike many of Sondheim's scores, in which both the words and music are dazzling, here both are extremely understated.

Sondheim is able to work at this ultra-refined level because he occupies a privileged position by dint of his extraordinary body of achievement. But his position, however much adulation it affords him, still doesn't guarantee him an easy path to production. *Into the Woods* was given workshop productions in La Jolla and at the Off-Off Broadway Playwrights Horizons before it was mounted on Broadway.

His only completed work after *Passion* is a musical he'd been toying with since the early Fifties, when he became enamored of Alvah Johnston's *The Legendary Mizners*, about two brothers: Wilson, an enormously successful Broadway playwright and con man of the early decades of the 20th century, and Addison, who was the visionary architect of Palm Beach. Johnston's book had been serialized in *The New Yorker* in 1952 and remains the longest work ever carried in its pages. Unfortunately at that time Irving Berlin also became enamored of the book and secured the rights. Despite the fact that the young Berlin had been a friend of Wilson Mizner, he was unable to translate the material to the stage.

Sondheim's first attempt to create a musical about the Mizners, *Wise Guys*, was presented at the New York Theatre Workshop in 1999, directed by Sam Mendes, a year after his triumph with the revival of *Cabaret*. Sondheim was so unsatisfied with *Wise Guys* that he refused to allow the press to see it. When it closed there ensued a long and ugly period of litigation as Sondheim recovered his rights to the material from producers who'd hoped to move it from NYTW to Broadway. In the spring of 2003 Sondheim presented a new version at the Goodman Theatre in Chicago with the title *Bounce*. This time it was directed by Harold Prince, their first collaboration since *Merrily We Roll Along*, twenty-two years earlier. The press was barred from seeing it in Chicago on the condition that they might come to see a further revised version at the Kennedy Center in Washington that fall.

Bounce covers an exuberant era in American life, beginning with the Yukon Gold Rush in the 1890s, proceeding to the excesses of the

Florida Land Boom and coming to an abrupt and dispiriting end with The Great Depression. It's possible that had Sondheim tackled the material around the time he wrote *A Funny Thing Happened on the Way to the Forum* he might have captured its dizzy energy quite naturally. Among its many virtues, in fact, was a song, "The Best Thing That Ever Has Happened," which you could hum as soon as you heard it in the overture. Sondheim has often been accused, unfairly, of not writing "take-home tunes." Well, here was an unmistakable example of the genre.

The score had Sondheim's customary lyrical intelligence and musical sophistication. It was also full of dramatic tension. All these qualities, however, which Sondheim had honed in the course of nearly half a century long career, were rather at odds with the breathtakingly vulgar life force of the Mizners. *Bounce*, for all its virtues, remained a work in progress, too demanding for the breathtakingly vulgar taste of current Broadway. At some point one of New York's not-for-profit theatres can revive it and give Sondheim another chance to realize what he set out to do long before he became the revered Sondheim.

Because his work is so idiosyncratic, Sondheim isn't really an appropriate model for young composers, but he is the only living theatre composer to whom they are likely to gravitate. If they're intelligent enough to see that there's no model for them to imitate in contemporary pop music, inevitably they turn to Sondheim. Having neither the verbal nor the musical background he does, their work is likely to sound imitative and hollow.

There are exceptions. In her 1977 *Violet*, Jeanine Tesori was able to create a theatrically viable style out of country music. Maury Yeston's 1982 *Nine*, which Yeston began in the BMI Workshop, has a distinctive style that alludes only occasionally to the Italian setting of his musical version of the Fellini film *8-1/2* (or to its soundtrack score by Nino Rota.) But it's hard to think of many scores that do not fall under the heading of pastiche.

This is a crisis that will not soon be resolved. It reflects a much deeper cultural malaise, the fact that the omnipresent entertainment industry is oriented toward the minds and tastes of adolescents rather than adults. The unavoidable corollary of this situation is that there are fewer and fewer adults who demand to be treated as such. This situation has grave implications for a democracy, knottier perhaps than any of the dilemmas of the musical theatre.

The problem of musical style is not helped by the attitudes toward composition prevalent in academic circles, which is where young composers may get their training. In academia the emphasis is on innovation and harmonic experimentation. Earlier, I mentioned that the musical idiom that was still predominant in the theatre as well as popular music 50 years ago was one that was kin to as simple but profound a piece as "Danny Boy." One does not require musical education to listen to this melody and be attracted to it. That attraction deepens when one listens to the words, realizing it is the farewell of a mother as her son goes off to war. In fact the words were not added until long after the melody had gained currency, but the fit seems entirely appropriate and absolutely natural.

Whether or not such a thing can be taught, it often seems that the academy has no interest in even trying. In the 1980s the marvelous (I mean the word in its most literal sense) Canadian novelist Robertson Davies told me of his dismay when, as the head of McGill University, he thought it would be nice to commission students from the graduate school in music to write something festive for the university's Christmas celebration. "Something festive" was not in their musical vocabulary. The closest one of them could come was a cerebral piece whose atonal machinations were suddenly interrupted by an ironic allusion to the Hallelujah Chorus. After this self-conscious break in decorum the work returned to its intellectual pretensions.

Morton Gould once lamented that a generation of American composers—himself, Aaron Copland, Marc Blitzstein, even their predecessor Charles Ives (whom Ned Rorem once called "the most overrated of our underrated composers")—were all striving for a style that could be called American. But after World War II their efforts were almost instantaneously discredited by the arrival of 12-tone music, which became the only acceptable mode for serious composition. Even Copland, whose style, exemplified in such works as "Appalachian Spring" and "Fanfare for the Common Man," is the most immediately recognizable American strain, began composing serial music.

Interestingly, no comparable crisis exists in the world of movie music, which has maintained certain traditions and standards since the glory days of the child prodigy Erich Wolfgang Korngold. The son of an influential Viennese music critic, the young Korngold spent a decade as a serious composer, writing string quartets, instrumental music and an opera. He arrived in Hollywood in the mid-30s, a refugee from Hitler, happy to take any work he could. He created the exhilarating scores for movies such as *Robin Hood* and *The Sea Hawk*, and in his spare time continued composing "serious" work like his ultra-romantic violin concerto, which remains one of the most often played and beloved works of the 20th century.

It is unlikely that when Steven Spielberg asked John Williams to compose the background score for *Schindler's List* that Williams proposed that since Arnold Schoenberg was the dominant composer of the period in which the story took place perhaps his theories about music should underline the score. In fact, when Spielberg screened the scoreless film for him Williams said, "This requires a far better composer than I am." Spielberg said, "I know, but they're all dead." Williams proceeded to create a score—often relying on the solo violin—that heightened the extraordinary emotional impact of the film.

A movie composer knows that his job is to underscore the emotions on the screen. Theory plays no role whatsoever in the proceedings. Perhaps because the clarity of the undertaking is related to the commercial success of the film itself, the composer's task is easier. An ego trip is out of the question. Even if a film composer creates a signature style—as the great Nino Rota did—the music is always at the service of the material.

Moreover, there are no limitations on what he can use to achieve his aim. If he feels his score would be most effective with a full symphony orchestra, he gets it. No one tells him the public will not tolerate an old-fashioned musical onslaught of strings. In the theatre producers are constantly trying to whittle down the size of the musical forces at a composer's or orchestrator's disposal.

For a young theatre composer, there are no simple answers. Neither the utter banality of what passes for music in pop circles nor the lofty theorizing of academia is any guide to writing music for the theatre.

COMEDY

> **It is very difficult to be wholly joyous or wholly sad
> on this earth. The comic, when it is human, soon
> takes upon itself the face of pain.**
>
> Joseph Conrad
> "A Familiar Preface"
> *A Personal Record* (1912)

I know of no workable musical that does not contain comedic elements. Both *Carousel* and *West Side Story* are "serious," yet in both there are comedic sequences which by contrast add strength and poignancy to the central themes. Throughout *Carousel* the bright-colored thread of Carrie and Mr. Snow provides a contrast to the inevitable sad tale of Julie and Billy. In *West Side Story* early in the play there is a scene in the drugstore that is simultaneously threatening and humorous, and there are two great comedy songs in the otherwise dour second act.

These elements are integrated—not merely inserted—in the principal plots, and aside from their own intrinsic values they complement the basic plot lines. Historically, this integration is new, for it did not exist in earlier American musicals, where comedic elements were only garnishments. Earlier writers failed to understand the nature of comedy, so it emerged as labored and unfunny and was kept like a contagious disease far away from the pure young romancers. Comedy was indeed so threadbare and hopeless that many producers during the first two decades of this century employed established comedy "teams" who inserted their own material regardless of subject matter and performed it themselves within the musical. The team was generally assigned two or three spots at fixed intervals in the show, and it was the team's problem to "take" stage after a book scene, solder themselves loosely to some existing situation, and deliver the stage after the allotted time back to the continuing musical.

By the mid-Twenties, operetta librettists were writing all of their own material but were still failing to create real and durable comedy. In *Rose-Marie, The Vagabond King, The Desert Song, The Student Prince,* and others, the songs were fated to endure for an indefinite time. The simple, if sentimental, plots of love, nobility, and sacrifice won every heart, but the laughter was muted from the beginning.

However, in more highly developed later shows, the two princi-pals became so humanized and so three-dimensional that they themselves embodied both romance and comedy. This was due to the fact that in maturing, comedy grew out of character and situa-tion rather than buffoonery, or jokes.

Much of what had been truly comic in our past was purely visual. The early silent movies—Chaplin, Fields, Keaton, and others were deathless examples. And these men were grim or sad or expression-less. They behaved in no way that seemed to say, "I will make you laugh." To the contrary, much of what they did was either an act of cruelty or we saw them as victims of a cruel life. W. C. Fields made us laugh when he wanted to kill a defenseless infant.

To quote an example from Walter Kerr's distinguished book *Tragedy and Comedy*:

> One evening I sat with a friend during a showing of Chaplin's *The Circus*, and when Charlie, having surrepti-tiously managed to eat the whole of a small child's hot dog, solemnly searched for a napkin and most thought-fully wiped the child's lips, my friend, clapping his hands in astonishment, fell back on his seat.... I thought he was going to fall out of it ... exclaiming, "He believes it! He believes it!"

It is the character truly in the situation which allows him to believe it, and as a result, we laugh.

It must be remembered that our musical theatre, on emerging from its operetta chrysalis, was dubbed "musical comedy." Today we find ourselves unconsciously employing this same label when what we actually refer to is a variety of things involving drama with music. But from the start, comedy was an importantly sought after and too seldom realized part of the scheme of things, and today our continuing in pursuit of it is not at all because we think that "bright-ening things up a bit" can make a show more commercial. (In my opinion, everything that works is also "commercial.") Rather we employ comedy for its contrasting mood values and theatricality, but also because musically a score consisting of ballad after ballad, occasionally lightened by a balladic relative—a charm song—is a deadly bore. The show becomes a mere thread for a lullaby recital.

The elements of comedy *and* romance or pathos or other lyrical components are present in all good musical shows.[11] Again Shakespeare, the poet-playwright-librettist, found comedy an essential concomitant to his otherwise most tragic plays. *Hamlet* has for comedy its gravediggers as well as Polonius, Rosencrantz, Guildenstern, and, on occasion, Hamlet himself; *Macbeth* has its gatekeeper, *Romeo and Juliet* its musicians. In the comedies, the same contrasts exist. *The Merry Wives of Windsor* has its Falstaff, who is bawdy and laughable but also profoundly pitiable; *As You Like It* has its melancholy Jaques. *A Midsummer Night's Dream,* with its high fantasy, poetry that leaps from star to star, romance to satisfy all lovers, also has its Bottom and its Pyramus-Thisbe scene. The work is a great tapestry blending all the colors and emotions, delighting the eye, the ear, the mind, and the heart, and when this tends to be gossamer there is fun on the lowest, bawdiest, and most comprehensible level for all people in all times.

Again Walter Kerr in *Tragedy and Comedy* writes: "Comedy [exists] not in order to give the lie to the occasion but to complete it. . . . All truth is whole, one," and "the clown's tribulations are enacted rather than reported." Both the classical and the modern examples to which I have referred—in all cases—become more complete and whole because of the comic inclusion, and in every instance what is funny to an audience is indeed the tribulation of the character who enacts it.

Kerr also wrote: "Comedy is not lyric, not rhapsodic. . . ." Does this not describe situations and characters who are obdurate if not impossible for use with music? These people do not sing. That is one good reason why the combining within characters who are basically romantic with a comic facade is of inestimable value in a musical. It is also true that some forms of comedy obviously may lend themselves to musical adaptation while others eschew it. Of the existing, workable musicalized comedies, we recall *Annie Get Your Gun, Wonderful Town, A Funny Thing Happened on the Way to the Forum,* and, if I may be forgiven, *Fiddler on the Roof.* All of these in one sense or another (speaking quite generally) are romantic, which means that they contain the element that enables them to sing.

The farces of Feydeau and Labiche cannot accommodate music because they are extremely complex without the additional and probably more confusing burden of another element. Also they are swift and the inclusion of songs would only slow them down. Without speed, they would fail to make their incessant—almost unrelenting—comedic points. As they are—musicless and full of "sight jokes"—they seem to me best described as ballets without scores. And the scores are neither necessary nor missed.

There is something else of prime importance: the troubled character is likable, naive and usually charming. This is certainly true of the Gatekeeper, the Gravedigger, Adelaide, Ado Annie, and the "Officer Krupke" boys. However, a question must here be raised.

The most successful of all contemporary writers of comedy is Neil Simon, and to me his work leaves a great deal to be desired. Douglas Watt in the New York *Daily News* (February 1, 1970) articulated, "There is something a little disturbing about Simon's people; they are very often completely devoid of charm." My own feeling is that this observation is not only true but it accounts for what I think would make the musicalization of Simon's plays undesirable if not impossible, and in spite of their present overwhelming success this charmlessness of character will ultimately throw the plays into an early discard. I find it difficult to care about the people or the outcome of their situations.[12] Scenes read like monologues rather than exchanges among different personally identified people, and actually, in most of Simon's plays, scenes are indeed dialogues rather than multi-character discussions. The material is almost exclusively "banter"—exchanges between two or more people who never fail to recall the goings-on between the end men at a minstrel show. The subject matter skips around helter-skelter in many directions or wherever a "joke" can be made, suggesting a game of tennis played without boundaries, perhaps in outer space. The "jokes" are *outside* the characters, not generated through them as individual human beings. Furthermore, since their subject matter is not homogeneous they would not lend themselves to any single specific lyric theme—the germ of the song.

It has been suggested that the Simon characters are perfect roles for "personalities" because they can become almost anyone their performer wants them to be. Allow me to quote a portion of a scene from Neil Simon's *The Odd Couple,* which I feel will illustrate the points I have tried to make. In Act Two a poker game is in progress.

> OSCAR: Close the kitchen and sit down. It's a quarter to twelve. I still got an hour and a half to win this month's alimony.[13]
>
> ROY (*Sniffs*): What is that smell? Disinfectant! (*He smells cards.*) It's the cards. He washed the cards! (*Throws down cards, takes jacket from chair and moves above table. Puts money into kitty box.*)
>
> FELIX (*Comes to table with OSCAR's drink, which he puts down and then sits in his own seat*): Okay ... What's the bet?
>
> OSCAR (*Hurrying to his seat*): I can't believe it. We're gonna play cards again. (*He sits.*) It's up to Roy ... Roy, baby, what are you gonna do?
>
> ROY: I'm gonna get in a cab and go to Central Park. If I don't get some fresh air, you got yourself a dead accountant. (*Moves toward door.*)
>
> OSCAR (*Follows him*): What do you mean? It's not even twelve o'clock.
>
> ROY (*Turns back to OSCAR*): Look, I've been sitting here breathing lysol and ammonia for four hours! ... Nature didn't intend poker to be played like that. (*He crosses to door.*) If you wanna have a game next week ... (*He points to FELIX.*) either Louis Pasteur cleans up after we've gone ... or we play in the Hotel Dixie! Good night! (*He goes and slams door.*)

Simon's characters are anything but lyrical. Oscar is brittle and lacks humanity. What he wants or says he wants is truly unimportant. He is uncomfortable but not much more than that. He is terse and hard-workingly funny. I think that in order for it to really matter or for a lyricist to be able to write a comedy song, the situation has to be of *primary import to the character who sings.* The scene needs to be serious. We laugh because of the tragic or pathetic or frustrated nature of the character in the specific situation. Kerr, again, wrote: "Comedy, it seems, is never the gaiety of things; it is the groan made gay." Eliza Doolittle is "groaning" in "Just You Wait,

'Enry 'Iggins"; so is Ado Annie in "I Cain't Say No" and Meg Brockie in "The Love of My Life" and Miss Adelaide in her "Lament."

Oscar and Roy in *The Odd Couple* are making with jokes. They *intend* to be comic. These jokes succeed as they are (for a time), as do all good jokes, but they are not "truthful." In Simon's plays the actors are observers rather than doers. They are the Greek chorus minus the principals. While the subject matter is always a "complaint," it is not real or serious or sincere enough to engage audiences deeply in problems, which are ever so slight. What causes the laughter—and there is plenty of this during the prescribed period of the plays' lives—is the rapid-fire succession of jokes. Once heard, these are dead. They do not engage audiences repeatedly. This is not true of the material given the Krupke boys, Ado Annie, Miss Adelaide, the Gravedigger, etc., all of whom represent situations and people so basically real, empathic, *and* charming that experiencing them on one single occasion does not preclude the desire to experience them again and again. None of these latter (or the many others like them) make "jokes." In one way or another they *suffer*[14] and their plaints are very real outgrowths of this suffering, all of them relating directly to all of us.

As Neil Simon's characters are not human beings they are incapable of suffering. As they lack definition, reality and dimensions, their existence is short-lived. Most of their greatest supporters in the audience will be fickle enough to have "had" them once, and then no more. Because of the many omitted human qualities in all of Simon's plays, the "haste to the joke" frenzy and many other factors, it is my considered opinion that none of Simon's plays could be successfully converted into musical libretto form. Simon of course did not compose his plays for that purpose, but it seems odd that commonplace and basically typical characters would fail in adaptation to the musical stage. The most serious omission among the many in all of these plays, however, is heart. This alone renders these works useless as partners in musical treatment.

Recently Noël Coward's thirty-five-year old comedy *Private Lives* was revived and proved to be younger than springtime. The very opening stage directions *predict* laughter: There will be two sets or characters and we can quite easily guess who they will be. All four prove to be charming and real. Couple A—newlyweds—includes the former husband of a much discussed lady. They exit inside the hotel, and we know that we are fulfilled when Couple B—also newlyweds—including the former wife of the husband of Couple A, enter. The scenes given each pair are nearly identical. We are made to *want* them to be so. Each one of the four people is a sharply etched individual. The entire play engenders warm and knowing laughter and there are no "jokes." The fun is produced by the specific characters in their specific situation.

The following segment occurs in a scene between the characters comprising Couple A.

> SYBIL: (*Coming down to the balustrade*): She was pretty, wasn't she? Amanda?
> ELYOT: Very pretty.
> SIBYL: Prettier than I am?
> ELYOT: Much.
> SIBYL: Elyot!
> ELYOT: She was pretty and sleek, and her hands were long and slim, and her legs were long and slim, and she danced like an angel. You dance very poorly, by the way.
> SIBYL: Could she play the piano as well as I can?
> ELYOT: She couldn't play the piano at all.
> SIBYL (*Triumphantly*): Aha! Had she my talent for organization?
> ELYOT: No, but she hadn't your mother either.
> SIBYL: I don't believe you like Mother.
> ELYOT: Like her! I can't bear her.
> SIBYL: Elyot! She's a darling, underneath.
> ELYOT: I never got underneath.

Notice that this entire scene has only a single subject: Amanda.

Even in so brief an exchange we know that Elyot is not in love with Sibyl (they are mismatched), that Sibyl is prudish, that Elyot is vain and selfish and that both of them—now on their honeymoon—are anything but happy, It seems quite appropriate that *Private Lives* might lend itself successfully to libretto treatment for music. The people are charming, engaging, identifiable, and unhappily in love. These are subjects that quite easily skip hand in hand with music.

I have not attempted to show the kind of inverse relationship in size alone between the "topic" or basic subject matter in a play and its expanded outgrowth as a lyric in a musical. Let me now illustrate the latter. Look at Shaw's *Pygmalion,* Act Two. A marvelous comedy song grew out of Higgins's speech.

> .... I suppose the woman wants to live her own life; and the man wants to live his; and each tries to drag the other on to the wrong track. One wants to go north and the other south; and the result is that both have to go east, though they both hate the east wind. So here I am, a confirmed bachelor, and likely to remain so.

Shaw's topic here is the impossibility of a woman in this man's life; Considering Higgins' selfishness, which permits him to comprehend no point of view other than his own, Alan Jay Lerner employed in his *My Fair Lady* song ("I'm an Ordinary Man") the subject matter given by Shaw expressed in Higgins' first-person-singular attitude. The lyric is a vast expansion of the above capsule, consisting of three eleven-line verses, five seven-line choruses, and three four-line "interludes"—a total of eighty lines on this single topic. Despite Higgins' erudition and snobbishness and worldliness on this subject of his own "ordinariness" and women, he is also naïve. His "naïveté" plus his vitriol produce, in his case, charm.

Similar craft went into Frank Loesser's "Adelaide's Lament" from *Guys and Dolls.* However, additionally this song illustrates again and even more clearly a very important point: Of all types of musical numbers, comedy songs are the most personal. Personal problems usually work best in comedy songs because the complaint (always expressing some kind of misfortune or frustration) is more humorous when delivered in first-person singular. By so doing the audience experiences something felt as opposed to something observed. It is a matter of conjecture as to why we laugh at Miss Adelaide and her "Lament," but I have a feeling that it is due to a mixture of at least two things. First, of course, is the quality of Loesser's writing—his hilarious narrative, its sharp and amusing images, its suave rhymes and Loesser's outrageous choice of subject matter—"psychosomatic symptoms," which is obviously "far out" for poor Miss

Adelaide's comprehension. Then too in life we have all heard such plaints all too often, though not so deftly phrased. But on such boring occasions we cannot and we do not laugh at the would-be pathetic creature who tells us of her troubles. Now, in the theatre, when it comes to us on a person-to-person basis, we are free to react as we will and we do indeed laugh. Also perhaps we see our own foolish selves in a related predicament, and our laughter is slightly nervous. We *were* foolish and now we know it.

We don't laugh at happiness, only at pain, discomfort, sorrow, catastrophe, or embarrassment. Hiccoughs are painful. Tripping over something unseen or falling downstairs can be fatal. Scratching can be uncomfortable. Sneezing can be unpleasant. Knocking over a glass of liquid can be embarrassing. Snoring is objectionable. Opening a can or a bottle when it spurts all over someone can be outrageous. Seeing someone wipe gravy off his mouth with his necktie (thinking it is his napkin) is distasteful. Watching a waiter drop a trayful of dishes is catastrophic, Belching is repulsive. Seeing someone spread shaving cream on a toothbrush is disgusting. The failure of a magician's trick, pages of music sliding off a music stand during a concert, a chair collapsing under someone, seeing a string break on a violin or cello *during* a performance, someone slipping on ice, on roller skates, skis or on a banana peel are all terrible. Someone pulling out of his pocket a dollar bill when he believes he has a much-needed handkerchief. Watching someone struggle into a coat (the wrong one), which is in the end far too small or too large. Seeing somebody make a would-be dignified exit, but going *into* a closet instead of out of the front door, putting the wrong end of a cigarette in his mouth, dropping a forkful of food just as the mouth is open to receive it, etc.

"A chair collapsing under someone." Notice that for its humorous effect it is not pertinent to describe the person as to age, sex, or size. The kind of chair is not mentioned. It might be of any size, period, color, or type (folding, non-folding). The background of the person involved is of no concern, nor for that matter is the result of the accident, which might have been of no consequence or might have resulted in a broken leg, a smashed finger, or a heart attack. All that does matter is the simple fact: a chair collapsing under someone. That is an invariable maker of laughter. Or if the person involved were—let us say—a very dignified and formal man, the result would be especially funny because the man's dignity and his out-of-character sitting on the floor in a heap of rubbish are so unrelated and so out of style, the one with the other. All of these aforementioned things and booksful of others are productive of laughter as the immediate reaction.

It must be remembered that these mishaps—large and small—are not amusing to the person involved in them but only to the observer—the audience. Also all of them are to be *seen* and do not involve creative writing. The most serious problem is to be able to know how to translate similar events into a song or a scene. Describing any of them is a bore.

I believe that there are only certain mechanical suggestions that can be of any help. First, as to the person who is to sing the (if it is to be one) song. These qualities have been pointed out earlier, but it will do no harm to reiterate them. The character must have charm, naïveté, sincerity. The subject matter should be personal, unfortunate. In creating the lyric for such a song (the music alone is incapable of being precisely funny) the writer should work backward: know where he is going and he must make that point the very last syllable of that "joke." Having established this—the what and where be is going—he needs to *set up* the joke in relation both to it and to the performing character and to create the separate setting of the song in which the "incident" occurs (as distinguished from the actual scene at the moment in the show). What is chosen as subject matter—it should go without saying—must unquestionably be compatible with the capacities and probabilities of the performer and his possible experience. The tone should be wry. Rhythm and rhyme should be of invaluable help in making the end result amusing. And under these circumstances and for purposes of laughter *only* can self-pity be employed as a workable theatrical element.

It might conceivably be of additional help if the writer considered using some of his material as descriptive of a picture, a scene, circumstances surrounding his character's personal misfortune. Consciously or not such descriptions—knifelike precise—exist in most of the workable and lasting songs to which I have already referred. Adelaide says, "when *they* get on the train . . . ." Tevye describes the house he would have if he were rich. Meg is detailed in depicting the four men she encountered in looking for the love of her life, where she and they went, what they did, and why (to her) they all went awry. Ado Annie delineates the precise nature of the disease that makes it impossible for her to say "no." Professor Higgins is a torrent of locution in attempting to prove his own ordinariness—a complete and detailed antithesis of reality and truth. Eliza Doolittle is most graphic about her proposed conversation with the King regarding the fate of Higgins. All of these are descriptions of scenes which help to pinpoint the emotions that trigger the laughter.

In the creation of a comedy song the librettist often has the problem of creating a scene—a frame—which never existed in the original source material but one which nevertheless enjoys the credibility of having existed. Rodgers and Hammerstein based their *King and I* on *Anna and the King of Siam,* a semi-biographical novel. In no section of this book is there any remote suggestion of comedy, and yet *The King and I* contains two comedy songs, "A Puzzlement" and "Shall I Tell You What I Think of You?" These were in no way suggested by any line or any specific situation in the book but *were* "dreamed up," as it were, out of the reasonably *possible* behavior of the characters. *The King and I* also contains a 'musical scene," "Shall We Dance?", which is not a comedy song but allows comedic staging as the schoolmistress attempts to teach the arrogant king how to dance. Because the choreography here becomes more and more amusing, the dramatic situation which interrupts sharply becomes even more tense than it would otherwise be. This illustrates another important function of comedy, planned and executed, though not written as either a scene or a song but is peculiarly a unique property of musical theatre.

The characters in plays under consideration for adaptation into musicals may or may not possess a comedic potential, but I believe that inherent possibilities do exist in essentially naïve characters. Martha *(Who's Afraid of Virginia Woolf?)* and Blanche *(A Streetcar Named Desire)* are neither naïve nor are their problems universal. Tevye *(Fiddler on the Roof),* Adelaide *(Guys and Dolls),* and Ado Annie *(Oklahoma!)* are universal, personal, charming, and naïve.

For lyric clarity comedy songs are almost necessarily solos. ("Officer Krupke" in *West Side Story* involves a group of boys, but all of the material important in the exposition of the ideas and the "pay-off" of the humor is sung by a single character.) While music itself is incapable of being explicitly and universally comedic, it can emerge as a valuable ally. First off it should be discreet enough to support but never overpower in calling attention to itself. It should best "frame" the lyric. Furthermore, it can assume a more active role by setting up a form that will literally "trumpet" in its pattern the "This is where the laughter will come. Listen!"

As I said at the beginning: I know of no workable musical that does not contain comedic elements. To attempt to create a musical show without knowing how this all-important element is to be employed is, I think, suicidal. While charm, cheerfulness, delightfulness and the rest are useful, none of them nor anything else is a proper substitute for comedy, which is essential.

COMMENTS ON COMEDY

One of the most beguiling soundtrack scores in recent decades was by the English composer Richard Rodney Bennett for Sidney Lumet's treatment of the Agatha Christie mystery *Murder on the Orient Express*. Bennett has some eerily orchestrated chords that remind us that someone has been murdered, but the score is best remembered for a glorious waltz that suggests what's taking place on the fashionable train is also an exercise in nostalgia for a time when people of a certain class carried themselves with an elegance now exceedingly rare. This elegance contributed enormously to the "investigation" that constitutes the drama, and Bennett thought the music should underscore that.

Years afterward, he learned that Bernard Herrmann, who'd written the scores for many of Alfred Hitchcock's greatest films, told another composer, "Bennett got it all wrong. This is the TRAIN OF DEATH."

Needless to say, it would have been fascinating to hear how Herrmann might have scored *Murder on the Orient Express*, but one can't help feeling his high seriousness, even the sardonic quality you hear in some of his scores, might not have served a film in which, after all, even the revered detective Hercule Poirot is played (by Albert Finney) with tongue firmly in cheek.

One of the most important theatrical theorists of the 20th century, Bertolt Brecht, understood the uses of comedy. One reason his savage indictment of the mercantile instincts, *Mother Courage*, seldom works is that the people who present it generally yield to the bourgeois emotions Brecht despised. *Mother Courage* is played as a heroic, maternal creature rather than the simple monster she is.

The only time I've ever seen Brecht's so-called "alienation effect" work was in a production of a one-act, *The Exception and the Rule*, directed by Isaiah Sheffer, about forty years ago. Terrible things were being done to a widow and orphan, but the audience, instead of reacting with conventional middle-class outrage, were laughing themselves silly, fulfilling Brecht's wish that the theatre not indulge us in sentimental piety.

Comedy can play a far more important role in the theatre than simply eliciting laughter. There was no Brechtian subtext to *Murder on the Orient Express*, but Bennett's music, by its unexpectedness, may have made the events of the plot more chilling.

One of the most effective scenes in Stephen Sondheim's problematic *Merrily We Roll Along* is the one toward the end (the plot, remember, moves backward) in which the three friends who bonded in high school write and perform a satirical sketch in a Greenwich Village cabaret in the early Sixties, "Bobby and Jackie and Jack." The number has an innocence that conveys the Camelot years perfectly. It's lighthearted, sweet, but, in its ability to evoke deeper memories, far more powerful than any solemn invocation of that time.

Similarly, in a little-remembered Kander and Ebb musical *70, Girls, 70*, a vaudeville set in an old people's home, the issue of death is skirted for much of the evening. (*70, Girls, 70* is little remembered because it had the bad luck to open a few months after another musical featuring old people, *Follies*.) Death is alluded to directly only very late in the score in "The Elephant Song," a lilting ditty that asks, "Where does an elephant go?" As one of Fred Ebb's verses explains,

> When a pharaoh finally met his doom,
> They would lay him out in a swanky room,
> But an elephant takes so much damn room . . .
> Where does an elephant go?

> When the coffin's shut and the lid is firm
> A man's consigned to the pine and worm
> But what kind of box fits a pachyderm?
> Where does an elephant go?
> When an elephant sees his final dawn,
> When an elephant's final breath is drawn,
> It's a cinch there ain't no Forest Lawn,
> Where does an elephant go?

The very silliness of the images, especially sung in the unmistakably weathered voice of Mildred Natwick, had unsettling reverberations.

In February 2004 New York City Center *Encores!* presented a concert version of the Gershwins' 1933 flop *Pardon My English*. Before this universally praised revival, if the show was remembered at all, it was because of the poignant standard "Isn't It a Pity?" But the show was written only a year after their wildly ambitious *Let 'Em Eat Cake*, which had an incredibly rich score, and only a year before their monumental "Porgy and Bess." The *Encores!* team was wise to give it a second look.

Pardon My English, it turned out, had a wonderfully silly book by Herbert Fields and Morrie Ryskind (to which David Ives, who did the adaptation, contributed much of his own wit.) In the context of a plot that was akin to the contemporaneous absurdist movie *Million Dollar Legs*, the high-spirited score, which had been shaped with extraordinary care by musical director Rob Fischer, took on a kind of delirious quality. John Kander, who happened to be sitting in front of me, turned and said, "Isn't it a shame we no longer call it musical comedy?"

I was reminded of something the humorist S.J. Perelman said when I interviewed him in 1974 on the occasion of a revival of his failed Broadway comedy *The Beauty Part*. In his years as a Hollywood screenwriter he had been forced to attend previews of his films where the audience would laugh heartily while they were in the theatre, then declare on their way out, "Wasn't that silly?"

"People don't have the courage of their laughter," he said.

The audience laughing at *Pardon My English* couldn't help itself. That was the force of the material. They were also indulging in a kind of nostalgic laughter, laughter at an innocent world, mired in an economic depression but about to tumble into a much graver chaos.

The material in no way adhered to any of Engel's principles. As we have seen, those principles were at work a few years earlier, in the 1927 *Show Boat.* They were certainly at work a year later in *Porgy and Bess.* But here the rules did not apply. Is it inappropriate to praise something so far in spirit from Engel's vision? Perhaps, but we should always bear in mind that when a work is at a certain level of inspiration the rules seem irrelevant. In the introduction to the Mercury Theatre editions of Shakespeare's plays that I read as a youth, Orson Welles dealt with Shakespeare's frequent inattention to proper grammar with a very wise observation: "Fences are made for those who cannot fly."

In the case of humor there are no formulae. And when we pontificate about musical theatre it is sometimes useful to remember that the genre began with the simple desire to amuse.

So far we have looked at comedy as a way of dealing with serious issues, but of course most of the time comedy is intended merely to be comedy, as Engel discusses in "Comedy and Entertainment."

6

Comedy and Entertainment

One's roused by this, another finds that fit:
Each loves the play for what he brings to it.
Goethe, "Prelude to the Theatre"
in *Faust, Part One* (1808),
translated by Philip Wayne

Considerable confusion has always existed between the terms "comedy" and "entertainment," which, in the minds of too many people, are thought to be synonymous. Webster defines entertainment as "the act of diverting, amusing or causing someone's time to pass agreeably." The single aspect "amusing" is the chief cause of this confusion because that is a chief attribute of comedy. On the other hand tragedy also can "cause someone's time to pass agreeably" provided the observer (audience) is sufficiently involved to be entertained by it. The factors that account for precisely what entertains different people are unlimited, but they can be narrowed down to a few generally pertinent ones:

1. Background (including place of residence)
2. Average age (physically and mentally)
3. Kind and degree of education
4. Amount of exposure to various forms of entertainment
5. Need for entertainment
6. Effects of general audience and umpire reactions
7. Relationship to time present

This list would seem to indicate that *quality* is unimportant, and for these purposes I think this is so. The quality of an entertainment is important to me, but what entertains me, a farmer from Kansas, a traveling salesman from Detroit, a professor of literature, a once-in-a-lifetime visitor to New York, a man who has never read a book or seen a play, a man who does not read a daily newspaper, what entertains is going to be different in every case. And it is this difference—the dichotomy which channels the preferences of recipients rather than what is actually presented on a stage, in a sports arena or anywhere else or in whatever media—that allows anything to qualify as good or bad entertainment: how it is seen through the eye of the beholder.

Take, for example, the case of some non-representational picture by Picasso in a museum. One man, lacking any cultural background, previous experience with or interest in this kind of painting, might pass it by quickly, having received nothing from it, with a contemptuous, "My four-year-old daughter can draw better than that!" Another man, with the opposite background, interest, and experience, may look long and with considerable interest at the same picture. His attention will be focused on particular aspects of the work: the use of color, its style and form, its relationship to the past and present, to earlier works by the same artist, what it communicates to him, etc. All of this simply because the second viewer has in himself the means to become engaged with or "entertained" by this picture. In the end he may for this or that reason even reject it in favor of another work of Picasso's which he prefers. He might after careful scrutiny dismiss it, thereby in a sense agreeing with the first viewer. But meanwhile the first man will have seen nothing, not have been engaged, while the second will have been absorbed, in spite of his ultimate negative verdict.

The differences between the two viewers may very well illustrate what I mean by "background," also "kind and degree of education," possibly "place of residence" and "amount of exposure." One factor that can work either for or against involvement of a listener or viewer is familiarity. This does not mean that because he derives the pleasure of pure recognition that may come from familiarity his obvious reaction makes the product—what is seen or heard—good or high art. Nor is the reverse—boredom due also to familiarity—proof that the end product is poor. To illustrate the "pleasure of pure recognition" (one half the result of familiarity), watch the audience in the last act of *Götterdämmerung*. Most of the people are somewhat titillated by the childishness of the horn exchanges. (Siegfried's hunting party has strayed from Hagen. Each of the two leaders pretends to sound his own motif, which, of course, a four-year old knows is something actually going on either in the orchestra pit or backstage by two men wearing spectacles and carrying a union card.) The sound of the two motifs grows nearer and finally the two principals with retinue rejoin one another.

Lots of dull things happen after this meeting, the longest and dullest of which follows Hagen's plunging his spear into Siegfried's back. After some all too clearly understood remarks by the male chorus *("Hagen, was tust du?")*, the dying Siegfried, who now understands *everything*, proceeds to spell it all out to us—not forgetting a single detail of his complex if brief history. At long last he runs out of breath and dies. Remember that this is late in a long opera. Act One has lasted two and a half hours. (Who remembers the length of Act Two?) And this is at the conclusion of Act Three, Scene 1. (You can imagine how depleted the average audience—not to mention the orchestra and singers—is.) All at once there is the sound of the "Funeral March." Many people have tried to play it in high school or in the navy band, have it on records and have heard it over many years at concerts. Now at long last familiarity, and for about the next fifteen minutes ecstasy. This is not so much due to anyone's regard for Siegfried's "Funeral March" (which might be pretty high) or its clashing cymbals, which are always good for a goose pimple or two, or the fortissimo brass, but to simple recognition—the face of a friend in a wilderness.

Actually this same thing happens with much truth in *Midnight Cowboy*, a contemporary film, when the young hero, now penniless, is walking aimlessly across 42nd Street late at night and suddenly sees the only man he had ever met in New York sitting in a beanery. The man had done the boy out of money at their last encounter, nevertheless the boy's *first* reaction upon seeing the man was "Friend!"

The same thing happens with the same thrill to non-museum addicted tourists who stroll sadly if manfully, as when your mother forced you to take a dose of castor oil, through the Louvre. The poor fellow sees Davids, Poussins, Delacroix, and many others I cannot just now recall, but be sees nothing because he *recalls* nothing except the way his feet feel until—bingo!—there, my friend, is a familiar face, and of all things and in all places, it's the Mona Lisa, just like it was in an old schoolbook, only bigger! The Mona Lisa, Siegfried's "Funeral March" and *Midnight Cowboy* contain, in these cases, happy recognitions. They are the upper half of familiarity. The lower half also does not furnish any proof that the product is poor, although *this* half may more often lie nearer the truth. Familiarity through incessant repetition is most of it. The usher who is forced to hear *Fiddler on the Roof* at eight weekly performances fifty weeks in the year for seven or eight years cannot conceivably be expected to do other than vomit at mere mention of the show. The orchestral players who rehearse and then perform *Die Walküre* some eight or ten times a season, especially at the slow Von Karajan tempos, can never be interested in attending a performance of the same work. These are two obvious examples of the ill-effects of familiarity. And yet both *Fiddler* and *Walküre* are at least decent works of art.

In the theatre—especially the musical theatre—at a first exposure to a new show, even the most attentive audience must deal with time, which cannot possibly allow (critics to the contrary) a thorough comprehension of the various elements which go racing by simultaneously: music, lyrics, orchestrations, libretto, costumes, scenery, direction, performance, lighting, and individual actors or singers.

Becoming more and more familiar with distinguished shows such as *Fiddler on the Roof, My Fair Lady,* and *West Side Story* can only clarify them—all elements—and enhance the pleasure of an attentive audience. Each time one enjoys them more and more, one sees details missed on previous visits, and the long road from beginning to end is filled each new time with anticipated enjoyment. I feel the same way about *Hamlet,* although by now I know the play so intimately that the *new* interest is the cast and how it fulfills or fails to fulfill (in its own way) the great work. And *Meistersinger, Wozzeck,* and *Pelléas.* On the other hand, when I have attended successful theatre pieces which I have not liked (contrary to nearly everybody else) I return again and again, feeling that perhaps I had been too tired the first time or had had indigestion or just anything of my very own that had prevented my enjoyment. After seeing *Man of La Mancha* four times I concluded that nothing altered my original feeling: I did not like the idea of the play-within-a-play; I thought the music was artificial "Spanish"; I could not buy as a show what I had bought in its parent novel, *Don Quixote*—the "wisdom" of a pathetically senile man; I loathed to the point of nausea the lyrics, which were strictly from Woolworth's. I did like—and I liked it again and again—the scene with the mirrors in which the Don saw his true and pathetic self. The death scene, which never took me in, I thought was lugubrious, and I know that it defied all principles of dramaturgy which deal with matters of proportion (this was endless) and the successful transmission of emotion to an audience. For the death scene in *Man of La Mancha* begins with the hero dictating his will, the forced entrance of the heroine, who is at first unrecognized by the senile Don Quixote, then the long-ago dull business of recalling the past, the girl's reprise of "Dulcinea" (oh! happier times!), followed closely by the Don's reprise of the would-be inspirational "The Quest," followed closely by the Don, the girl and Sancho's reprise of the title song, followed by the Don's death (what a time *that* took), followed by the Padre's intoning of a *De Profundis* in Latin (of course). At last the Don (only the author Cervantes acting the part) has really died. Not long after this, Cervantes becomes himself again (what a relief!) and closes the show with the *third* reprise of "The Quest." In this case familiarity engendered boredom, just as it has for me with *Die Walküre,* the symphonies of Schumann, Mendelssohn and Tchaikovsky, and a great many plays of the Twenties and Thirties. These things become transparent, and when you see through them and you see nothing, you must become bored.

In all of the arts it is the same. I have a very good Piranesi engraving—one of the set of architectural "Imaginary Prisons." I have lived with it now for many years. Every time I focus on it, I observe something I am certain was never there before. This is an example of art in depth, which is art's concomitant, and the enjoyment of seeing it again and again—instead of diminishing—grows greater. Each time I see El Greco's "View of Toledo" I have a new experience. Also most of the plays of Shakespeare, the poems of Walt Whitman, Emily Dickinson, and e. e. cummings. When works of art in any media can stand up to this repetitive experience and continue to offer a fresh enjoyment, the fortunate beholder has achieved a maximum pleasure: "Hello, old friend." Only art can measure up to this.

Again and again the question arises in relation to a theatrical production: Does it entertain? And among the varying answers all are necessarily personal and too frequently have little to do with the quality of the product. Such reactions, when expressed by professional critics, are too often misleading to audiences—especially to those unknowing ones seeking guidance—who lack the experience of a day-to-day acquaintance with this or that judge—a factor which would enable them to recognize the judge's special foibles, limitations, and prejudices.

If one reads the newspaper and magazine critics daily or weekly —year after year—certain predilections, background (or lack of), a sense of nostalgia for the past and complaints about the present, limitations in technical comprehension of this or that element begin to emerge and assert themselves like neon signs. Some critics stand out so engagingly simply as writers that it is possible to become more fascinated and stimulated by *how* than *what* they say. This man finds it difficult to dislike anything with an attractive girl in it. Another knows a great deal about playwriting and nothing about direction. Another contradicts himself so thoroughly that no one can be certain of his conclusions. Still another knows about direction and little about music, etc., *ad nauseam.*

These differences are similar to and no more bigoted than those found among the members of an audience, with one single exception: Professional critics attend and have attended for years ("amount of exposure") nearly everything on the stage, while many of those who buy tickets, because of geography, lack of money or interest or habit, or a thousand other things, attend a theatrical performance this one time (first and last) or sporadically as they stumble on the occasion, opportunity, money, or urge to do so. Most of the time, if the theatregoer is dependent for his choice of show on the chance reading of a favorable criticism or a quote from one in an ad, he is going to be bitterly disappointed, because he is not going to be entertained as he had expected to be. This is due to inexperience with faulty communication.

All of us have been aware for too long now that critical language is in dire need of a more precise vocabulary which would clarify for all theatregoers exactly what the reviews mean and would differentiate an "entertainment" on this or that precise level from a more serious attempt or (unfortunately less often) complete achievement on another. The current imprecise vocabulary makes it appear on the one hand that critics toss garlands continuously at primitive though nearly perfectly made frolics when in most cases these turn out to be empty, uninventive, ephemeral, and going nowhere new or special. On the other hand, a grudging and worthless E for effort is given (like a bone to a dog) to something that sets out honestly and seriously (this fact does not necessarily make it humorless) with some fresh ideas, in an effort to chart a newer path, which may not quite arrive where it altogether intends. Even with this failure to achieve an ideal everything, the latter project may deserve attention and may be engaging.

It is in this situation that the critical vocabulary breaks down. The gods are unwavering. They mete out swift sentences of death to all who dare, who have the courage to try and who are very often able to show us a tiny but brilliant opening in the otherwise cloud-ridden sky. But the death ballot has been cast. It is irrevocable and the sentence is carried out. The show closes because nobody has been sufficiently stimulated to see it. The critics cannot be accounted wrong because indeed they have given E for effort and they would perjure themselves to say that (in their opinion) an imperfect piece were otherwise than imperfect. But somehow the language has to be able to say "This is imperfect but fascinating and stimulating and it ought to be seen," but say it in such a way that at least theatre-oriented people will be moved to run to the box office.

The result of this present situation—not of opinion but of language—is that some perfect piece of nonsense continues to run indefinitely and too soon gives birth to more rubber-stamp items of the same quality, while the imperfect some-sense folds its little tent and disappears at once and forever. There is surely something wrong here.

There are two factors which make this method of criticism almost inevitable. The first is the high price of tickets. With little need for conscience on the critic's part, he is honestly telling his readers which is the more perfect of the two gems, so that his readers may buy only the best. The other factor lies in the pressure from producers and the public to sell and be sold products because of their "entertainment" values. The majority of ticket buyers are from the outlying regions of the U.S. They come to New York two or three times a year to buy merchandise for their stores and, incidentally, to let Broadway amuse them. The corporations which sell to these buyers frequently provide them with theatre tickets. As these buyers or merchants usually live far from New York it follows that their theatregoing is limited. They have most often had a high school education, not had the interest, habit, or the opportunity to become acquainted with anything much more than the most rudimentary "joke" and are thirsty for entertainment, which for comfort should be as nearly as possible an extension of what they see at home on TV.

For this majority rhinoceros citizen, life itself is too sad to warrant an evening in the theatre containing less than—whee!—fun and games. But there are other considerations. These people have heard about this or that sell-out show in New York. Joe and Estelle from back home were in New York last month and couldn't get a seat for love nor money. They *know* it's good because Johnny Carson said it was two weeks ago (or was it three weeks?). Then, glory be, the "house" we buy from comes up with a pair. Hot dog. (They love it as they walk down the aisle to their seats.) Now *if* (and it's not a likely one) these seats were not available, the same eager people (many of them also, by the way, live in New York City) would, if given the choice, go to Radio City Music Hall, the Copacabana and / or a baseball or football game, or a taping of their favorite TV show.

These people who are—like it or not—the majority reside far from New York (even if they actually live there), are mentally young (listen to the jokes they tell), have had only the most elementary educations, in lieu of substantial inner resources, seldom if ever read a book, become active in (if made president of) a nonprofit public-interest enterprise that could fulfill some purpose in life, are not creative in any way—therefore they are in need of entertainment to fill a great void. What they look forward to is in a sense what conventioneers of non-professional organizations look forward to when they convene: a helluva "good" time that in no way involves the mind or challenges the nonexistent inner resources.

The theatre experience which promises them the most is the musical. It would seem to have everything: girls, costumes, an abundance of scenery, comedy, dancing, *and* music, which eases pain and sugar-coats the possibly otherwise bitter pill.

This large part of the musical-theatre audience is analogous to the unprepared man in the museum having a bout with Picasso, but with one enormous difference: If the musical "works," if it involves the audience ("entertains"), the audience need only consist of ordinary human beings capable of being communicated with. The show does not require a cultural background; the theatregoer has only to give himself to the experience.

If the foregoing seems to indicate that the musical theatre is a primitive stone pile, it is not meant to do so. In the past, the plays of Aeschylus, Sophocles, and Euripides did appeal to everyone, including the tired businessman (or so history leads us to believe).

We know that Shakespeare wrote for the majority audience of his day (without scenery or stars or even girls as added attractions) and that similar phenomena have occurred in other times and places. Sometimes these have resulted in a variety of individual, often serious, lasting works, not the least of which has been the immensely popular opera in Italy.

Any discussion of entertainment must be incomplete without some reference to its opposite number—boredom, alluded to earlier. The same factors which entertain some and fail to involve others are at work. For the insufficiently educated or for those who too frequently from childhood and through grade and high school are forced to read Shakespeare, whose language they cannot possibly then understand and enjoy, there arises such antipathy that the mere mention of any of the Bard's plays serves as a reminder of ennui, dullness, and dreariness. In this connection I am reminded of a scene in *Carousel* in which Mr. and Mrs. Snow, having recently returned from a trip to New York, are having an unhappy exchange.

> ENOCH SNOW: We also saw *Julius Caesar*. Wouldn't that be a better play to quote from?
> CARRIE SNOW: I don't remember much of that one. All the men was dressed in nightgowns and it made me sleepy.

It would seem that the operettas of Gilbert and Sullivan are at the opposite end of the spectrum from Shakespeare, but identical mental associations link the two in the minds of those people who during their formative periods were required to perform the great English operettas without comprehending them. By adulthood these same people have developed such a dread of Gilbert and Sullivan, such a deep recall of boredom that they can seldom be persuaded to attend a performance.

The modestly educated, theatre-oriented adult is bored by the too obvious, while the opposite kind of person is amused by the same thing. The first group will most likely not be wearied by the sheer length of a performance *(Hamlet, Die Meistersinger, Who's Afraid of Virginia Woolf?)* because he has the necessary background to become engrossed in what happens all along the way. Those in the second group generally will find the same lengthy works tiresome to the extreme. The first group members have learned a language that remains largely meaningless to members of the second group. The latter simply comprehend so little of what is being said, sung, or enacted that in the end they feel excluded, become inattentive, and are finally left behind in a state of boredom.

One of the chief qualities in a workable musical (intellectually simple) is its ability to communicate to the emotions (happy or unhappy) of just everybody. "Everybody" would include the intellectually "prepared" as well as those less developed. This quality is not a part of many slight, musicless comedies which appeal to one group and not the other. These shows have a way of becoming very big for a period, then becoming quickly dated and unworkable. The same situation exists among many "intellectual" musicless plays which appeal to the much smaller other group—the better educated. These can also go quickly out of style.

I believe that this is an important point, and if it is true, then the musical, at its best, today stands in a unique position and represents our time, since it can relate to all people as once did the plays of Euripides and, much later, those of Shakespeare.

It would be unfair to fail to examine briefly the first group—those who have background, reside geographically close enough to our theatre, who are able to attend at will (and can afford to), the intellectually better developed who have had more extensive experience in theatregoing, and whose reasons for going (these, how-ever, can be manifold) are to be found to coincide *exactly* with what the other group also seeks: entertainment. Here, however, the word takes on an enlarged meaning. It is irrefutable that the mem-bers of the less-oriented group look upon "entertainment" as "amusement." For the other group "entertainment" is a matter of being interested, stimulated, and involved. These people do not fault being amused, but if they are really knowledgeable and expe-rienced they are bored with the too familiar, too shallow, obvious, laborious attempts at humor that end up being predictable reruns of many, many other things from the past. Since as a group these peo-ple are educated, mature, backgrounded, and experienced in enter-tainment-seeking, they often look forward to intellectual plays, sometimes avant-garde ones, serious problem plays, ballet, opera, well-done classical revivals, etc. On the other hand, if they want revue-type nightclubs they will largely avoid the broad Copacabana in favor of the more "special" Plaza 9 and the Upstairs at the Downstairs.

In a broad sense Group B is not inferior to Group A; it has for a variety of reasons simply not enjoyed the advantages of the Group A people. And what is important to this discussion is the fact that what entertains one usually bores the other and vice versa. The exception, stated a bit earlier, is to be found in the best of the musicals, which can engage *all* people, and this is frequently even true of people who do not necessarily understand the English lan-guage. But the characters are who they seem to be and are univer-sal. The plot is essentially uncomplicated, and the music requires no translation. An example of the very big—but now you see it, now you don't—is a musical like *The Music Man,* which opened in 1957 and ran for 1,375 performances. This was a hit and one which you needed no background to be entertained by. In fact, the less background, the better you liked it. It was corny, brassy, and puerile, a mindless circus parade without the inner excitement. After Broadway it became a movie. The stage company toured here and there, then it was available to the amateur theatres, where it thrived for a short while. And now it is nearly dead, unlike *My Fair Lady,* which opened a year earlier, ran approximately twice as long on Broadway, movied itself, still plays in nearly every country of the world, and has lost none of its appeal in both amateur and professional revivals. *The Music Man* is a traveling-salesman joke straight out of Joe Miller, whereas *My Fair Lady* is an enchanting, witty version of Cinderella created with taste, style, charm, and containing not "Seventy-Six Trombones," which will draw out the cheering crowds for a moment, but "I've Grown Accustomed to Her Face," which will touch the hearts of every kind of human being here, in Ankara, Timbuktu, Tel-Aviv, and Spitzenbergen. Both shows entertain; the lights went out on the coarse one some time ago.

In the end, the best musicals will continue to operate for and relate to all kinds of people over such a long period of time and in so many different environments that even the financial returns will outdo the less good but temporary smash hits, just as the novels of Proust and Thomas Mann will continue on and on, long after Jacqueline Susann has disappeared. Do you recall Elinor Glyn's *It?* Do you recall Elinor Glyn?

The truth is that art has never been created successfully in a vacuum. Nor has workable theatre. In fact, obviously no theatre (and especially today's costly one) can exist without an audience. It is economically impossible and also undesirable. But it is also artistically unthinkable. Leonardo, Michelangelo, Orlando di Lasso, Mozart, Thomas Morley, J. S. Bach, Shakespeare, Dryden, and all the rest worked for specific audiences. It was only in the most decadent part of the nineteenth century that artists created almost exclusively for themselves and to very little if any other purpose. All of the aforementioned creative artists made their works to please, to satisfy, to fit into current needs, or to suit a definite purpose at a definite time. Although the taste of patrons who helped to make the work possible was the first to be considered, it was fairly predictable that the majority of people would also react favorably to what had been ordered.

Those works made to complement religion were aimed at heightening the spiritual experience. The profane or secular works were aimed at providing pure entertainment. In both cases, the aim was directed at engaging or involving the viewer or listener. When religious music became so complex and self-interested that the public no longer comprehended it, the Reformation occurred. (The music was only symptomatic, of course.) For a while it reverted to healthy simplicity. Thus everyone could again participate and comprehend. The average human being once again received what was offered. He was included.

Recently there was a musical (off-Broadway) called *Whispers on the Wind*. It was a lovely show, charming, fresh, and wonderfully acted and sung. It died within a week without ever having been able to find its audience, which surely exists somewhere, though the show could have appealed only to the educated, imaginative, and theatre-oriented. It is my feeling that the language of Clive Barnes, our No. 1 man on the No. 1 paper, *The New York Times,* pulled the trigger that killed it dead, and certainly Mr. Barnes's review was anything but con. I feel sure its writer was filled to the brim with love when he did the deed. But just look at *the praise* this review is filled with:

OFF-BROADWAY MUSICAL SHOWS GENTLENESS
A gentle musical is something of a rarity, and, yet, gentleness is the pervading quality of *Whispers on the Wind*, which opened last night at the Theatre de Lys.

Does anybody want to rush to buy a ticket to a gentle show? This makes me recall the old Charles Ray movies and a flock of sheep and something that will soothe me to sleep.

The show is an imaginatively staged biography of a young man who is born, grows up in a Middle Western town, goes to school, drops out of college, comes to New York, succeeds in publishing and gets married.

Nobody in the world can fault this as an accurate *reporting of* the plot. Yet the reader of this *New York Times* review is just very likely going to say, "Well, what's new, Babe?" and turn to the sports page to see who is in the hospital (exciting!) this morning. Barnes's account is true, but since he seems to like and respect this show, he ought to be at some pains to *make* the public want to anticipate seeing it, and as Mr. Barnes is not naïve, he *knows Whispers on the Wind* isn't going to live unless the audience rushes to it and fast. The plot as he sketches it (you can't really do justice to this show or any element of it without all of its concomitants right there to give it its fundamental quality) is plain dull because it's been done many times before—just about beginning with *Everyman* (late fifteenth century).

> The book and lyrics are by John B. Kuntz and the music is by Lor Crane, and both words and music vary in quality more than they should, but when good they are very good. Mr. Kuntz's concern is with nostalgia. He writes with some of the free-flowing imagery although far less vividly—that Dylan Thomas used in *Under Milk-Wood,* and, particularly at the beginning, perhaps, there is a certain similarity to Thornton Wilder's *Our Town.*

Here Barnes sends us fast just anywhere but to *Whispers on the Wind.* The music, lyrics, and book "vary in quality more than they should, but when good they are very good." It so happens that I agree with Mr. Barnes, but if I don't want to kill the horse, I don't pull the trigger. Then he tells us, and not maliciously but poorly calculated for helpfulness, that the writer writes "far less vividly" than Dylan Thomas. (Did he forget about Shakespeare? Why the need for this and the next comparison?) " . . . at the beginning, perhaps, there is a certain similarity to Thornton Wilder's *Our Town. (That* will make us all hurry to the box office.) And was Thornton Wilder the first playwright to employ this device?

> Mr. Kuntz has a nice way with the salient detail that can evoke a time and a place. A boy in the woods, a warm day and furry caterpillar crawling leisurely over his hands. Or a boy being sent to stay with his grandmother, and the smell of the leather upholstery in the car as he is led by uncles to that adventure of that first trip away from home.
> The difficulty with this kind of writing is the ease with which it can slide into sentimentality and a kind of fey self-satisfaction with its own poetic verbiage. And this does occasionally happen with *Whispers on the Wind.* The author wants simplicity but he does occasionally settle for banality. I liked, however, the humor of the piece—wry and aware and very warm. Mr. Kuntz

> makes fun of life, not people, and this is pleasant, and,
> unfortunately, unusual.

The fourth paragraph will send the incipient poets running for free tickets, having smelled a failure if indeed a poetic one. In the fifth paragraph we are further encouraged by "sentimentality and a kind of fey self-satisfaction with its own poetic verbiage." (I just can't wait, Mother. Give me a nickel for some pot.) "The author wants simplicity but he does occasionally settle for banality." (It's only a little gas, honey. Just take an Alka Seltzer.)

The vocabulary problem of this critic was never more clearly illustrated than with "I liked, *however,* the humor..." This is the dead giveaway that, in all honesty, Mr. Barnes didn't like *anything.* He grudgingly, *however, did* like the humor. It's a bit like telling an actress on opening night of her performance, which you thought stank, that her costumes, however, were divine.

> Lor Crane's music is a notable plus for the show. At
> times, it is something like Simon and Garfunkel, but it
> has its own character and its own sound. There is a melo-
> dious sweetness here that is never allowed to become
> cloying, and yet the music supports the action with
> deftly dramatic finesse.

Very nice and sweet. The music is like somebody else's, but it has its own character and its own sound. Which is it? You can't really have it both ways at once.

> Burt Brinckerhoff's staging is fluid, stylish and, like
> the setting by David F. Segal and the happily modish cos-
> tumes by Joseph G. Aulisi, has a neatly spare elegance.
> The setting is nothing but handsome ramps and screens,
> which is beautiful in itself but purposely anonymous.

The " . . . staging ... like the setting . . . and ... costumes . . . has a neatly spare elegance." That recalls for me the discomfort of staying in a palace. "The setting is *nothing* but handsome ramps and screens, which is beautiful in itself but purposely anonymous."

Screens and ramps have thrilled me since Robert Edmond Jones. Certainly anybody in the theatre knows what Mr. Barnes means, but why make it sound, to those who don't know and who matter most, so unattractive and poverty-stricken? I simply *love* the "purposely anonymous." Makes you want to be equally purposely anonymous out of the audience.

> Into this arena, the actors create their world. Apart from the hero, all the actors play many roles according to the exigencies of the story, and Mr. Brinckerhoff and his cast manage these protean changes with clarity and charm. It is, luckily, a very strong cast.

Very nice, but what about "luckily"? Doesn't that convey the feeling that, but for this (and it *is* the meaning), *Whispers on the Wind* would sure be in trouble? (They were, but they might not otherwise have known it for a few days.)

> David Cryer, with his powerful voice and presence, is superb as the detached and, yet, compassionate Narrator, and a gleaming Nancy Dussault, his co-star, is equally good in a myriad of roles ranging from the very young to the very old.
>
> The cast's versatility is exceptional. R. G. Brown, at his best as a hilarious New York cab driver, Mary Louise Wilson and, as the hero, Patrick Fox, are all not merely accomplished but thoroughly likable. Indeed, *Whispers on the Wind* is a thoroughly likable show.

Bully for the cast—and I should hope so—but then why end with "a thoroughly likable show"? This is the sort of thing you say about your great-aunt whom you have to kiss mercifully only on one day a year. It is not what you say about a very good picture, poem, novel, or musical—that is if you care for it.

In all honesty I have no idea how a show such as *Whispers on the Wind* could have survived. My point is that it was not given the chance. Critical words such as "special," "attractive," "touching," "lovely...... endearing," "unique," and many more were, I think, all applicable and I even believe Mr. Barnes would agree. But without a *strong Times* as opposed to a *gentle Times,* this poor out-of-the way show was dead when it began.

Another show that by no means shared the fate of *Whispers on the Wind—Hair*—began off-Broadway in 1967 when it ran eight weeks. It was hailed as "brilliant entertainment." At that time it had twenty songs. *Hair* was moved to a discotheque, retained its popularity, trimmed much of what plot it had and added more songs. After a few weeks it trimmed off dialogue still more and now with twenty-six songs (despite deletions of six of the original ones) and the addition of some nudity, it is playing in its third year in New York with great success. The fact that *Hair* is entertainment is indisputable. That it is a "musical" is highly questionable. It is chiefly a song recital in which many of the songs and the lyrics are highly workable.

Despite its success, I cannot believe that it is important in the stream of our musical-theatre development. It may be important as an "opening up" of the musical theatre as we have known it. It entertains mostly the young, who need bring nothing to it, as what is seen and heard is primitive as well as overpoweringly noisy. It assaults many older people and at least for a while it was a "must" for theatregoers if for no reason other than the much publicized momentary and quite unsensational nudity.

Another "entertainment" which comes immediately to mind—this time a revue with sketches and songs all with well-defined beginnings and endings, which *Hair* usually eschews—is *Oh! Calcutta!,* the *real* nude show. The sketches here are unfunny to the extreme. The music is thin and puny. The show has to be boring to everyone who possesses even a fragment of mentality. The nudity, presented *in toto* in the very first number, palls in a matter of minutes, and you wonder perhaps for the first time at the profound importance of costumes in the theatre.

When I saw *Oh! Calcutta!* and was deeply bored and then resentful of its childishness, the laughter and applause (not much) came from middle-age people (frustrated is my guess) who giggled with a sense of wicked embarrassment at what they saw.

The big girlie revues of the Twenties and Thirties entertained general audiences made up of people from both kinds of backgrounds. The sketches were truly funny and new. There were great stars and great clowns. The girls—often the central attraction—wore opulent quasi-costumes that suggested without revealing what must always be less appealing than the imagination is capable of manufacturing.

The smaller intellectual revues of the Twenties and Thirties lacked the girls and the expensive wardrobes but had newer music and funnier sketches. Also new-to-be stars. *Oh! Calcutta!* has none of that and nothing as an adequate substitute for it. A dull thud for all but the pathetically frustrated voyeur. Entertainment not for the theatre but for the peephole.

And so there are shows which obviously appeal in some way to one group and not another. Some of them have a way of becoming very big for a period and then vanishing altogether—unlike authentic art.

All art provides entertainment-involvement, largely through personal identification. Sometimes that "entertainment" that art alone can communicate is limited to those who, due to their own relationship to time-present, are able to perceive what is, always has been, and always will be there—able, therefore, to comprehend and enjoy. The latter is another of those conditions which turns on or shuts off the possibility of communication. For example, today Berg's opera *Wozzeck,* written in 1925, seems to many people to be so far in the future that it communicates nothing to a majority of listeners. To those who are *au courant* (due to background and concurrency of time)*Wozzeck* is a wonderful theatre experience and a musical masterpiece. But the barrier to comprehension due to lack of relationship to time-present is constantly disappearing like a mirage, only to turn up again in future time. Wagner's *Tristan und Isolde* at its premiere in 1865 was received with the same hostility that greeted *Wozzeck* sixty years later. Today's ardent defenders of the Wagnerian faith—having progressed in time so that they have come full circle—are among the *Wozzeck* detractors.

But *Tristan* is art and so is *Wozzeck,* and the centuries will pass by bidding them farewells just as they have the Hermes of Praxiteles (fourth century B.C.), the David of Michelangelo (late fifteenth century), the Greek classic plays, those of Shakespeare, etc. All of these examples are art—some received at first with contentiousness, others with love. The best art is entertaining and has the power to impart its meanings as well as its mysteries to all people at all times and in all places. Just so the best musicals seem to be surviving this period of violent change and will most likely continue on their way around the world and again and again there and at home.

The enormous success *of Show Boat* in London (1971) calls attention to at least one aspect of the fate of this show since its debut in 1927. *Show Boat* has had (besides the current London version) one major revival in New York in 1946, another in 1966, a published version which uses part of both, and the original vocal score which agrees with none of these *in toto.*

The list of differences among these versions would fill books, although the essential structure remains the same in all. Songs and scenes have been added and deleted and the dialogue has been cut, "improved," and even, in some instances, added to.

In my opinion, all of this fussing only proves that producers, directors, and performers so admire *Show Boat,* and at the same time are so aware of its book weaknesses in the face of its musical strength, that the attempts at "improving" it are testimonials to the general high esteem in which it is held.

In America we grew out of the artificiality that immediately preceded us and finally we matured in a theatro-semi-realistic way that represented us, our country, and our lives—and in time, all lives. This is one of the most important achievements of the best musical theatre: the ability to involve all people, the astute and the non-astute, because what all people have in common is the capacity to feel. Drama and non-musical comedy are often non-productive of feeling. Musical theatre, by its nature, cannot be.

While the best opera retains its place in world repertory because of the quality of the music, the best plays because of literary and dramatic achievements, the best musicals survive because of simple universality largely propagated through feeling. This is our contribution to entertainment.

Although the ambiguity of the critical language and often the opinions themselves of some of the umpires have shortened the lives of too many serious if somewhat imperfect plays due to a misunderstanding of "entertainment," the same factors have tended to make successes out of not really so good musicals, but have never thus far harmed the best of them. The best of the musicals reach and involve everyone—even the umpires.

COMMENTS ON COMEDY AND ENTERTAINMENT

When Engel wrote *Words with Music* the term "musical comedy" was still the standard way of referring to the subject he was exploring. In that context a chapter entitled "Comedy and Entertainment" seemed entirely natural. Nowadays it requires some explanation. Around the time Engel was writing his book, comedy was changing radically, in response to the frenzied world of the late Sixties and early Seventies.

As for entertainment, in the context of that world, it was vaguely disreputable, associated as it was with the bourgeois world American youth was both attacking and, in theory, transcending.

Even disregarding the huge cultural changes that were occurring, comedy often loses its luster because the things that make people laugh in one period often leave them cold in another. Think how difficult it is to perform Shakespeare's comedies, with their word play that must have seemed hilarious 400 years ago but now strikes us as merely tedious.

Centuries aren't required to make humor seem stale and unfunny. Even the jokes of fifty years earlier can strike us as lame, although a lot of the comedy in classic musicals still works surprisingly well. When country singer Reba McEntire played Annie Oakley in *Annie, Get Your Gun* on Broadway in 2001, the jokes, more than half a century old, seemed entirely fresh. And the resounding laughter that filled the theatre made it clear I wasn't alone in thinking so.

When I last saw *Kiss Me, Kate*, in early September 2001, there was plenty of laughter all through the house. But a young man sitting near me cracked not a single smile during "Brush Up Your Shakespeare" until the rhyme suggesting that if you want to give a woman pleasure show her your "Measure for Measure," accompanied by a gesture to the crotch. This elicited a hearty guffaw. I had the feeling all the wit based on Shakespeare play titles was meaningless to him.

Similarly, a lot of Lorenz Hart's cleverness must elude contemporary audiences. In its time it was topical, and the range of allusions in a song like "Bach, Beethoven and Brahms" in *On Your Toes* suggests that audiences were conversant with a wide range of references.

One of the jokes, for example, requires an awareness of what was a new opera in 1937, Shostakovich's *Lady Macbeth of Mtsensk*, which Hart ribs in his line about "Lady Macbeth from Minsky's," referring to the burlesque house. That the audience would know Minsky's was to be expected. That they would catch the reference to the opera, which aroused great controversy at its Moscow premiere but was hardly an everyday topic in New York, suggests the audience was extremely knowledgeable.

In his discussion of comedy Engel draws on a wide variety of sources, making reference to Feydeau, Labiche, Shaw, Noel Coward and Neil Simon. He's harsh on Simon, many of whose plays he considered simply collections of wisecracks. In the thirty years since *Words with Music*, however, Simon has matured as a writer. Many of his early comedies have a desperate quality, as if he were uncomfortable not hearing the audience laugh and was trying energetically to fill every moment with yocks.

In part the nearly hysterical quality of the writing stemmed from the medium in which Simon got his start, television, in which a lull in laughter might induce the viewer to switch channels.

Late in his career, however, Simon felt comfortable enough with his reputation and with his experience in the theatre to use it as a medium for autobiographical exploration (in the three plays whose titles all begin with B—*Brighton Beach Memoirs*, *Biloxi Blues*, and *Broadway Bound*). His most remarkable play may be *Lost in Yonkers*, in which whatever autobiographical elements there are have been deeply submerged and in which serious issues are raised without hitting the audience on the head, specifically the issue of how to survive in a dangerous world, which Simon had addressed more narrowly in *Biloxi Blues*.

Curiously, given his enormous success, Simon has written few musical theatre books. One, back in 1966, was for *Sweet Charity*, a Cy Coleman show based on the Fellini film *Nights of Cabiria*. Another was for the Marvin Hamlisch score, *They're Playing Our Song*. Neither was an unqualified success, perhaps for the reason cited by Douglas Watt early in Simon's career—his characters, though they make us laugh, lack charm.

In recent years the tenor of TV humor has changed radically. Simon, for example, began writing for an early Fifties comedy program, *Your Show of Shows*, starring Sid Caesar and Imogene Coca. In the early days of television, when not every American home even owned a TV set, the humor was directed toward an upper-middle-class audience, which shared certain cultural knowledge and awareness.

It was also directed toward adult viewers. Today it's aimed, as is much entertainment, toward a teenage mentality, which is yet another reason why musical theatre, which has traditionally assumed its audience was adult, is at a great distance from popular culture. The humor of *The Simpsons* has had a great impact on the movies, not to mention other TV shows. But it's an adolescent sensibility, not suitable for all subjects.

Engel cites Chaplin's as a style of humor with universal appeal. Time has not dimmed the brilliance of Chaplin's comedy. Nor has it diminished the effectiveness of, say, the gravediggers' scene in *Hamlet* or the porter's monologue in *Macbeth*. All of these styles fall under the heading "adult," which is why the boisterous, rowdy humor of the gravediggers does not seem amiss in what is otherwise a grim tragedy.

Correctly, Engel notes that even in as serious a musical as *West Side Story*, the humor of "Gee, Officer Krupke" fills a great emotional need. The characters in *West Side Story*, of course, are supposed to be teenagers, and certainly the lyrics reflect their youthful anger, but the sensibility is not adolescent. It's clear that adults (that is, Bernstein, Laurents and Sondheim) are in charge. In recent decades we've cultivated an adolescent frame of mind. At no time in history has such a mentality served as a foundation for theatre.

Apart from this major shift in sensibility, which broadens the gap between serious and comic elements, there's another reason why comedy plays a decreasing role in musicals. Often nowadays musicals are produced not as commercial ventures, which they always were in the old days, but as offerings by not-for-profit theatres.

When musicals were commercial entities—and all the classic musicals, from *West Side Story* to *Porgy and Bess*, fell under that heading—comedy was an essential selling point. When they're part of a not-for-profit season, however, they can be presented as Art. Comedy might detract from their pretensions.

Looking back over musicals of the last few decades it seems remarkable how few outright comedies there have been—a notable exception was the Larry Gelbart-Cy Coleman-David Zippel *City of Angels*, with its witty juxtaposition of "real life" in Los Angeles and a film noir plot. (The emphasis on comedy did not preclude Coleman and Zippel writing an absolutely heartbreaking ballad, "With Every Breath I Take.")

A more recent instance is *Hairspray*, based on the John Waters film of the same name. Set in the early Sixties in Waters' native Baltimore, it's a tale of racial understanding based on the appeal to both white and black of black-based music. The score by Marc Shaiman and Scott Wittman tells the story in a tongue-in-cheek way that never lets it slide into ponderousness or sentimentality.

In recent years many musicals have attempted greater seriousness, seldom with satisfying results. If someone had come to Arnold Saint Subber, who produced the original *Kiss Me, Kate*, with the idea of presenting a musical based on the lynching of Leo Franks in Atlanta on the eve of World War I, it's unlikely he would have signed on. I mention him because he did produce Porter's masterpiece rather than *Hellzapoppin*. He was a man of great taste. But it probably would have struck him as exceedingly strange to do a musical about a lynching.

Parade, Jason Robert Brown's musical about Leo Franks that was produced by the Lincoln Center Theatre in 1997, did have humorous elements, like an extended number in which Franks, who was accused of having lascivious thoughts about the young women who worked for him, performs in a fantasy dance based on his enemies' lewd idea of him. Only an audience conditioned to accept the bizarre and unsavory as evidence of "transgressive" Art would stomach such a number unquestioningly. Nor was its score of a depth or audacity that justified the unorthodox choice of material.

It's possible that had the book for *Parade* been written by Bertolt Brecht, there might have been some bite to the material, but here the conception of the musical added little to our understanding, emotional or historical, about this deplorable incident. Many who saw *Parade* probably knew going into the theatre that lynching was not a good thing. It's hard to imagine the musical in any way enhanced this perception.

This, I fear, may also be part of the legacy of rock, which lectured its listeners in a self-important, solemn way, generally informing them of things they already accepted. You didn't hear a lot of rock songs, for example, extolling the virtues of small businesses.

Parade, however, also owed a lot to its director, Harold Prince, who, for a period in the mid-Eighties, seemed to be drifting without a clear sense of purpose. After his two triumphs, *Evita* and *Sweeney Todd*, Prince experienced a profound setback in the most important of his collaborations, that with Sondheim, in their uncompelling version of *Merrily We Roll Along*.

In 1982, a year after the financial failure of *Merrily*, Prince collaborated with Betty Comden and Adolph Green and composer Larry Grossman on a sequel to Ibsen's *A Doll's House*. The show had a picaresque, aimless quality in stark contrast to the relentless inevitability of Ibsen's play. In 1985, with Grossman and lyricist Hal Hackady, Prince conceived *Grind*, set in a Thirties burlesque house but intended to dramatize American racism. As with the later *Parade*, it told us things we already knew, and in a strident way that only pointed up the obviousness.

Starting with *Show Boat* in 1927, the American musical theatre has not shied away from seriousness in subject matter, but recently it has lost its ability to treat weighty issues without losing its sense of humor or its ability to entertain the audience.

Admittedly it has become harder to be humorous because the audience has become more fragmented. In the Thirties, for example, it could be assumed that the humor of the Marx Brothers or of the so-called "screwball" comedies would cut across all barriers.

A few years ago, in a tribute to Jack Benny on Public Radio a writer who grew up in Greenwich Village reminisced about being sent on an errand by her mother on a Sunday evening in the Forties, when the Jack Benny show was on the radio. As it happened, it was a summer evening. Air conditioning was rare, so every window was open. As she wended her way through the Village streets, she recalled, she missed nary a word of the Benny program since every radio was tuned to it. That is a phenomenon that can only be paralleled by the final episodes of such shows as *M*A*S*H* or *Seinfeld*.

In recent decades there has been a huge invasion of British humor into American television through PBS, which imports such shows as *Monty Python's Flying Circus*, *Fawlty Towers* or the Patricia Routledge (it's pronounced "Bouquet") series *Keeping Up Appearances*. All these are alternatives to the sitcom humor that dominates American TV. Not all of it is breakthrough comedy, though the Pythons achieved a huge following with humor that in no way condescended to its audience. (Imagine an American network comedy offering a sketch based on the "All England Proust Recitation Competition.")

Given the correlation between people who write musical comedy and those who watch public television, it's strange how little of such humor has influenced our musical theatre. The closest it has come is some of the broad jokes in the musical adaptation of the film *Thoroughly Modern Millie*, like the use of subtitles in Chinese. If one wants to analyze this material one might even consider it courageous. The point of basing musicals on old movies (*Millie* opened a few weeks after a musical based on *The Sweet Smell of Success*) is that they're relatively safe. So to introduce a whole new style of humor implies an element of risk. In this case it also flouts, though gently, the rules of political correctness.

When *The Producers* had its triumphant opening in the spring of 2001, Mel Brooks was proud to reintroduce burlesque to Broadway. At a time when humor was not the strong point in musicals the power of low humor was especially noteworthy. Forty years earlier there'd been a similar reliance on burlesque in *A Funny Thing Happened on the Way to the Forum*, but at that time, the spring of 1962, comedy itself had not yet gone out of fashion in musicals. So *Forum* seemed regressive—happily so—rather than remarkable.

As for the other word in Engel's chapter title, Entertainment, which often implies crass, mindless pleasure, we have broadened our understanding of what it can mean. *Pacific Overtures*, which draws on Asian theatre conventions as well as Western traditions, can be entertaining. So can *Falsettoland*, a musical in which a leading character dies of AIDS.

Today's audience is more fragmented than the theatre audience of 1950, most of whom watched the same TV shows, listened to the same radio programs, read the same newspapers and magazines. There was a lot of common ground for theatre writers to build from. TV is still the major frame of reference, but even it offers an infinitely greater palette than once it did. For a writer trying to reach a broad audience, this can be a challenge as well as a drawback.

7

The New-Old

Psychologists tell us that we live forward, think backward; a formula that really divides the past from the future; two aspects of one and the same thing.

James G. Huneker
The Outlook, 1921

Having discussed the developed form of musical theatre to which we came about 1940, I find it interesting to note that although it influenced nothing that was eventually accomplished here in America, there existed here in full bloom nearly two and a half centuries ago a great musical comedy, and the model for all librettos existed even more than a century earlier.

John Gay's *The Beggar's Opera* (1728) is generally considered to be the first musical comedy and has seldom been off the boards since it opened. In the words of Simon Trussler, *The Beggar's Opera* is "comedy, farce, satire, ballad-play and burlesque all at once."

John Gay's ballad-opera was written and presented during the corrupt administration of Sir Robert Walpole, who, under George II, was the first Prime Minister of England. It successfully lampooned Walpole, who nevertheless took no action against it. By the unique use of characters of the underworld employed satirically, Gay made it abundantly clear that he was in reality concerned with the upper classes, with whom he equated the scum of the earth. *The Beggar's Opera* is unique satire because while it was written about and for Gay's particular time and place, it escaped these and became universal and timeless, exactly what Aristophanes was unable to do.

The music consists of an original overture composed by the musical director, Dr. Pepusch, *and* sixty-nine short songs, all adaptations of everything from folk songs to excerpts from a Handel opera. The show is also a satire on Italian opera, which was becoming more and more popular in England through the talents of a German composer who wrote them profusely—George Frederick Handel.

The show was divided into three acts, and its plot was wisely tailored for the two breaks. The characters were pickpockets, gangsters, whores, and fences who were not only operating against the law but doing everything possible to "rub out" each other.

The plot is essentially simple, although no characters, setting, or comparable satire existed prior to it. All of the lyrics are models of particularization—all are a part of the play's action.

The Beggar's Opera might have been a model for *Guys and Dolls.* Its satire of people in high places, the humor in both dialogue and lyrics are unequaled by any show since. It has already had a long history, which seems to imply that it will live on indefinitely. In our own time it has had many revivals everywhere. It was badly mangled as a movie with elaborate orchestrations and some new music by Benjamin Britten. Just before 1920 Bertolt Brecht transformed it into *The Threepenny Opera* with music by Kurt Weill. This, too, was and is a great success.

It is interesting to compare the difference between the Gay-Pepusch version and the Brecht-Weill one. Principally, the original is lighthearted, gay, funny, and free. However, Brecht used Gay's characters and situations with different beginnings and endings and, of course, all new music and lyrics, and it is full of bitterness, "drama," jaundiced at the society which the first version lightheartedly lampooned. The two versions are at opposite ends of the same pole. Gay's work contains clear-cut subplots, romance, particularization in the sixty-nine lyrics, comedy, and satire. The characters are two-dimensional because—like *Guys and Dolls*—this is a fable and the players recognizably represent their likes in a much higher social strata. The songs are full of contrasts, and it must be remembered that the tunes were already well known to the audiences even without the aid of phonograph records, radio, and TV.

The Beggar's Opera is a one-of-a-kind, unique model of style, humor, and workability. We have seldom strayed far away from it, never topped it. And so John Gay and his immortal *Beggar's Opera,* even performed here in America in the eighteenth century, gave us little more than an unforgettable evening's pleasure. We had to go all the way to Vienna to gain the inspiration for our own theatre when what we needed to know was already fully developed more than a century earlier.

While John Gay created a full musical comedy form in 1728, Shakespeare, a century earlier, was already the model librettist, for his plays alone today are the archetypes of what is needed in the musical "book."

To go from the outside in, Shakespeare's plays are all multi-scene, as are all of our musicals. It is curious that our reasons for this practice and Shakespeare's were the results of opposite conditions. In Shakespeare's theatre there was no scenery, but most information as to time and place was contained in the dialogue. On the other hand, in the twentieth-century American musical theatre the stage machinery is so fully developed that we are able to employ an almost unlimited number of sets, following one another with split-second rapidity. The author has only to dream the sequence of places and the designer will provide the machinery for their realization.

Although the nonmusical theatre in our country has infrequently gone in for multi-scene production (exceptions to the contrary), the current tendency—what with the rising costs of production and operation—is proceeding in the opposite direction: unit sets, representational or abstract set-in pieces which can mean all things to all people.

But is it not curious that the sceneryless theatre of Shakespeare and the sceneryful theatre of today's musical should result in similar writing practices? However, the shape and the content of the musical librettos which define the shape follow the basic form of Shakespeare's plays.

In all of the Bard's dramas, in the "cells" (scenes) which make up the acts, there is a consistent technique which could serve as a model for contemporary librettists. One by one these "cells" terminate strongly with an exclamation point while—at the same time—they thrust the observer ahead: What is going to happen next? That is why it was not actually necessary for Shakespeare to write any indication of time. We *know,* for example, at the end of Scene 2 after Hamlet has been told of his father's ghost that he will go to confront the ghost. ("I will watch tonight; perchance 'twill walk again.") We *know* at the end of Scene 3 in *Macbeth* that the antihero, having been named Thane of Cawdor as prophesied by the witches (the first of the two prophecies has materialized), that Macbeth will help himself to realize their second prediction of his becoming king. As a matter of fact, this was fate's trap for Macbeth. As if this *idea* of moving ahead were not enough, Shakespeare often concluded scenes with lines which baldy *stated* what it is we should expect. As in *Macbeth,* prior to the murder of Duncan, the king:

> MACBETH: I go, and it is done; the bell invites me.
> Hear it not, Duncan; for it is a knell
> That summons thee to heaven or to hell.

Later in the same play, in a scene largely between Malcolm and Macduff, the latter has learned of the savage murder of his wife and children. Malcolm ends the scene with:

> Come, go we to the king; our power is ready;
> Our lack is nothing but our leave. Macbeth
> Is ripe for shaking, and the powers above
> Put on their instruments. Receive what cheer you may;
> The night is long that never finds the day.

One of the most important factors common to musicals as well as Shakespeare (and there are many others) is that the principal characters are identified as such immediately. As pointed out earlier, in the miniature Scene 1 of *Macbeth* (the witches) Macbeth is named. In Scene 2 we learn of a new honor that has come to him, and in Scene 3 we meet him and learn much more. He is ambition-ridden, sometimes weak, often pitiable, and a human being. Our very first encounter with his wife tells us unmistakably who and what she is: Lady Macbeth will manage things as she wishes. In *Julius Caesar* the title character enters in Scene 2 (following a brief introduction) and *dramatized* in that scene we are given all we need to know. King Lear enters shortly after the play commences. Prior to his entrance, however, we have heard about "the division of the kingdom" and as he is about to appear we hear "the king is coming." In what follows the king himself states his aim and we immediately sense the disaster which will sit upon the entire play.

Hamlet, Romeo, Falstaff, Othello also are all clearly defined when we first encounter them. Everything that is to happen to them proceeds in a straight line and we are carried along—sometimes breathlessly—to experience the unfolding and the denouement.

In Shakespeare's plays there are no character ambiguities. To the audience, even the villains and dark plotting are made clearly known. Iago tells us directly of his evil intents. The Macbeths make no secret of their murderous plan. Brutus proclaims his intentions and so do all the others. Characters are always (to the audience) precisely who and what they seem to be.

In musicals again, it is essential that this same order of things be observed, that there be no tricky character surprises to confuse, no complexities to be unraveled. (Is not this one sound reason for our not having developed any "horror" or "mystery" librettos?) In Shakespeare, the songs—exquisite as they are—are largely decorative, external to the drama (important exceptions to be noted) and usually assigned to minor characters, drunks, or urchins commanded to vocalize. Often these songs—especially the sad ones—prepare the color or heighten the mood of the scene ("Blow, blow, thou winter wind," "Orpheus with his lute," "Hark, hark the lark," etc.), but in no way detract from the plot line.

Curiously enough, in the most romantic of Shakespeare's plays, *Romeo and Juliet,* there isn't a single song, nor is there any in two of his best frolics (not only suggestive of musical comedy but actually, in our time, employed as such), *The Comedy of Errors* and *The Taming of the Shrew.* So the pattern for song inclusion or exclusion in no way clearly emerges. They simply are or are not. Most often the songs are non-functional as regards the characters who sing them.

Of the fifty-one songs in all of Shakespeare's plays, nine are sung by drunks, six by fairies, and twenty-seven by minor (often nameless) characters. The remaining nine are given to principals. The fools or clowns in *Twelfth Night, King Lear,* and *Hamlet* (two gravediggers) are among the lesser characters with eight songs among them.

All of these songs are introduced as such. They do not emerge as integral parts of the plays unless the characters (sometimes) are drunk. (Ophelia's and Desdemona's songs are the exceptions.) A typical and clear example of the "announced" song is to be found in *Henry VIII,* in Queen Katherine's apartment at the opening of Act Three. The queen says (addressing one of her women at work):

> Take thy lute, wench; my soul grows sad with troubles.
> Sing and disperse them, if thou canst. Leave working.
> > *Song*
> "Orpheus with his lute made trees," etc.

This method of employing songs is the sole one of Shakespeare's practices that is antithetical to song usage in our shows where they are chiefly assigned to principal characters and are—more and more—an integral part of the action and frequently a furtherance of the plot itself.

In Shakespeare it is the soliloquies—not the songs—that are the counterparts of operatic arias and show songs in that they usually are developed virtuoso pieces for the performer and are germinated by the characters in the situations. It should be noted that these "soliloquies" spring out of different moods. There are the scherzolike Queen Mab speech in *Romeo and Juliet,* the tormented outpourings of Othello, the vicious plottings of Iago, the reflective narratives of Hamlet, the gay descriptive ones of Puck, etc.

Indeed the Shakespearean soliloquies, operatic arias, and the best show songs are the outgrowth and climax of much—sometimes everything—that has been said or has transpired in the scene leading up to the "song"—often concluding with it. In opera and musical theatre as well as in the soliloquies of Shakespeare, these lyric climaxes gather together the loose ends of the scenes and focus them in one direct emotional line. Sometimes they form moments of anger, excitement, or violence, but in all cases they function as climax and synthesis. They spawn action.

Some earlier-noted exceptions to Shakespeare's generally nonfunctional use of songs are to be found in Ophelia's mad songs and in Desdemona's "musical scene," which includes the "Willow Song." In *Othello* when Desdemona is preparing to retire and is in conversation with Emilia, her waiting woman and wife of Iago, Desdemona says:

> My mother had a maid called Barbara;
> She was in love, and her sole love proved mad
> And did forsake her; she had a song of "Willow"
> An old thing 'twas, but it expressed her fortune,
> And she died singing it, that song tonight
> Will not go from my mind; I have much to do
> But to go hang my head all at one side,
> And sing it like poor Barbara. Prithee, dispatch.

After several brief nervous exchanges with Emilia, she sings. "The poor soul sat sighing by a sycamore tree," etc.

Desdemona interrupts herself three times during the song in a most dramatically effective manner. The realistic excuse is that she is anxious that Emilia leave her alone according to Othello's wishes and before the latter's return. What ensues is nervousness and fear in the audience and each interruption heightens this effect.

In Act Four, Scene 5 of *Hamlet,* Ophelia is mentally deranged. Her songs, unannounced, happen as integrated parts of the play. The subject matter is so expertly drawn as to provoke the precise pitying audience reactions which were intended.

The first song with three stanzas is wistful and delicate. "How should I my true love know?" etc. "He is dead and gone, lady," etc. "White his shroud as the mountain snow," etc. Ophelia's dialogue and that of the other characters present are an integral part of the song scene.

The second song erupts in a senseless, happy way, "Tomorrow is St. Valentine's Day," etc., and bursts the emotions of the audience because of its very oppositeness to the situation and its pathetic cheer. And finally Ophelia sings a sadly reflective song: "And will he not come again?" etc.

What is probably genius-accounting on the playwright's part is his ending of this song which leads to Ophelia's final exit. The last of the sung lines—"God ha' mercy on his soul!"—is followed by *spoken* words: "And of all Christian souls! I pray God. God be wi' ye!"

Speech is barely possible when, under emotional stress, song becomes impossible.

This *calculated* integration of song and speech is fabulously effective. This is what we, in our time, have striven to learn, to arrive at in our work. It *is* the dramatic-musical experience.

The song scenes in *Othello* and *Hamlet* have their more recent counterparts in "Shall We Dance?" (*The King and I*), "One Hand, One Heart" (*West Side Story*), "I've Grown Accustomed to Her Face" (*My Fair Lady*) and "If I Were a Rich Man" (*Fiddler on the Roof*). In all of these (and in Shakespeare) much of the effective power is derived from the back-and-forthness between song and speech and in the examples from *The King and I* and *Fiddler on the Roof* the further inclusion of dance.

Other elements should also be noted. The Ophelia songs are spun around and include related dialogue spoken by other characters as integral parts of their total scene. In *The King and I*, the resolution of "Shall We Dance?" at its gayest height is interrupted by the dramatic entrance of the Kralahome with his announcement of Tuptim's apprehension; and the scene, dialogue, and choreography of "One Hand, One Heart" combine to make a unique contribution to musical theatre. None of these is merely a song, although a song is at the root of each.

This inclusion of several theatre elements—speech, song, and dance—make for "total theatre," and when they are employed in their most eloquent togetherness we have musical theatre at its most effective best. Shakespeare practiced this more than three centuries ago, and the American musical theatre, out of its own peculiar evolution, has employed it and made something unique in our own time.

COMMENTS ON THE NEW–OLD

Shakespeare is seldom regarded as a source for thinking about musical theatre, but it seemed perfectly natural for Engel to discuss him because Engel grew up at a time when Shakespeare was an integral part of the theatre. During Engel's youth, after all, two Shakespeare plays were turned into musicals—*The Comedy of Errors* into *The Boys From Syracuse*, whose first recording Engel directed, and *Taming of the Shrew* into *Kiss Me, Kate*.

Audiences until a few decades ago were familiar with Shakespeare both from reading him and from seeing productions.

Nowadays, alas, people are equally unfamiliar with Shakespeare either as readers or as viewers.

A few years ago, in fact, when the Metropolitan Museum of Art mounted an exhibit of Delacroix's drawings of *Hamlet*, I watched two middle-aged women standing before a depiction of the bloody final scene. One of the women, wearing a pair of overalls of high quality fabric, suggesting a wealthy kindergartener, was narrating the grisly events of the final scene to her friend with an astonished smile and a breathless tone that suggested Shakespeare's true genius lay in his ability to devise so many macabre ways for his characters to die.

I was both amused and saddened by this moment of instruction. Nevertheless I was pleased that at least the aged kindergartener was familiar with the play. When I recounted the moment to a friend she chided me for not having realized the woman who was conversant with *Hamlet* had probably not read the play. She'd more than likely just seen the recently released film version starring Mel Gibson. I realized my friend was correct.

Shakespeare is no longer, as he was once called, "our familiar." His plays have become exotic, which in some ways makes him a more logical counterpart to musical theatre. Because we don't know the plays as well as we once did they now strike us as extravagant, which is, to a certain extent, also true of musical theatre.

When Engel discusses the structure of Shakespeare's plays he inevitably calls to mind the famous essay in which the great Russian film director Sergei Eisenstein compared the technique of montage in cinema with the storytelling technique of Charles Dickens. The example he gave was the fairly early novel *Oliver Twist*, in which scenes of comedy alternate with scenes of brutality that were extremely stark for readers of the 1830s.

In both Shakespeare and Dickens, the alternation throws the different sides of the drama into high relief. Needless to say, this sort of alternation can also be highly effective in a musical, assuming that the story being told is indeed dramatic.

Engel is correct in noting that Shakespeare makes very clear who his major characters are and what they intend to do. The point seems obvious except that when Engel wrote the book the theatre had become infatuated with playwrights whose intention was to confuse the audience. Mystification was the order of the day, and Engel was correct to state it would be of little help in musicals.

If Engel's discussion now seems a little shortsighted, it's in suggesting that Shakespeare's songs are less important than his soliloquies as dramatic devices. There's no doubt that the soliloquies advance the plot directly. A character addressing the audience to explain his intentions—even his motivation—is a device the contemporary theatre associates with 19th century melodrama. (Shakespeare was more familiar and popular in the 19th century than the late 20th—Shakespeare parody was a staple of minstrel shows. It could only have worked if the audience knew the originals.)

There's something artificial about a soliloquy because in "real life" people seldom take us aside and confide their deepest thoughts and aspirations to us, especially if they're on the order of, "Since I cannot prove a lover, to entertain these fair, well-spoken days, I am determined to prove a villain and hate the idle pleasures of these days . . ." A song is also something unnatural, but we can accept the song as a convention in which all sorts of things that don't happen in "real life" can take place.

In the era of the book musical, in which every song advanced the plot, there was no room for what we might call "throwaway" songs, something that might be pretty or clever but had no organic relationship to the whole, like "Quiet Night," the atmospheric nocturne in *On Your Toes*. It has nothing to do with the plot about dancing. It has nothing to do with the character of the Russian impresario who sings it. But it casts a magic spell, and the show would be poorer without it.

It was one of the many inspired songs Rodgers wrote with Lorenz Hart. For many years these songs were somewhat undervalued because they didn't fit the "rules" Rodgers developed with his subsequent partner, Oscar Hammerstein II.

Few of their songs followed those rules better than "Some Enchanted Evening," from *South Pacific*. The plot involves an elderly French planter whose former wife was a native woman. He's fallen in love with a young American nurse at a naval hospital during World War II. This is an extremely specific story. But when the planter sings "Some Enchanted Evening," suddenly the situation is one everyone can identify with.

Shakespeare's songs fulfill a similar role. "Blow, blow, thou winter wind" does not grow out of the specific scene in which it appears in *As You Like It*, but its theme of ingratitude certainly resonates within the play's complicated plot.

Sometimes the songs serve as counterpoint to the themes of the play. It seems odd that one of the most spirited of Shakespeare's comedies, *Twelfth Night*, should have the rather somber song, "Come Away, Death." Many of Shakespeare's early comedies are about people fearing to embrace life. The reminder of mortality, which also occurs in "O Mistress Mine," a much lighter song in the same play, thus serves a cogent dramatic purpose.

Shakespeare, after all, was no less canny or serious about putting his plays together than the practitioners of musical theatre. He was also part of a culture of which music was a key component, as it always has been in America. (During the period of classical musical theatre there was no difference between theatre songs and pop songs.) According to the distinguished historian A.L. Rowse, 16th century England was considered one of the most musical societies in Europe. England, he says, sent its music masters to Italy, where the students, of course, soon bettered the instructors.

Shakespeare's stage directions are filled with references to instruments, some of which simply announce the presence of royalty. But we must not forget that Shakespeare's audience was not as saturated with music as we are. The very sound of the instruments, some of which connoted the hunt or were associated with dances that struck those listeners as lascivious, evoked powerful responses hard for us to duplicate.

Perhaps the most important reason to think about Shakespeare when discussing musical theatre is that his characters and stories have size. Shylock bedevils and perplexes us 400 years after he was created because Shakespeare took a stage caricature—the Jew—and turned him into a man of flesh and blood. Similarly, in Falstaff he took a character with slim historical antecedents and created an archetypal figure of fleshy selfishness.

Looking back, we see that the American musical theatre was once peopled with characters who, if not exactly Shakespearean, are nevertheless of heroic scale, like the prairie men of *Oklahoma!* or the title characters of *The King and I*.

One of the interesting phenomena of recent years is the huge success of a musical called *I Love You, You're Perfect, Now Change*. Despite largely mediocre reviews, it has been doing solid business, at the time of writing, for eight years. Its situations and characters are no deeper than those on TV sitcoms. Suburban values, of course, are the ones that predominate in our society, so it's entirely natural that they should be the subject of plays or musicals.

But if we look back to the Depression, when "the common man" was the subject of the theatre, we see that, however accurately a writer like Clifford Odets understood the proletariat, he was at least striving for something grander, something heroic. This attempt to create on an epic scale is apparent in a forgotten musical like Kurt Weill's *Johnny Johnson*. Admittedly, Weill was hardly an average Broadway composer, but for a fellow from Weimar, Germany, he fit in surprisingly snugly with his American counterparts.

The heroic eludes us these days, in part because we don't aim for it. Billy Bigelow, in *Carousel*, is heroic, even in his failings. Another heroic character in musical theatre is Sweeney Todd, the vengeful barber. Interestingly, both men are criminals, but they have a kind of stature. Perhaps it's related to what Norman Mailer wrote in his infamous essay "The White Negro," when, in defending street kids who've murdered a candy shop owner, he suggests there's a kind of heroic element to their act, because they've passed beyond the boundaries of conventional morality, which requires a kind of courage. The street kids, of course, do so without any intellectual hesitation. What makes Billy Bigelow and Sweeney Todd interesting is that they do what they do with an accompanying anguish, which, especially in the latter case, is reflected in the harrowing music.

It is arguable whether Boublil and Schoenberg's version of Jean Valjean attains the stature of Hugo's, but perhaps one explanation for the huge success of the show is that at least it strove for something monumental.

Engel's invocation of Shakespeare is a reminder that when he was the norm in our theatre the writers aimed higher because they were used to thinking of the theatre itself in grander terms.

8

Response

Applause is the spur of noble minds, the end and aim of weak ones.

> Charles Caleb Colton
> *Lacon* (1825)

The public simply reacts to various forms of theatre from moment to moment. The reaction to plays as opposed to musicals is in many ways as different as these two forms basically are. A sense of approval, approbation, satisfaction, and rousing excitement—often momentary—have stirred audiences, mobs, and other assorted collections of people to handclapping and/or cheering long before the beginning of recorded history. This response is usually not the result of contemplation but is an instantaneous emotional reaction.

History tell us that crowds gathered in the Roman Colosseum carried on enthusiastically when a lion devoured a Christian. At sports, we witness the vigorous reactions of both approving and disapproving crowds when almost anything happens. A burst of fireworks produces a similar effect. In the theatre, the machinelike precision of a dancing chorus line, such as the famous one at Radio City Music Hall, always creates a kind of mass hysteria. It must be recognized that each of these examples is widely different from the others, and yet all of them are productive of one single similar effect.

I dare to codify some of the many causes of applause not because I am a psychologist but because during a lifetime of incessant performing and attendance at other performances, of laboring to help improve theatrical productions that have often been too consciously aimed at eliciting response of this kind, my observations should have a certain validity of their own. I do not exaggerate when I claim that during some 160-odd productions I have witnessed at first hand the reactions of some 15,000 audiences and have myself been a member of at least 2,000 others.

It is no secret to anyone that applause occurs more frequently during the performance of a musical than a play. The reasons are not mysterious. The average play is divided into three acts and usually asks for approbation only at the very end. If one or two stars are included in the package, they can usually count on nightly rounds of handclapping on their entrances, and if it is made clear in the play that their exit—prior to the end of the play—is their finale (sometimes preceded by verbal fireworks on a grand scale), they may again be applauded. In a play there is usually so little expectation of audience demonstration at the ends of Acts One and Two that the house lights snap on simultaneously with the fall of the curtain. At the play's end the house lights remain discreetly dark, inviting applause, while the cast members take bows. A majority of the audience are either sufficiently taken with the play or grateful for the performances, or well-mannered enough to remain politely in their seats and clap their hands in spite of bunches of eager departees, who risk life and limb beating hasty retreats up dark aisles, stumbling over umbrellas and one another.

While the latter condition unfortunately exists at all types of performances, at musical shows even unwilling hands become exercised quite frequently during the course of an evening. The appearance of stars is still a big occasion, and the show's end is another. But the conclusion of songs (*some* songs), dances (ditto), the frequent apperance of *new* sets, dazzling costumes, the end of an occasionally rousing overture create audience "happenings" that don't exist in the non-musical theatre.

A personality—real or manufactured—produces its share of applause on sight. The real kind, the indefinable, individual, unique, magnetic something that is radiated by a particular human being, has the special power of creating wild excitement when he simply appears. This rare jewel, when he is a performer, usually becomes a legend in his own time, and sometimes legends outshine real ability.

Beauty is not necessarily a concomitant; talent often manifestly plays an important role. But whatever it is, it is obviously present on *sight*. In our time, Arturo Toscanini, Leonard Bernstein, Lotte Lehmann, Laurette Taylor, Ezio Pinza, Leopold Stokowski, Judith Anderson, President Kennedy, Greta Garbo, Marlene Dietrich, Alla Nazimova, and a few others not instantly recalled here have had this "something." What I refer to is not accomplishment but personality—what they stir on sight in audiences before they have performed: animal magnetism, if you like. If their performances are commensurate with their promise, so much the better, but a failure to measure up to expectation in no way interferes with their images.

Then there is the "manufactured" personality, which is in no way native or genuine. Of course, there has to be something to begin with—physical beauty, good looks, sexual attraction, a popular identification with TV, films, government, royalty, wealth, society, etc.—but basing their relentless campaign on one or a combination of several of these things, skillful public-relations people mold an image that is fed to the public through press (columns, feature articles, photographs, interviews), TV, etc. This kind of campaign can create a figure which, though quite unlike the real human being, nevertheless emerges as someone intimately known to such a large part of the public that at his live appearances he takes on the aspect of a *real* personality with the attributes of the former manufactured solely by the audience, owing to the elaborate and relentless build-up.

Either of these two kinds of personality-people is able to elicit hysterical applause. The real kind—strange to say—has usually a more limited audience than the manufactured, because the latter is usually made more personally known to everybody.

Many years ago an aunt of mine used to come from the movies saying, "I hate that Edward G. Robinson. He is so mean!" and an old family friend always talked about how good Lucille Ball was to her children. These serve to illustrate other common examples of things that help to condition audience reaction: the kind of role an actor plays (again and again) and the human-interest stories—not even necessarily true—the public swears by and passionately devours.

In my opinion no general audience acclaim has—sad to say—very much to do with the quality of what is seen or heard. Any instantaneous outburst has to be a thoughtless, judgmentless emotional response. Much of it is due to conditions in advance of this particular performance, not necessarily of public-relations making. All of the critics have praised the show. As a result tickets are nearly impossible to come by, but somebody has an "in" somewhere, or the calendar has rolled around at last to *our* theatre-club or party night, or to that eventual golden time months after *the* opening when the date on our tickets coincides with the calendar and here we are!

In these circumstances the lowering of the lights in the theatre activates the applause of glorious expectancy. By now, too, the tunes of musicals have been inescapably memorized because of incessant repetition on radio, TV, at discotheques, through home-owned recordings, etc., and applause greets the *start* of each tune in the overture. (There's not so much at the end.) Then the scenery, the star, the costumes, and the jokes.

I believe that most audience reaction is contagious. If there is warm response it affects nearly everybody in the theatre. On the other hand, when the audience is chilly, this feeling too is generally communicated. The "nearly everybody," however, does not always include myself when I am on the listening end, and I cannot believe that I am a loner in this respect. To the contrary, when I really enjoy something that is perhaps caviar to the general I try hard to compensate for the lack of audience response. I am sickened by a good deal of the enthusiasm I hear when I feel it is misplaced, gauche, or says that the majority of people are suckers for falling into cheap traps laid by tasteless showmen.

Example: When I attended the opening of *My Fair Lady* I cringed at the violent laughter (always accompanied by applause—an increasingly common practice and a deeply disturbing one). When did people start applauding "jokes" instead of being sufficiently satisfied by *laughing* at them? My cringing was due frankly to a looking down my nose at the laughter of discovery. After all, I had read Shaw's *Pygmalion* a thousand years ago and had enjoyed at least three different productions of it within twenty-five years. Didn't *everybody* know *Pygmalion*? Obviously they did not because most of the people in the audience wouldn't have been caught dead at a musicless play.

While I smiled at the great comedy that had long been familiar to me, I was appalled by the raucous laughter which told me that these uninitiates required the sugarcoating of music if they were to be dragged into the theatre at all.

In a consideration of entertainment versus boredom there is one factor that has caused me to bristle, and after much soul-searching I have concluded that my personal reactions have been incorrect.

Because of my age (I was born in 1910 and was first exposed to the New York theatre in 1929) I have had occasion to see certain gimmicks and devices, or have heard certain dialogue—all received by present-day young audiences gleefully, a reaction I have found myself resenting. A very good example of this is a high-camp song in which a very girlie girl sings while swinging, seated in a crescent moon. This precise device (I know through old photographs) has been used again and again since the middle of the last century and in my personal experience was employed marvelously by Beatrice Lillie in a 1930s revue, then in 1958 by Elaine Stritch in *Goldilocks*, by Jean and Walter Kerr. At the Broadway opening of *Mame* (1966) it was *again* used. I was far from amused by it and was finally disgusted because of the hysterical laughter from a young "camp" audience.

Similar examples have caused me a great amount of worry: Was my reaction reasonable or not? I have concluded that it was not and was entirely due to my earlier theatregoing. The hysterical audience had right on its side. I have an idea that this attitude is one which all getting-to-be senior citizens (including the critics) must incessantly remind themselves of, and they then must shrug off the present new reaction as "the way we felt when we first saw it."

The aforementioned Beatrice Lillie brings up still another point: the effect of incongruity and surprise, which is undoubtedly a legitimate and prime applause-getter. In one of the *Little Shows* (popular revues, 1929–31), just prior to the end of the opening nuber when a curtain was pulled aside, Miss Lillie was "discovered" standing center stage dressed in a glamorous beaded evening gown. After a single line she lifted her full-length skirt and the audience saw that—quite incongruously—she was wearing roller skates which carried her off stage. This was a shocker and a great applause-laughter-getter.

As this is an example of visually produced applause, it might not go amiss to list a few quite dissimilar others in the same category. Peter Plan "flying" is an assured provocateur. The appearance on stage of just anything that seems incongruous is sure-fire: an automobile (my, didn't anyone *ever* see a car?), an old person or a fat one doing a dance routine (how *does* he do it?). Any child (aw, isn't she cute?) or any animal (just "aw"). A self-respecting star will commit anything just short of murder to prevent competition with a child or an animal because she knows that either will victimize her.

The same day or night of the week—surprisingly—produces similar audience responses. When the show is known to be a hit, Monday-, Tuesday- and Wednesday-night theatregoers are most likely to be "regular" patrons. Their reaction as a group is likely to be intelligent, and if the show itself merits enthusiasm, they will provide it. As Thursday is a stores-open-late night, many suburbanites come to the city to shop, then go to the theatre. The response from these people is likely to be more muted, possibly because they are tired. Friday night may be attended by people less subtle than Monday's and Tuesday's, and comedy produces mindless hilarity. Saturday night's audience, a sleepy one, is part of a weekly or bimonthly ritual. Husband has played golf. Wife or girlfriend has spent the entire day being beautified. They have dined too heartily and drunk a weekly cocktail that makes everything on stage appear a bit fuzzy. The unmarried couples are often on their most formal behavior while nevertheless hand-holding under a coat. The married ones applaud or laugh when they are awake.

Wednesday matinee audiences are famous among performers for their lethargy. They are almost exclusively female and the average age runs somewhere between fifty and eighty. They talk loudly throughout. As they wear gloves, their applause is inaudible. They fall asleep—row by row—their sea of decorated hats resting left or right, but seldom topside up. But they invariably awaken in time to start a noisy mass exodus somewhere in the middle of the second act, possibly to reach their waiting cars before the general theatre break, which is nearly simultaneous everywhere in the neighborhood, or to get cabs, etc. But they go and fast for their years and with no regard for whatever is happening on the stage.

Saturday's matineee usually provides the one audience most

eager to see this particular show. The tickets are somewhat less expensive, workingmen are free, teachers and students are out of school, and interested families can attend together. They listen, react normally, and applaud vigorously.

The lighting has a good deal of bearing on audience attention and applause. In the theatre, the star entrance is "spotted." Attention is focused along with the light. Sometimes a conductor is fortunate enough to enter into a waiting spotlight. When this happens, he is usually greeted with applause. When he is simply darkly present, he is ignored and receives neither attention nor applause.

At the opera it is probably tradition that reverses the conductor's reception. The auditorium lights are taken out. There is a pause. The conductor enters the pit. Immediately there is considerable applause and this is followed by abrupt and complete silence along with real or feigned interest in the music. In any case there is blessed silence and the music *can* be heard. Like everything else, this too is changing. In America today operagoers are made up of a wider variety of people than formerly. Many of these have neither the tradition of operagoing or enough native taste sufficient to tell them that the music being played is the *feature* of the performance and that any interruption of it with applause, talking, etc., is an infraction and one which is distasteful to music lovers. As a result, they applaud scenery, entrances of stars, and all kinds of other things while the composers' ideas lie buried. It is nice to know that even today at Bayreuth the audience maintains complete silence even after the curtains have closed until, at the end of an act, the last note of the orchestra has died away.

I have found that in a musical a song may be excellent, it may be performed well, it may be staged and lighted effectively, but its reception is largely dependent on the very last few bars in the orchestra or on the singer's very last note; the rest passes by acceptably enough, but the effect can be totally changed by the ending. An unsatisfying conclusion can negate the effect of the whole. Sometimes it is not clear enough that the song has ended. This may be due to improper exposure of the song so that the audience lacks sufficient opportunity to become familiar with it. Sometimes, due to improper staging, the performers continue to move at the song's end—a stupid disregard of tradition. A loud brassy ending is not the only way of conveying the idea of finish. Sometimes (Joshua Logan always demands this) there need be only a quiet but definite "button"—a single pizzicato in the bass will do it; however, the audience needs to be told that the number has been concluded. Then usually it will applaud in some fashion with, of course, varying degrees of enthusiasm: *something* will happen in response to "The End."

Three examples within my own experience will help clarify these points about ending and insufficient song exposure. When *Fanny* (1954) first opened in Boston, Walter Slezak sang one of Harold Rome's tenderest songs, "To My Wife." In rehearsal everyone working on the show had been melted by it. On the opening night, Walter finished the song to complete audience silence. At a meeting later the same night I think it was I who suggested that the song needed lengthening, and what was added by the next performance was an orchestral reprise of most of the chorus played under a spoken sentimental "toast" to Fanny, which in turn concluded with Slezak's singing only the very last phrase. From then on, there was always applause. In *Illya Darling* (1967), none of the songs except the well-known "Never on Sunday" had the kind of ending—quiet or noisy—that prepared the audience that it was approaching and that now it was actually here. Period. The result: sporadic and diffused applause, if any.

The now celebrated but then unknown Barbra Streisand made her theatrical debut in *I Can Get It for You Wholesale* (1962). She had a single song, "Miss Marmelstein." In rehearsal—due to lack of experience—Barbra did not understand at first that she must "freeze" all direction, that she must practice the precise staging and interpretation arrived at carefully through the combined efforts and experiences and talents of the stage director (Arthur Laurents), composer (Harold Rome), choreographer (Herbert Ross), and me. Barbra "stopped the show" nightly with "Miss Marmelstein." She received much attention in the press because of this plus her unique personal quality. A few weeks after the opening the various directors and authors were away, and one night Barbra asked my permission to try "Miss Marmelstein" her "own way." I refused, which was ethically proper for me to do, and I reasoned with her that she did indeed stop the show nightly and what more could she want?

Performance after performance she continued to bug me to let her try her song her way. Finally, because of my growing impatience, I told her she could do as she pleased. When the song was finished that night, the audience was unaware that it had concluded and instead of receiving much applause, Barbra got none! Within the same disastrous week she came again requesting me to rehearse her. I knew that one of the simplest crimes she had committed was at the end of the number when she had not stopped still—an invariable custom—incidentally, based on experience. She had continued to fidget. Was the song really over?

The set-up of a song in a show often governs its response. For example, if the singing character has been able, through both the writing and his own performance, to gain audience empathy, and the situation out of which the song grows strongly creates audience identification, then the song—whether it is a lyrical ballad or a comedy song—will more effectively reach and engage the audience's attention than a song which is merely stuck in loosely and lacks some definite reason for being. This is a principal reason why situation ballads such as "You'll Never Walk Alone" (*Carousel*) or "I've Never Been in Love Before" (*Guys and Dolls*) or "You Can't Get a Man with a Gun" (*Annie Get Your Gun*) or comedy songs like "Adelaide's Lament" (*Guys and Dolls*) or "The Love of My Life" (*Brigadoon*) work so well. We have been given the opportunity to know the character and become engrossed in the situation which produces the song, and so we become involved in it. What we hear is not merely a song but a piece of theatre—a segment of an entire continuing fabric.

I know of no better examples of songs in a show presented without character and situation set-ups than those in old revues. I remember one revue starring Fanny Brice and Willie and Eugene Howard. These were great performers who appeared in as many marvelously comic sketches as time permitted. Alas, between these sketches and occasional spectacular production numbers, an agreeable male or female singer (sometimes both), attractively dressed in evening clothes, would step in front of a curtain cold (no set-up, no character introduction, no situation) and sing a song. Some of the songs were first-rate and the singers usually sang them well. But few people in the audience paid them any attention. What they performed was meaningless. The song was obviously "stuck in" while sets and costumes were changed. The singers commanded little attention, sang against loud conversation, and received little applause.

High sound—volume along with other quantitive considerations—masses of people on stage, enormous glittering scenery have invariably "grabbed" audiences. The big brassy song finishes which used to be called "Paramount-Publix Endings" worked effectively for too long a time. I had begun to believe mercifully that they had blown themselves completely out of style until I saw *George M!* (1968), which was abominable, because it contained every vulgar, noisy cliché ever known. In the specific case of *George M!*, nostalgia very likely played some part. For the old, it was a simple matter of remembering; for the young, seeing things they had heard about but never experienced.

The Palace Theatre which housed *George M!*—once the home of vaudeville—again rang with the sound of endings, and once again audiences responded like suckers to something nauseatingly vulgar, out of style and over-obviously calculated to produce such a response. The Roxy and Capitol theatres died because this kind of formula, served up as a regular daily dish, had become insupportable to audiences. In reality it can be equated with the old parade routine of brass and drums and fifes and flags which I had thought was universally rejected. But I was wrong. It rode once again in *George M!* and if you want to be frightened, see a print of the Riefenstahl movies of Adolf Hitler, which did the same thing. The cause, the mind, reason are non-functioning. Rabble-rousing, enormous masses of people moving in march tempo; the glories of brass and ensign accomplish the trick. It is my guess that this same tired stimulus will go on and on producing the identical reaction from the undiscriminating who will always find it irresistible (the young may find it new). It is theatricality at its lowest, oldest, most primitive, and most predictable.

Equally obvious and well known at the opera is that one powerful, endless high note that a capable vocalist can manage to deliver at the end of an aria. The performance can lack meaning and subtlety, but that last pearl of a high tone will come to the rescue and instantly all else is forgotten and forgiven. True—this note and ending will be accompanied by a gesture of wide-open arms that beg the ovation—Al Jolson–like. But again, success.

There is one quite opposite cause of applause that is familiar if weak, but it should not go unmentioned. When a song in a musical ends unsatisfyingly—but nonetheless ends definitely—gestures and all, I have many times been a witness to sporadic applause which is a result of audience embarrassment and a feeling of obligation: let's help out the poor soul. While no one believes that what they have just heard merits any response, there is nevertheless the applause of pity. It carries little weight, but it occurs.

Most applause comes as a result of feeling. Since feeling is foremost among the many things the best musical theatre is about, audience response in varying degrees will result. The greater the feeling engendered, the more spontaneous will be the response.[15] What I believe to be of great significance is the number of years approbation for a single show can continue. This is one of the surest yardsticks by which, given the perspective of time, one can measure the effectiveness of musical-theatre art.

COMMENTS ON RESPONSE

The narrator of Wright Morris's 1956 novel *Love Among the Cannibals* is the manager of a second-rate singer. At one point he expresses amazement at how well his client is invariably received but goes on to explain that the reason is the way he presents her. "There you have the new show business in a nutshell," he says. "You tell them what they're going to like. They like it. Then they stand and applaud themselves."

Interestingly, 1956 is the year *My Fair Lady* opened and Engel found himself appalled by the opening night response, what he calls the "violent" laughter and the applause for the funny lines. What both Engel and Morris were decrying was the arrival of the synthetic audience, which by now is so established we hardly see it as something even worth noticing.

Given the year, it's not hard to see what created the audience that offended both the novelist and the musical director. By 1956, television had begun to dominate the entertainment world. Until television, an audience was expected to do its own laughing. Television absolved its viewers of that obligation.

The laugh track, one of the most fascinating inventions of the 20th century, served two purposes. One, of course, was to signal what was supposed to be funny, though the humor was seldom so subtle or ambiguous that someone watching at home might be likely to miss it.

Secondly, and perhaps more important, the laugh track set a tone of excitement. A moment of silence might jeopardize the sense of momentum a comedy is supposed to maintain. The laugh track might almost be regarded as a musical element, a kind of percussion that keeps the beat strong.

The mood of forced hilarity that characterizes much of television humor is the standard by which other entertainment is likely to be judged. Even the use of amplification can be chalked up to a quality of sound people are used to hearing at home and to the need for a level of volume that underscores that a good time is being had by all.

The relationship with the audience was always crucial to the creation of musicals. That was why shows used to have out-of-town tryouts, to calibrate the give and take between stage and audience. Moreover, although the tryouts were all in Eastern Seaboard cities—Boston, New Haven, Philadelphia, Washington—there was an understanding that a show had to work with more than a New York audience.

One of the most interesting stories about how a show was altered to take into account the audience's needs was the 1959 *Gypsy*. Stephen Sondheim invited his friend and mentor Oscar Hammerstein II to a performance of the show on its pre-Broadway tryout tour in Philadelphia, when "Rose's Turn" didn't end but merely segued into a scene between Mama Rose and her daughter Gypsy. Sondheim was convinced that not having a climactic coda was the dramatically correct way to handle the situation. Hammerstein agreed in theory. But, he cautioned Sondheim, sometimes what's strictly truthful isn't the best way to go. The audience also has needs, and in this case they needed to applaud Ethel Merman's performance. Their frustration at not being able to do so would cloud their response to whatever happened afterward.

It's unlikely that anyone but Hammerstein could have persuaded him to make this compromise. Given the brilliance of its book and score, doubtless *Gypsy* would have been the classic it is even without this alteration, but this consideration makes the show more satisfying for the audience. This practical viewpoint tends to be overridden at a time when musicals are regarded, as they so often are, as works of art. It's a paradox that we now regard Golden Age musicals as works of art when they were created under an extremely practical mindset.

Engel's anecdote about Barbra Streisand wanting to do "Miss Marmelstein" *her* way is instructive. Here's an artist of extraordinary talent and limitless feeling whose instincts aren't necessarily infallible. Carol Burnett once recalled that, on *The Garry Moore Show*, when Streisand was presented with the brilliant Peter Matz arrangement of "Happy Days Are Here Again" as a study in melancholy, she balked at singing it that way. It required strenuous persuasion to make her do what eventually became one of her signatures.

At the time these incidents took place Streisand was a very young, audacious but relatively inexperienced performer. Nevertheless, there was a whole community to support her outsize talent, a community that had been formed at a time when pleasing the audience was still considered paramount.

In 1980 there was an Off-Broadway revival of Arthur Miller's 1967 play *The Price*, which featured Fritz Weaver as a brother short-changed by the vicissitudes of the Depression and Joseph Buloff as the owner of a pawnshop whose monologue about the values we place on things invariably steals the show. Buloff was one of the great actors of the New York Yiddish theatre but he occasionally worked on the main stem, most notably as the original peddler, Ali Hakim, in *Oklahoma!*

Weaver and Buloff shared a dressing room. Weaver was always fascinated that Buloff would arrive early and then, a little after 7:30, disappear every night. One night he followed Buloff and found him in a tiny alcove above the stage, concealed from the audience but within earshot. He came there every night to listen to the audience as they filed in, to try to gauge their mood, which would help him shape his performance.

There are many reasons why this attitude of solicitousness toward the audience, seldom as heightened as Buloff's, has changed, some of them valid, but the lack of trust in both directions can only hamper the theatre experience.

There was, after all, a time when the trust was invariably repaid. When *Brigadoon* was on the road the choreographer Agnes De

Mille, who'd certainly demonstrated her prowess in the work she did on Rodgers and Hammerstein's two seminal works, *Oklahoma!* and *Carousel*, found her fellow creators hesitant to allow her to do a solemn, very un-Broadway funeral dance. It was intended for the sequence after Harry Beaton, who wants to destroy the magical hamlet, is killed and laid to rest. Finally she asked her colleagues for one performance out of town to let the audience response determine whether her dance would remain in the show.

"All I want is real people," she said. "No *experts!*"

The out-of-town audience totally vindicated her request, and the powerful dances she created raised *Brigadoon* to a level far beyond what was then the norm in musical comedy.

9

Opera

Again I think it necessary to remind the reader that although the spoken word came first, musicalization followed it closely down through the ages. The word has always been the basis of communication between human beings. When it clothed itself in the more formal styles of poetry or prose, it still functioned as communication but with some added elements. As poetry, rhythm was attached and along with this the concord of sounds at planned intervals which was called rhyme. With the further addition of music, the communication of feeling—already present—was intensified and dramatized.

During the varied history of word-music combining, one or another of these two elements has often taken priority. The medieval minstrels and troubadours were poets first who improvised musical accompaniments to their love songs and their dramatic ballads. The verses were heightened rhapsodically because of these musical trappings. There also flourished in all countries a wealth of simple and more formal songs that had grown out of the people, and these become known as folk songs.

As the *art* of music began to assert itself, rules—many of them handed down from the ancient Greeks—became better known.

Music gradually developed as a mathematical art, and, in relation to words (most music until the seventeenth century was vocal), it was still used for expressive purposes in which there was a vivid inter-relationship; but sometimes the words might as well have been only abstract syllables, so overpoweringly complex was the musical structure.

In the first case, wonderful madrigals, written to lyrics of a high order by composers of enormously inventive talent, flourished in all European countries. In the second case, especially in the many-voice (polyphonic) music of the Church, purely technical complex-ities often obliterated the words which provided only general ideas rather than shifting specific meanings.

Amid this frantic activity on both the sacred and secular fronts, various kinds of mystery and miracle plays employed music and movement and these were performed in cathedrals. They were also secular folk plays with music, called by many different labels in each country.

By the sixteenth century musico-dramatic activity was feverish and its eventual eruption, first in Florence, was in error in that it became something different from what it set out to be. Count Bardi, a wealthy nobleman wishing to revive Greek classic drama, surrounded himself with poets and musicians. Stage works were created and presented. The subject matter was adapted from Greek mythology and history as employed in the fifth-century-B.C. dramas.

The Florentines, aware that music had played an important part in the originals, were anything but certain (neither are we) as to just how or to what extent. Their products were called "Monodies" because one voice (character) sang at a time, as opposed to the simultaneous singing of many voices. These were accompanied by a varied orchestra, and scenery and costumes were employed. The vocal lines were non-melodic; they were indeed what later came to be called recitatives. There were no arias, although lyrical orchestral interludes did exist. This meant that the words were of extreme importance, and their musical setting in no way interfered with nor distorted them. And every word was sung.

In much less than a century creation and performance of these music-dramas spread throughout Italy. They became known as operas, and not too gradually the music emancipated itself from the speech-inflected monody and re-endowed itself with all the elements that nature and evolution had already provided: melody, rhythm, cadence, and shape. Within less than a century after its inception opera had become extremely popular not only in Italy but also in France, Germany, and England. Distinguished composers were caught up in the movement, the elements of spectacle and dance were added, and by the middle of the eighteenth century nearly every self-respecting court in Europe was commissioning works in celebration of every occasion.

The use of classical tales continued for more than a century, but gradually composers began using contemporary plays for their librettos. Mozart and Rossini used Beaumarchais. Shakespeare afforded librettos for at least ten operas. Dumas, Sardou, Goethe, Hugo, and nearly everybody else made his contribution to adaptation in this form. Words were employed for their meanings. The operatic form settled down for a long period to sung dialogue (recitative) to tell its story and song (aria) to expose its characters (first person singular) to express their emotions, and to forecast action.

In opera, from its very inception, composers were impelled by the word in the writing of their music; but it was the music—when it was full grown—that became the more important to the listeners. Today the two prime elements—the words or libretto and the music—work together in importance. Since words have always been important in opera, audiences should understand them. Music-drama has been understood and loved by the masses of people in every European country. Many small towns in continental Europe have always had opera houses.

The international repertoire is sung in the language of the country in which it is performed. Ordinary people in Italy, France, Germany, Russia, and many other countries go to the opera as we in America go to the movies. No preparation is needed because everything is understood. In the United States we perform many operas in their original languages. Our audiences attend lectures of explanation, read synopses and librettos, and even then can only comprehend the dramatic outline. This is very much like an English-speaking person, familiar with *Hamlet*, attending a performance of the play in

Russian. The Englishman knows the story and *sees* where the soliloquies come but cannot possibly feel or appreciate properly the nuances of the performance since the specific inflections are incomprehensible. He witnesses *Hamlet* in outline only.

I believe by now that most grand opera is a European antiquity. We present it here as though it were being given in a museum where it is sometimes exquisitely embalmed. But I believe that the *form* as we inherited it can never take root creatively in our culture. This is not to imply that I do not enjoy the operas of Gluck, Mozart, Verdi, Wagner (when they are visible with the naked eye), Puccini, Strauss, and others. I believe wholeheartedly in the validity of Alban Berg's and Debussy's contributions to lyric theatre. But opera is an artificial form foreign to American audiences, which need to hear the words translated and the style explained. *All* opera everywhere is not made from the same pattern, and I believe that by pointing out some of the main differences as well as the relationship of librettos to plays I might perhaps be able to draw some useful conclusions.

First as to different patterns. The recitative-aria style, while containing some of the noblest music ever written (Mozart especially), is today the most artificial of forms. It is, in outline, anti-dramatic. Only the musical covering makes it bearable as drama. Not the words. Not the fragmented form. We impatiently await the arias.

Wagner did away with these earlier practices when he wrote his music-dramas,[16] which contained neither recitative nor aria, but a continuous movement of words and music as these might occur in a play. Form as such was obliterated. It was the (slow) progress of the drama alone that defined the musical outline. This dramatic "philosophy" has survived although there have been alterations in style and forms have been created whereas for a while none existed. The overblown static quality of most of Wagner's music-dramas gave way to something nearer to realism. Richard Strauss followed his ancestor to a great extent but advanced the musical style, humanized the people, often provided them with humor, and managed to reach his audiences on a more personal basis. The lofty Wagnerian gods succumbed to human beings who communicated to other human beings.

Opera in France meanwhile possessed a simpler texture. The aria remained; the vocal line was accompanied by a quiet orchestra with few comments of its own. The simplest and most successful of the "new"

French operas was Georges Bizet's *Carmen*—an *opéra comique*. Here was theatre. The dialogue was at first spoken. Bizet wrote only preludes, interludes, songs, and dances. *Carmen* has an outline similar to the later American musical. The music is vital, attractive, and compelling. It is tuneful in a simple way. The text is comprehensible and also compelling. Twenty-five years after *Carmen*, Charpentier's *Louise* (1900) followed in its path as a realistic musical-theatre piece. Its *hundredth* performance took place one year later! Most of its text is in prose. Only two years after *Louise*, Debussy's *Pelléas et Mélisande* had its premiere.

Pelleas is vastly differently in style and point of view from *Carmen* and *Louise*. It is drama first, with shadowy music that reflects an unreal impressionistic world. It renounces the thickness of the Wagnerian orchestra and the sweetness and formal shape of popular Italian and French aria. The drama is fragmentary. There are multi-scene acts. The music is continuous, delicate, occasionally "dramatic" in the old sense. But the music was new and it exhausted its own limited coloristic vocabulary, leaving no progeny.

To quote from Oscar Thompson's *Debussy, Man and Artist* (the quotation marks indicate Debussy's own [translated] words):

> Debussy would not follow the plan of the lyric drama "in which the music arrogantly predominates" and "there is too much singing in musical dramas." He believed that music "begins where speech fails," music "intended to express the inexpressible."[17]

Although *Pelléas* did not follow the usual plan of the lyric drama, it is ironically true that in its subtle, gray, quiet way, the music is the entire *raison d'etre*. Maeterlinck's play without Debussy's music would no longer exist.

As to there being too much singing in opera, it is nearly continuous in *Pelléas*. However, the vocal line is largely in recitative style (many words on a single note), which in effect is a reversion to the earliest Florentine opera. Nevertheless, the vocal line often soars as it does in all lyric dramas, except that the quality of *this* soaring was unknown earlier. What Debussy *said* and what he *did* were two different things.

The year 1925 saw the first performance of Alban Berg's *Wozzeck*, a monumental opera based on Büchner's nearly century-old expressionistic play, which is as fragmentary as Maeterlinck's *Pelléas*. But Berg added musical form, which had been conspicuously absent in nineteenth-century opera. Neither the complexities of the orchestra nor the celebration of many small forms intruded upon the drama. All of the elements are interrelated and interdependent. This *was* music drama as it had only hitherto been dreamed of.

Although *Pelléas et Mélisande* and *Wozzeck* have many things in common libretto-wise their points of view are diametrically opposite, the former being *impressionistic* ("use of detail, sometimes brief, intended to achieve a vividness . . . more by evoking sensory impressions [as of mood and atmosphere] than by representing an objective reality"), and the latter *expressionistic* ("the practice of seeking to depict not objective reality but the subjective emotions and responses that objects and events arouse in the artist—with the wide use of distortion, exaggeration, and symbolism").

Impressionism, expressionism, Dadaism, twelve-tone technique, pure classicism, and all the rest came into being as revolts against the then existing establishments. Each of them set up their own milieus, their own sets of rules for their own creativity as well as staunchly negating the *immediate* past. Everything except the new *then* was passe. And so each one of them, while creating something positive and contributing to the always progressing line, also became imprisoned by the stringencies of newly created rules: new prisons for old.

In the first scene of *Pelléas et Mélisande* (libretto by Maurice Maeterlinck in fifteen scenes) there is an exchange between Melisande and Golaud—both lost in a forest:

> MÉLISANDE: What is it that brings you here?
> GOLAUD: I cannot tell myself.
> I was hunting in the wood,
> And I was following a boar,
> And I went out of my way.
> You're very young.
> How old are you?
> MÉLISANDE: I begin to feel so cold. . .

In spite of vagueness and non-sequiturity, both characters and their relationship to place and each other are defined.

In the second scene of *Wozzeck*, libretto by Alban Berg based on Georg Buchner's play (also in fifteen scenes), Wozzeck and Andres are cutting sticks in a field in the late afternoon.

> WOZZECK:This place is cursed! See how the mist is
> floating above the grass there where the toadstools are
> springing up. There rolls at dusk, a head! Once a man
> did lift it up, thought it was a hedgehog. Three days and
> three nights then, and he lay in his wooden coffin.

This style is of poetic prose against realistic action.

Maeterlinck's *Pelléas* and Büchner's *Wozzeck* presented their situations continuously and with leanness, developed their plots directly, had beginnings, middles, and ends, and presented characters with whom we could readily empathize. The musical trappings heightened the dramas and never interfered with either the action or the words themselves. Both *Wozzeck* and *Pelleas* were in a broad sense reactions against the lushness of Wagner, and in both the vocal lines are almost a complete relinquishing of aria in favor of a truly lyric—if often fragmentary—recitative. Both librettos are non-realistic, and the characters are on a superhuman (as opposed to a personal) level. Wozzeck himself is *all* simple, abused, bedeviled mankind, not a mere individual. Melisande is the quintessence of young love, full of mystery, delicacy, unreality, insubstantiality—with the uncommunicative, fearful yet dazzled qualities of adolescence—but she is not real and is neither girl nor woman.

All the while Debussy and Berg were struggling with new ideas, the fecund career of Giuseppe Verdi, begun in the old Italian tradition, was concluding on a very high new plateau with *Otello* and *Falstaff*, both of course based on Shakespeare; and Puccini, always theatrical and simple, was enjoying international successes with his operas based on successful contemporary plays. His scores contained memorable melodies, and the dramatic propositions were more in line with the realistic contemporary theatre than operas heretofore had been.[18]

Il Trovatore (libretto by Cammarano), produced in 1853, and

Otello (text by Boito after Shakespeare), produced thirty-four years later, show not only enormous advances in Verdi's remarkable musical capabilities but a change of taste in his choice of libretto. The earlier opera belongs to the recitative-aria style that was still the fashion in 1853. The words scan and rhyme and belong squarely in the melodramatic mold of the time. Two lyrics from the opening scene will serve as samples: "Jealousy's fierce serpents are writhing in his breast" and "Ah! the wicked, unspeakable woman!/It fills me with both rage and horror!" (English translation by William Weaver.)

On the other hand, *Otello* is a music-drama. It climaxed Verdi's long career and pointed toward the future. Henry W. Simon has written, "The principal problems faced by Boito were based on two very obvious facts. First—it takes much longer to say anything with music than to say it without music. Second—simple emotions and emotional problems lend themselves well to the lyric theatre; complex ones do not." (The present author has made both points in an earlier chapter.) It is unnecessary here to quote a sample of Boito's text because it follows Shakespeare's play as closely as possible.

There had to have been many different styles of librettos to accommodate these different styles of music. (Percy Scholes has written that more than 42,000 operas and operettas have been written.) Those librettos which came about in the eighteenth century to serve Mozart and Rossini (slightly later) and others of their periods were formal. The recitative (dispatching the action in sung dialogue) was generally followed by the aria (solo, duet, terzette—in any case, the tune), the emotional expansion of a single idea. While the recitative propelled the drama forward in *words*, the aria became the promised musical climax. This alternating sequence defined the form of opera—roughly 1650 to 1850. Recitative of this kind (accompanied usually by harpsichord to allow freedom for the singer) was called *secco*, or dry.

A quite different kind of recitative called *stromentato* (instrumental) was the inevitable more sophisticated development. Because this was accompanied by the orchestra, the singer was more restricted, the accompanying texture became more interesting—even more independent—melodically, rhythmically, and harmonically. Instead of the dramatic weight having to be conveyed almost exclusively by the text and through the vocal-acting of the singer, the orchestra added substance and its own comment.

Wagner's early operas—*Rienzi, Der Fliegende Holländer*, and *Lohengrin*—employed this new kind of recitative. As Wagner's style progressed, the musical outline became blurred partly because there was a lesser line of demarcation between recitative and aria. In fact, both of these merged into a single dramatic fabric. The recitative became by turns more lyrical or dramatic, while the aria became less formal and less separate.

Wagner (his own librettist) arrived at his most developed style in the four Nibelungen dramas and in *Tristan, Meistersinger,* and *Parsifal*. These have the epic as their model. Everyone talks and talks, tells all, including all personal history and background. The style of the verse is so "lofty" and "superhuman" that it is difficult for us—poor lowly mortals—to care about what is said except as it imparts to us the circumloquacious information we so desperately require as guideposts—lights in the murkiest of worlds. This is especially true in the Ring operas and *Parsifal*. In these and in *Tristan* it is the music only that allows us to care. In it we are surfeited with emotion which emanates as much from the restless orchestra as from the singing characters themselves.

In the one "comedy" Wagner wrote, *Die Meistersinger von Nürnberg*, everything is more humanized. Full human beings provoke laughter and tears. The music comes to life because of its more classic quality and its form, in contrast to the nauseating chromatic meanderings ever present in the other music-dramas. The self-imposed formal musical restrictions in *Die Meistersinger* caused Wagner to achieve in this one work what he most wanted to achieve in all of them.

The librettos provided for Richard Strauss are all terse and stage-worthy. They introduce the characters at once and with impeccable clarity. The two "classic" tragedies *Elektra* (von Hofmannsthal) and *Salome* (libretto after Oscar Wilde) are each in a single act—following the Greek pattern. Both are dramatic and race breathlessly from beginning to sharp terrifying end. Both are dramas that immediately claim the attention of the audience and hold it relentlessly until the end. Nothing is extraneous. The style of the Strauss librettos is conversational, modern. Most of the lines neither scan nor rhyme. All conversational, naturalistic, non-"grand." Structurally the librettos employed by Verdi and Puccini cling closely to the plays from which they were adapted. In *Madama Butterfly* alone there was a first act added to the two original ones in Belasco's short play, and in *Otello* Boito cut out Shakespeare's Act One.

The formal recitative-aria kind of opera written by composers from Mozart to early Verdi are more closely akin to the scene-and-soliloquy of Shakespeare than anything else I know. The aria is synonymous with the soliloquy.

A word now about the second point I alluded to earlier: operatic "tableau" versus continuation of action in a musical. In many operas there is "space" especially between the acts. George R. Marek writes:

> . . .[the libretto of] *Manon Lescaut* may hold the record for the between-curtains broad jump, since at the close of the first act Manon and Des Grieux elope to Paris not yet lovers, and at the beginning of the second act Manon has not only terminated her idyll with Des Grieux and taken a second lover, but has already tired of that second lover.

This sort of thing happens sometimes in plays but never in the librettos of musicals, which are more compact. Furthermore there are many hopelessly complex plots in grand opera which no *honest* operagoer can claim to comprehend. (*Il Barbiere di Siviglia, Die Zauberflöte, et al.*), especially at a single hearing-seeing; and there are other overly simple ones such as *Tannhäuser*.

Take, for example, *Carmen*, a rather simple but tableau-type libretto (based on Prosper Mérimée's novella).

ACT ONE. Before a cigarette factory, Seville. Heroine (Carmen), a gypsy, and hero (Don José), a soldier. Micaela (Don José's childhood sweetheart) brings Jose a letter from his mother. Carmen becomes involved in a fight. Jose arrests her, then allows her to escape.

ACT TWO. A tavern. Carmen is *told* Jose was imprisoned on her account, but now has been released. Escamillo, a popular matador, tries to interest Carmen but she is aloof. Two smugglers ask three gypsies (Carmen and two of her friends) to join them in a venture, but Carmen refuses, saying that she is expecting a "friend" who did her a service and in return she will make him her lover. When Jose arrives Carmen picks a fight with him. He hears Retreat sound and when he tries to leave, Carmen accuses him of cowardice. Jose's lieutenant enters and orders him to the barracks. A fight ensues which is broken up by the smugglers. Jose has no choice but to go away with the smugglers.

ACT THREE. A rocky mountain pass. Jose is remorseful for having dishonored his rank and his mother. Carmen taunts him. Micaela comes to try to persuade Jose to return to his home. (By the way, how did Micaela know where to find Jose?) Just then Escamillo comes in search of Carmen. (It's like Grand Central Station.) Jose fights with him, but Carmen intervenes. Escamillo invites Carmen to his next bullfight. Micaela tells Jose his mother is dying and he must come with her. Jose warns Carmen that he will return to her.

ACT FOUR. Outside the bullring in Seville. Meanwhile (between Acts Three and Four) Carmen has taken Escamillo as her lover. Carmen's two gypsy friends warn her of her death and tell her that Jose has been seen. Carmen waits outside the bullring to "face her destiny." Jose appears and pleads with Carmen to take him back. As Carmen proclaims her love for Escamillo (we hear the crowd inside the arena celebrating his triumph), Jose stabs her.

The "space" between Acts One and Two is considerable. We are *told* in Act Two of Jose's arrest and his having regained his freedom. We are *told* in Act Three of Jose's dying mother, a circumstance which causes him to leave Carmen. We are *told* (after the fact) in Act Four that Carmen has become Escamillo's mistress.

This method of storytelling more nearly resembles the one generally employed in musicless plays. In *My Sister Eileen*, for example, we are told many things that we do not see in the play but *did* see in the libretto *Wonderful Town*, made from the play.

I think it is only fair to examine the libretto forms of a couple of other operas in order to clarify my view of the "tableau" form. Take *Tannhäuser*.

ACT ONE. Tannhäuser, a knight and a minnesinger, is enjoying the carnal love of Venus, the embodiment of physical passion, but he has a desire to forgo these pleasures of the flesh and return to earth. Venus warns that he will return to her to beg for her love. As he says, "My salvation is with Mary," Venus and her surroundings dissolve and Tannhäuser finds himself before a Madonna near the Wartburg.

The Landgraf and his hunting companions ask Tannhäuser to join them. Wolfram tells Tannhäuser of the spell he has cast on the Landgraf's niece Elisabeth, and Tannhäuser asks to be taken to her.

ACT TWO. The great hall at Wartburg. Elisabeth is joyous because Tannhäuser has returned. Nobles and guests arrive to attend a song contest. The subject of the songs is chaste love, and the Landgraf announces that the winner may have a prize of whatever he chooses. Tannhäuser sings of sensuous love (there is considerable disturbance). The knights would slay Tannhäuser but for Elisabeth's intervention. The Landgraf banishes him but tells him he can find salvation by going to Rome. Tannhäuser joins pilgrims departing to Rome and is threatened with death should he return without absolution. Elisabeth offers her life to God for Tannhäuser's redemption. He kisses the hem of Elisabeth's gown, cries "To Rome!" and leaves.

ACT THREE. Elisabeth is wasting away at prayer for Tannhäuser. Pilgrims return from Rome and Elisabeth looks anxiously for Tannhäuser. She begs God's forgiveness for her sins so that if she is taken to Heaven, she may pray for Tannhäuser's salvation.

After Elisabeth's exit, Tannhäuser appears. He is searching for the Venusberg. The Pope has damned him. There will be no forgiveness as surely as the Pope's crozier will never sprout leaves.

The Venusberg appears. Wolfram prevents Tannhäuser's rejoining Venus by mentioning Elisabeth's name, at which point, Venus disappears. At that moment Elisabeth's funeral procession enters. Tannhäuser kneels at her bier and prays that Elisabeth will pray for him.

Young pilgrims return bearing the Pope's crozier, which has sprouted leaves. Tannhäuser, redeemed, dies.

Here is a theological tract. No character is real, nor is any situation. Surely there is nothing here unless it be the music. At times, there *is* music, but dramatically it is a foolish oratorio. We do not meet the heroine until Act Two. Between Acts Two and Three the hero has gone to Rome for absolution and returns without it. The heroine seems robust early in Act Three and is dead by the middle of the act. Tannhäuser dies without apparent cause.

How can anybody regard this as a stage piece? Elisabeth is a nun, not a woman to be loved. She has lost Tannhäuser before the start of the opera because she is so unworldly, and apparently it is unworldliness that kills both the hero and the heroine. Is there a moral here?

If—if the music communicates enough and from time to time it succeeds, then *Tannhäuser* provides at least that much interest, but there is no theatre.

Having recounted librettos of one French and one German opera, let me briefly touch on an Italian one, Verdi's great *Otello*, libretto by Arrigo Boito based on Shakespeare's tragedy.[19] This is *not* a tableau opera. In general outline the original play was in five acts (fifteen scenes), while the libretto is in four, each act taking place in a single set. In constructing the libretto Boito remained remarkably faithful to Shakespeare in spirit; however, cutting on a giant scale and character simplification were essential, while subtle details had to be sacrificed in the interests of over-all proportions as well as of clarify, above and along with the music.

Bianca, mistress to Cassio, and Brabantio, Desdemona's father, were eliminated. The entire first act of the play disappeared in the libretto, though essential elements of it crop up elsewhere. The storm scene which opens the opera is a rearrangement of a small dialogue exchange occurring in Shakespeare at the beginning of Act Two. The play's Act One, which Boito eliminated, sets up Iago's hatred of Othello; also it announces the hitherto secret marriage of Othello with Desdemona, which the latter's father would have prevented had he been forewarned. The Iago set-up is stated again and again, and from the beginning of the opera we know that the hero and heroine are married.

Boito closed his Act One with a memorable love duet, a perfect idea since the audience is aware of Iago's plot and is given the feeling of its inevitable success. Now *prior* to its beginning to take effect the hero and heroine are given a blissful lyrical moment together without which much of the ensuing drama would be meaningless. The material for this duet is ingeniously taken from the third scene of Shakespeare's Act One but there it is exclusively Othello who speaks to the Duke and Desdemona's father, describing his love for and winning of Desdemona. In its duet form in the opera, the same material is divided between the couple and becomes a powerful musical climax and end to the act, providing a point of departure for the rest of the opera.

Although Shakespeare cast his Act Two in three scenes, Boito based almost all of his Act Two on a single scene in Shakespeare—Act Three, Scene 3, in which Iago hacks away at Othello, arranges for Cassio to speak with Desdemona, then shows them innocently together to Othello. He arranges for Emilia to pick up Desdemona's handkerchief, which he will plant with Cassio. As Act Two ends Othello is convinced of Desdemona's duplicity.

In Act Three, Othello savagely confronts Desdemona. Then Iago arranges to hide Othello so that he can overhear a conversation between himself and Cassio in which the latter tells of (and shows) Desdemona's handkerchief. The tension within Othello leads to an epileptic seizure.

Act Four is in Desdemona's bedchamber. This is a greatly condensed version of the scene in the play, and I believe it is more dramatic. Desdemona sings the "Willow Song" to Emilia, then left alone, she sings the "*Ave Maria*." She retires, Othello enters, has a brief violent scene of accusation, and kills her. Emilia enters and reveals Iago's perfidy. Othello stabs himself and kisses Desdemona as he dies.

Otello is one of the greatest of all operas. Its libretto, tastefully adapted, is based on a great play. The action follows itself precipitously, not as in a majority of operas or plays but as in librettos such as *West Side Story*. The characters are sharply defined and simple. The machinations of Iago are clear and their effects properly obvious. Desdemona's innocence is indisputable and her victimization—step by step—inevitable. The compression of the play works admirably for the opera.

In the best operas (and the most successful) of the past half century, drama has become more alive and has through the characters succeeded in making the audience care about the stagework as a whole. In the best musicals (1940–1965), the libretto became for the first time the compelling force, although music, as in *Carousel, Fiddler on the Roof, West Side Story, Guys and Dolls, South Pacific*, and a few others, also made unique contributions.

The librettos of the majority of repertory operas are foolish, laughably melodramatic, old-fashioned (sung in a foreign language

that not too many Americans know, and the long stretches of boredom are anticipated and accepted *in advance*), but in America those
who attend in order to listen bring with them some prior acquaintance which they use desperately to heighten their enjoyment of
many facets that necessarily elude the non-prepared.

Even to these latter people it is the arias and the star performers
that give pleasure. The general drama is predictably shrugged off
pretty much as the drama critics withdrew from serious consideration of the librettos of the new American musicals in the Twenties
and Thirties.

It is true that many people attend the opera for reasons other
than enjoyment. These people are generally annual subscribers,
often inheritors of their seats from ancestors, have no idea of what
opera they will hear on a given date and none as to who will sing in
or conduct it. It is inconceivable that any human being—regardless
of background—could anticipate with equal pleasure attending *La
Forza del Destino, Romeo et Juliette, Götterdämmerung*, and *Wozzeck*. The
first two on this harum-scarum list are indeed threadbare. A seasoned Wagnerite may be well disposed toward Götterdämerung,
and *Wozzeck* is a *chef d'oeuvre* for the nearly up-to-date listener.
Nevertheless, many of the subscribers (the guaranteed method of
hanging onto choice seats) go to *all* of them (perhaps fifteen in one
eight-month season) even if they do stumble up the aisle in the
darkness of the third or fourth act.

Why do they go? The answers are many and varied, but they
include habit and only occasionally pleasure. Many of these "regulars" have heard many of the operas again and again over a twenty-
to fifty-year period. Surely anyone who has heard *La Forza del
Destino, Roméo et Juliette, Un Ballo in Maschera, Don Carlo, La
Sonnambula*, and a carpetbag of others—all drear candidates for any
season's repertoire—twice cannot possibly look forward to enduring them for a third time. Of course if luck is running, the listener
may occasionally hear Birgit Nilsson, Franco Corelli, or Joan
Sutherland sing, or Herbert von Karajan or Karl Böhm conduct.
This sometime casting indeed provides another interest despite the
opera in which the stars perform.

The regular operagoers as a class do not go for entertainment or
enjoyment, although I believe that the majority of people who buy

tickets for a play or a musical have a genuine desire to see the performance they have selected, and what they want is indeed entertainment, whether it is to be *Hello, Dolly!* or *Hamlet.*

So—what's new?

The Metropolitan Opera began commissioning operas from reputable American composers in 1910 with Frederick Converse's *The Pipe of Desire.* It has commissioned and produced a total of twenty-two new operas. All of them have had "patronizing" receptions, but not one has been in any sense a success. Certainly in our own time Samuel Barber and Gian-Carlo Menotti are men of considerable talent, and the latter has had significant operatic successes but *not at the Met!*

I believe that in this observation there lies a bookful of truth. Allow me to spell it out by beginning elsewhere.

The Russian people know and love the operas of Glinka, Moussorgsky, Borodin, Rimsky-Korsakoff, and others, which continue everywhere—decade after decade. The musical style of these works grew out of very simple and well-known Russian folk music. The librettos originated in Russian history and fairy tale. This period of Russian operatic creativity sprang up suddenly. It was immediately preceded by only Italian opera (later French), which had been imported by the Russian Court as early as 1635 and had continued successfully for two centuries.

In Italy, there is a scarcely a barber or a farmer who has not been breast-fed on the operas of Rossini, Donizetti, Bellini, Verdi, Mascagni, Leoncavallo, and Puccini. Rossini's best-known work, *Il Barbiere di Siviglia*, is based on a French classical play by Beaumarchais and set of course in Spain. His *William Tell* is set in Switzerland. Donizetti's *Lucia di Lammermoor* is based on Sir Walter Scott's poem "The Bride of Lammermoor" and set in Scotland. Bellini's great *Norma* concerns the Druids in England. Verdi's *Aida* was an Egyptian commission with an Egyptian setting. *La Traviata* is based on a French play (Dumas) and laid in France. *Otello* and *Falstaff* both have their roots in Shakespeare, and the latter is set in England during the time of King Henry IV. Puccini's *La Boheme* is based on a French novel, set in Paris; *Madama Butterfly* is based on an American play set in Japan; and *Tosca* was a French play (Sardou) in its original state but set in Rome. Bizet's *Carmen* has a French book but is set in Spain. Gounod's *Faust* is based on Goethe's poem and set in Germany. Delibes' *Lakmé* is set in India. Thomas' *Mignon* is laid in Germany and Italy. Wagner's *Tristan* is based on a Celtic legend and set in Cornwell. *Der Fliegende Holländer* is set in Norway, and the Nibelungen Ring is based on a famous Icelandic saga. Weber's *Der Freischütz* is Bohemian, and although his *Oberon* comes from a French romance, its characters were also the basis of Shakespeare's. *A Midsummer Night's Dream*. Strauss's *Elektra* is Greek in origin, and *Salome*, based on a translation of Oscar Wilde's celebrated play, is Biblical.

And so, where are we? The whole thing is an international ring-around-the-rosie but with one vast difference. All of the Italian operas referred to are profoundly Italian in style, the German operas *echt-Deutsch*, the French, including Carmen, French, etc. Of them all, only the Russian operas have their roots—book as well as music—in Russia. The same is true of the operettas. Strauss was nothing if not Viennese, Offenbach French, Gilbert and Sullivan English. And the musicals of Gershwin, Rodgers, Porter, Kern, and the others are totally non-European: American and inimitable.

I think that this all adds up to something as plain as anybody's nose on anybody's face. The Metropolitan's American commissions were given to composers reputable in their own times, and yet out of all of them not one *durable* "American opera" has emerged! Nothing has rooted, nothing has survived.

It is my considered opinion that "American" and "opera" (in the traditional sense) are qualities which are at odds with each other. If we are to have opera as it has evolved in Europe—its birthplace without question—we have a form belonging to another time and to other places. I'm not even certain that time has anything to do with the case, because even today we have Benjamin Britten's wonderful *Turn of the Screw*, Stravinsky's *Rake's Progress*, Ginastera's *Bomarzo* (South American, but with European artistic parentage), etc.

Of course in the United States we have had "operas" other than those at the Met, and these have been birthed (and show for it) in two general and quite different places: the New York City Opera and Broadway. With all due respect or whatever *that* means, I can't ascribe much importance or originality, basic distinction or "nativeness" to any of those which have emanated from the New York City Opera. This is of course not the fault of that enterprising organization. I think that all of these so-called operas have failed to find any empathic public at home or anywhere else, and I believe this is a fact of considerable importance. I do not feel that any of them has either real theatrical, musical or locally representative distinction, and it occurs to me most seriously (if respectfully) that the fault lies not in the skill of some of the composers, or in their high-mindedness, but in the *fact* of opera of this kind being created in America! After all, the Europeans have not been able to create (try as some of them have) the kind of musicals on Broadway that we have done better than anybody else in the whole world. It should therefore not be so out-of-the-question farfetched that we, for one reason or another, cannot come up with bona-fide operas as created by Europeans for three centuries. (Certain wines, cheeses, and perfumes are miraculously made *only* in France; certain beers *only* in Czechoslovakia; cigars *only* in Cuba; best caviar found only in Iran and Russia, etc.)

However.

On Broadway—which is only a name of a filthy, garish avenue of non-theatres by now—there have been since the late Thirties certain unique and laudable and apparently lasting as well as universally praised musical stage pieces, some of which fulfill the dictionary's definition of opera (all sung and all that) and some not quite which in my opinion are in several of various ways America's own *version* of opera.

No matter what anybody has to say to the contrary, *Porgy and Bess* (1935) is by definition and in spirit an opera. It began on Broadway, has gone through revivals everywhere, and has succeeded in opera houses as a repertory piece all over Europe and the Middle East and here and there in Asia and in fact just everywhere *but* at the Metropolitan Opera House, which is located in the United States of America. In its thirty-six years *Porgy and Bess* has not gone out of style.

When *Porgy and Bess* opened originally it was attended by both the drama and the music critics. It is interesting to note that the music critics liked the choruses and recitatives; they shied away from the songs as being a bid for popularity! The drama critics, more exposed to musical shows, loved the songs and were bored by the artificiality of the recitatives. Both sets of notices generally found fault with what each reviewer was least familiar with. Today, thirty-six years later, the songs, though "popular" then (they were never "pop" songs), have become a permanent part of our national heritage. The choruses are still first-rate and the recitatives are dramatic.

Then there have been in successful sizable runs (not five, six, or seven performances in a single season and then no more) beginning on Broadway and then in many other places Menotti's twin bill *The Telephone* and *The Medium*, and *The Consul*. By now, roughly twenty years, these have "traveled" well and are in the repertory of opera companies here and abroad.

Since the general concern of this book is with librettos, it is essential that I say something about American librettos versus those which have succeeded in other countries. As pointed out before, Russian opera is the only one which sprang full grown from the head of Zeus. Not only is the music Russian but the subject matter, the text of the librettos and everything else are thoroughly homemade. And they work in Russia and everywhere else. They are honest.

In all other countries there was a kind of warm-up period in which new composers and their librettists were at first shy, then they grew stronger and more secure and finally the best of them, having written some six to twelve operas (more or less in each case), knew precisely where they were going and made it there. Examples are Verdi: *Il Trovatore* (1853) versus *Otello* (1887); Wagner: *Der Fliegende Holländer* (1843) versus *Die Meistersinger* (1868); Puccini: *Manon Lescaut* (1893) versus *Turandot* (1926), etc. In most of these works and booksful of others, the music grew stylistically and the librettos leaned over to become stage pieces, not poetic hemorrhages. Furthermore the earlier works were largely local, whereas the more mature ones became universal. More: The "between-curtains broad jump" that George Marek has referred to in relation to *Manon Lescaut*—a generally recognized schism in too many operas—is *not* present in the mature ones. *Meistersinger* happens in two days, and the action in *Otello* and *Turandot* is precipitous. This is one thing that happens in good librettos for our native musicals—already pointed out.

Now as to language—and here I do not refer to English as opposed to French or German but English versus English! Have you ever noticed that if someone said (foolishly, to be sure), "Go to the window and open it" with careful *equal* stress on each and every syllable, you would find it more difficult to comprehend than if he said, "Go to the *win*-dow and *o*-pen it." The ear transfers to the mind quickly the *key* sounds which tell all. I referred to this when I said, "English versus English." Not just words, but tempo, cadence, and everything else that we say by nature.

Now *if* we are to sing as we speak—and God knows we should— librettists first need to write as simply as we speak, and these writers must stop being put off by the term *grand* opera, which should be only descriptive of a kind of result, not a classification in a card catalogue.

The next item on the writer's agenda would be "kind of subject matter." It does not matter a tinker's dam whether the idea came from Hawthorne, Arthur Miller, or Bill Smith's *History of the Susquehanas*. If the subject matter were American, all to the good, but that is not what I have reference to. What I do mean is that the subject matter must have flesh-and-blood characters if the writers mean to involve the audience and if they also mean to give their composers half a chance to make them sing in grief, in love, happiness, fun, or any other way that communicates any emotion.

And the words must allow the characters to sing and must be comprehensible through being simple. Not "thee" and "thine" and "thou," which is only the style of King James's (inaccurate) version of the Bible (date: 1611) but by no means the way people speak. Speak-sing. One and the same thing, only the latter elongates the vowel. Nothing more.

Oh yes, one thing more that all singers must learn. (The money wasted on fraudulent singing teachers could set the U.S. economy straight.) We sing as we speak. The Italians, French, and Germans do. Why not the Americans? Do we say "*thees* is my beloved" or "this"? "Give me your hahnd" or "Give me your hand"? "Brrrrrreast" or "breast"? And on and on. Singers must give the writers of words in English a break or the writers might as well do their lines in Icelandic. (This is why in Puccini's *The Girl of the Golden West* in the first scene all those Italian opera singers dressed up like Western

American cowboys are especially absurd as they sing "Meenee" for "Minnie" and "Dick Yahnson" for "Dick Johnson" and "Goooodbye" and a few other would-be Americanisms. Of course, in the first place they shouldn't have been written there. It's an Italian opera. Now it is and now it isn't, and that was Puccini's cute little hang-up.)

One other thing that brings me back full circle to characters. In spite of the fact the Strauss-von Hofmannsthal *Der Rosenkavalier* is in German, which I do not understand, I am able to laugh at Baron von Ochs (even out loud) and to weep at the end of Act One—when the Marschallin sees herself in the mirror and realizes that she is no longer young. And at the Act Three trio when the Marschallin behaves with heartbreaking dignity and surrenders her boy to the girl he now loves. This is theatre and what all opera—especially today's—must be if it is to engage and hold audiences on its own account only. It is theatre because these are life-size characters.

Another fact ought to be faced. When a work is commissioned for performance in a big opera house, everybody *expects* to lose money. A handful of performances is scheduled for that "debut" season. If the newspapers have been kind or generous, the opera may be seen the following season for another handful of performances.

To the contrary on Broadway. There is no commission. The work has to succeed in every sense of the word. It must find its own sizable audience and a large enough one to keep it going long enough (hopefully) to pay off its producers' investment and possibly even earn some profit. If it fails, it closes. Menotti has had both experiences.

But just look briefly at the conflicting psychologies: the paid-for opera that can be sandwiched for a time in between *Il Trovatore* and *Tannhäuser* (imagine what that idea must do to the composer's thinking!), plus the advance knowledge that there will be only a limited number of performances to a probably hostile public and hopefully patronizing press *versus* the other composer who must succeed all the way or die immediately.

I think that the former luxuriates for a moment in unreality which says "The sky's the limit, kid" and writes as nearly as possible to please himself without ever much thought as to what might engage the audience, which is an ill-defined group not wholly interested in music. The second composer's first thought must be—

especially in regard to the libretto and the characters—"What will make them [the audience] care?" This second reasoning is realistic and undoubtedly played a significant part in the life of every serious opera composer in every age.

Earlier than Menotti, Virgil Thomson's *Four Saints in Three Acts* was produced. In the original production and two subsequent revivals it played sixty-five performances. It didn't reach so extensive an audience as the most successful Menotti operas, but still many times as many people saw it as those non-operas given in the established museums.

Also there was on Broadway when for political reasons it was disavowed by the WPA Marc Blitzstein's *The Cradle Will Rock*, an anti-opera that nevertheless by definition *was* one. It had a checkered career, if an altogether successful one. Later Blitzstein set Lillian Hellman's *The Little Foxes* to music, which, as opera, was called *Regina*. It had a good press and for an opera a not disastrous run of fifty-six performances. Kurt Weill, who had been a "serious" composer, then became successful with Broadway musicals, made an opera based on Elmer Rice's *Street Scene* that had a run of 164 performances. Both have been opera-house repertory pieces from time to time since then and both originated on Broadway.

I must not proceed any further without laying claim to something in which I firmly believe, which is that American opera, which many writers discuss in the future tense only, has already existed for some time. In addition to those listed above, I believe that Rodgers' *Carousel*, Bernstein's *West Side Story* and *Candide* and Loesser's *The Most Happy Fella* are operas in the same sense that *Carmen* is, and their librettos do not suffer from the silly matricentricity so nauseatingly present in *Carmen*.

But I am not alone in feeling that here in the United States we do have our own opera. The Sadler's Wells Opera in London opened *Kiss Me, Kate* (December 26, 1970) as a repertory piece and after twenty-two years it met with great success. I myself opened *Porgy and Bess* in Ankara at the Turkish State Opera in 1968, and it met with acclaim. This sort of thing will happen more and more and again and again. But note that what is given is what we know how best to do and it comes from Broadway, not what we know nothing about and occasionally dish out as imitation ragout. Lyric theatre that is authentic lyric theatre is one thing whether it be baroque, romantic, epic, or popular. And that is what the rest of the world continues to tell us about ourselves.

The differences between our own genuine form of music-drama and the traditional ones from Europe are extensive, and there is every reason to suppose that they would be. Our workable operas—never those at the Met—are based on characters that everyone knows and therefore cares about. The plots are simple and comprehensible. Their composers dress them in our very own peculiar way in music which communicates to everybody.

Should we try to be intellectual snobs, and if we succeeded what purpose would that serve? To exclude our audiences would be, in the end, to isolate ourselves.

The Greek dramatists, the Florentine monodists, Shakespeare, Mozart (court then to public), Bach, Verdi, Puccini, and all the other rememberable names wrote for times, places, and people. And for money. Was this a disgrace?

Then let us try to discover what it is that opera-house audiences care about—aside from the social aspects referred to previously. I believe in large measure that it is the *reputation* of the particular opera.

"*Traviata?* Oh, goodie goodie." Gleefully.

"*Simon Boccanegra?* Oh, what is that?" Less gleefully.

And not least of all, the singing star. Nilsson, Price, Corelli. Yum yum. I'm certain that most audiences don't care about Leonora or Elisabeth or Senta. Nor do they care about how things turn out since there is usually a mass exodus long before the end.

Anyhow there's always next Thursday.

On Broadway the audience has to care about the characters and about how it all turns out, or there are no other performances.

The libretto in opera, as in musical, is the thing, although as it has turned out it is the music in opera that in the end dominates. However, the degree of this domination depends not solely on the talent of the composer but on how forcefully the libretto stimulates and motivates his writing. Also, if the libretto *really* works, as in the cases of *Otello* and *The Consul*, the audience can be expected to have a full experience—one of *total* musical theatre, not merely of waiting in agonizing boredom from aria to aria through musical "talk" that is neither comprehended nor stylistically acceptable in our own time and place.

The writer of opera ought to come to grips with several other questions he may not have considered at all.

1. Whom is he writing for? Mozart knew the answer precisely. He knew the date, place, cast, and audience. Also how much he *hoped* he was going to be paid for it. Wagner knew. So did Verdi and Puccini and Strauss. But does today's opera composer know it? (I speak of opera as it is generally defined.) If he does not know *whom* he is writing for, how can he write anything vital? Self-expression is a destructive form of pseudo-artistic masturbation and should have been discontinued with the death of the romantic nineteenth-century French schools. If the opera composer does not know whom he is writing for, he is either an ostrich with his head—such as it is—buried deep in the sand or an idiot for slaving away for several years over a single project that may never see daylight, or, if it does, perhaps only for that once-in-a-school-or-work-shop production without pay, or without pay commensurate with the time he has spent. But is this a life's work?

2. Does he think that this operatic form, as he inherited from Europe, belongs to this time and place? Does it have an audience here? Does this kind of stage musical reach any appreciable segment of our population? Does it not seem today either museumlike or contrived? Does it speak for our time and place? Does it communicate anything to anybody? Has it ever grown any roots here in the nearly three quarters of a century since any American began to write opera?

3. Has he ever been seriously aware of what has been evolving on Broadway musical stages?

The answer to this latter one is extremely important, and I know from experience that it is a resounding "No!" (nose in the air or sand and all). And there's the rub.

It's time that the self-martyred going-nowhere-fast failures took their heads out of the sand and looked around fast (the light will be blinding) at the creative work that has been done by the best composers working within the mainstream. Mozart was no less great because he worked for his specific audience, as did Bach, Palestrina, Verdi, and Puccini—all theatre-wise and artists working for a living to be paid them while they still lived by living people who were privileged to enjoy what they were given.

What those who opine to create opera might learn from Broadway is precisely what it is that does work on the musical stage, and why. And why not.

Does anybody truly care about Manrico and the final truth that he was not a gypsy's son but the child of a count? Haven't we laughed about that same one in operetta? Of course we simply loved the aria as sung by Antonienativa, but was that honestly worth putting on a collar and a tie to go and hear? Did we feel better because the Pope's staff sprouted leaves and Tannhäuser's soul was saved? And by the way, what did the poor man really die of? And what did Elisabeth die of a scene earlier—and she looked so well only fifteen minutes before her dead body was borne across the stage on a litter?

These and similar queries are endless. But the performances go on and only the very few can really say just what they heard. Of course the language is "foreign" and so some of it seemed as silly as most of it *is* because it wasn't understood in the first place and the soprano was marvelous and everybody—but everybody—was there.

When the show was half that bad, nobody—but nobody—was in the theatre. And it is in the theatre where apprenticeships are to be served. Without these, nobody is going to learn anything. The best of the theatre writers all began there, and when they had talent they knew what to do with it. Then, and only then, is God in His heaven!

COMMENTS ON OPERA

To utter "opera" in connection with musical theatre in 1972 might have been considered dangerous in some quarters (it would scare people off!), pretentious in others. Today, however, it seems perfectly natural.

There had been several operas written for the Broadway stage by the time Engel wrote *Words with Music*, the most notable being the one for which Engel had himself conducted the first operatic recording, *Porgy and Bess*. *Porgy* had been heavily cut when it was first presented on Broadway in 1935, but even then it was apparently hard to reckon with. Theatre critics found it too operatic, music critics found it not operatic enough. When it was produced seven

years later as a musical comedy, with most of the music excised and
more spoken recitative, it didn't require the "approval" of the music
critics. The theatre critics now accepted it readily.

Interestingly, decades before Gershwin wrote *Porgy*, an
extremely popular and influential American composer who happened to be African-American, Scott Joplin, tried his hand at opera
in *Treemonisha*, which had no full scale production until 1972, sixty
years after the composer's death. (In the 1975 Broadway cast was a
young understudy, Kathleen Battle, who went on to a great career
in opera houses all over the world.)

It's fascinating that often when Broadway intersects with opera
the characters are African-American. When Oscar Hammerstein II
translated *Carmen* for Broadway, in his *Carmen Jones*, his lyrics are in
African-American dialect. It stems from a perception that the
extreme conditions of black life are more suited to the grandeur of
opera than those of paler Americans.

Although the influence of African-American musical styles on
pop music has often been noted, a parallel movement in which
African-American performers explored the world of traditional
classical music is less well known. From the late 19th century
onward there were African-Americans studying "serious" music in
American conservatories. Many, like the composer Will Marian
Cook, took their knowledge and aspirations to Europe.

The most famous and influential of these figures was the singer
Roland Hayes, born in 1887 to parents who were both ex-slaves.
He showed musical talent at an early age but didn't want to pursue
singing as a career until, as a teenager, he heard a recording of
Enrico Caruso. He gave his first concerts in Boston, then went to
London, where critical praise for a recital he gave at Wigmore Hall
in 1920 led to an invitation to Buckingham Palace to sing for King
George V and Queen Mary. His program included works in
German, French and Italian as well as traditional spirituals. The
royal recital, which lasted two hours, opened many doors, and he
went on to score triumphs in Austria, Czechoslovakia, Italy and
France.

When he appeared on the stage in Berlin he was greeted with 10
minutes of hissing, but when he waited his audience out and sang
Schubert's "Du Bist die Ruh," they were enraptured.

Among his engagements when he returned home was one at Constitution Hall in Washington, D.C. in 1931. Before his concert—the first in that hall with a mixed audience, a condition he insisted on—there was a racial incident. This led an administrator to institute a policy of not allowing black performers there, which led to the incident in 1939 in which Hayes' student and friend, Marian Anderson, was not allowed to sing at Constitution Hall. (After her iconic Easter Sunday concert for an audience of 75,000 before the Lincoln Memorial, the rules were changed and she subsequently sang there numerous times.)

Just as Joplin showed that ragtime, once considered as vulgar and dangerous as rap, could be raised to an eloquent level of discourse in *Treemonisha*, Hayes showed it was possible for African-Americans to pursue careers in classical music. Were it not for a generation that followed his example, there might not have been a suitable cast for Gershwin's *Porgy and Bess*, whose score required classical training. In 1935, when Todd Duncan, who was enjoying a serious if not a lucrative career in Washington, D.C., was invited to New York to audition for the title role, he treated Gershwin, whom he regarded as a Tin Pan Alley composer, a little condescendingly.

Gershwin was impressed that, unlike other singers, who had brought spirituals or "Old Man River" to their auditions, Duncan brought an obscure Italian art song. Duncan's first intimation that Gershwin might be a serious musician came when he saw that the composer had memorized the accompaniment after only one playing.

After Gershwin heard Duncan sing he asked, "Will you be my Porgy?"

"Well, I don't know," Duncan replied. "I'll have to hear your music."

Porgy and Bess did not succeed in its original 1935 operatic version. It entered the popular consciousness in a scaled down version, without sung recitatives, that Cheryl Crawford produced on Broadway in 1942.

Several operas now performed with regularity in opera houses were first presented on Broadway stages—Kurt Weill's *Street Scene*, and Marc Blitzstein's *Regina*, a musical treatment of Lillian Hellman's melodramatic *The Little Foxes*. Another Weill work with an operatic sweep is *Lost in the Stars*, his 1949 adaptation, with Maxwell Anderson, of Alan Paton's novel *Cry, the Beloved Country*.

In 1954 at the Phoenix Theatre on Second Avenue, known for their sterling productions of classical plays, T. Edward Hambleton and Norris Houghton presented *The Golden Apple*, an Americanized retelling of *The Odyssey* with lyrics by John Latouche and music by Jerome Moross. It received rave reviews and became the first production to move from Off-Broadway to Broadway, where it quickly died. The reason given at the time was that the show had no spoken dialogue, which to the suspicious ear meant opera. The suspicious ear recalled the New Yorker cartoon of the 20s, with a child telling her mother, "I say it's spinach and I say the hell with it." My hunch is that there were other reasons, mainly the inconsistencies of the score, that doomed *The Golden Apple*, but its being perceived as an opera didn't help.

When it opened in 1956, Frank Loesser's *The Most Happy Fella*, a musical version of Sidney Howard's Pulitzer Prize winning 1926 play *They Knew What They Wanted*, raised questions about whether it was an opera, simply because it offered so much music. In those days the score to a musical could easily fit on one 12-inch vinyl record (about 30 to 40 minutes' worth). The brilliant record producer Goddard Lieberson issued *Fella* in two formats, the standard highlights album and a two-record set that offered virtually the entire score.

Opera or not, nobody regarded *Fella* as too highfalutin for the theatre. There was no question but that its music—from the hit tune "Standin' on the Corner" to the choral "Song of a Summer Night," even to its ambitious, harmlessly discordant ensemble numbers—all fell within the Broadway vernacular. The ensemble number, for example, that begins, "I don't like this dame," although it flirts wittily with fugue, never sounds unduly "learned," perhaps because its lyrics are so down to earth.

Later that year one of the most impressive works ever to be created for Broadway, *Candide*, opened. It had music by Leonard Bernstein, book by Lillian Hellman and lyrics by Broadway veteran John Latouche and the distinguished poet Richard Wilbur (not to mention a few by Bernstein himself).

No one called it an opera but that was how it was perceived and

I still remember the first time I attended *Phantom of the Opera* and saw a bedraggled fellow enter the men's room with an expression suggesting he'd been bamboozled. "I didn't know this was going to be an opera!" he wailed (the presence of the dread word in the title notwithstanding), barely able to contain his anger. I realized at that moment, however, that one thing destined to make *Phantom* a success was its operatic veneer. Even people who claim to hate opera have a certain pretentious respect for it. They know that sitting through an opera constitutes a kind of cultural "merit badge." Many artistic institutions benefit from this notion of culture as a painful but ennobling, status-enhancing duty. When the original cast album of *Phantom* was issued on compact disc in London there were no individual numbers. Lloyd-Webber wanted it to be listened to as a whole, not in bits and pieces. The show itself has a clear flow, enhanced by Maria Bjornson's sets, especially a sumptuous series of curtains, which seem to have been designed as a kind of tribute to 19th century theatricality. Although a few numbers are clearly contemporary rock, for the most part the score is an unabashed look backward at the full-throated romanticism of another time.

The "through-composed" British musicals did have a significant impact on the structure of musicals. Until then there'd always been a sense of give and take in musicals. The performer gives a great performance, the music builds to a climax, and the audience responds with fervent applause. The ensuing dialogue is, in effect, a cigarette break, and then the lovers resume their embrace. There are remnants of this structure in *Les Miz*, especially in a comic number like the duet of the Thenardiers, "Master of the House," which cries out for applause. But much of the evening proceeds without any such give and take.

Well before the British established their beachhead on Broadway, a similar "through-composed" momentum infused the 1981 *Dreamgirls*. Two years before that *Sweeney Todd* had long passages that seemed operatic, but its individual numbers all had climaxes. They didn't blend seamlessly into the next number. Moreover, there's no sense that the music creates its own world or that anything about the material is realistic or natural—the lyrics always presuppose an audience. *Sweeney Todd* never lets us forget we're in a theatre.

It was interesting that Sondheim's mostly "through-composed" why it languished, largely un-produced, until 1973, when Harold Prince had the happy idea of doing it in the round in a slapstick, totally non-operatic way. It was not a version that served the music well, but it removed the fear factor from the material, and now it gets performed a lot, though most of the time in opera houses, where its knockabout style is not really necessary—presumably people who subscribe to the opera aren't afraid of it.

Lest anyone imagine the theatre world has a uniquely built-in fear of opera, it seems instructive —and amusing—to note that in the spring of 2003 the Minnesota Opera did an operatic version of Margaret Atwood's novel *The Handmaiden's Tale*. Its success at drawing a large audience, many not regular classical concertgoers, was attributed to its marketing campaign, in which the word "opera" not once appeared.

There's something comical about all of this. Opera, after all, is an older form of musical theatre. It has the same aim—to tell a story using music. If the connection between opera and musical theatre has often seemed weak it's because until recently the dramatic values of opera were shortchanged in production. Properly performed, Rossini's *Barber of Seville* and Verdi's *Falstaff* can draw belly laughs, but too often comedic skill has not been something opera singers cultivate.

Some operas use music exclusively, linking arias by sung recitative. (There are good reasons for this—it's harder to project the voice speaking than singing, especially in a large opera house.) Nevertheless many operas separate the musical numbers by spoken dialogue. Is *The Magic Flute* less of an opera than, say, *Andrea Chenier* because it uses spoken dialogue? Even one of the most beloved of all operas, Bizet's *Carmen*, was originally written with spoken dialogue.

Does that mean that *Les Miz* is an opera, since most of it is sung rather than spoken?

The only way to describe the soaring love songs or the combustible energy of the "Tonight" ensemble number in *West Side Story* is operatic. To my mind the score of Jerry Bock and Sheldon Harnick's *She Loves Me*, which tells its story with extraordinary musical and lyrical artfulness, is operatic, especially the way it utilizes Barbara Cook's incandescent voice in "Ice Cream."

Does it matter?

revenge tale of early 19th century London did require unconventional Broadway voices—not in the role of Mrs. Lovett, most of whose material is patter, but in the role of the ingénue, Johanna, who needs traditional training to make her aria, "Green Finch and Linnet Bird," work.

So does the title character, who cannot project Sondheim's passionate outbursts without a proper husbanding of the voice. It's not surprising that such a powerful dramatic role attracted the interest of one of the great dramatic baritones of our time, Bryn Terfel, who was supposed to sing it with the New York Philharmonic in 2000. He was medically unable to do so but he did perform it in Chicago several years later. For the Philharmonic performance, which was recorded, George Hearn, who had taken over the role from Len Cariou in the original production 20 years earlier, was called in at the last moment. His voice was still astonishingly powerful, his performance likewise—a testament not only to his talent but to his classical vocal training.

The choral numbers have a harmonic richness that also demand serious musicianship. They cannot be "belted." Yes, *Sweeney Todd* has enough music and little enough spoken dialogue to constitute an opera, but its unending flow of verbal brilliance places it firmly in the theatre. Beautiful voices will not make the material work unless wedded to firm dramatic technique.

This interplay between the demands of opera and those of the theatre has grown in importance in recent decades. Adam Guettel's *Floyd Collins* makes great demands on the voices of its cast. Nevertheless, much of the time it's written in a down-home, entirely American idiom. Even its ventures into unexpected intervals and harmonies are often offset by the sound of a harmonica or a country fiddle, which never lets us imagine we have wandered into some abstract, operatic mode.

Michael John LaChiusa's *Marie Christine*, a reworking of the myth of Medea, also has a grounding in the American vernacular, in this case Creole harmonies and rhythms. But some of LaChiusa's earlier ventures, especially his *First Lady Suite*, four one-acts about American presidents' wives, sound unnatural in the mouths of average Americans. They have a "learned" style that sounds comfortable only in a theatre with a subscription audience.

It seems a pity that the Broadway production of Puccini's *La Bohème*, directed by Baz Luhrmann, who'd directed opera in his native Australia, didn't have greater success. One of the many virtues of Luhrmann's work was that he understood how much humor there was in the original. The laughter of the audience at the subtitles showed an involvement in the work you seldom sense in the opera house, where the audience all too often is waiting for "the big numbers" and regards all interstitial material as a hindrance.

Had Luhrmann's *Boheme* been as successful commercially as it seemed in its initial months, it might have led to other such productions and hence an even greater understanding of the relationship between the "old" musical theatre and the new.

10

Adaptation to Libretto

An adaptation clearly deserves to be judged in its own right, though for the initiated the prototype will inescapably be present in the mind.

Richard Gilman

Common and Uncommon Masks

Nobody would dream of trying to build a bridge or fly a plane without first having had a considerable amount of study and experience. This is due to a matter of personal safety that is of major concern. However, there is no village in the United States in which there is not at least one person dreaming the impossible dream, who does not write a complete musical libretto that is most often replete with tunes and lyric copyrights. These "shows" are then dispatched in envelopes covered with postage stamps to people like me.

The enclosed letters *ask* for an opinion but really underneath *expect* a production for which they offer me 10 percent to 50 percent of the profits. I used to read these manuscripts, return them with carefully (and I think kindly) considered critiques. All of the shows were hopelessly bad. If I had any letter in response to mine, it was to accuse me of *preventing* production, a pox on me. Now I don't read these, although this does not mean that I don't read hundreds of others from members of my BMI Musical Theatre Workshops, or from writers of some experience who sincerely want opinion and advice. I stopped reading the unsolicited ones when I began perusing the cast of characters in one script, the first of whom was "George Sand—a lady writer."

Some of the submitted material was supposedly "original" ("where angels fear to tread"), and some were based on previously known properties—Broadway-like, but as far away from Broadway as the theatre at Epidaurus and nothing like as wonderful.

The all-pervading notion even among professional writers is that *anybody* can write a successful musical and become rich and famous overnight. Once a famous symphonic composer asked my advice about *his* writing a musical so that he could make lots of money. He was certain that he could do such a simple thing with one hand tied behind his back, and it would be *better* than those written by such simple-minded people as Irving Berlin. I was quick to assure him that he couldn't—he had never ever *seen* a musical show—and that the basic difference and an all-important one between him and Berlin—talent aside—was that the latter *believed* in what he was writing. This composer thought of himself as "slumming" in this field and his slip would show. Also I once saw the manuscript of a musical that Shostakovich wrote. He shouldn't have.

The writing of a good musical is one of the most complex undertakings ever conceived by man. It is a many-sided collaboration, and each person working on it must be talented, knowledgeable, experienced, and be the possessor of such selflessness that he can know when he is proceeding in the wrong direction or can coolly evaluate criticism from his co-workers which might wisely lead to his removing the poorer material he has fallen in love with.

The practice of adapting librettos based on previously known properties in other media is not an evil one, nor is it new. The only "trick"—and it is a neat one if it works—is to recognize what properties contain the germs of useful ideas and then what needs to be accomplished in conversion. That is all; but it is a mighty all.

By way of warning: Any play, story, film, or novel under consideration for adaptation to libretto which does not already contain all five elements discussed earlier—feeling, subplot, romance, particularization of character and situation, and comedy, or would not permit of their introduction and assimilation—is antithetical to the requirements of a workable musical show. To disregard this warning is to fly in the face of disaster unless in the absence of any one or several, the adaptor can feel positively that he has created satisfactory replacements which can fill adequately the void their omission will have left. To be sure, there is no arbitrary way one can, should, or must employ any one or all of these elements. The method is dependent on the quality of characters and situations as well as the personal taste and skill of the creative writer and the style. But a careful consideration of them is urgently recommended.

The truth is that for any of a number of possible reasons there have been, to date, no truly successful and lasting librettos that were original, *Lady in the Dark* (1941) and *Company* (1970) excepted. This does not mean to imply that an original book is a total impossibility, nor that the contemporary musical theatre is a dependent copy-cat. On the other hand, the fact that a libretto is based on some previously known work in another media does not guarantee its success. The list of poor musicals based on successful plays and novels is limitless. To name a few, not mentioned elsewhere: *Come Summer* (Esther Forbes' novel *Rainbow on the Road*), *The Education of Hyman Kaplan* (short stories by Leo Rosten), *Here's Where I Belong* (John Steinbeck's *East of Eden*), *A Time for Singing* (Richard Llewellyn's *How Green Was My Valley*), etc., *ad infinitum*.

Somehow the misconception has been generally accepted as fact that present-day musical creators have *invented* the practice of grave-robbing. This is of course farthest from the truth. The Greek writers of tragedy used *only* well-known legends and histories as the bases of their plays. All of Shakespeare's plots had earlier origins. Shaw based his *Pygmalion* on an ancient legend. Mozart and Rossini based operas on plays by Beaumarchais. Monteverdi, Rameau, and Gluck employed Greek legends. Verdi used Dumas' *The Lady of the Camellias* for *La Traviata* and Shakespeare's plays for *Macbeth, Otello,* and *Falstaff*. Puccini based *Madama Butterfly* on David Belasco's play, which in turn was based on a story by John Luther Long. This list also is endless.

So, Cookie, what's new?

In consideration of material for adaptation the element of feeling is first. Little if any is to be found in Elmer Rice's *Dream Girl*, or Shaw's *Caesar and Cleopatra*, yet they were translated for musical usage as *Skyscraper* and *Her First Roman*.

Subplot. To *Skyscraper* and *Her First Roman*, which had none, can be added *Billy* (*Billy Budd* by Herman Melville), *House of Flowers* (Truman Capote, an original), *Coco* (based on the life of Coco

Chanel. Yes, I know there is a young couple, but they have no plot and are made of tissue paper, *I Can Get It for You Wholesale* (based on Jerome Weidman's novel), *Destry* (based on a film, *Destry Rides Again*), *Baker Street* (based on Conan Doyle's *Sherlock Holmes*), *Ben Franklin in Paris* (largely historical), *Tovarich, What Makes Sammy Run?*, *Dear World* (based on *The Madwoman of Chaillot*), and many, many others.

Romance. *Caesar and Cleopatra (Her First Roman)* has an ersatz romance made up (not in the original), which was unbelievable and repulsive; *Ben Franklin in Paris* ditto. *Mame* and *The Happy Time*— fade in, fade out, inconsequential, etc.

Particularization of character and situations. This is to be found wanting in parts of shows rather than in any show as a whole. But even in its momentary absence the audience is lost. Very often the sudden and unrelated creation of a ballet can be a signpost that says that something more relevant could not be thought up. Nobody knows where to go, and so a red herring is introduced in an effort to cover up a bald spot. *Maggie Flynn, Silk Stockings, Tenderloin, Mr. President, Out of This World, Redhead* are examples.

Comedy of the workable variety. *Camelot, The Gay Life, Golden Boy, House of Flowers, Kean, On a Clear Day You Can See Forever, Redhead, Saratoga, Skyscraper, What Makes Sammy Run?*, etc., were notably bereft of laughter.

In choosing material the adaptor should locate those factors capable of immediately grabbing the audience's attention and empathy: Why should they care? It may be the situation, or a character, alone or within the situation. One mistake too often made by adaptors is that they are too "faithful" to the original, while the original is in fact much better left in its primal state if it is not to accommodate other uses.

The adaptor of a property for use as a musical libretto should comprehend some universal quality within it which makes contact with people in general, interests them, can entertain them with characters which contrast one another, a plot line (preferably several) that concerns audiences because it relates to general experience, and a resolution wanted and therefore satisfying. People and events must be in focus sufficient for the communication of feeling of any sort.

As to a satisfying resolution: *My Fair Lady* provides a perfect example. Shaw ended his play *Pygmalion* without bringing his two principal characters together romantically. He was so well aware of the general disappointment that would result that he (old Foxy Grandpa) bothered to carry on' for an additional sixteen pages of explanation—non-dramatized—as to what became of Higgins and Eliza after the play's end.

Alan Jay Lerner concludes a Note to the printed edition of the libretto for *My Fair Lady* with:

> I have omitted the sequel (epilogue) because in it Shaw explains how Eliza ends not with Higgins but with Freddy and—Shaw and Heaven forgive me!—I am not certain he is right.

Secondly there should be a careful examination of the characters and a decision that there are too many (in which case some deletions will be desirable) or that there are too few when additional ones will be created but only for precise functional reasons. (*Oklahoma!*)

Then the proscenium must be thrown open so that the action is always on stage and not simply muttered about, after the fact, back in the girls' apartment. (*Wonderful Town* versus *My Sister Eileen.*)

The three crucial moments in the show are the opening, the end of Act One (if it is in two acts), and the conclusion. The opening must be functional. It can predict the show as a whole: "Comedy Tonight" (*A Funny Thing Happened on the Way to the Forum*). It may introduce and characterize a principal role, as in "Oh What a Beautiful Mornin'" (*Oklahoma!*). It may introduce the theme and the principal character of the show, as in "Tradition" (*Fiddler on the Roof*). It may introduce separately *all* of the characters, as in *Fiddler on the Roof*. It may introduce only a place and secondary characters while preparing for the entrance of the stars, as in "Christopher Street" (*Wonderful Town*). It may introduce one of the two protagonists and show him to be both attractive, untalented, and stupid, as in "Chicago" (*Pal Joey*). Or set up an important situation in pantomime against music, as in the opening waltzes of *Carousel*. Or excite an air of mystery about which we are made curious, as in the chorus-in-the-dark of *Brigadoon*, or provide a charming playful duet involving two Eurasian children who will be the innocent causes of a major conflict, as in "*Dites-Moi*" (*South Pacific*). It can define a place, period, and style of a whole show, as in "Fugue for Tinhorns" (*Guys and Dolls*). And the show also may open—for the moment—*without* music, as in *Kiss Me, Kate* and *My Fair Lady*. (Yes, yes, there is an underscoring to take up the curtain, but this is incidental even if it is also effective.)

The end of Act One is particularly crucial in that it may determine whether or not the audience is sufficiently entertained or involved to return for Act Two. The following are a few of the many workable Act One endings.

Joey has been provided by Vera, his "benefactress," with his own nightclub, and he envisions himself as a very successful and fine performer. (The affair with Vera has just got going.) What will happen?

Laurey is going off to the social with Jud, her psychotic farmhand, and, looking back, sees Curly, her friend, standing helplessly by.

Billy Bigelow has gotten a large knife under the guise of getting his pregnant wife a shawl. Everyone is going off gaily to a clambake from which Billy and his evil friend Jigger plan to depart in order to hold up a ship's paymaster.

Annie Oakley receives a note left by the love of her life saying that he has gone away.

In *Brigadoon* there is a condition that if any inhabitant of the town leaves, the townspeople will die, and out of spite a disappointed suitor has run away.

Sky Masterson and Sister Sarah have at last fallen in love. After their return from dinner in Cuba, as they stand before her mission late at night, police whistles shriek and gamblers scamper from the mission like so many mice. Sister Sarah believes that Sky took her away so that gamblers could use the mission.

Eliza Doolittle is dancing at an Embassy Ball with a speech professor who has bragged that he can always detect a phony by speech defects. Will he unmask Eliza, the flower peddler?

The end of a show—the third most crucial moment—in the old days was an occasion for a huge vocal and orchestral finale. In more recent and better times this practice has almost completely disappeared.

Laurey and Curly go off on their honeymoon to a reprise of "Oklahoma!"

Billy has at last, as a disembodied spirit, been able to tell Julie that he always loved her. His daughter, among the high-school graduates, is singing "You'll Never Walk Alone"—the school song we associate with Billy's death. Billy now exits, expiated, to heaven.

The hero of *Brigadoon* has impulsively returned to the place where the village existed. The head of the town appears, takes the hero's hands and leads him into the now disappeared town, saying, "Love is stronger than death."

Emile de Becque returns safely from the war to find a chastened Nellie playing with his Eurasian children. "Some Enchanted Evening" swells in the orchestra as the curtain falls.

Eliza Doolittle returns to Higgins' house, which she had left in a fury. Higgins, lying in a chair, appears not to notice her and says, "Eliza, where the devil are my slippers?" Eliza comes toward him, slippers in hand, as "I've Grown Accustomed to Her Face" crescendos and the curtain descends.

The rival gangs—Jets and Sharks—jointly pick up Tony's dead body and exit. (*West Side Story*)

A few other important details come to mind in no particular order. Choreography has replaced dialogue in at least four shows. At the end of Act One in *Oklahoma!*, when it made history, Agnes de Mille created a kind of nightmare in dance. In *Carousel* the same Agnes de Mille created a beach ballet in Act Two in which Billy sees his daughter Louise dancing happily on the beach until the haughty Mr. Snow parades by with his many children and all of them snub her. The sight of this—Billy's fault—distresses him.

In *Fiddler on the Roof* Tevye, acceding to his eldest daughter's wish, consents to let her marry the poor tailor instead of the rich butcher. He is nervous about his wife's reactions, and so he invents a tale about the butcher's dead wife coming to him in a dream to threaten their daughter with dire consequences should she marry the butcher. This is achieved with dance, pantomime, dialogue, and music. The mood is hilarious. This and the next in *West Side Story* are the work of Jerome Robbins.

In the latter, a disembodied voice (with orchestra) sings "Somewhere," on which is built a dance of such quiet ecstasy that it becomes perhaps the most moving part of the entire show. In it, the members of the two rival gangs dance together freely in country fields: It is the momentary realization of the impossible and the ideal.

In most shows dance is used for realistic purposes. In *Pal Joey, Guys and Dolls,* and *South Pacific* there are dances in shows within the shows. In *My Fair Lady* (choreography by Hanya Holm) one dance is at the Embassy Ball, another at Ascot, and one which is an elongation of the Alfred Doolittle song "Get Me to the Church on Time." All of these are "show-type" dances. There is another mood dance in Act Two when Eliza, having left Higgins, returns for a visit to the old Covent Garden flower market.

Besides the one major dance number mentioned in *West Side Story*, there is a threatening one by the Jets near the opening of the show, in which a sound pattern produced by snapping fingers and fragmentary music is most effective. There is a charming "musical staging" of "America," the pavane in the gym, and much else throughout the show, giving it additional vitality.

In *Guys and Dolls* (aside from the two show-within-a-show song-and-dance numbers) there is a crap shooters' ballet set to a song, "Luck Be a Lady Tonight"—all male—which ends abruptly as Sky Masterson rolls the dice. It creates moderate suspense.

Jerome Robbins created an out-and-out show piece, an unconcealed ballet—"The Small House of Uncle Thomas"—as well as a thoroughly amusing, dramatic, and integrated number for the two principals, "Shall We Dance?" in *The King and I.*

Time is usually an important element in musicals just as it is in Shakespeare. Generally scenes rush after one another. *West Side Story* begins late one afternoon and concludes the following midnight. *Brigadoon* covers the span of a single day. *Oklahoma!* occupies two days. *Carousel seems* to last two days, but there is a moment when Billy arrives in heaven when the Starkeeper tells him his daughter is fifteen. An entire tour of Europe occupies the intermission between the two acts of *Annie Get Your Gun. Guys and Dolls* takes place in less than one week. *My Fair Lady* needs to occupy months during which Eliza is learning to speak correctly. While there are certainly no rules governing this, large lapses of time seem to belong more often to plays and operas rather than to musicals.

It is interesting to note parenthetically that Shakespeare, like the best librettists, pushes his time along continuously. Allow me to list the first five scene endings in *The Merchant of Venice*, chosen at random.

> SCENE 1. "Go, presently inquire, and so will I,
> Where money is; and I no question make,
> To have it of my trust or for my sake."

> SCENE 2. "Come, Nerissa—Sirrah, go before—
> Whiles we shut the gate upon one wooer,
> another knocks at the door."

> SCENE 3. "Come on: in this there can be no dismay;
> My ships come home a month before the day."

> SCENE 4. "First, forward to the temple: after dinner
> Your hazard shall be made."
> "Good fortune then!
> To make me blest or cursed'st among men."

> SCENE 5. "And I must to Lorenzo and the rest:
> But we will visit you at supper-time."

What occurs here and everywhere in Shakespeare and in the best musical librettos? As the scene ends there is a specific promise of action. Something immediate will be. The drama of other writers of all periods (non-musical) is far more leisurely.

While I do not think it necessary to begin a musical at a high point, such commencement can certainly be helpful. I *do* think that with few exceptions the schism between the principals is essential and we have no time to waste. Joey is seen, defined, and characterized at the opening of his show. In Scene 2 we see him try to "make" a sweet girl. In Scene 3 we meet Vera Simpson. Joey is for Vera. They fight. She is well bred, rich, and mentally bright. She is going to have him. What will happen?

In the first scene of *Oklahoma!* Laurey and Curly in a scene together; it is clear that they were made for each other. Rather irresponsibly and a little cutely Laurey refused to go to the social with Curly. No real reason. She will (later regretfully) go with the repulsive Jud. What will happen?

Julie and Billy are mutually attracted in the first (pantomime) scene of *Carousel*. In Scene 2 she deftly wins him but not before we see he is undependable, egocentric, independent, lazy, and many other things that do not include the happy working out of a marriage. What will happen?

Annie Oakley, an ignorant country girl, falls in love with a celebrated shooter whom she outshoots. What————?

At the start of *My Fair Lady* a snobbish gentleman, a speech authority, is to be pitted against a dirty flower girl who speaks atrociously. Mrs. Anna and the King of Siam—charm and democracy versus selfish, absolute monarchial cruelty divide the principals in *The King and I*. In *West Side Story* only, the two young lovers fall instantly in love without any thought of the fact that each belongs to a different warring faction. What will come of them?

I have grave doubts that any leisurely musical can work because I believe that pressure (sometimes hidden) is a necessary ingredient. Since there are so many elements in a musical show, everything that can be whittled down or eliminated is so treated. Superfluous dialogue may tend to exclude songs which must be properly exposed if they are to work best. Superfluous dancing is going to curtail plots or characters or songs which must have time for proper exposure if they are to work at all. It is the director's duty to give each of the elements its proper proportions in relation to the whole.

There have been "gentle" musicals as opposed to "brassy" ones. *Brigadoon, My Fair Lady, Kiss Me, Kate* and the new and important *Company* are among these. But wait! Examine! Their gentleness is a matter of quality but never of tempo. It is possible for a show to be gentle and swift, and it is my belief that swiftness is an inevitable concomitant of all musical shows. They may not *seem* swift, but on examination they will reveal themselves as seldom pausing for breath.

It would constitute a serious omission if, at this point, I failed to pay even brief homage to the craft and artistry of scene designers who, among other things, have made the swift movement of musicals possible. These began with the late Robert Edmond Jones and

Lee Simonson and continue today with Jo Mielziner, Oliver Smith, Donald Oenslager, Boris Aronson, David Hayes, Jean and William Eckart, Isamu Noguchi, Raoul Pene du Bois, Ming Cho Lee, Ben Edwards, Rouben Ter-Arutunian, etc. They have raised the art of theatre designer to an even higher and more imaginative level, have (when permitted) given us larger-than-life representational forms in place of the older limiting realism. They have imparted a sense of style to productions which at any earlier time we had not looked for since we seldom had cause to see it. Firstly, they have made their designs and the resultant sets an important part of the total collaborative effort that is a show. No author or librettist need be concerned about sequence of scenes and the *possibility* of their realization. Today's best designers turn dreams into accomplishments.

Out of the dozen or so longest lasting musicals, six were based on plays, seven on collections of short stories, three on motion pictures, three on biographies, three on novels, one on a single short story, and one on history. I would like to examine first five of the six that were converted from plays to note the changes that were made: *Oklahoma!* from *Green Grow the Lilacs* (Lynn Riggs), *Carousel* from *Liliom* (Molnár), *The Most Happy Fella* from *They Knew What They Wanted* (Sidney Howard), *West Side Story* from *Romeo and Juliet* (Shakespeare), and *My Fair Lady* from *Pygmalion* (Shaw).

Oklahoma! followed its parent play closely. The major change in the scenes was near the end. In the play, after the hero has accidentally killed the villain on the hero's wedding night, there is one subsequent scene. The hero has been arrested at the end of the penultimate scene, and the final one takes place at Laurey's farmhouse a few nights later. Curly appears, having broken out of jail. A group of neighbors who have been deputized come to take him back to jail. As in the musical, Aunt Eller coyly "blackmails" the men into allowing Curly to spend the night with his bride.

Rodgers and Hammerstein also created one character not in Riggs's play, Will Parker, a young man who becomes Ado Annie's opposite number. With him and Ali Hakim, there is a full subplot and a considerable amount of comedy which is not in the original. In *Green Grow the Lilacs* Ado's character had been dull. She existed only as a friend of the heroine's. In *Oklahoma!* she was infused with a vivacious and mischievous life of her own. The villain Jud (Jeeter in the original), through his one song (soliloquy), "Lonely Room," is made into an understandable human being without any loss of repugnance.

The libretto's sequence follows that of the play. At the very opening of the show (Riggs's idea, but unheard of in a musical), the hero enters singing a folklike ballad *unaccompanied* and begun off stage! How revolutionary can one musical be? One song establishes him more thoroughly than ten pages of dialogue might have done. The songs are fresh and tuneful, and lyrics are vivid and precise, and an enormous amount of humor that was oddly lacking in the original play is injected into the musical.

My Fair Lady generally follows Shaw's play, which, contractually, it was obliged to do.[20] In it there are five acts using three sets. Fortunately the shape of the original could be sequentially adhered to without damage to the musical. However, the proscenium was opened up in *My Fair Lady*. We are twice shown Doolittle outside a pub, a scene near Ascot and one outside a club tent at Ascot, three times in front of Higgins' house, the flower market at Covent Garden, the Embassy promenade, the Embassy ballroom, outside the Royal Opera House, Higgins' study (five times), and the upstairs hall in Higgins' house. All of these are spoken of in Shaw's play, but in the musical all of them are seen.

Comedy is shared by all characters and there is no subplot—a fact which I have endeavoured to account for in another chapter. Romance is ever present largely because the audience wills it; none is articulated.

Molnar's *Liliom* was a celebrated play in the first quarter of this century and has today been totally superseded by its musical counterpart, *Carousel*. Rodgers and Hammerstein made considerable changes when they adapted *Liliom* as a libretto. The play was immersed in the spirit and aura of middle Europe (Budapest, to be exact) about 1919. This aura, all important to the play, was totally eradicated and replaced by one appropriate to the coast of Maine about 1873. These drastic changes of time and place had equally drastic effects on the characters. The hero became less psychotic, the heroine less willowy. The drab couple known in *Liliom* as Mr. and Mrs. Beifeld became Carrie and Mr. Snow, two amusing

American prototypes: the roguish girl who worships security and the humorless man she marries.

The play, in a prologue and seven scenes, became a two-act musical with the single act break occurring at the point when the hero has consented (he has just learned of his wife's pregnancy) to go with his pal to commit a hold-up. This threat to safety hangs over the intermission and the opening scene of Act Two. *Liliom* was done with two intermissions, the first occurring just after Liliom hears that his wife is pregnant, the second after Liliom's exit to heaven. Liliom's scene in heaven in the play is a long, serious one, dark and predictable. The same scene for Billy—his counterpart—is charming, bright, and brief, but it does not fail to achieve the essential point.

Then, too, the functioning of Rodgers' music adds immeasurably to the total effect. The opening pantomime to a suite of waltzes, the musicalized "Bench Scene," the warm comedy songs, the stoic "You'll Never Walk Alone" reprised so effectively at the end, Billy's "Soliloquy," all add other dimensions to the play, and the beach ballet is a model of inseparably integrated dance which shares with the play the burden of storytelling. The play ends after Liliom's anonymous visit to his wife and daughter. In *Carousel*, on the other hand, there is a final scene at the daughter's graduation. Here Billy (Liliom) does implicitly communicate love to both his daughter and his wife, and we are given the feeling, on his exit, that he will go off to heaven.

Frank Loesser transformed Sidney Howard's old-fashioned play *They Knew What They Wanted* into a fresh musical (perhaps opera), *The Most Happy Fella*. First he threw open the proscenium (the original takes place in a single set) and then he began the libretto two scenes prior to the beginning of the play. We *see* what previously we had only heard about. Most importantly, he altered the character of the leading lady, who was a rather tired, somewhat tough and more mature lady of too easy virtue, to a vibrant young girl in need of love. To be able to expose her more fully (for one reason) Loesser created a girl friend for her, Cleo. Then Cleo needed an "opposite number," and Herman, a farmhand, was created. In addition, the middle-age hero, Tony, plagued by feelings of insecurity, inadequacy, undesirability, is given a sister, Maria, who voices these doubts so that they are heard without their becoming introspective philosophical monologues.

Here again the musical score intensifies the feeling—romantic, comedic, and emotionally turbulent to a far greater extent than the text of the play could have, even in its heyday. It is interesting to note that *The Most Happy Fella* is a musical in three acts, and it works well with the double break.

Last but certainly not least is *West Side Story*, closely patterned after Shakespeare's *Romeo and Juliet*. While the latter is in five acts with a total of twenty-four scenes, *West Side Story* was elided into two acts with a total of fifteen scenes. A scene-by-scene comparison follows.

ROMEO AND JULIET ACT ONE	*WEST SIDE STORY* ACT ONE
1. *A Public Place.*	1. *The Street.*
Establishes warring factions. (Montagues/Romeo's family/and Capulets/Juliet's.) Prince of Verona intercedes in a street fight and orders the Capulets to go with him, leaving the Montagues to see him later. The Montagues speak of Romeo. Where is he and why is he sad? He enters. He is in love	Establishes warring factions. (The Jets/Tony's group/and the Sharks/Maria's brother's.) Officer Krupke and a plainclothesman Shrank intercede and order the Sharks away. Officers exit. There will be a "rumble." The Jets need Tony, who has not been with them lately. Riff will go to re-enlist him.
2. *A Street.*	2. *A Backyard.*
Capulet will give a party. Gives list to servant who cannot read. Paris asks Capulet for Juliet's hand. Servant encounters Romeo (a stranger) and asks him to read list. Finds it's Capulet's party and Romeo's love, Rosalin, will attend.	Riff (Mercutio) tries to persuade Tony to rejoin the Jets. Tony finally agrees to join them at the dance that evening. He is obsessed with the feeling "…there's a miracle due, Gonna come true, Coming to me!"

Romeo decides to attend also. "I'll go along. . . to rejoice in splendour of mine own."

3. *A Room in Capulet's House*.

Lady Capulet tells Juliet of Paris' suit, asks her to consider it.

3. *A Bridal Shop*.

Maria with Anita (functions much as the Nurse). Latter is fitting the excited Maria in a dress for tonight and the dance. We meet Bernardo (Tybalt). For Maria it is important that she have a wonderful time at her first dance.

4. *A Street*.

Romeo and Mercutio en route for Capulet's party. Romeo has premonitions of death.

5. *Capulet's Party*.

Romeo and friends wearing masks. Romeo sees and is instantly in love with Juliet. Tybalt (Juliet's beloved cousin) recognizes Romeo and wants to fight but Capulet forbids it. Tybalt exits. Juliet is smitten with Romeo, who says "Is she a Capulet? O dear account! My life is in my foe's debt."

ACT TWO

1. *A Lane by the Wall of Capulet's Orchard*.

4. *The Gym*.

Members of the rival gangs are present with their girl friends. A "social director" (Capulet) tries to draw them together: "You form two circles: boys on the outside, girls on the inside.... When the music stops, each boy dances with whichever girl is opposite." Tony and Maria meet and are instantly in love. Bernardo (Tybalt) observes and berates both, ordering Maria to go home with Chino (Paris). The Jets and Sharks will meet in half an hour at Doc's Drugstore (Tony works there) for

Romeo enters Capulet's orchard.
Mercutio and Benvolio realize
that he has climbed the wall into
the orchard.

2. *Capulet's Orchard.*
  (Balcony Scene)

Romeo and Juliet, with
interruptions by the Nurse.
Romeo arranges to send for Juliet
next day to be married.

3. *Friar Laurence's Cell.*

Romeo tells of his love for Juliet
to Friar Laurence, who will marry
him. Friar Laurence thinks the
wedding might heal the rift
between the two families.

4. *Street Scene.*

Mercutio says Romeo has a letter
awaiting him from Tybalt. The
Nurse comes. Romeo arranges
with her to bring Juliet in the
afternoon to Friar Laurence's cell.

5. *Capulet's Orchard.*

Juliet impatiently awaits return of

a "council of war." Tony is thinking
only of Maria.

5. *A Back Alley.*

Tony has love scene from street;
Maria above on fire escape.
Mother's voice interrupts from
time to time. Tony agrees to meet
Maria next afternoon: he will
come to bridal shop—back
door—at sundown. Bernardo and
Anita enter (Tony has just gone).
Anita is opposed to Bernardo's
warring attitude.

6. *The Drugstore.*

The Jets are edgily awaiting arrival
of Bernardo for the "council of
war." Bernardo arrives and is
taunted. Tony bursts in happily,
understands what the meeting is
about. He shames both sides into
an agreement that one man (the
best) of each will have a fair fight
without weapons. Lieutenant
Schrank enters and threatens all of
them if they rumble. After he
leaves, Tony left with Doc, says
how much in love he is.

Nurse, who finally arrives and tells her of the wedding plans.

6. *Friar Laurence's Cell.*

Romeo and Friar Laurence await arrival of Juliet. After she joins them they exit for the wedding. Friar Laurence: "Come, come with me, and we will make short work;…"

7. *The Bridal Shop.*

Anita is about to leave when Tony arrives. Anita doesn't object to his seeing Maria, but she is worried. After she leaves them, Maria begs Tony to stop the rumble and he promises that he will. There follows a wedding ceremony (minus a minister). "One hand, one heart—Even death won't part us now."

8. *The Neighborhood.*

A musical scene in which all of the characters appear, but separately and "abstractly." All are waiting expectantly for the night, but for very different reasons.

ACT THREE

1. *Verona. A Public Place.*

Mercutio and Benvolio speak of avoiding the Capulets—not wanting to fight, but when Tybalt enters, Mercutio picks a quarrel with him. Romeo enters and tries to dismiss Tybalt's taunts. Mercutio draws his sword. Romeo tries to prevent the duel, but it occurs and Mercutio is slain. Romeo takes up the fight and Tybalt is slain. Romeo flees. The

9. *Under the Highway.*

The gangs are waiting to begin the rumble. As Bernardo and Diesel move to fight, Tony enters and stops them. He is taunted from both sides. Little by little he is insufferably angered. General fighting breaks out. Bernardo, then Riff, reach for their knives. Tony persists in trying to stop them. Bernardo stabs Riff. Tony grabs Riff's knife and stabs Bernardo. A free-for-all has

Prince arrives, outraged, and sentences Romeo to exile.

broken out. Police whistles sound. Everyone disappears quickly, leaving a stunned Tony standing over the bodies of Riff and Bernardo, crying out "Maria!"

ACT TWO

2. *Capulet's Orchard.*

1. *A Bedroom.*

Nurse tells Juliet of Tybalt's death (Juliet loved her cousin Tybalt) and of Romeo's banishment. Juliet sends Nurse to Friar Laurence's cell to find Romeo.

3. *Friar Laurence's Cell.*

Romeo hears of his exile. Nurse enters and Romeo says he will come to Juliet.

4. *Capulet's House.*

Disturbances over Tybalt's death. Paris is promised marriage with Juliet on Thursday. (This is Monday.)

Maria with her girl friends. She is happy. There will be no rumble. The girls exit as Chino enters from the rumble. He tells Maria that Tony killed Bernardo, and leaves. Maria kneels at prayers when Tony enters from the fire escape. Maria is bitter as Tony recounts Riff's death, then Bernardo's. Tony will give himself up to the police. Maria relents and forbids. Tony will take Maria away: "Suddenly they are in a world of space and air and sun." Others join them "making a world that Tony and Maria want to be in, belong to, share their love with." Jets and Sharks are joined together.

2. *Another Alley.*

The Jets. Where is Tony? Officer Krupke enters, wanting to question them. They elude him and regroup. (Comedy song.) All decide to look for Tony, fearing that Chino will kill him.

3. *The Bedroom.*

Maria and Tony are asleep. There is knocking at the door. It is Anita. Tony says he will go to the drugstore to hide out and climbs out of the fire escape. Anita enters and comprehends the situation. She is savage to Maria, but, in the end, turns to help her. (Together):

"When love comes so strong,
There is no right or wrong,
Your love is your life!"

Shrank comes to question Maria, who asks Anita to go to the drugstore (she says she has a headache) to tell Doc to hold the medicine there until she can come for it herself.

ACT FOUR

1. *Friar Laurence's Cell.*

Friar Laurence gives Juliet vial. If she drinks the contents the night before her projected marriage to Paris it will make her appear dead. Paris also comes to Friar Laurence's cell and speaks to Juliet of their marriage.

2. *Capulet's House.*

Juliet returns, tells her parents she consents to the marriage with Paris.

3. *Juliet's Chamber.*

Juliet drinks potion.

4. *Capulet's House.*

Marriage preparations.
"To waken Juliet."

5. *Juliet's Chamber.*

Nurse discovers "dead" Juliet.
(Peter and musicians have comedy
scene.) (This comedy scene
corresponds with *West Side Story*
Act Two, Scene 2, song, "Gee,
Officer Krupke."

ACT FIVE

1. *Mantua——a Street.*

Banished Romeo. His servant
Balthazar tells of Juliet's "death"
and Romeo resolves to go to
Juliet's tomb and brings poison
for suicide.

2. *Friar Laurence's Cell.*

Friar John returns with a letter
that Friar Laurence had written
Romeo about Juliet. Friar John
had not been able to deliver it.

4. *The Drugstore.*

The Jets are standing by. Tony is
hiding out in the basement. Anita
comes to deliver Maria's message.
The boys mistrust and taunt her
savagely. She becomes angry and
blurts out, "Tell the murderer
Maria's never going to meet him!
Tell him Chino found out and—
shot her!"

5. *The Cellar.*

Doc tells Tony what Anita has said. Tony rushes out in the darkness yelling "Chino? Chino, come and get me, too, Chino."

3. *A Churchyard.*

6. *The Street.*

Paris arrives to keep guard at Juliet's tomb. Romeo enters with Balthazar. Paris challenges Romeo and is killed. Romeo takes poison and dies. Juliet wakens, discovers Romeo and stabs herself. The warring houses (Capulets and Montagues) renounce their enmity.

Tony is still yelling for Chino. He sees Maria. As he runs toward her, Chino appears and shoots him. Members of both gangs appear and lift up Tony's body as they exit.

As to plot differences. In *Romeo and Juliet* there is the thread of Juliet's approaching marriage to Paris which does not exist in *West Side Story*. (Chino is a small part and one which vaguely resembles Paris.) There is also the involved business of Juliet's being given a potion by Friar Laurence so that she will appear dead. She will avoid the projected marriage to Paris (she is already secretly married to Romeo), and it is Friar Laurence's plan to inform the exiled Romeo of Juliet's apparent death so that the latter will be present in the tomb upon her awakening. When Friar Laurence's letter is not delivered to the banished Romeo in Mantua, matters become dangerous. Romeo then hears that Juliet is dead, goes to her tomb, poison in hand, slays the vigilant Paris, poisons himself, is found dead by the awakening Juliet, who then stabs herself! This stream of melodramatic complexities—common in the seventeenth century and effective in *Romeo and Juliet*—is dispensed with in the more realistic adaptation of the plot in *West Side Story*.

By the simple elimination of Paris, the threat of Juliet's impending second wedding does not exist, and both the potion and the poison become unnecessary. In *West Side Story* Tony also hears erroneously of Maria's death and, due to this, offers himself to the avenging Chino, who kills him. In both treatments of the plot, however, the sting of the avoidable-unavoidable tragedy is haunting. In the libretto it is brought about more simply than in the play.

It is my guess that Shakespeare avoided the actual wedding ceremony because it would need to have been an exact reproduction of the Church liturgy. It could not have been created by him, and so he rid himself of the need by Friar Laurence's brief speech, which points ahead to the actual ceremony.

In *West Side Story*, the twentieth-century authors could be as free as they liked, and they succeeded in creating a touching theatrical scene—original, simple, poetic, young, and, in one sense, unique in that this scene of marriage is performed alone by the consenting couple themselves.

It is my feeling that *West Side Story* is a superb example of one kind of libretto adaptation. The parallel with *Romeo and Juliet* is basic. Its change of time and place are clear and valid and of course strongly pertinent. Because it elides or deletes certain elements that were present in the original so successfully and with such excellent taste, it has been brought closer to our life and time and given a shape as a libretto which works with and requires music

These five examples of play conversion to libretto will, I believe, suffice. However, many workable musical books have been based on short stories, novels, and films. Since the material employed in these had not been organized previously in dramatic form, the librettist was freer to create the form best suited to all musicals as well as to his own.

Fiddler on the Roof, South Pacific, Guys and Dolls, and *Pal Joey* originated in collections of short stories. In every case, the librettists combined several stories in order to give substance to their plays.

An excellent libretto made from short stories is *South Pacific*, which originated in James A. Michener's collection *Tales of the South Pacific*. Oscar Hammerstein II and Joshua Logan (I am told) began with "Fo' Dolla'," the tale about Lieutenant Cable. Liat, and her mother, Bloody Mary. Deciding finally that this single story failed to provide sufficient material for their libretto, the authors turned to a second very short tale, "Our Heroine," which concerns Ensign

Nellie Forbush and Emile de Becque. To these was added the character of Luther Billis, who appeared in several of the other tales,
and he became a foil for Bloody Mary. The Forbush-De Becque
affair became the framework for the libretto, while Lieutenant
Cable and Liat provided an important interior secondary plot, and
Bloody Mary with Luther Billis were intertwined among the others,
furnishing comedy and other colorations. The musical begins with
the Forbush-De Becque romance, then introduces all of the others.
While all six major characters (and several minor ones) develop
intermittently we arrive at the end of Act One and with it the break
between the two principal older lovers. The curtain is held up in Act
Two through further developments of all characters (the two principals are separately involved) until the end, by which time the
Cable-Liat romance is terminated by the death of Cable, and De
Becque, returning from a dangerous war mission, is reunited with
the now less bigoted Nellie.

There has been a very curious turn-about in our musical theatre,
and by all laws of pendulum and history and crystal balls, this turn-
about should happen again but in the opposite way. What I am talking about is the survival of the music (the songs, if you prefer) in our
shows—operettas and musical comedies—between 1925 and
1940. The books of *The Student Prince, Rose-Marie, The Desert Song*,
and a few others are between bad and worse. Yet today amid all the
musical uncertainties, revolts, anti-the-day-before-yesterday, etc.,
the songs in these operettas still persist in performance, recording,
Muzak, and every other way. (In the hinterlands, even the whole
shows are revived and usually horribly "updated.")

In the following years to 1940 when I reckon that the musical
comedy was coming into its own, Rodgers and Hart, Porter,
Gershwin, Youmans, Kern, Berlin, Schwartz, Rome, Arlen, and
others were composing some of their best songs to librettos that
were worthless after a single season or "a little bit over."

Today those songs—the list is endless—together with those
from operettas comprise our "standards." The books (*Porgy and Bess*
excepted) at once became useless, and, despite some efforts to
"redo" them, they don't and can't be made to work. What is left is a
gigantic stack of songs that is heard everywhere and in all kinds of
new arrangements, with "contemporary" rhythms, harmonies that

often make them unrecognizable, and melodic "freedoms" that would do credit to the muezzins of the world.

(This, in many ways, is like the old popular tune "*L'Homme Armé*," which originated in about the tenth century but continued on and on in the damnedest places, such as the basis (*cantus firmus*) for solemn Masses undertaken by all of the greatest composers for about two hundred years!)

Now here is where my question arises: The books of the best shows from roughly 1940 to 1965 were the first good books for American musicals. It occurs to me to ponder the possibility that one day a new generation may "whistle" the librettos and compose new music and lyrics to them! This sort of thing has happened a number of times in grand opera.

COMMENTS ON ADAPTATION TO LIBRETTO

When Lehman Engel addressed the issue of adapting a libretto from another source he was talking about a time when narratives, regardless of the form, shared certain concerns, especially the one that preoccupies him throughout *Words With Music*, character. Contemporary novels, movies and plays shared this preoccupation, although, as we've seen, there was a powerful movement in the years after World War II to downplay the importance of conventional psychological motivation. Interestingly, this movement was more pronounced in the theatre than in fiction or cinema.

Engel was by no means slavishly devoted to any particular models in adapting a narrative from a pre-existing source. In his lengthy analysis of the relationship of *West Side Story* to its source, *Romeo and Juliet*, he notes the changes in character and plot, most of which are parallel. A digression like "Gee, Officer Krupke" doesn't exactly fit the schematic presentation. It exists to fulfill a need in musicals similar to one in Shakespearean tragedy, the need to relieve accumulated tension.

There's a comparable moment earlier in *Romeo and Juliet*, Mercutio's "Queen Mab" speech and even the lighthearted jest he makes when he's been stabbed to death. A closer parallel with "Krupke" occurs in *Macbeth*. In the middle of all the bloodshed you have the night porter's scene, an injection of low comedy that, whatever emotional solace it provides, also sets the horrifying events that surround it in stark counterpoint.

Nowadays a different dramatic logic applies. When Julie Taymor adapted *The Lion King* to the stage she wasn't dealing with a plot akin to *Romeo and Juliet*. She was transferring a plot that had its basis in folk art but whose success hinged on visual effects. She translated these effects to the stage with astounding artistic ingenuity.

Similarly, *Nine*, Maury Yeston's musical version of Federico Fellini's *8½* has a source that exploits all the possibilities of cinema, its ability to leap in and out of reality with no cumbersome transition, to create rich, deep visual images in a matter of seconds, to resemble the "logic" and structure of dreams far more readily than the stage or even fiction. Yeston recreates Fellini's concerns in expanded musical numbers that have a dramatic power and melodic beauty that are the equivalent of scenes of dialogue.

The impact of the cinema, with its fragmented narrative, was only partly understood when Engel wrote *Words With Music*. The year it was published, 1972, was not a notable one in the history of Broadway musicals. It did have a disaster, however, that, in retrospect, can be seen as a harbinger of things to come. *Via Galactica*, a science fiction musical, had a score by Galt MacDermot and a book by the team of Ragni and Rado, all of whom had concocted *Hair*. *Via Galactica* inaugurated the Uris Theatre, subsequently renamed the Gershwin. Its material was thoroughly unmemorable but some of its stage effects were quite striking—as an intergalactic pilot Raul Julia would occasionally get into the cabin of a spaceship that would extend beyond the proscenium into the audience. On one of the planets he visited there was a lack of gravity. So the stage had a huge trampoline, on which the citizens of that planet were constantly "lifting off." If this sounds pretty silly, it should be remembered that the director of this nonsense was no less than Sir Peter Hall. Sir Peter understood that visual effects were going to be more important, especially if the material was as negligible as it was in *Via Galactica*.

In addition to the visual orientation of the cinema, another influence on the course of musicals was the theatricality of rock concerts.

When Boublil and Schoenberg set out to translate Victor Hugo's massive novel *Les Miserables* to the stage, they followed the lead of

Tim Rice and Andrew Lloyd Webber, who first presented their epics about Jesus and Eva Peron in what might be considered "oratorios," concerts rather than fully-fledged dramatic presentations. In other words, *Les Miz* was originally conceived as a series of numbers that crystallized key moments in the plot. In such a context the interstitial material was secondary.

Making a stage presentation of the concert was the idea of a young English producer, Cameron Mackintosh. Given the complexities of the novel, Boublil and Schoenberg had condensed it quite adroitly. Moreover, the musical material was abundant. Adding more or adding book scenes to clarify the plot would make it even more unwieldy. Hugo's novel had been condensed more succinctly and cogently in the Frederick March-Charles Laughton movie, but those two titans also made a contribution that deepened the material.

Here the main concern was to transfer an existing score to the stage, which Trevor Nunn did with a brilliant succession of stage pictures. In a visual age the broad sweep matters more than dramatic consistency. Someone of my acquaintance enamored of *Les Miz* saw it five times and described it as a musical about the French revolution. Given the splendidly staged street fighting and heroic waving of flags, this misunderstanding is easy to explain. The French, who may still not yet be ready for self-government, have had more than their share of revolutions, not all of which have strengthened the force of liberty. In fact the events of Hugo's novel take place before and after the Revolution of 1830.

Is it dramatically essential that the audience grasp the niceties of this particular revolution to understand the story? Yes and no. If we think that theatre exists to deepen our perception of how we've reached a particular moment in history, then, yes, it would be good if we saw the events of 1830 as an attempt to redress the problems that had accrued since the revolution of 1789.

But *Les Miz* wasn't a theatre work in the mold of Friedrich Schiller, whose historical dramas distort the events of history in the interests of his powerful intellect. *Les Miz* was a romantic entertainment. Even in Hugo, the politics of 1830 are merely a backdrop for the story of one man's redemption in the eyes of God. Here they provide one of the obstacles to the course of true love. We may have intellectual objections to the oversimplification, but we should bear in mind that *Les Miz* may not have told Hugo's story very well but it told a derivative story in a way that has satisfied audiences, if not critics, all over the world.

Lloyd Webber's *Phantom of the Opera* is also based on a 19th century French novel. It has none of the intellectual underpinnings of Hugo's, but it's a work that casts an undeniable spell. In translating it into a musical Lloyd Webber and lyricist Charles Hart have not created a compelling narrative but rather a series of arresting moments, some of which, like the chorus that opens the second act, are musical. Others, like the candelabras rising from the watery Opera house basement floor or, of course, the fall of the chandelier, are purely visual. Dramatically speaking, however, a lot of dots are not connected.

Long before *Phantom* the set designer Robin Wagner, who created the starkly simple set for *A Chorus Line*, the inventive moving pillars of light in *Dreamgirls* as well as the dazzling tribute to the golden age of rail travel in *On the Twentieth Century*, complained that he'd sometimes been offered musicals in which the score was not yet complete but the scenic demands were already in place. The producers had determined the material's potential for spectacle and that had taken precedence over its dramatic needs.

He lamented this state of affairs well before he worked on a mid-Eighties musical called *Merlin*, whose selling points were Wagner's sets and magical effects devised by Doug Henning. These assets were not enough to counteract the ineffective book and score. Few musicals of the British era were as scenically lavish as Lloyd Webber's *Starlight Express*, whose dangerously high raceways required three months to install. As in the case of *Merlin*, the impressive effects were no guarantee of success.

It's possible to point to shows in recent decades that have been very workmanlike adaptations from film to stage. Two that spring to mind are *Applause*, based on *All About Eve*, and *Woman of the Year*, based on a Forties film of the same name. Both were adapted for Lauren Bacall, whose star power assured them decent Broadway runs. In both cases the creative teams made logical, sensible decisions on adapting the material from one form to another. One can pronounce both shows successful in achieving their goals. Neither, however, is inspired. Neither recreates the vitality of the original.

A similar case is the 2002 musical *A Man of No Importance*, based on a modest film with Albert Finney as a Dublin bus conductor who stages amateur theatricals. Here too the adaptation was workman-like, logical but, if anything, it called into question what about the material needed to be sung.

While it's possible to suggest several overall trends that have influenced the adaptation of material from other forms into musicals, sometimes it's simply bad judgment that blocks a successful transfer from one form to another. Robert Sherwood's delightful *Idiot's Delight*, a great Broadway success in the late Thirties when it starred the Lunts, seemed like a logical piece to turn into a musical. Its leading character was a song and dance man. It had comedy and romance in spades.

One of my fondest theatre memories is of attending an audition in which Charles Strouse, Alan Jay Lerner and members of the cast, including Len Cariou, George Rose and Lerner's wife, Liz Robertson, performed the material for an audience of the ladies who book theatre parties. Strouse, an enormously winning performer of his own material, was at the piano. He sang the two ballads from the score that ought to be better known, the title song "Dance a Little Closer" and "There's Always One You Can't Forget," the song and dance man's anthem.

Lerner narrated the afternoon. Although he was apparently an exasperating collaborator, he was a deeply appealing man. A few years earlier I'd interviewed him on the occasion of the publication of his memoir, *On the Street Where I Live*. I was thrilled at the opportunity and, on my generous *Women's Wear Daily* expense account, took him to lunch at Lutèce. While we lunched members of the staff came to our table to greet him and regret how long it had been since they'd seen him. I was in awe of the man who sat across from me, one of the most brilliant lyricists of the American musical theatre. If, however, you didn't know who he was, you might not have realized he was an important figure. He had the aura of a wounded bird.

At the audition this intense vulnerability was a great asset. As he was describing the alterations he'd made to Sherwood's plot, notably the change in the villain from a munitions manufacturer to a character modeled on former Secretary of State Henry Kissinger, you sort of winced. You assumed, however, that this gentle, wise man would understand how to make the change from a generalized villain to a topical one amusing. Alas, he did not.

That enchanted afternoon made me look forward intensely to the opening of *Dance A Little Closer* a few months later. It had a short, effective prelude that enhanced my eagerness for the show to begin. As soon as the curtain went up on a stage full of people disco dancing in rather vulgar Seventies clothes, I knew that none of the problems had been solved. *Idiot's Delight* was clearly a more fragile property than it had seemed. Sherwood's naivete about war was possible in the years before World War II. No such naïveté was possible afterward. Nor could the premises of the show be transferred to as coarse a time as the Seventies.

The show opened on a Thursday and closed on Saturday, suggesting that Lerner's vulnerability did not have the same impact on the theatre party ladies that it had on me. Had enough parties been booked, it might have lasted longer. Nor did the sets (which included an ice skating rink) or the costumes save it from its dramaturgical frailties.

Around this same time Galt MacDermot adapted William Saroyan's World War II novel *The Human Comedy* as a musical. The material was full of potential, but MacDermot's surfeit of music didn't always capitalize on it. Here was a case where an old-fashioned craftsmanlike book might have given the material a sense of structure, a spine. The music, which was not without its own felicities, wasn't strong enough to make the characters or situations compelling. Here too the story was linked to a specific time that translated ineffectively into the musical idioms of forty years later.

These casualties by creators with plenty of experience and success show how difficult it is to build a seaworthy vessel even from proven material. Nonetheless, it does seem unfair that these efforts should have failed when less conscientious ones succeeded thanks to lavish sets.

Although Engel was certainly aware of musicals that had succeeded despite their dramatic shortcomings, he failed to foresee a time when his insistence on logic could be so flagrantly flouted. In a time that does not stress narrative consistency, "the rules" Engel considered helpful if not obligatory seem not to matter—though it should be borne in mind that not every neophyte creating a work that flouts "the rules" is guaranteed a multi-million dollar production to "help" the audience overlook his shortcomings in logic.

11

Failures

... endurance, though it may be a fallible test, is the only test of excellence.

Maxwell Anderson

Not nearly everything in the musical theatre that earns a profit—even a large one—can be considered a success, even if its earning power continues for, say, about ten years. (I can hear authors and producers laughing uproariously as they deposit their profits in Swiss banks, hoping always to be blessed with such "failures.")

Lest there be any misunderstanding, let me assure the reader that the opposite of my first statement is untrue: box-office failures are not implicit artistic successes.

I do not believe in art for art's sake. Every creative work must be directed toward an audience that already exists in the artist's own time, and the work must produce an experience for each of the many kinds of individuals comprising our polyglot audiences.

In the musical theatre, nothing completely workable has ever failed with critics and public. On the other hand, a great many productions have enjoyed success—even enormous success—although they have been stereotyped in idea, shabby in construction, dull in content, and poorly crafted. Some of these shows have a way of creating a kind of instant frenzy which causes them to sail on for several years. Then when they are made available to stock and amateur companies, they are snatched up avidly and reproduced over a period of another several years, and finally they take their places on the shelves along with Nehru jackets, seldom to be used again.

It should also be mentioned that a few poor shows succeed for a time because of novelty—particularly of the shock variety. *Oh! Calcutta!* is all nude if all nothing. There have been others.

There is another large group of shows which open and quickly fold. These are obviously weak as they totter briefly across the stage. Few people try to pinpoint their faults, and this failure to examine carefully is expensive because it needlessly allows similar—sometimes identical—projects to begin, labor, hope, and die.

An out-and-out failure should not be shrugged off as "let's not flog a dead horse." This time of abject failure should not also be a time for sympathy which we are accustomed to expressing at other funerals. The death of a human being is usually unavoidable, whereas the death of a bad show is foreseeable before money-raising, casting, and rehearsals. Too often authors are advised of shortcomings in their shows, pointed out by knowledgeable professional friends, but the authors and producers proceed in the face of storm warnings with "We'll fix that in rehearsal." No bad show has ever been truly "fixed" in rehearsal. Some have been improved a bit by cutting, or a fleeting illusion has been created that a new director or choreographer replacing the original one will resolve all problems; but the fundamental idea, when it is wrong, cannot be altered sufficiently to produce the all-important difference between failure and success or workability.

The causes of failure are manifold, but true success is a result of talent plus knowledge and an impersonal perspective of the project at hand. Please notice that I did not refer to "formula." I do not believe in formula. I do, however, believe in the wisdom that comes of a careful study of the past—success and failure—and in the possibility of obtaining a biopsy which might indicate the causes of both.

To begin with, let us refer again to the most exemplary musicals in order to list certain qualities they share with one another. The musicals I have in mind include *Pal Joey, Oklahoma!, Guys and Dolls, Carousel, The King and I, South Pacific, Kiss Me, Kate, Brigadoon, My Fair Lady, West Side Story, Fiddler on the Roof*, and *Company*.

All of these except *My Fair Lady* have at least one subplot. *South Pacific, Kiss Me, Kate*, and *Brigadoon* have two each. *Fiddler on the Roof* has four. My reasons for the successful working of *My Fair Lady* minus a subplot have been stated earlier. All these shows employ romance in one form or another as an essential core. All of them engender in the audience an empathy due to the prototypical definitions of the characters and the universal relationship of the plots to most human beings. This latter quality eschews the use of stereotypes and promotes interest and credibility.

In the light of these observations, I would like to examine briefly some of the success-failures and some of the failure-failures and attempt to codify some of the causes which contributed most strongly to both. In musicals—strange to say—the quality of music and lyrics has little to do with the total result. These help or hinder, make memorable or are bypassed as a negligible contribution to the end product, but the libretto must carry the prime responsibility for success or failure precisely as in a nonmusical. It is the workability of the play that accounts for the end results.

It is my hope that by categorizing book deficiencies to be found in less than ideal musicals some attempt at lifesaving future writers and producers may be made. If my thinking is less than rational, I can hope that my errors in judgment may at least produce *better* thinking or *some* thinking that may lead to fewer flops and better shows.

First I would like to examine some of the shows I would call "success-failures," which is to say shows that enjoyed a certain instant success running on to something less than infinity, whose internal limitations have circumscribed the extent of their "after-life," and whose permanent demise is and was predictable. Not so incidentally—even from a purely commercial point of view—shows like *Carousel, Fiddler on the Roof*, and *Guys and Dolls* fare much better over an extended period than *The Music Man* or *Cabaret* and not because of any obvious commercial appeal (two of the three shows are "sad") but because they are better made. They go where they mean to go.

I would place squarely in the success-failure category *The Music Man, The Unsinkable Molly Brown, Candide, What Makes Sammy Run? Jamaica, Mame*, and *George M!* This is only a partial list, but these particular shows—perhaps not strange to say—all lack subplots. Of these, *Candide* has no continuing romance, and both *Mame* and *George M!* contain none. (I can hear screams, but I would still claim that the bits of romance tossed into the latter two shows are mere crumbs—brief and integrally unimportant to anyone in or outside either show.)

Then, too, the characters in *The Music Man, The Unsinkable Molly*

Brown, and *George M!* are such stereotypes involved in such ordinary
and predictable situations that it is quite impossible to empathize
with them. All suffered from old age long before they were contrived, and they were presented in no situation less subtle than W.C.
Fields' nose. The makers of *Music Man* must have felt that they were
in trouble when they resorted to an exercise in Terpsichore involving a number of fat ladies in Grecian costumes, and the music
reached for adrenalin in the form of an old-fashioned American-
type march, "76 Trombones." The tried-and-true tricks were in full
operation.

On the other hand, the characters in *Jamaica* invited no sympathy
and for the very opposite reason: They never achieved the status of
human beings. It was the contribution of Lena Horne and David
Merrick that created a kind of simulated success.

In *George M!* there isn't a single situation about whose outcome
you could give a damn. The production was nearly as vulgar as the
resuscitated songs by yoo-hoo know who-oo, with those red and
white in-stripes all over everywhere and a man programmed as
"George M"—once very talented—making like a fetus. This show,
in the words of one critic, was a string of finales.

But there are more serious considerations which authors and
producers undertaking a project like *George M!* should ask themselves before abandoning it. Why choose George M. Cohan as the
hero of a musical? Of course I can surmise the quick off-the-cuff
principal answer: We can employ for the show an endless rabble-
rousing dysentery of antique songs which Cohan once composed.
But there are two *other* reasons that come to mind, without involving profound thinking, why *not* to have embarked on this project.

From the libretto point of view Cohan was hardly an heroic character. He did send "our boys" into World War I with "Over There" on
their needlessly dying lips, and Congress rewarded him with a dec-
oration and royalties poured lavishly into his bank account. He was
also regarded as an impossibly difficult man to work for and with, a
selfish tightwad and a supreme egotist. He also—almost solely—
held out against the formation of Actors' Equity (the actors' union)
and never did relent or change his position as long as he lived.

There have been excellent musicals that employed anti-heroes at
the top. *Pal Joey*, Billy Bigelow (*Carousel*) and to an extent the King

of Siam are good examples. However, George M. Cohan seems to have been (and was) an out-and-out villain, several whole staircases beneath the lowest anti-hero. At least Joey and Billy had charm. Both provided their respective ladies with what they most wanted. Billy Bigelow had some special attraction, and his wife Julie contrived their wedding ever so subtly.

The King of Siam-in his own limited way-was trying to help his wives and progeny by importing a Welsh teacher to instruct them. Because the latter was not easily ordered about, the dramatic conflict occurred in *The King and I.* Throughout the King was privately trying to learn, to change, to become humanized. But George M. Cohan-unlike the three above-mentioned anti-heroes-had no redeeming qualities. Whatever charm he was able to exercise was limited to Cohan the performer and not Cohan the person.

From the musical point of view the successful score for a show is a collaborative effort. Since Cohan's songs were frozen by death and a lingering nostalgia which still infects a not very large group of very old souls, it follows that the music had to be simply "stuck in" here and there between random speeches and scenes and assigned to characters for whom they could never have been intended.

Clive Barnes, the *New York Times's* guardian and proponent of Only-the-Newest and Loudest-Music-Is-Good-Enough, tossed *his* hat into the air, and *George M!*, which is the oldest of all old hats in the world, staggered along for a not very long time. Perhaps there is a reason for Barnes's enthusiasm: He was an insular Englishman unacquainted with earlier American theatre and therefore *George M!* was new to him.

Another of the success-failures lacking subplot and appreciable romance is *Mame*, based on Jerome Lawrence and Robert E. Lee's adaptation of their soap opera *Auntie Mame* (based on Patrick Dennis's novel), which as a play ran along successfully starring Rosalind Russell. The play worked despite its mawkish sentimentality, because the central character was well motivated. You cared about the lady who inherited a young orphaned nephew. You cared about the boy and their mutual attachment. But in making the musical there had to be considerable chopping-out, and it is my feeling that this was unwisely done. I suspect that everyone took the audience's prior exposure to the characters too much for granted.

Almost the only thing that Mame taught her nephew in the musical was how to make a dry martini—a sufficient reason for the child's lawyer to remove him from her clutches. Also there had to be music? And production numbers? The show should've been presented by Hallmark, because every production number celebrated an occasion: Christmas, New Year's, Thanksgiving, an engagement, etc.

The tip-off is to be found in the very opening lines.

> VERA: Mame, what the hell are we celebrating?
> OTHERS: Yeah what's the occasion, Mame? What *are* we celebrating?
> MAME: A holiday.

There were so many production numbers that insufficient time remained to develop the essentially important if soapish relationship of aunt to nephew. The play made the most out of a very tender love between aunt and nephew. It was this kind of "romance" that held the play together and held the audience's empathy. (By the way, this *was* a new role for romance in the musical theatre except that it was so truncated that it failed in effectualness.)

This suggests another unhealthy factor. The once musical-comedy young romantic pair now have too frequently been reduced to half a pair, or a total of one. That one is usually female, often grotesque and not young. The leading ladies of *Mame, Gypsy, Hello, Dolly!, Coco*, and many others will illustrate this point. In *Man of La Mancha* it was a feeble old man.

This upward thrust of the age bracket makes a caricature of romance and throws the usual burden of including it on minor characters. This again was *one* of the many miscalculations to get in the way of artistic success in *Cabaret, Zorba*, and *Dear World*.

Back again to *young* love in *Mame*: There must have been something wrong with the nephew, whom we hardly meet and certainly never know, if he could fall in love with such a "careless" girl in the first place and then allow her to be taken away from him under such shockingly offhand circumstances without uttering a single protest or taking a single step forward.

Among success-failures, if more often on the list of failure-failures, one will find strong ideas that defied suitable adaptation. The source material worked with distinction in another medium but could not be forced to function properly in conversion. In this group among the success-failures belong *Candide* and *What Makes Sammy Run?* (both based on novels); and on the casualty list *Her First Roman* (Shaw's *Caesar and Cleopatra*) and *DearWorld* (*The Madwoman of Chaillot*), both adaptations of plays.

Candide has Leonard Bernstein's very best score with a book by Lillian Hellman based on Voltaire's satire. It is a philosophical travelogue which has worked well as a literary piece for more than two centuries, and I think it might be made to work as a motion picture, but on the musical stage it is in trouble.

On the positive side and in addition to the glory of Bernstein's score and the glowing lyrics by Richard Wilbur, John Latouche, and Dorothy Parker, it must be said at the outset that *Candide* is an illustrious failure. The imperfections of Lillian Hellman's libretto are nevertheless not without quality. Unhappily what is important for the theatre is that it does not really work. It has style and it reaches for stars undreamed of by writers who are glib about same. It is a distinguished attempt that was doomed to fail at the very outset.

Lillian Hellman said in an interview recorded in *Writers at Work*: "*Candide* and *My Mother, My Father and Me* were botched, and I helped do the botching. You never know with failures who has done the harm. . . ."

The failure is implicit in the very choice of Voltaire's satirical novel *Candide*,[21] and I would like first of all to describe the original.

Voltaire called his witty novel *Candide* or *Optimism*. It is written as a narrative in thirty short chapters. The sole constant character is Candide himself, a rather dull-witted young man. It was necessary for Voltaire to give him this non-attribute because this work is a philosophical satire and it allows the hero to question many things about life, love, God, etc., which a bright young man couldn't possibly ask, not out loud.

Candide's female opposite, Cunegonde, appears fleetingly near the beginning. In Chapter VII, Candide *happens* to find Cunegonde. In Chapter XIII, he leaves her again. He finds her—ugly and undesirable—in Chapter XXIX.

During these thirty chapters the hero is guided by the philosophy of his teacher, Dr. Pangloss (mostly in absentia), whom he catches up to in Chapter IV. Candide witnesses the hanging of Dr. Pangloss in Chapter VI. In Chapter XXVII, the doctor reappears; he has not died.

In keeping with the style of this great satire, there are no fewer than ten impossible if witty coincidences. Candide is an inveterate traveler *supposedly* always and only in search of Cunegonde. Although Voltaire wrote his piece more than two centuries ago and therefore long before planes, fast ships, trains, etc., Candide seems to have covered the entire world. There are a great number of characters, many of them important if only briefly present, and each one relates a full-fledged autobiography. There are no fewer than sixteen of these.

Voltaire's hero lives by but often naively questions Dr. Pangloss' philosophy, which is that ours is the best of all possible worlds and everything that happens—no matter how catastrophic—is for good. This is the intentionally absurd theme, and it is subjected to much merriment in the course of disprovement.

The plot is simple: Candide is turned out of his home with a baron in Westphalia. He endures many terrible plights and is always in search of his love, the baron's daughter, Cunegonde. When he finally locates her and can settle down, he does so because he believes it is his duty; but he no longer loves her because she is ugly.

I think that Voltaire's wanderer (and largely for this reason) is the least likely character to be used for anything less than an epic motion picture. As originally written Cunegonde occupies, to a large degree, the position of *cause*. As a character she is nearly non-existent. Dr. Pangloss, whose words of questionable wisdom become the *modus operandi*, is largely absent. There are an abundance of tales from the minor characters, but considering the unimportance of the tellers, it is unlikely that any of them could be well-enough integrated to form a subplot.

Lillian Hellman's approach to her formidable task was the best one in any circumstance. She took Voltaire's characters, his philosophy and the fact that Candide is in constant pursuit of Cunegonde in a variety of places and created a plot. She kept Candide and Cunegonde together in many more scenes. In Act One (there are two acts) the hero and heroine appear in Scenes 1, 3, 3A[22] and 4, the final scene of the act. In Act Two, they are together throughout.

Dr. Pangloss, who was so infernally sporadic in Voltaire, appears in Act One in Scenes 1 and 2 as himself, the incurable optimist ("This is the best of all possible worlds"), and then Miss Hellman pulls off a neat trick: She uses the same actor to play Martin, a beggar, street sweeper, etc., who is an incurable *pessimist*. He appears in Scene 4 of Act One, the last of the act. In Act Two Martin is in Scenes 1, 1A, and *then* is Dr. Pangloss *also* in 1A, 2, and 3.

A fourth character, the old lady who is associated with Cunegonde, first appears in the third scene of Act One, then in 3A and 4. In Act Two she appears throughout.

By keeping the four leading characters closer together in time, the story line is tighter and the audience is made to care more about them. Also for the same reason the narrative appears more "normal" in that it actually does concern people, not merely the tacit disproof of a philosophy. All of this constitutes a particularly skillful achievement, but alas, more is needed if it is ultimately to work. There is no subplot here, although the frequent changes of place would seem to make a subplot unnecessary. The musical moves from Westphalia to Lisbon, to Paris, Buenos Aires, Venice, and back to Westphalia. In this way the audience is provided additional entertainment. However, a subplot here was essential because what the characters do is repetitious in spite of frequent costume and scene changes. Nevertheless, Candide is always behaving stupidly, except in the final scene when, without transition, he becomes assertive. Dr. Pangloss is always a sunrise of optimism, and his other half, Martin, is too predictably (of course this was intentional) cynical. The old lady is practical, greedy, and ambitious. There is almost no change to any character within this limited spectrum.

The "movement" in nearly every scene becomes monotonously predictable because it involves only repetition. Candide is always going to be duped, Dr. Pangloss is always going to find good in the evil that befalls them both. Cunegonde is always going to take advantage of each situation because it promises worldly goods and/or security for her despite the fact that this action militates against Candide, whom she continuously and unbelievably professes to love.

In my opinion the most serious flaw in the libretto concerns

Cunegonde. She is a selfish, ridiculous trollop despite the fact that what she does is obviously satirical. We cannot wish her well especially if we accept Candide as our hero. However, that too is dubious. We can laugh at him, empathize with him in a limited way, wish to Christ we could help him by teaching him some worldly sense. But then the laughter becomes weaker through repetition, his predictably foolish decisions become boring, and finally his sudden violent change in the very last scene seems highly unreal. He is an atheatrical figure.

By the time he is reunited (and we can feel assured that it is to be forever) with Cunegonde, she is far less than desirable, and we can only conclude that once again poor Candide has been duped. Candide: "And I am not young, and not worth much. What we wanted we will not have. The way we did love, we will not love again. Come now, let us take what we have and love as we are."

Dr. Pangloss offers to marry them, concluding with "Thus we promise to think noble and do noble"—to which Candide replies (with force), "No. We will not think noble because we are not noble. We will not live in beautiful harmony because there is no such thing in this world, nor should there be. We promise only to do our best and live our lives. Dear God, that's all we can promise in truth. Marry me, Cunegonde."

Finally the entire cast brings down the curtain with an optimistic jingle.

We don't care about the Merry Villagers as they try to make it all appear innocent, sweet, happy and all that is not possible. We do not care because we have not been given anything sturdy, attractive, or honest enough to generate any feeling whatsoever. Pity, but nothing that anyone has the right to look arrogantly down his nose at. (I feel this way also about *Anyone Can Whistle*, by Arthur Laurents and Stephen Sondheim, because it tried hard and knowledgeably to go off in a new direction, which it never was able to conquer.)

What Makes Sammy Run? was originally a biting novel of ruthless ambition. Stripped of its descriptive and commentating material in its libretto form, it was reduced to a too simple plot impossible of sustaining interest for an entire evening in the theatre. Obvious comparisons are to be made between Sammy Glick, Joey Evans (*Pal Joey*), and J. Pierrepont Finch (*How to Succeed in Business Without*

Really Trying), all of them basically heels, yet Joey and Finch are endowed with charm. You are fascinated to see what will become of Joey, and you are satisfied when he is dispossessed. He is no worse off than at the start. This is neatly managed without resorting to lessons in morality.

You know from the outset that Finch is *going* to succeed in business, and you want him to in spite of his high-handed methods because he is likable, and perhaps most of all because he is not real but a farcical representation—a cartoon. The authors always took care to keep him charming, and in his not so mythical quest for power and position, no heads rolled. There was nothing to detest about him because no one was hurt. He was a delightful spoof of an animal whom in reality we despise.

I think perhaps the most serious flaw in *What Makes Sammy Run?* was the fact that Sammy Glick *was* real. He lacked charm. Heads did roll. He was the real McCoy, and this fact alone would prevent his being even the anti-hero of the piece. (The same was true of Harry Bogen in *I Can Get It for You Wholesale*. Billy Bigelow is the anti-hero of *Carousel*, but the audience is satisfied because of his eventual expiation. Joey Evans, witless boy without sense enough to rob a piggy bank, is easily disposed of. Nobody is hurt. Not even Joey. But Sammy Glick goes after everything with hammer and tongs, and the sight we see is neither pretty, unexpected, nor entertaining, and nothing is added to whet our interest along the way. He is an unstoppable steamroller.

Then too *What Makes Sammy Run?* is thin for the stage. The three-cornered story of Sammy, his nice *amour* (plus her other friend), and his boss's conniving daughter are not enough. There was no attempt made to remedy this by creation of a real subplot, and so we were stuck for a full evening with people we didn't care about and a far too familiar situation. In Budd Schulberg's novel the author had pungent comments to make, and he always made them sharp. In the musical, comment had to come as a result of what we saw, which was not enough. The sole reason *What Makes Sammy Run?* enjoyed a decent run was the presence of Steve Lawrence as the anti-hero. Nothing could have worked except this popular singer who was also an untrained but highly talented actor. He was happily provided by the composer Ervin Drake with two songs which were reasonably appropriate and were hits for quite a time.

I think it altogether fitting that I come to grips with *Man of La Mancha*—a great, great success (as the crow flies) based on the celebrated novel of Cervantes, and to my way of thinking and that of a few of my colleagues, it does not work. (I introduce it here because, like the four aforementioned shows, its libretto is an adaptation of a masterpiece.) The musical has a book by Dale Wasserman, music by Mitch Leigh, and lyrics by Joe Darion.

Cervantes' original novel is distinguished by the quality of writing.[23] It can describe brilliantly and narrate with pathos. As a musical, description is an impossibility. Pathos in the original becomes sugary sentimentality in the musical which also failed in credibility. I cared nothing about the girl or her being "uplifted," and *seeing* Don Quixote—blithering idiot—made me discredit all that he had to say, obviously the product of senility. I could not fail to agree with the hostile Dr. Carrasco's words: "There are no giants. No kings under enchantment. No chivalry. No knights. There have been no knights for three hundred years."

Are we being itsy-bitsy, or is this not true? And later: "Hold! Thou ask my name, Don Quixote. Now I shall tell it. I am called— the Knight of the Mirrors! Look, Don Quixote! Look in the mirror of reality and behold things as they truly are. Look! What seest thou, Don Quixote? A gallant night? naught but an againg fool! Look! Dost thou see him? A madman dressed for a masquerade! Look, Don Quixote! See him as he truly is! See the clown! Drown, Don Quixote. Drown—drown in the mirror. Go deep—the masquerade is ended! Confess! Thy lady is a trollop, and thy dream the nightmare of a disordered mind!"

To all of this reality and more, Don Quixote replies in the sugary generalities of an impossible song cast in the "inspirational mold." Pure Woolworth! From the inimitable jewelry department. It seems to me that the cultlike embracing of this "inspirational" song indicates only too clearly the extraordinarily low taste that millons of people everywhere enjoy. The pile of cliches here included "impossible dream," "unbearable sorrow," "unrightable wrong," "to follow that star," followed by "no matter how far," "heavenly cause," "I'm laid to my rest," "The world will be better," "last ounce of courage," and finally "unreachable star."

These non-images are so time-worn, so common, so vulgar, so sugary, and such generalizations that I should have thought that even people who regularly attend "do good" club luncheons, listeners to the phoniest, tritest political orators, and devotees of TV soap operas would have been revolted. They have not, and more's the pity.

Also one of my pet abominations is inconsistency of language. How is it possible for Dr. Carrasco to say (and everyone else does throughout the *spoken* parts of the show), "Thou ask," "What sees thou," "Naught but. . .," "Dost thou," "Thy lady," "Thy dream," etc., and *then* we have lyrics following with normal pronouns: "Your arms," "This is my quest," "And I know, if I'll only be. . .," "That my," "When I'm laid," etc. Inconsistent?

The whole thing is an imitation. Don Quixote was really Cervantes with costume and make-up. An imitation. To what purpose? The music was imitation Spanish when it remembered what it was supposed to be. Why not real Mitch Leigh if there is a real Mitch Leigh? Why should we care? Personally, I didn't. Obviously I and a few friends of mine are outside these who were touched by this masquerade. It therefore works for them. I believe that an audience as large and as universal as *Man of La Mancha's* must have the right on its side. It usually does. I deeply regret that in the four times I have witnessed performances during each of which I tried to find the light (as it were) I came away only more convinced that it did not exist.

And so it goes.

It is too often forgotten that narration, description, and comment are among the principal elements of the novel and that all of these are inhibited in the theatre. A single song may utilize any one of these elements, but in length alone as well as perhaps in depth the result can in no way compare with what, say, Dostoievski, Proust, Mann, O'Hara, Maugham, or Mailer would come up with in a similar situation and in the employment of their own art.

It is precisely because of this kind of essential concession which adaptors must determine that decisions governing what can or cannot be made to work in transposing a novel to play or musical must be made. If the loss is a too grave one and the gain not sufficiently compensatory, the project should be abandoned. Otherwise failure must be the result. If on the other hand characters and story lines are the principal issues, strong, interesting enough, meaningful, perhaps the inclusion of songs and dances will compensate sufficiently or even abundantly for the other elements necessarily sacrificed in the transference.

It seems important now to examine three shows in this category which I felt lacked the essential stuff that should lie at the very core of lyric librettos—feeling.

First, there is *Sweet Charity*. We are told at the outset in neon signs that the girl is looking for love. Boy #1 pushes her into a lake (it was the orchestra pit and no one was fooled). She recovers quickly enough to encounter a romantic Italian movie star. In this encounter she is preoccupied with collecting souvenirs so that her friends will believe the experience really happened. She encounters Boy #3 in a stuck elevator and he leads her almost to the altar but not quite. But Pollyanna isn't altogether dead, and she finally assumes *that* role as she disappears upstage into—was it a sunset? It usually is. *Finis*. Well, in her search for love she suffers not a bit. She has opportunity after opportunity to sing touching ballads, but they are not provided.

In the scene with the movie star, their almost love scene in his apartment is interrupted by a knock at the door. He hides her in a closet in which we can clearly see her. The knocker enters and she is his temporarily estranged girl friend. They make love and go to bed while our too-brave-to-be-true girl spends the night in the closet performing a would-be comedy routine, smoking a cigarette, then blowing the smoke into a cellophane clothes bag. No feeling here, no sir. The next morning, while the girl friend still sleeps in a curtained bed, the romantic Italian actor spirits our heroine out of the closet. Her parting shot is an unfunny wisecrack. The writer (Neil Simon) blew that *one* obvious opportunity to make us believe that poopsie Chaplin had a heart. So now we'll never know. But I fail to see in the circumstances how anyone could care. I didn't.

Sweet Charity is a perfect example of our recent equating of stage and screen. In film, frequently the audience (particularly the psuedo-intellectual audience) can accept and believe in an anonymous character because of the way the director points to or comments on that character. (The feeling for the character is all in the point of view of the lens.) In film, it isn't the feeling that counts; it's the artsiness of the director. In fact, film is a lazy audience's medium. They don't have to work at anything. However, the stage is of necessity a writer's medium. It is the point of view that he creates in the writing of the work that makes it possible for the audience to suspend its disbelief and makes the audience work to understand what's going on. *Sweet Charity* attempted to impose artsy film techniques on the stage. And the audience couldn't care less.

I listed "subplot" as an element essential to a successful musical. Because I do not feel academic about anything, I also said that *any* element might conceivably be omitted *provided* the writer was aware of the omission and was able to supply a satisfactory something to replace it. In *Sweet Charity*—which is, in my opinion, a success-failure—there is no subplot. Okay, let's see what replaces it. Certainly there are many devices already invented and others to come which could fulfill such a need. *Sweet Charity*—minus a subplot—however, had something that *might* have worked successfully in its place. It supplied all the assets of a good subplot except rest for the star member of Plot A, for in this case the opposite number was always another character.

Sweet Charity consisted of three separate vignettes. Each involved the girl in search of love (this idea was the cobweb that was intended to hold the whole thing together—the idea plus the girl). The trouble was that none of the three men opposite the one girl was clearly enough defined or sufficiently developed. The first was seen and heard only briefly at the very beginning. The second—the Italian actor—and the third were mere foils for the girl. The third was more an excuse for a big production number (dancing) than anything else.

This use of several separated plots (in this case not nearly inventive or developed enough) might conceivably have substituted for a running, parallel, or contrapuntal subplot. However, what these accomplished in *Sweet Charity* was insufficient. The underdeveloped men were never more than foils, and the girl, her character, purpose, search (lacking in credibility), and dynamics were unwaveringly the same. *Sweet Charity* on the stage "made it" because of Gwen Verdon (and Bob Fosse's dances) just as *What Makes Sammy Run?* made it because of Steve Lawrence. However, neither of them really was more than a success-failure.

Both *Cabaret* and *Zorba* were created by the same composer (John Kander) and lyricist (Fred Ebb), were produced and directed by Hal Prince, but had different authors. *Cabaret* had, by far, the highest potential of all shows in the success-failure category, and perhaps not strange to say both it and *Zorba* had identical weaknesses. Both were great wastes because they could have been fully realized, and had they been—especially *Cabaret*—they might have been added to the roster of the very best. The failure in both cases stemmed from a lack of feeling, and this in turn was due to a lack of "particularization" and a great underdevelopment of characters. There was also no decision as to precisely what kinds of shows they were to become, a false reliance on what the audience could supply out of its own experience, and both had ill-defined musical scores (discussed previously). It is true that all of these serious faults are interrelated.

The initial idea of *Cabaret* was excellent, but why take Christopher Isherwood's marvelous Berlin stories and John van Druten's often workable dramatization (*I Am a Camera*) if what is to result is not enough like either to suggest a plagiarism suit? In Couple Number One Sally Bowles (heroine?) might as well have been a dish of goat's cheese. She was a blob. The boy (Isherwood himself) was a darn nice American kid. This boy and this girl have an affair? Well, the absence of sex between them was precisely one of the dramatic and most original features of what Isherwood wrote, because the boy was homosexual and not in any way responsible for Sally's eventual pregnancy. This made a situation.

Couple Number Two consists of an elderly rooming-house keeper and a shy, lovable Jewish fruit-store owner who lives in her pension. The audience is supposed to see the rise of Hitler through the effects on four human beings and gasp at a dissolute society as presented in a cabaret. But "supposed" is the entire distance traveled by the audience. The boy and the girl never develop, and who were they that we would weep for them? Two innocuous (if sometimes attractive) ice cubes who melted before they could become a part of our memories. They were conceived and played in such a way as to suggest that they were unaffected by the dissolution around them. In fact they had nothing whatsoever to do with the play's theme. (This also was the reaction to the young couple in *Dear World*.) *Cabaret* lost out on its "theme," which is engagingly pointed

out by the emcee. But the young couple are untouched by the dissolution, and the old couple are affected only by Nazism, which is
only one symptom of the dissolution, not the dissolution itself. The
writer did not *focus* in on his *theme*, thereby having three separate
shows, each promising something different.

The old couple had the biggest natural opportunity of representing exactly what was intended, but there was nothing believable
about them and they too never evolved. Plotwise the old man is
seen by a resident whore coming out of his lady friend's room. In
order to prevent gossip, he announces lacklusterly that they will be
married in three weeks. Then there is an engagement party during
which 1) a brick is thrown through the window of the Jew's shop and
2) a card-carrying Nazi armed with a swastika makes his position
known. In a subsequent scene the old lady announces to the
fruiterer that she is afraid to marry him because she might lose her
pension license, and the old man unselfishly decides to move to
another part of Berlin in order not to embarrass the lady. End of *this*
plot.

Its unbelievableness stems from the fact that their relationship is
never meaningful. It isn't anything at all. It is impossible that they
were truly in love or that in any way they meant a great deal to each
other. The events leading to their engagement and disengagement
were meaningless and never interlaced with anything resembling
feeling. What you witnessed was more of a timetable than an affair
charged with love, fear, and distress. And so you didn't care. No
feeling whatsoever.

In *Zorba* I find the same failure to arouse interest in people. Hal
Prince's production is often fascinating. Sometimes it is almost original. Everything works mechanically well except the people, who
cannot be mechanical. The title character is pleasantly if vaguely
foolish. The young man who hires Zorba to work for him has to be
an idiot to do so on such a short acquaintance. The young man's
romance with the young widow is so underdeveloped that when we
see the widow stabbed before our very eyes, it makes no difference
to us—neither the fact of her death nor its emotional impact (was
there any?) on the young man. We care a bit more perhaps for the
older lady, probably because she is more fully defined, less mysterious, better known.

Again the question of transference from one medium to another is not thought out. While the problem with both *Candide* and *Man of La Mancha* lay in the things that must be sacrificed and/or lost in moving from novel to musical play, in *Zorba* and *Ilya Darling* the movement was from film to stage musical and in both cases it was wrongly assumed that you can do the same thing on the stage that was done in film. Wrong. Considerable change is essential if it is to work. Lost are the close-up, the fast cut from one scene to another, the time out for costume change, the capsule building of character by the lingering and following camera, which reveals the actor in quick succession in varied situations and places.

Walter Kerr in *The New York Times* (November 24, 1968) wrote similarly about *Zorba*. Of the title character he said, "…we don't greatly care." Of the young man he wrote, "[he] is no one we know at all." Kerr's first sentence in summarizing the show was "Call it honestly ambitious and emotionally bleak." I feel that this is a fair appraisal and that "emotionally bleak" is perhaps the only character- istic which cannot exist in any thoroughly workable musical. We must know the people and be made to care about them. If we do not know them, how can we care? We care about Tevye, Billy Bigelow, Mrs. Anna, Emile de Becque, Annie Oakley, and many more. That is why their shows worked so well and will continue to work.

I charged earlier that the kind of show *Cabaret* was to become had not been decided on in advance. The cabaret scenes themselves were always entertaining (you could have counted on that in Boston), and so there were eight of them. They were like the eight "acts" of a single floor show. Oh, the young principals bobbed in and out, and the Nazi strode about, and there was so-called "decadence" represented by girls receiving propositional telephone calls at tables. So what's new? You didn't and don't have to be a Nazi living in Germany to be so shockingly decadent. The people involved in creating *Cabaret* had—especially with Boris Aronson's fine set—a very entertaining thing going, but I think they reiterated it beyond the call of necessity at the expense of character development. After all you can only care about people. The result was a series of floor shows interspersed with two ersatz love stories.

I also charged that the creators of *Cabaret* and *Zorba* relied "on what the audience could supply out of its own experience." As the war with Germany ended twenty-five years ago and as none of my best friends was a Nazi, I did not go "Eek!" at the sight of an armband with a swastika. I know it as a dirty fact of history that hordes of such people perpertrated terrible crimes, but this itsy-bitsy representation of Nazism in *Cabaret* did not scare me.

In *Cabaret*, with four principal characters living in such a turbulent era, there is nearly nothing of Hitler's rise communicated to the audience—only the facts that the boy is going back to America (he is not compelled to) and the old lady will not marry the old man. Who ever said she really cared to marry him in the first place? Without this caring, there is no relating to the Nazi rise, only a stage convenience and a weak one at that.

In the case of *Zorba* it is my guess that everyone connected with escorting it to the stage was so saturated with both the novel and the motion picture that they lost sight of the fact that not even nearly everyone else had had part of the same experiences. (I, for one, knew nothing of either.)

Cabaret's reliance on the audiences' knowledge of history is a common pitfall. Just try someday when you are lecturing to a group of young people to tell a story about Nellie Melba or William S. Hart. Eyebrows like giant question marks will fly through the air with the greatest of ease.

The failure-failures, of course, simply perish. They open and close. I would like to consider briefly ten recent musicals in this category. Since I have pointed out in the earlier chapters of this book certain principles none of which I invented, I would like to measure these failures against some of them—all present and obvious as a spotlight in *every* workable and best musical.

Of the ten to be scanned here evidently not a single one thought it necessary to employ a subplot or anything else that might successfully replace it. Five of them contained no real romance. Two of them made ugly thrusts at romance which rendered them highly unattractive. Two attempted to "librettize" distinguished plays which in no way lent themselves to such ill-advised maltreatment. One garbled a basically excellent story idea. Most of them were old-fashioned. Five had stereotyped characters and situations which allowed for no audience sympathy. One based itself on a poor play which in a thousand millennia could obviously not have been converted into a good musical. None of them should have been attempted, as all of them were doomed at the very outset. Nobody but nobody could have made them work. They were *Maggie Flynn, Darling of the Day, On a Clear Day You Can See Forever, Dear World, Ben Franklin in Paris, Her First Roman, The Happy Time, House of Flowers, Skyscraper, Billy.*

Maggie Flynn was plain ordinary. It dealt with a lady who was especially very good (Civil War times) because she kissed Negro orphans. Then this lady is in love with a snobbish young army officer who quite predictably—cad that he is—is not going to come to her rescue when she is in trouble. (He doesn't.) Opposite the lady is her ex-husband, now a circus clown, who re-endears himself to her but not to the audience. This is thin, thin, thin, and all the "serious" ballets just before the end of Act Two (a dead giveaway that there is considerable trouble and that everybody knows it) are just not going to put Humpty Dumpty together again. (They didn't).

The biggest and most inexcusable of the "red herrings" employed in *Maggie Flynn* was the starting with and almost ending with Negroes. At this time in our history we have the right to expect a comment, but there was none. There was no idea of one. This is careless. Then there were baskets full of schmaltz—enough to fill *The Student Prince* and *The Chocolate Soldier*, both long-ago pieces. Then there was a villain! Heavens, I thought he died a century ago. Worst of all, the author never settled on a theme. He never let the audience in on what he was getting at, and this is only half excusable if the whole thing is somehow meant to be entertaining. None of it ever was.

Then there was *Darling of the Day* based on *Buried Alive*, the novelette by Arnold Bennett. This is the one about the celebrated snobbish English painter who had lived in seclusion on an island for twenty years accompanied by his valet and is now returning to London. He finds society so revolting that when his valet dies, he exchanges identity with him. This means, of course, forfeiting wealth, position, and all. He then persues a very inferior lady (socially and intellectually) who had corresponded with but had never met the valet. Now we are unsuccessfully led to believe—and we *must* believe—two things implicitly if this charade is to work: that this snob (the painter) is wildly in love with this plain, artless lady and that his exchange of identity is a carefully thought-out decision.

In *Darling of the Day* the artist's decision is made with such happy mercurial idiocy as to rob the artist of any believability (given him once upon a time by Bennett), and when one considers the high-flown taste of the artist and the gaucherie of the lady, the situation becomes insanely preposterous. The trouble here is waste in that the original material contains a high libretto potential, but when the adaptors (unlisted in the program) carelessly throw away a great opportunity I am once again reminded that in the musical theatre a majority of "adaptors" are amateurs.

In *On a Clear Day You Can See Forever* there are similar incredulities and deficiencies. Again there is no subplot. The leading lady is involved in a triangle consisting of, besides herself, a timeless psychoanalyst (who appears alongside her in earlier centuries wearing the same suit) and a stereotyped boy friend. The plot and action are slanted to keep the doctor sympathetic while making the boy friend appear even more stupid than necessary. There is pretentious carrying on about "time" (flashbacks to other periods), and the heroine to me is a bore. The whole show is wrapped in a saccharine mysticism that I found nauseating despite some lovely music and lyrics. There is the possibility that it could have succeeded as a movie (it didn't) or TV show because, handled with imagination, the material begged for effects, montages, fancy camera twirling, fades, overlaps, etc. None of this is possible on the stage, and so it all comes down to a foolish choice of medium. But dull it was too and unbelievable. Without an audience's being made to believe and being entertained along the way, what do you have?

Dear World was adapted from Giraudoux' unique play *The Madwoman of Chaillot*. Why was it ever considered likely as libretto material? The original is a delightful comedic-philosophical play about an old lady (and two of her cronies) who save Paris from certain destruction and the world from the avarice of "big business." Everything essentially revolves around these three quite mad elderly crones and a sewerman who helps them in their plan. There is an unimportant young romantic pair. The central characters and their plot are fairly stylized and satiric. It is clear from the start that the Countess Aurelia is persistent and unrealistic enough to accomplish anything she sets out to do. The success of the play is achieved by means of the delightful wit and satire given the old ladies.

The libretto version called *Dear World* had, of necessity (for music), to delete much that was the lifeblood of the original. There was a vain attempt to promote boy-girl to a more prominent position. Nothing worked, including most of Jerry Herman's music, which failed to approach the style of the play. In the end, what we saw was a denatured comedy with too little that was new and/or relevant. Nothing that was added helped to sustain the quality of the original or to compensate for the losses except the luminous performance of Angela Lansbury in the central role.

The failure of *Dear World* ought to have been predictable the moment the librettists made up their minds to tackle so obviously unadaptable a play—unadaptable because it offers nothing that is essential to the well-being of a musical: romance, subplot, and lyricism of a non-philosophical nature. In my opinion nothing at all should have been added to this already self-sufficient play.

Footnote: If anyone else in the future should decide to musicalize *The Madwoman of Chaillot*, I hope he will be sensible enough to use it pretty much as Giraudoux wrote it, and, if he must, superimpose on it only the trappings of grand opera. Prima donnas can be as old or as fat as necessary, and it's a simple matter for an audience to understand their lack (at least on the stage) of romance.

It was pointed out to me recently that *The Madwoman of Chaillot*, which is dear to many of our hearts, was a failure as a play in Paris, London, and New York. Even more recently it failed horrendously as a movie starring Katharine Hepburn. I still enjoy the play and cannot account for its consistent failure.

The idea that the world might be saved by a lunatic, a misbegotten dream, is an intriguing one, but hasn't that something in common with *Man of La Mancha*, which I did not like and for both of these reasons?

Skyscraper, based on Elmer Rice's *Dream Girl*, another unlikely basis for a libretto, has been described earlier.

The Happy Time had handsome Robert Goulet and his beautiful voice. End of review. He seemed to be looking for something (he was a photographer), but whatever it was it didn't seem to matter. A girl was thrown in for a little while, and then she disappeared as mysteriously as she had come. Obviously she wasn't supposed to mean anything, and God knows she succeeded. There was a unique lack of feeling throughout. The production was "interesting" in that it fused still photographs, motion pictures, and live action. But how much did these contribute to something that was basically lifeless already? Did anybody care?

The Happy Time seems to have started with a director's or set designer's gimmick. "Hey, Joe, why don't we do a show about a photographer with photographs of all kinds—stills and movies—as shifting backdrops?" This they did do at the expense of plot, suspense, theme, and anything like arousing the audience's sympathy for just anybody. All of these missing elements—the most important parts of a show—were a gigantic gaping parenthesis.

Actually the starting point here—photographs because of a photographer—is the wrongest possible kind of start because—believe it or not—it has nothing to do with anything. It's like starting a play about Dr. Christiaan Barnard with a valentine. What I am trying to say is that neither of them is more functional than the opening chorus of a Vincent Youmans show. (This, by the way, was missing in the successful "revival" of *No, No, Nanette*.)

Her First Roman and *Ben Franklin in Paris* were both about old men and young girls. Both lacked romance, subplots, and any success. *Her First Roman*, made from Shaw's *Caesar and Cleopatra*, was an obvious attempt, because of *My Fair Lady*, to mine gold from another Shaw play and to jump aboard the current bandwagon by using a glamorous black girl in the female lead. The adaptation even had Caesar, the "old" man, having an affair with the child Cleopatra, which is an unpleasant idea, supported by history[24] but not by Shaw. This *play*, in its original form, is a witty debate. Nearly all the wit was chopped out to make room for the songs, which, good or bad, were so numerous and so underexposed that I doubt anyone's ability to get a clear impression of a single one. I didn't.

Ben Franklin in Paris could only be described as a show about a dirty old man, even though that man may have been the founder of the *Saturday Evening Post*. Franklin, in his seventies, is in Paris making with a pretty young girl who can help him get to the King of France, where Franklin hopes to gain recognition for the new American nation. The picture of the very old man and the very young girl is bad enough, but when it is clear that Franklin, though undoubtedly enjoying himself, is chiefly interested in using the girl for purposes other than sincere personal ones, the tale becomes grim. It is appropriate to point out the fact that although both Peter Stuyvesant in *Knickerbocker Holiday* and Emile de Becque in *South Pacific* were considerably older than their girls, in both of these latter cases the men were endowed with enormous charm, and as seen by the audience through the eyes of the girls, there was attraction and involved romance. The girls themselves let us know and in no uncertain terms how much *they* cared. And we understood and empathized.

On the other hand, Shaw's Cleopatra thought of Caesar as an "old man," and she saw nothing romantic about him. Nor did Caesar regard the Queen of Egypt as more than a child. Shaw went to considerable lengths to make this relationship anti-romantic and his play about them a witty tract about war, politics, power, and everything else *except* romance. The introduction of romance into the libretto was destructive of the original material, was inconsistent, out of place, and failed to suit the characters or the situation.

Her First Roman is another excellent example (though not the only one) of a show that could not in any circumstances have been made to work. Someone in command (director, producer, or composer) might have chucked Leslie Uggams and brought in an aging ingénue as Caesar's opposite. Then he might have created a pair of young lovers (it worked in *The King and I*) among the many servants. Dancing might have played a bigger part with more and more elaborate production numbers. This helped put over a thin and second-act-less *Pajama Game* and helped to make a subplot needless in *Annie Get Your Gun*. Or they might have made Cleopatra's younger brother a bit older so that he could have plotted with his dearest love in a truly menacing way for the throne of Egypt. (History is meant for alteration when it interferes with theatre.) But nothing contained in the above nightmare would have or could have made *Caesar and Cleopatra* work as a musical. Shaw wrote it as a discourse and a very lively one at that, and for musical adaptors it carries the curse of the great sphinx.

Something needs to be said about *House of Flowers* on two accounts. First, its composer, Harold Arlen, writes attractive, distinctive, and often memorable songs. They have invariably been anchored to unworkable librettos. Second, because the songs in *House of Flowers* were remembered fondly after the initial production of the show, there was a somewhat general and unusual insistence that this or that, or he or she, in the original production had ruined an otherwise marvelous show, and so it had its *second* chance more recently in an off-Broadway revival.

The book by Truman Capote could not have been more ruined by anybody than by its author, who demonstrated beyond any possible doubt that he knew nothing about the requirements of a libretto.

I would like to insist at this point on the inescapable importance of introducing and clearly defining characters in a musical at the outset. At the start of *House of Flowers*, the heroine (a black prostitute) is having a happy, continuing relationship with a thoroughly likable, titled white Englishman who wants to give her everything. She responds to him warmly. It is impossible for the audience not to accept him as the hero. However, sometime later, the girl sees a dull native black boy and she tells us that she is in love with him. He represents nothing and is endowed with no visible qualities to support such a foolish notion.

At the end of Act Two, Scene 3 of *House of Flowers*, the following exchange occurs between Ottilie, the heroine, and Royal, the man she has just recently married.

> OTTILIE: Oh, Royal…you ain't goin' to whip me, is you?
> ROYAL (*advancing toward her*): Not right away. To begin with, I just goin' to tie you to the bamboo tree. (*He takes* OTTILIE's *hand, starts to guide her into the yard*)
> OTTILIE (*pulling back*): What you talkin' 'bout…tie me to a tree!
> ROYAL (*pauses, looks at her*): When a man got to punish his wife, that's the first thing he do. Tie her to a tree and give her time to ruminate.
> OTTILIE (*struggling with him*): Let me go, Royal. You ain't goin' to do it. Let me go…
> ROYAL (*lifting her, throwing her over his shoulder*): This distress me as much as it do you.
> OTTILIE: Put me down! You hear what I say, Royal? (*He does; but it is only to stand her against the tree*) Royal, I'm

givin' you yo' last chance. You tie me to this tree…I'll run away. Sure as my name is Ottilie, I'll be gone tomorrow. (*Calm and whistling,* ROYAL *begins to wind the rope around her.* OTTILIE *does not resist, but, cold, final*) All right, Royal. You had yo' opportunity. From now on, I never gonna speak to you again.

(ROYAL *hums as he knots the rope, and then exits.* OTTILIE *wiggles inside the rope, swells up with air, inhale-exhale; then she begins to gnaw at the rope with her teeth*) CURTAIN

How can the audience want to see this relationship turn out well? This supposedly main event comes off like a parenthesis, after which you expect the amiable Englishman to return and win out. He does return. He does not win out. All motivations are deep secrets. Romance is a muddle. There is no subplot. There are songs. There is no show.

Walter Kerr made an observation (*The New York Times*, December 8, 1968) which applies to all failures: "A playwright can always do what he wishes to do. But he must first take steps to insure the audience wishes him to do it, too."

It may seem foolish at the outset to dwell on a Broadway musical that lasted for a single performance in 1969, but *Billy Budd* as a musical show failure offers a unique opportunity for discussion here since the novelette by Herman Melville is a classic, and eighteen years before the Broadway musical it was successfully treated as a play on Broadway and, in the same year, as an opera in London. The novelette contains three principal characters, and little of what the original said was used in the musical. The shape of Melville's story is more like that of a Greek tragedy. Everything physical is set up at the start. There is a theme but little plot. The novelette concerns itself chiefly with the dénouement.

The three-cornered story-such as it is-deals with a beautiful young sailor of few words who stutters when he is excited, whose parentage and history are unknown even to him. He is impressed for duty on an eighteenth-century man-o'-war whose Captain Vere is Godlike, with divine qualities of innocence and quietude for whom justice is absolute. The third principal, the master-at-arms, James Claggart, is the exact opposite of Captain Vere and Billy. He is hated by the men and punishes them sadistically.

Simply told, Claggart "has it in" for Budd, who is adored by everyone else. As the result of a small accident (Budd's spilling a bowl of soup) Claggart orders him to appear before Captain Vere. At the confrontation, Claggart accuses Budd of plotting an insurrection among the members of the crew. Billy, so angry that he is unable to speak, strikes Claggart, who falls dead. This is a fact, and Captain Vere—much against his will—must try Billy and, finding him guilty of lawlessness—even unintentional—must sentence him to be hanged.

As Billy approaches his execution he says only, "God bless Captain Vere!"

This is scarcely a plot or it is at most a minuscule one. What is to emerge from it as a drama has to, more than anything else, develop Claggart's motive in trying to be rid of the angelic and blameless Billy. Many scholars have made a case which hinges on Claggart's homosexuality. This would indeed establish a motive for his wishing to be rid of Billy, a temptation. (Melville again and again dwells on his beauty.)

In 1951 coincidentally there appeared on Broadway a dramatized version by Louis O. Coxe and Robert Chapman called *Billy Budd* and in London an opera by Benjamin Britten, with libretto by E.M. Forster and Eric Crozier. Both were well received. In the least successful of these three versions—the Broadway musical—everyone is two-dimensional. A girl, Molly, is introduced in fantasy with Billy six times! (This is a new addition and out of place.) Vere is given much greater importance than Claggart, who is an unmotivated villain.

One specific instance should serve to illustrate the lack of sensitivity and quality—and the wrongest kind of departure from Melville. An utter violation of character from among the many—and serving no purpose—comes near the end after Billy's sentence to death when Billy screams, "No! I will not die." For the record, the irresponsible parties to this catastrophe of a single performance were book by Stephen Glassman, concept by Ron Cowen, music and lyrics by Ron Dante and Gene Allan, a production of Vanark Enterprises, Inc. (in association with Joseph Schoctor).

In both the play and the opera the authors centered their adaptations on much developed discussion about good and evil. Melville's plot, as such, is intact—but every small segment is tremendously expanded.

The theme of Melville's novelette, significant, universal, and deeply moving, with all of its many implications of love, hate, justice, fate, and many other things, is bypassed in the insignificant throwaway musical called *Billy*. The reader should know by this point in this book that I have no resentment per se against adaptation of a libretto from another medium for use with music on the stage. Nor do I believe in "faithfulness" to the original, which is to say the use of all characters in the new treatment, the forbiddance of adding others who never existed before, or changes in plot or structure. To the contrary, these two latter procedures are often most necessary. But I *do* object to discarding elements of the original which define the core of its idea, without which little or nothing remains. Why, then, use Melville at all? In the musical, Claggart is a senseless, unmotivated Simon Legree. Billy is a gabby cuckoo clock and Vere is national chairman of the Boy Scouts. As if this were not enough, the highly inappropriate introduction of the dream girl Molly is as unthinkable, tasteless, and as antithetical to the spirit of Billy Budd as introducing a female into the shower room of the Swiss Guard at the Vatican.

One of the most moving things about the hanging of Billy is Billy's simple, uncomplaining, nearly silent going to his death. In the musical, he is loquacious. He protests his unfair sentence, regrets his not having run away. Then to make matters even more lugubrious, Billy sings a song *after* his death (the end of the show). In this he says, "Is that the green of home I see?"

What home?

What musical?

The foregoing sections of this book have contained liberal examples of what has worked, the methods of adaptation, and two detailed examples of what did not work and why. I have no doubt that important changes in the outer garment of a libretto are lurking like a hurricane somewhere in the wind, but I believe equally strongly that the roots of whatever it is to be are contained germinatively in the best of what the past has offered. To be sure, audiences for which all theatre must appeal have never basically changed. It is highly doubtful that they ever will. They have discarded togas for various other kinds of clothing throughout many centuries.

Goethe's hair was long. Hemingway's short. Byron wore chains and medallions about his neck, as did Shakespeare about two centuries earlier. These "signs of the times" are constantly changing, going back and forth at dizzying speed, but feeling and people do not change basically. Since the theatre and the musical theatre in particular appeal first to feeling, the working innards of what is created for the theatre and its audience will not basically change.

The out-and-out failures are clearly unarguable: Now you see them, now you don't. But they do incredible needless harm to the entire theatre. Their small *actual* audience feels frustrated and cheated. Their potential *almost* audience is put on guard against everything. Their backers lose everything and withdraw as backers of future shows either because they cannot afford additional losses (fools to have become involved in the first place if they cannot afford to lose!) or because they feel too cheated and regard all other and perhaps better shows with a jaundiced view. The poor performers more than anyone else needing success that creates continuing jobs and having been made to work harder, to go through senseless, useless, frantic daily changes in an always vain effort to change bleak disaster into the shining Holy Grail are precipitously unemployed. Now you see it, now you don't.

The success-failures are arguably good for everyone except, in the end, the theatre itself, the self-deceived authors, and the next generation of writers in search of new models. "New models" actually at this moment in history do not exist. "New" in a limited sense does. In today's newest musicals certain hallmarks appear. They invariably include rock music in some form and always ear-splittingly amplified, use of four-letter words, nudity, use of multimedia devices. Not much else of the present except perhaps plotlessness and cliché references to pot, sex, and Vietnam is in evidence. All of these elements symbolize the here and now, and together they constitute in a loose sense a kind of style.

When recent failures have become aware of their predicament, their authors or producers or maybe the stage doorman begin to clutch at one of the above-listed devices, insert it just anywhere and necessarily without reason in a vain attempt to infuse new life into a dead body.

In *Jimmy*, Frank Gorshin, the actor impersonating the title role, made a swift and embarrassing entrance and exit entirely nude. In

Coco Katharine Hepburn opens Act Two with a single word: "Shit!" In too many recent shows an otherwise conventional score suddenly erupts with a *single* rock essay. These abortive insertions fool nobody, change nothing that is basically already poor and old-fashioned, and, to the contrary, help point up existing weaknesses. The people—whoever they are—who are responsible for these tasteless insertions demonstrate without doubt a recognition of weakness, a futile bid for critical and audience favor, and a failure to comprehend the simple fact that "One swallow doth not a summer make." Consistency and style are Siamese twins.

In every decade in our musical-theatre history the success-failures have, for a time, outshone some of the more basic successes. What remains of *Better Times, The Big Show, Cheer Up, Follow Through, The Gingham Girl, Happy Days, Little Jessie James, A Society Circus*, or *Under Many Flags?* Yet all of them enjoyed runs of over 400 performances at a time when 150 spelled success. On the other hand, Coward's *Bitter Sweet* in the same period had 159 performances; *Girl Crazy*, with one of Gershwin's best scores, 272; Herbert's *Mlle. Modiste*, 202; *Naughty Marietta*, 136; and *Cabin in the Sky*, 156. To go a big step farther, the very best musicals enjoyed success their first time around and have continued on and on through our own era: *Oklahoma!*, 2,248; *My Fair Lady*, 2,717; *Annie Get Your Gun*, 1,149; *Kiss Me, Kate*, 1,077; *South Pacific*, 1,925; and *Fiddler on the Roof* (still running everywhere), 2,843 in New York alone as of July 18, 1971, on which date it became the longest-running musical in Broadway history.

Of the shows chosen at random for discussion in this chapter, five were big box-office successes. Several of the others for varying expensive reasons were kept alive weeks after they ceased paying their own ways.

As to subplots, which I feel are essential to musicals, only two of these had any: *Cabaret*, and *Zorba*. Neither was a disaster at the box office.

There is no calculable romance in seven (one third) of them: *Ben Franklin in Paris, The Happy Time, Her First Roman, Darling of the Day, Mame, Dear World*, and *George M!* (I hear screams of disagreement.) There is no continuing romance in *Candide*. The romantic duos in *The Music Man, The Unsinkable Molly Brown, Skyscraper, Maggie Flynn*, and *On a Clear Day* were too stereotyped and predictable to beguile anyone. The romantic situations in *House of Flowers* and *Jamaica* were too contrived for credibility, and those in the highly potential *Cabaret* and *Zorba* were too underdeveloped. The emotional involvements in *What Makes Sammy Run?*—because the central character was so distasteful—were unpleasant and never emerged as more than nightmares.

Do these factual tabulations prove nothing? Is the subplot really a non-essential parasite in the making of a good musical? Is romance dispensable?

The best, most successful, and longest-lasting musicals contain both. Omitting them without offering adequate workable replacements is, I think, demonstrably suicidal.

It must never be forgotten that all of these "properties"—novels, plays, etc.—were resounding and undying successes in their original forms. Failure here was due solely to not understanding the ways they needed to have been treated in another medium.

There are, however, two other elements that may figure largely for or against the box-office success or failure of any show. These are. . . [Engel continues in Chapter 12, Producers and Stars.]

COMMENTS ON FAILURES

In 1965, a few days before the opening of *Flora, the Red Menace*, the first musical by the then unknown team of John Kander and Fred Ebb, the show's producer Harold Prince set a date a few weeks hence when they'd start their next joint venture, a musical version of Christopher Isherwood's Berlin stories. He assured them the new project would proceed regardless of the reviews for *Flora*.

The reviews were not positive, but they did not impede Prince, Kander and Ebb from beginning work on *Cabaret*. The story is relevant because it provides the context in which Engel understood failure. Some of the flops he lists were by first timers; most were by writers who'd go on to do other, more successful work. In this context failure can be instructive. Today failure isn't a step on a longer journey; more than likely it signals the end of the journey.

Some failures achieve legendary status, like *Carrie*, the outrageous show based on Brian de Palma's film, which had an opening second-act musical number about "the kids" killing a pig. Or Gower Champion's one night stand, *Rockabye Hamlet*.

Some fill one with sadness, like the 1976 *1600 Pennsylvania Avenue*, with lyrics by Alan Jay Lerner and music by Leonard Bernstein. Bernstein, who'd not composed for Broadway in many years, never did again. Lerner wrote one more show, *Carmelina*, in the ten years before he died. An attempt to narrate the first century of American history as if the White House were a Yankee version of the British miniseries *Upstairs Downstairs*, the show was full of sophomoric ideas by Lerner. There are a few memorable songs, especially "Take Care of This House," but the show has never had a significant revival because, despite its creators, it doesn't merit one.

One of the most perplexing of failures is Jerry Herman's *Mack and Mabel*, which has some of his—or anybody's—best songs, like "I Won't Send Roses" and "Time Heals Everything." There have been several versions since the original Broadway production, which starred the unmatchable Robert Preston as Mack Sennett and the radiant Bernadette Peters as Mabel Normand. But their story ended in an ugly way, and no ingenuity can undo the shadow that ending casts on an otherwise effervescent evening.

The show opened in the fall of 1974, at a time when its producer, David Merrick, had lost interest in the theatre. Twenty years earlier he'd taken a show with comparable problems, *Fanny*, and turned it into an undeniable commercial hit. Had he had the will, he might have worked similar wonders with *Mack and Mabel*, but the will was lacking.

A 1982 flop I am surprised has not found a successful revival is Craig Carnelia's *Is There Life After High School?*, which had one song after another that beautifully captured the awkwardness of American adolescence. But its Broadway production was ludicrously lavish, with a huge two-level set. The simple, straightforward material was painfully overshadowed by an attempt to transform its intimate quality into something brashly commercial. Here is a case where a low budget production would have served the score much better. Given the current economics of producing theatre, it's surprising no one has done so.

There's certainly no more legendary failure than the 1964 Arthur Laurents-Stephen Sondheim *Anyone Can Whistle*, though if everyone who claims to have seen it actually had it might still be running. It received a thorough critical lambasting (the one excep-

tion was Martin Gottfried in *Women's Wear Daily*) and lasted only a
week. But its score has found many devotees. Its title song remains
one of Sondheim's most profound utterances.

In Engel's time it was standard for half a dozen musicals to open
on Broadway every season. In the mid-Fifties the number was even
higher. The 1954-55 season, for example, in which the Harold
Arlen-Truman Capote *House of Flowers* flopped, also produced *The
Boy Friend*, *Peter Pan*, *Fanny*, *Plain and Fancy*, *Silk Stockings* and *Damn
Yankees*.

Most of these titles still signify something even to non-musical-
theatre aficionados. Two other musical shows that opened on
Broadway that season were *Three for the Show*, a revue featuring
Marge and Gower Champion and an up-and-coming Caribbean
singer named Harry Belafonte, and Gian Carlo Menotti's opera *The
Saint of Bleecker Street*. Among the nonmusical plays were *Bus Stop*, *Cat
on a Hot Tin Roof* and *Inherit the Wind*.

This level of activity reflected an economic situation in which
production costs were not so hefty that failure could lead to bank-
ruptcy. It was also a time in which theatregoing was still a significant
part of New Yorkers' routine.

Producer Jean Dalrymple once remarked that as late as the
Fifties if the reviewers called something a "good first play" you could
have a six-month run from a reservoir of New Yorkers interested in
hearing a new voice. You would at least recoup your investment,
maybe make a little profit. In any case a young writer would be
launched. When she made the observation, in the Seventies, the
phrase "good first play," she said, was "the kiss of death." The costs of
producing and theatregoing habits were no longer conducive to
good first plays.

Engel is correct that failure is invariably foreordained in the very
idea for a show. But that's not always easy to determine. Several
teams rejected the idea of turning Shaw's *Pygmalion* into a musical
before Lerner and Loewe showed that it could be done—brilliantly.

To go back to *House of Flowers*, to which Engel devotes considerable space, it was the work of a relative neophyte, Truman Capote,
a bestselling author, to be sure, but one whose previous play, *The
Grass Harp*, had flopped a few years earlier. This financial failure,
however, didn't deter the producer Arnold Saint Subber from per-

suading him to do another show. The short story—more accurately, the sketch—on which the musical was based was more subtle than the libretto Capote created for the musical. In the process of adapting his material for the stage Capote vulgarized it and created more narratives than the simple story of a young woman consigned to a bordello who discovers the bittersweet meaning of true love.

Earlier in this book, you will remember, Engel mentioned how disgusted he was with the laughter of the opening night audience at *My Fair Lady*, whose humor is hardly off-color. It's understandable he'd have found the coarser tone of *House of Flowers* offensive.

However vulgar the book may have been, the score by Harold Arlen had one of the great theatre songs of all time, "A Sleepin' Bee," introduced by the 18-year-old Diahann Carroll. In addition to this standard, there were at least two other memorable songs, the rhythmically bewitching "Two Ladies in de Shade of de Banana Tree" and the evocative "I Never Has Seen Snow," to which the curmudgeonly Alec Wilder devotes several awestruck pages in his authoritative *American Popular Song*.

Years later, Richard Rodgers, not noted for his generosity, wrote that every time someone at an audition sang Arlen's "Sleepin' Bee," he heard it "always with pleasure." He considered the score "gravely misunderstood and underrated."

Would that there might be more "failures" on this level!

But we've passed the point where such failures provide "compost" for better material. Interestingly, Arlen would go on to write the successful *Jamaica*, starring Lena Horne, and the extremely unsuccessful *Saratoga*, after which he wrote nothing more for the theatre. As for Capote, *Grass Harp* was turned into a musical in 1971 by Claibe Richardson and Kenward Elmslie. The score, particularly "Chain of Love," has won great admiration, but it didn't change "Tru's" theatre luck.

In 1966 Capote's novella *Breakfast at Tiffany's* became one of the legendary theatre fiascos when David Merrick hired songwriter Bob Merrill (who'd written the scores for *Take Me Along* and *Carnival* as well as the lyrics for *Funny Girl*) and the veteran writer/director Abe Burrows to turn it into a musical. When the show was floundering Merrick had the weird idea of bringing in Edward Albee to "doctor" the book, in the process turning a charming story into an absurdist nightmare.

Rather than risk the humiliation of certain catastrophic reviews, Merrick closed the show in previews, refunding $1 million in advance sales, which at that time seemed like a lot of money. (Early in 2003 a record was set when *Dance of the Vampires* closed at a reported loss of $12 million—some thought the actual figure was closer to $15 million.)

Whether *Tiffany's* was a learning experience for anyone is doubtful. It frightened its star, Mary Tyler Moore, away from the theatre for several decades. Around this time Capote enjoyed his greatest success of all with his nonfiction book *In Cold Blood*. His only return to the theatre was reading his "Christmas Memory" at Lincoln Center a year before he died. But none of those whose theatre careers were already solid was really affected. A few years later Merrill and Jule Styne gave Merrick another hit, *Sugar*. Albee's career was not deterred.

What seems interesting is that in 1966 *Tiffany's* was sunk by certain suppositions that might have made it a success, or at least a success *d'estime*, a few decades later. In retrospect, *pace* Lehman Engel, it still doesn't seem like a bad idea to turn Capote's witty, delightful novella into a musical.

Part of the problem in 1966 was that it had to compete with the very fresh memory of the film version with the irreplaceable Audrey Hepburn. Even Mary Tyler Moore, a popular TV star, fell short of Hepburn's overwhelming charm. Even so, she was too wholesome and cleancut to embody the character as Albee rewrote her. The movie had softened Holly Golightly. In Capote's story she disappears in the end, following the whims of her own eccentricity. In the movie she becomes susceptible to romance. She settles down with George Peppard.

By contrast, Albee's Holly is a much harsher, coarser woman. Rather than taking the expectations Hollywood had created and presenting a character with her own charms, Albee seemed to take pleasure in confounding those expectations. Those expectations had been heightened by casting another television star, Richard Chamberlain, opposite Moore. But Albee minimized any chance of creating romance in the Hollywood manner by making Holly a creature of Chamberlain's imagination, a fictional character rather than an endearing woman.

What had been an exercise in whimsy in Capote's original now became something out of Pirandello, hardly what a Broadway audience wanted in those days. Worse, Holly was no longer elusive. She was a creature of the rankest flesh and blood—at one point an FBI woman punched her viciously in the stomach, causing her to lose an illegitimate child.

In 1966 all this seemed a cruel joke on the audience. Tellingly, Albee later remarked that the experience taught him what it was like "to watch a dictator being disappointed in preconceived notions." The dictator, he clarified, was not David Merrick, but rather the audience, who were outraged by what he regarded as daring innovations in the musical form.

In those days you took a show out of town to test it, to modify it, to make the audience happy. By the end of the decade, as Vietnam cast a darker and darker shadow over everything, the audience came to be seen as the enemy. If before the Sixties the audience was seen as something to be pacified genially, by the end of the decade the audience had become something to be conquered militarily. Their bourgeois tastes were not to be accommodated but thwarted. When Albee articulated his distaste—his contempt—for the audience, his views seemed revolutionary. Nowadays that attitude seems quite normal.

What made it increasingly easy to *epater* the bourgeois audience was that by the Eighties musicals were seldom done in the traditional manner of tryouts in Boston and Philadelphia before a New York opening. The cost of such a procedure had become prohibitive. The new technique was to present new musicals in not-for-profit theatres with subscription audiences.

The subscription audience is a very different creature from an audience that pays for a specific show. The subscriber signs up, in effect, for five pigs in a poke. The desired effect is that at least two or three pigs be tasty enough that the subscriber will sign up for another season.

By the Eighties the subscription audience knew it couldn't always expect to be entertained. Some evenings it would be edified. Others it would be affronted. Under such circumstances it seemed natural that an audience should be confronted, say, with a musical like Jason Robert Brown's *Parade*, about the lynching of Leo Franks, or Stephen Sondheim's *Assassins*, which, as its title warns, is about the assassins of American presidents.

The notion of fine-tuning a show to suit the audience's tastes no longer applies. The discomfort of the audience is no longer necessarily a sign of failure. It may be the proof of a show's success, though nowadays the audience is so accustomed to being assaulted there's not much excitement in it. It's almost a kind of ritual, performed as mechanically and predictably as most rituals. In any case, if either the Burrows or the Albee version of *Breakfast at Tiffany's* were presented as part of a subscription series, it might do very well.

Brian De Palma's early film *Hi, Mom!* has a scene in which some avant-garde actors actually pummel their audience. Rubbing his wounded head on the way out, one audience member mutters, "Makes you think!" What was satiric then, in the late Sixties, is now quite routine.

The templates that underlay Engel's assumptions about success and failure have been broken. The tastes and desires of the audience are no longer part of the equation. The creators have greater latitude, but there's no longer any guarantee the work will retain the affection or even the interest of a large audience over time the way the golden age classics have.

That dictator Albee was among the first to want to overthrow has indeed been toppled. As with most revolutions, however, the overall result is still in doubt.

12

Producers and Stars

Hello, Dolly! is, inevitably, the "new" hit in town, and if David Merrick can hold onto Miss Merman for longer than the three months to which she has agreed, he's going to make good his boast that the show would break the longevity mark for a musical set by *My Fair Lady* at 2,717.

Lewis Funke
The New York Times

The musical theatre is the most collaborative of all theatre forms, representing the combined efforts of writers, composers, lyricists, designers (costume and set), a director, a conductor, musicians, singers, dancers, publicists, a light designer, a stage manager with assistants, and, not the least, one or two stars and a producer. Perhaps the least appreciated because he is the least understood is the producer. In England producer is the name we give the "director," and in the past everywhere he has been known as "manager" or "deadbeat."

1971 seems a late date for trying to clarify the producer's functions. He has to find a property (new play, new musical, or revival); then he must set about deciding on or learning the availability and/or interest of an appropriate director—the single most important person to the production. Perhaps a star or stars will be needed. They have to be interested in playing in the "property." Money has to be raised (today for a musical around $1,000,000). A theatre has to be engaged in New York, and, going backward like a crab, dates must be set for out-of-town tryouts, which usually occur in at least two cities. The producer engages press agents, a scene designer, a custome designer, wardrobe personnel, company manager, stage managers, and, in musicals, a conductor, rehearsal pianists (three), ensemble people who sing and/or dance, actor-singers for small parts, etc.

Dates are always important items. The New York theatre is available on such and such a day. Will the director be free then or busy in Hollywood with "retakes"? Will the stars be free of other commitments? Etc.?

The matter of contracts (next to the choice of property and director) is the first test of the producer's ability and experience. (In time past, a producer was perhaps first a director, which he arrived at after acting; he knew the problems at first hand.) I recall well that *Wonderful Town* got great and unanimous reviews. It should have run forever. The billing—a most important problem for the producer—had four words in neon lights:

ROSALIND RUSSELL
WONDERFUL TOWN

However, Miss Russell's contract was for a single year. She refused to renew. When she left, the show continued only a very short time.

Another case involved Jackie Gleason in *Take Me Along*. The one-year situation was the same. The star refused to extend. He was replaced by the movies' William Bendix. Within a few weeks, no show.

Avoidable or not, this is inadequate producing. It's the long shot that didn't work out. In the case of *My Fair Lady*, the stars were committed to a minimum employment of two years. The producer used one of these years to open the production in London with the same two stars. But *My Fair Lady* was always *the thing* even though Rex Harrison and Julie Andrews were praised and adored. When they were no longer available, the show went on merrily with others. It may surprise many people to learn that many stars refuse to sign two-year agreements. For some, it's the idea of repetitious boredom. For others, well, they've got the most they can get out of the opening, what with potentially good press reviews and much hoopla and publicity, and perhaps they can afford to go elsewhere to do something else.

These are various reasons why producers have had bad reputations. Before the formation of the actors' union (Equity), players were left without salary and return-trip railroad tickets to New York when they were touring. Often they were underpaid, treated rudely, and done out of money. Today, contracts have done away with all of these evils except perhaps rudeness, but then that is personal and not necessarily a concomitant of producing.

But there are other things I believe differentiate a good from a bad producer.

1) His choice of property; 2) his choice of director; 3) his "feelings" about when and where it should open; 4) his skill in raising money; 5) his skill in drawing pivotal contracts; 6) his knowledge of promotion; 7) his holding back expenditures so that he has a reason for going ahead for a while at a financial loss *when he thinks honestly he has a* "fighting chance"; 8) his judgment and willingness to close his show, *even* with a reserve when he knows that its future is hopeless.

In the first case, his choice of property may be a good one at a bad time (summer, newspaper strikes, etc.) or a bad one which he knows is bad but which, in his opinion, will work. This is where the business end intrudes on the artistic. If he is a successful producer—or in direct order of his success   he will be given first choice of everything by authors and their agents. This is a distinct advantage. Perhaps he will admire the property but not be *interested* enough in it to devote two or three years of his life to get it on stage.

Quite often a good producer and, in this case, one who is also creative will buy rights to a story or play, then engage a composer, lyricist, and book-writer or librettist to transform the original into a musical. Often—since producers are human beings—they will fail to comprehend the particular qualities in this or that script, and another producer, comprehending them, will have a success.

Brigadoon, one of Lerner and Loewe's best musicals, was offered to every producer in New York with negative reactions. Just about the last on the list was Cheryl Crawford, who immediately adored it, produced it, and enjoyed her greatest success with it.

The second proposition—choice of the proper director—this takes considerable foresight and experience *and* good fortune that the good director respects the producer to the extent of becoming an employee and that the director is available at the right time, or that the producer values the director to the extent that he is willing to suffer an even drastic postponement.

The feeling of when and where the show should open depends on theatre availability, availability of performers and director *and* the season. Some producers possess so much invincible optimism as opposed to solid judgment that they have scheduled a late-May Broadway opening! Everybody knows that the show *must* be a blockbuster or its life span will be limited if not immediately ended at a late season opening.

There are exceptions that should be noted. When a fall season has been poor, especially with unsuccessful musical shows, a wise producer may choose to open a light kind of musical, or one with a kind of commercial star, when New Yorkers are just leaving the city and out-of-towners are pushing their way in. If the show succeeds, the summer traffic will be enormous and of course the show will continue on indefinitely. The "where" of this choice has to do first with out-of-town, which can be a total loss without a reputable star, rave reviews, and a theatre with air-conditioning. Many of our theatres, especially out of New York, do not have air-conditioning.

The second part of the choice is availability of a theatre in the main line of the most popular theatres where buyers can go easily from theatre to theatre in search of tickets, near the well-known restaurants, and near all kinds of transportation.

The producer's skill in raising money obviously must be more than a wish, for without it, *and during a specific time limit* spelled out in all contracts, including the author's, there will be no production, or perhaps one later on by another producer.

In recent time some successful producers use mostly their own money (David Merrick and Richard Rodgers are examples, with perhaps a nod to old friends to invest a limited sum). Also a single company has more than once put up all the money. CBS did it for *My Fair Lady* and Columbia Pictures-Screen Gems for *Georgy*. Well, that's life, for the former made and still makes legendary millions and the latter closed in a single week as a total loss.

My fifth standard—"skill in drawing pivotal contracts"—has many meanings. It first of all implies that, due to experience as perhaps a former business-manager, the producer knows when it is most essential to spend and when it is not. There are many things to be weighed before any conclusions in this connection can be safely made.

Then there is the previously mentioned aspect of the duration of the contracts. If the show is built around and needs a real star, catastrophe can all too easily occur if the star's contract expires and the general public whines, "Oh, why go to that? Judy Teasdale isn't in it any more." In this contract-making aspect, a knowledgeable producer will add together all the original production costs and then carefully consider percentages of in-take about to be assigned away to theatre owners (a large weekly chunk), star or stars, director, author, composer, lyricist, possibly choreographer, and very likely the scene designer. With all of this outgoing "off the top," what likely kind of overage can he hope for? For this "overage" is laughingly called profit, and it takes careful planning and a long time span (often more than a year) before the backers are reimbursed—that is, provided the show is a smash hit. For it is only after the backers have been repaid their investments, and only then, that the profits are split in half, half of which becomes the property of the producer. This is when he begins to make his profit—and not until (or possibly) then does he make any of it. This despite the fact that he may have worked on the show (rewrites), casting, money, backings, etc., two, three, or four years.

The next important thing about a producer is that he have some concept of appropriate promotion in addition to the engaging of the most expert public-relations office available. The producer will leave all the routine matters of ads, interviews, gossip-column notes, signs, etc. to his PR men, but as often as not he himself will come up with a new idea, such as moving signs in railway stations and airports in and out of New York. Or the producer (Merrick especially) will pick a fight with a critic. This commands public attention and can result in one of two things: The critic may feel that giving a poor review may seem personal in the circumstances, or he may be spiteful and pan the show. In the latter case the critic may very well lose face even if he is right in his judgment.

The matter of holding back expenditures is a result of experience and perhaps a certain kind of special genius. I have seen many a show built-particularly by David Merrick—from something quite small in its beginning into something large and in the end boasting a sizable run. But in these cases the shows had: substance, artistry, they were about something, were well produced, and they received enough quotable reviews that provided enough solid realities on which to build. This kind of achievement requires a property interesting enough to begin with, money to carry through the rough days, and lavish advertising. Also a feeling born of experience to know when, where, and to whom tickets must be *given* away so that the minority audience which actually paid for its seats is unaware that what they're seeing is actually at the moment a flop. Also the producer must know silently and precisely when to stop giving seats away.

The last quality—the producer's judgment and willingness to close his show in spite of some financial remains in the till—is again something that Merrick has always been willing to do. Personally, I believe that in his case, if he himself does not like the show he doesn't care what happens to it. However it comes about, when the obvious flop is closed quickly, the backers will have some token part of their investment returned.

For the past several seasons and especially due to off-Broadway, which in the beginning had no reputation, new producers mushroomed. Nearly all of them were young theatre-struck semi-businessmen who were able to raise small sums of money (all that used to be needed for an off-Broadway production) and with no experience or background in the theatre, they launched their careers as producers. Most of them failed. But it did prove—rightly or otherwise—that just anyone could get the curtain up for a show on opening night. Eventually they set up shop on Broadway, where they had to raise and thus lost more money, but still, for the most part, seldom "made" it.

Nevertheless, the more knowledgeable producers off-Broadway, those with a desire to do something more meaningful, more special, more adventurous than is usually offered on Broadway, have served a purpose even in failure. In having begun the careers of new playwrights, some of them have had a chance to show promise in revealing the very existence of new actors and talented new directors who doubtless would have had to wait out a longer period for the opportunity of introducing themselves.

Another thing. Because of some success in the off-Broadway theatre, a need has been created to have an even *less* expensive theatre for even *more* experimental productions, and this has accounted for a segment called off-off-Broadway. Both serve useful purposes in spite of the fact that only the smallest percentage of what they do was intrinsically worth doing at all. Nonetheless, the *one* playwright or actor or director who has been given his springboard makes the whole operation eminently worthwhile.

All producers watch Broadway business and trends precisely in the way that Wall Street brokers follow "the market." They cannot be faulted for this, because they are first of all businessmen and sometimes two or three years pass during which they must give lavishly of themselves, the while earning no money. Then comes the realization, and if they are successful, more than another year will pass before they begin to collect profits. The truly good things always succeed and even some pretty threadbare, old-fashioned ones make it for too long a time. The best shows have always been successful, but the producer's talents and his acumen can help them to hang about longer, or cause them to close up sooner than was inherently necessary.

While the librettist, composer, director, and producer are each of enormous importance in the putting together of a musical, the star, if indeed he or she *is* one, is also incalculably significant. A star is a number of very different things which have a way of undergoing the extremes of desirability and its opposite. Then too there is a vastly divergent use of the term in the minds of different kinds of people even at the same time.

As to the first statement: Alfred Lunt and Lynn Fontanne were stars in *The Visit*, a play by Friedrich Dürrenmatt produced in 1958. However, Rodgers and Hammerstein were the stars of *The Sound of Music*, and Lerner and Loewe (after the unprecedented success of *My Fair Lady*) were the stars of *Camelot*. Lauren Bacall was the star of *Applause*. What have these people—some actors, some writers—in common with one another? The answer, I think, is a very simple one: Their names cause people to rush to the box office to buy tickets. Had Lauren Bacall or her vehicle received bad reviews from the critics, it is a moot question as to whether or not she would be the star that she is today. On the other hand, Katharine Hepburn played the title part in *Coco*, a musical that received uniformly terrible notices, and was thought generally to be an awful show. Yet, *Coco* was a sell-out, and this was entirely due to Miss Hepburn's presence in the cast. When her role was assumed by Danielle Darrieux, *Coco* quickly closed. Miss Hepburn had not appeared on Broadway in twenty years. She has been adored in the movies for nearly forty years and has always played simple, touching, sympathetic roles—a fact that is not to be ignored. (Edward G. Robinson, often a "tough guy" in films, is not such a starry star.) Bits and pieces of her personal life have drifted about in various publications throughout these years, and all of them have served to endear her to a very large public.

The star business has more peculiarities than stars. At the turn of the present century a stage personality was a star. Then he was a movie star. Then only a radio performer achieved such status. Now he is a TV and/or recording performer, and the length of time he continues to shine is quite unpredictable. In fact, it's anybody's guess as to who is and who isn't a star at any given time.

David Belasco, the writer-director-producer who wore his collars backward and who created many stars in his time, forbade his famous ladies to appear anywhere in public *except* when they appeared on stage in his plays. Today, such a practice would seem to have an opposite effect, because the appearance of a stage star on a well-watched TV show could surely send the star's rating up a great deal. Although many well-known personalities appear on the TV talk shows, their hosts are usually better known, and for a longer time, than the guests. Johnny Carson, Dick Cavett, David Frost, and Merv Griffin seem to go on and on, while agents do everything in their powers to book their clients for appearances on these shows.

But strange things do and have happened to stars, and it's quite doubtful that they won't go on happening over and over again. George Abbott made Nancy Walker into a star by simply putting her name in lights above the title of *Look Ma, I'm Dancin'*. The same thing happened to Helen Gallagher in *Hazel Flagg*. Both of them are incomparably wonderful performers. Their vehicles did not succeed. Neither of these ladies has that special chemistry that makes the public fight at the box office for tickets to their shows. In my opinion, their well-meaning producers ruined their careers. Both were out of important work for some time, and it is only too understandable that it took some years to prefer positions a step or two down the ladder to remaining forever jobless.

Then there is a singular case of Ethel Merman, who sings up a storm, has succeeded in defining a style that is entirely her own, and yet seems to have a very slim and vacillating public. Outside of New York she is almost unknown. The state fair of Texas engaged her to star in a show during an extremely well-attended fair (about 1950) and people stayed away in droves. I conducted revivals of *Brigadoon* and *Flower Drum Song* at the Carter Barron Amphitheatre in Washington, D.C., about 1960. The place seated about 5,000 people, and we had in our two weeks audiences of between 2,000 and capacity each night. While we rehearsed, Miss Merman was performing nightly as the star of a show, the first half of which sported dancers and various vaudeville acts. The second half consisted of Merman-with-band, and she sang all of the songs she has ever been identified with. The audiences numbered about 500 nightly.

Recently she was the heroine of *Hello, Dolly!*, and she was perfect for it. She provided the kind of excitement one seldom finds in the theatre any longer. But the houses were far from packed.

The story is famous that when Jack Warner cast the movie version of *My Fair Lady*, so much money was involved that he used Rex Harrison in his original role but eschewed Julie Andrews because she was not a star. In her place he cast Audrey Hepburn, whose singing had to be dubbed. Before the film was released, Julie Andrews became a big star, first with *Mary Poppins*, and it was Julie Andrews who usurped that year's Oscar from Audrey Hepburn!

In earlier days, Tallulah Bankhead was a bona-fide star. In many productions she could be counted on to bring in audiences. During that period of her life and before she had to make a career of touring—mostly in *Private Lives*—she starred in Anouilh's *The Eagle Has Two Heads*, which had been a smash hit in London for two seasons with a new actress, Eileen Herlie, in the principal role. Mr. Anouilh's play is an excellent one in my opinion. It was murdered by the critics in New York, who could find fault only with it but *not* with Bankhead, who had literally destroyed it. This kind of "incident" has often happened.

There are more contemporary finer points to be made. A stage performer named Carol Channing first commanded attention in a little revue called *Lend an Ear* (1948). It and she were successful. The following year she was adored in *Gentlemen Prefer Blondes*. She succeeded Rosalind Russell in *Wonderful Town* (1954) and the show closed only a few weeks later. She starred in a flop, *The Vamp* (1955), but again achieved her biggest stardom in *Hello, Dolly!* (1964).

Another but quite different case in point is *Hello, Dolly!* When I first saw it I particularly disliked it because I remembered vividly the stylish production of Thornton Wilder's *The Matchmaker* on which it is based. Nothing in the musical approached the grand manner of the ladies as played by Ruth Gordon and Eileen Herlie. The play generated a delicious nose-in-the-air charm, naughty, a period piece, and, above all, the ladies were especially feminine. This was an all-important quality. I felt that the musical version was vulgar. It had one engaging production number in the staging of the title song. But it had two ladies who were about as feminine and believable as strong unsweetened iced tea. Carol Channing was still playing her nightclub act. She was not Dolly Levi, nor a charming female conniver. Mrs. Molloy (Eileen Brennan) was still playing *Little Mary Sunshine*. There was neither a unified style nor credibility nor fun in the entire thin evening.

Years and many changes of stars later, Pearl Bailey headed an all-Negro cast which I saw. Then, somehow, nearly everything worked. The ladies were ladies. The boys were masculine. Dolly Levi was deliciously concerned with her conniving—not merely with herself. Later. Bravo Ethel Merman.

The production of a musical is so complex and is made of so many elements contributed by so many different people, each believing absolutely in his own idea, that a single often unpredictable something can spoil everything or, to the contrary, can give the entire project an aura of success that it perhaps does not truly and intrinsically merit. *Hello, Dolly!* is pretty thin stuff. The pictorial-minded Gower Champion staging often had a way of making you overlook the faulty original casting and the music. But it was Pearl Bailey who pulled the wool over your eyes, and Leonard Bernstein's score for *Candide* nearly made you overlook the book. Here the composer was the star.

Then there is the case of Angela Lansbury, who, somewhat like Channing in *Dolly*, became a glamorous star in an even more threadbare vehicle called *Mame*. She was the toast of the world. Then she did the same creative team's *Dear World*, based on *The Madwoman of Chaillot*. Lansbury was incredibly good. The show was terrible and folded after a brief run in spite of the star.

The star department is not always accountable for good, and casting can conceivably harm a property. I recall attending a pre–out-of-town rehearsal of *A Tree Grows in Brooklyn*, which contained Arthur Schwartz's very best score. As usual at such a rehearsal there were no scenery, costumes, lighting, or orchestra, but the show was moving and impressive. With the addition of these other elements, the show failed to move or impress. I have often wondered about this, and as nearly as I can arrive at any conclusion (and from memory) I suspect that it was not the fault of these added elements that wrecked a most promising show but something else. The single star was Shirley Booth, who was wonderful. But she was cast in a role that actually lacked star proportions. I believe that unwittingly she destroyed the balance. The show was really about two young people who, lacking star quality in both writing and casting, were so dwarfed by the personality and power of a distinguished performer that the real values of the show were obliterated.

There is one fact: a star *is*. When I conducted *I Can Get It for You Wholesale* in 1962, the star was Lillian Roth, who was famous not only as a performer, but especially as a lady who had won a spectacular fight against alcoholism. There was an unattractive girl, undisciplined, untrained, who had a small part, her first in the theatre, named Barbra Streisand. She had one song to sing, and night after night she stopped the show with it. The show was not a success, but Barbra went on to become a superstar.

I believe it is true that a star can ruin a show and that he can also make it into a saleable product. From the star's own point of view, he should exercise the greatest caution in what he elects to do. Both Alfred Drake and Celeste Holm gave evidence of the right stardom ingredients in *Oklahoma!*, and yet, although each has worked often and diligently since, neither has even nearly equaled his first success, which is now twenty-seven years ago.

I know personally a dozen singing actors who look well, are

young, act well, sing well, and are extremely easy to work with. They have had opportunities. They are not unknown. They are large attributes to anything they appear in. The years pass. They are not stars. I do not begin to recognize the chemical ingredients they lack. They ought to be stars. I know now that for them it will never happen.

To recapitulate briefly: The play's the thing of more or less importance. The music of a musical can help enormously in its department but can seldom define the difference between failure and success. (Harold Rome's title song to *Wish You Were Here* had a great deal to do with that show's eventual success.) The director can ruin a property. In my opinion, the original stage director of John Kander's first show, *Family Affair* (book by William and James Goldman), which I much admired when reading it and hearing the score, turned it into a fancy catastrophe. On the other hand, Gower Champion made the definitive contributions to *Hello, Dolly!*, which he staged and choreographed. Good producers, given enough of a show and favorable enough reviews, can sometimes transform a stinker into a sweet-smelling rose. The star (who is it this season or is there any?) can help to ruin a show or send long lines of ticket buyers to the box office.

When the chips are down (as some people still say) it *is* the play or the libretto of a musical on which true success is pegged. With such a rare item, nothing else really matters. *Fiddler on the Roof* has had umpteen different stars playing it even in New York. Who cares? Jerome Robbins' direction of Joseph Stein's book, Jerry Bock's music, Sheldon Harnick's lyrics, and Boris Aronson's sets work so well together (Robbins piloting the craft) that what will last, go down in history, captivates the whole world now, and unquestionably to continue the show itself indefinitely is all that counts. Zero Mostel was great. So was Herschel Bernardi. So was Luther Adler. So were they all. Neither you, reader, nor I, non-actor could ruin it. The show remains and is, in this case, the star.

COMMENTS ON PRODUCERS AND STARS

Few chapters in *Words with Music* have the aura of ancient history as much as the one entitled "Producers and Stars." The two words retain few of the connotations they had when Engel wrote his book.

Of the two words, "producers" today has less resemblance to what it meant thirty years ago than "stars." If you were to look at a Broadway marquee in those days, there might be one or two names above the title. The most famous of those names for many years was David Merrick, who generally had solo billing. If he deemed their contributions essential, he might elevate one or two colleagues to a position just below his with the phrase "in association with."

Merrick isn't the only producer who got solo billing. Herman Levin, who produced *My Fair Lady*, felt CBS Records didn't rate producer billing, even though CBS had provided all the funding. They, after all, were getting the royalties, which turned out to be greater than anyone imagined. As for Levin's own contribution, it wasn't simply his brilliance in approaching CBS; it was also his tenacity over the years in securing the rights from the film producer Gabriel Pascal but also in persevering in the project when team after team had rejected the idea.

Only one man gets billing as producer for *Kiss Me, Kate*, Saint Subber, who dropped his prosaic first name Arnold and achieved a distinctive monicker. Subber was entitled to solo billing because his belief in Cole Porter was viewed as mistaken—the show had an unusual number of backers' auditions because many were convinced that Porter, then in his late 50s, was washed up. It took courage to swim against this stream, and Subber had it in spades.

Today producers' names rarely appear on Broadway marquees, not because there aren't any but because there are far too many. If you listed every producer's name there would no longer be any space left for the title. A popular game among theatregoers today is simply to open *Playbill* and count the number of producers above the title as well as those "in association with," who now generally appear somewhere in the middle. The numbers can be staggering.

When so many people are involved, the taste and experience of any single person matters little. The reason these consortiums have become necessary is that the cost of producing a musical is so high. Let's take as an example a relatively inexpensive show—*A Chorus Line*, which was produced at the New York Shakespeare Festival Public Theatre in the spring of 1975 for $250,000. For us this seems a pittance, but it was no small sum then. Moreover, when it moved to Broadway that autumn, the cost jumped to $1.2 million.

As an abstract number, $1.2 million also seems small, though it was not considered so at the time. As a point of comparison, the Harold Prince-Stephen Sondheim-John Weidman *Pacific Overtures*, which opened less than a year later in January of 1976, cost $600,000, and its recreation of 19th century Japan by set designer Boris Aronson and costume designer Florence Klotz was positively lavish—and exquisite. The only lavish thing in *A Chorus Line* was the snazzy gold costumes in the final number. Until then the cast wears blue jeans, leotards, and T-shirts. As for the sets, they consist of a long white line painted near the apron of the stage and, in the final number, a wall of mirrors. So how does this add up to $1.2 million?

In its time *A Chorus Line* was considered an unusually complicated show because, given its bare stage, it required extensive light changes to underline the emotional impact of the score. There were more than 300 individual lighting cues. Few things are more expensive in the theatre than paying a stage crew to be in attendance while lighting cues are set.

For the last fifteen years the standard cost of producing a Broadway musical has ranged between $10 and $12 million. David Merrick was able to pay for his last full-scale musical, *42nd Street*, entirely by himself. It cost $2 million, a record sum for 1980, but it was a gamble he was willing to take. These days Bill Gates might take a $10 or $12 million gamble to produce a musical, but Gates seems to have other concerns, and so it falls to armies of producers to raise the money for Broadway shows.

The result is that shows no longer reflect the taste or experience of a producer. Not surprisingly, they often reflect the sensibility of a committee. A useful way of understanding how things change is to look at the remarkable career of Harold Prince.

Prince began his career with a very traditional apprenticeship. His father was a stockbroker, among whose clients was the eminent Broadway producer/director George Abbott. The elder Prince called Abbott to ask a favor. His son, Hal, wanted to go into the theatre. If Abbott would hire him as an apprentice for a summer, surely the boy would get over this desire. Prince would even pay the boy's salary. Abbott agreed. At the end of the summer he called his broker to say, "I've got bad news for you. The boy has talent. I've offered him a job."

Prince worked for about five years in Abbott's office. In 1953 he and a friend, Robert Griffith, produced their first show, a musical about the garment industry called *The Pajama Game*. It was based on a successful novel, *7½ Cents*, and the novelist, Richard Bissell, wrote the book for the musical. The score was by two unknowns, Richard Adler and Jerry Ross. Even hiring Abbott to direct, the show was a gamble, but one that paid off handsomely. Two of its songs, "Hey, There" and "Hernando's Hideway," spent months on the hit parade. The show had an excellent run. A season later, Prince and Griffith produced another musical by Adler and Ross, *Damn Yankees*.

By now Prince shared an office with his mentor, Abbott, which he continued to do until Abbott died in 1996. In 1957 he produced *West Side Story*, which is now universally considered one of the great achievements of the American musical theatre. It was the work of experienced and respected creators—Leonard Bernstein, Jerome Robbins and Arthur Laurents—as well as a gifted newcomer, Stephen Sondheim. Given the iconic status of the show, it is hard for us to understand the enormous gamble it posed.

There was certainly no guarantee it would be a success. Bernstein's last show, *Candide*, however glorious its score, had been a flop. The original producer of *West Side Story*, Cheryl Crawford, had withdrawn, leaving Bernstein distraught. She was hardly your conventional commercial producer. Along with Harold Clurman and Lee Strasberg, Crawford had been one of the three founders of the Group Theatre. After its demise she helped finance its progeny, the Actors' Studio. The reason she was the logical producer for *West Side Story* was that she had devoted her enormously successful career to producing plays and musicals of merit, such as Lerner and Loewe's *Brigadoon* and *Paint Your Wagon* and two shows with scores by Kurt Weill, *One Touch of Venus* and *Love Life*. How many other producers might take on such a serious project?

Prince and his partner, Robert Griffith, took it over enthusiastically, but they had problems raising funds. One of the associate producers, Sylvia Drulie Mazzola, had what she considered a good idea. She approached Sondheim's father, a successful Seventh Avenue manufacturer, which angered his son. Sondheim *père* nevertheless made an investment, which turned out to be a very good thing.

The risk of failure was high, but no one was deterred. Ultimately *West Side Story* raised the stakes for the entire musical theatre and set the tone for the rest of Prince's career. In those days failure was no less a reality than it is today. Even though the sums were not great by our standards, they were not negligible. What has changed is that in those days the producers, Prince chief among them, saw their work as creative. They were not simply financing a commodity.

In the early Sixties, Prince began to direct, with Sheldon Harnick and Jerry Bock's *She Loves Me*. Earlier he'd produced their *Fiorello*, with Abbott directing. The show is one of the seven musicals to win a Pulitzer Prize. In 1964 Prince produced *Fiddler on the Roof*, directed by Jerome Robbins. Its huge success gave him an unparalleled power, consolidated a few years later by the success of *Cabaret*, which he both produced and directed. *Cabaret* was by John Kander and Fred Ebb, whose first show, you will recall, *Flora, the Red Menace*, Prince had also produced. Loyalty to creative teams was a hallmark of Prince's career as a producer.

For some time afterward he didn't need to go through the sometimes humiliating ritual of backers' auditions. He sent a letter announcing what he was going to do, and his loyal, grateful backers simply sent him checks. In the Seventies, however, tastes were changing. Of the creative artists whose work Prince championed none was closer to him than Stephen Sondheim. It was Prince's idea, based on seeing a famous photograph of Gloria Swanson in the ruins of the Roxy Theatre, to do *Follies*, and Sondheim and bookwriter James Goldman took material they'd begun in another guise and wed it to Prince's vision.

The last collaboration on which Prince worked as both producer and director was *Pacific Overtures*. It stretched the audience's adventurousness—and the backers' acquiescence—beyond where they would go. The next Sondheim-Prince collaboration, *Sweeney Todd*, was produced by the veteran producer Richard Barr, who resorted to a quite unknown method for raising money. He put an advertisement in *The New York Times* inviting people to invest money. What had for decades been a kind of insiders' game was now "open to the public."

It was a noble experiment. But *Sweeney Todd*, though it's often performed by American opera companies and was even presented in concert by the New York Philharmonic, wasn't a commercial success. So the experiment was not tried again. Eventually the problem of raising huge amounts of capital was solved by the consortiums that today are standard.

Producing theatre, however, certainly when Prince began in the late Forties, wasn't simply about raising money. A producer's office was a paternal institution. There were a host of character actors, for example, who turned up in one George Abbott musical after another, as if he were running a Hollywood studio with contract players. In those days, actors "made the rounds." That is, they paid frequent visits to the offices of producers just to remind them of their availability.

In the late Seventies, Harold Clurman lamented to a young actress that the theatre was no longer "a profession." When he'd started out, in the Twenties, a young actor—or writer—had to make an effort to be seen, but once that happened he had, in effect, stepped onto the first rung of a ladder, as Clurman saw it. After that there was a whole community to help him on his way up the ladder. When Clurman made his rueful remarks to the young actress, that ladder and the community around it no longer existed. Every step was now, in effect, the first step.

However much the theatre has changed, there are still producers whose commitment to a project is intense. Margo Lion spent nine years producing *Jelly's Last Jam*, a musical about Jelly Roll Morton by George C. Wolfe. It opened on Broadway in 1992 to admiring if uneven reviews, had a brief run and lost all its money. Another show she developed from scratch, *Triumph of Love*, based on the work of the 18th century French writer Marivaux, also lost all its money and didn't even garner good reviews.

By chance, she watched a video of John Waters' film *Hairspray*, set in her—and his—native city, Baltimore. When the movie first came out, in 1988, she had not liked it, but now she found herself responding to it deeply. She acquired the stage rights. She invited Marc Shaiman, of *South Park*, to write the score, with his companion, Scott Wittman, as co-lyricist. She knew she'd made the right decisions when, for almost the first time in her 25-year career, she didn't need to mortgage her apartment to raise the money ($10.5 million) to produce it.

Finally, in 2002, the same dedication and energy she devoted to her other shows paid off with *Hairspray*'s huge success.

The dedication of a single producer can still make miracles. That the musical about Ed Kleban, *A Class Act*, had a Broadway run is entirely because of the efforts and financial resources of another female producer, Chase Mishkin. She committed an equal amount of energy and money, along with that of many others, to *Urban Cowboy*, a musical version of the John Travolta film.

Sometimes the theatre benefits from producers who aren't necessarily devoted to Art. In the late Eighties, a play was produced on Broadway starring the young Denzel Washington that, it turned out, was financed by drug money. It had seemed odd that one of the producers, so eager to contribute to the production, hadn't attended the opening. Only later was it discovered he was unable to because he was in a San Francisco prison. No one has yet urged that easing drug laws might benefit theatre production, but here was a preview of it.

Similarly, in the mid-Seventies, much hope for the theatre was pinned on a producer named Adela Holzer, who was responsible for the Broadway production of Scott Joplin's opera *Treemonisha*. She was the major producer of a musical with the ominous title *Truckload*.

Among her other productions was a 1974 Murray Schisgal play, *All Over Town*, which had eighteen characters and an elaborate set with the multiple doors a farce requires. Among other things, *All Over Town* marked the Broadway directorial debut of Dustin Hoffman. Despite this apparent success, the show, which had a heavy overhead, lost $500,000 in its six-month run, as did *Truckload*, which she had the prudence to close in previews. These setbacks, however, didn't seem to deter her.

In addition to her theatre production, Mrs. Holzer, who'd been a major investor in *Hair*, had a commodities business that yielded extraordinary returns. Ultimately it was discovered she was involved in a pyramid scheme. Money for the commodities business was going into the theatrical productions, and money from "backers" was paying off the commodities investors. As inevitably happens, the pyramid crumbled, but not before it created a new respect for the achievement of Scott Joplin (as well as employment for many actors and singers).

A similar case might be made for Garth Drabinsky, whose financial dealings have come under government scrutiny. Unlike Mrs. Holzer, however, he was genuinely devoted to the theatre. In 1990 Harold Prince directed a new musical by John Kander and Fred Ebb, *Curse of the Spider Woman*. It was done in a program at the State University of New York at Purchase in which new works would be tried out presumably without the intervention of the press. The cost of the tickets, however, in a venue an hour from New York, aroused the watchdog instincts of the press. To protect the public from such high prices without any critical guidance, the press descended on *Kiss* to give it the kiss of death.

Drabinsky, who'd not been involved in this initial production, took up the *Kiss* cause. He produced it in London, where it proved successful. It transferred to New York in 1993, where it had a healthy run. Set in an unnamed, oppressive Latin American country, it had an extraordinarily powerful song, "The Day After That," sung by its protagonist, a political activist, with a chorus of "disappeared," those "inconvenient" people Latin American dictators occasionally must dispose of. The song became emblematic of the gay community in the midst of the AIDS crisis. This was heroic producing.

So was the lavish revival of Jerome Kern and Oscar Hammerstein's *Show Boat*, also directed by Prince, which Drabinsky produced first in Toronto, then on Broadway in 1994. Drabinsky had his hand in several other productions as well as the construction of a new Broadway theatre, the Ford Centre, on Forty-Second Street, helping spark the revival of that long forlorn thoroughfare.

He was, however, financially overextended, and when his production of the Terrence McNally-Lynn Ahrens-Stephen Flaherty musical based on E.L. Doctorow's *Ragtime* failed to win the rave reviews it needed to make it a blockbuster, Drabinsky's whole financial empire began to unravel. Whatever the consequences for investors, his disappearance represents a heavy loss for the theatre.

The most successful producer in recent decades—perhaps of all time—is the Englishman Cameron Mackintosh. Mackintosh began producing on a small scale in the late Sixties. One of his first successes was a revival of Cole Porter's *Anything Goes* in 1969. Although he became known for his lavish shows, one of his early ventures was a musical based on an Arnold Bennett novel, *The Card*, starring Jim Dale. In 1976 he produced *Side by Side by Sondheim*, a revue celebrating the American composer, whose *Follies* he gave a major revival in the West End in 1985.

He is, of course, best known for his mega-hits, *Cats*, *Les Miz*, *Phantom* and *Miss Saigon*, which transformed not just Broadway and the West End but commercial theatre all over the world. One of his most impressive understandings was that shows did better if they were marketed as shows, not as vehicles for stars. *Phantom* is known for its beautifully designed mask, *Les Miz* for its 19th century illustration of a waif weeping, *Miss Saigon* for its helicopter in the shape of an Asian pictograph. These iconic images exerted a power far greater than that of any star's name (not to mention requiring considerably less expense and ego massaging).

When Michael Crawford left *Phantom of the Opera* it had no impact whatsoever on the box office. When Andrew Lloyd Webber produced *Sunset Boulevard* on his own he linked its success to the presence of a star. When Glenn Close departed so did the big box office.

Which brings us to Engel's other concern in this chapter—stars. When he wrote his book there was still a clear memory of actors who'd spent their lives in the theatre and whose name on a marquee was guaranteed to sell tickets. Only a decade had gone by since Alfred Lunt and Lynn Fontanne had toured the country in Friedrich Dürrenmatt's *The Visit*. Carol Channing, whose greatest success had been in the theatre, opened *Hello, Dolly!* in 1964. When its fortunes began to flag, Pearl Bailey made it a hit again. (Despite a formidable night club reputation and TV track record, she had been first a theatre star.) At the end of its run Ethel Merman, for whom it had initially been written, took over the title role and gave it the momentum it needed to break the then record for longest-running musical on Broadway.

Now, however, the only stars who can carry a show are those from TV and the movies. But the financial burden their recompense puts on a production makes their presence a mixed blessing.

A playwright once explained to me that he was excited about having a play of his done at an Off-Off Broadway subscription theatre. The hope, of course, was that it would open to favorable reviews and then move to a commercial venue, either Off Broadway or On.

To bolster the commercial viability of the project—and to signal it was a play of some significance—it was agreed that it would be beneficial to have a TV star play the leading role. The star was amenable, and her career was successful enough that both she—and her agents—were willing to take a substantial cut in income during the noncommercial run. The $2000 a week she agreed to accept was pocket change to her, but a sacrifice she was willing to make because she liked the play. To pay her for her appearance at the not-for-profit theatre, however, the playwright had to waive his royalties, which he too was willing to do. Despite this cacophony of self-sacrifice, other problems submarined the production.

When Engel wrote about producers and stars they were both parts of an equation that didn't require higher mathematics to solve. Now the number of variables has multiplied geometrically, and neither element is sufficient to make the equation work. In some ways this is healthy. The closest thing to a star in *Hairspray* was Harvey Fierstein, and though he gave a great performance, his presence was hardly guaranteed to sell tickets. It didn't matter. The success of *Hairspray* hinged on the material, which, for people creating new musicals, ought to be encouraging.

13

Nonplot

To try to belong to one's own time is already to be out of date.

Eugène Ionesco
(translated by Donald Watson)

One of the many hallmarks of current rock nontheatre musicals is the employment of nonplot, which many critics have accepted with incredible equanimity as though a musical without a plot is a perfectly usual state.

But is this really true?

Unusual it is without doubt. Impossible, I would say, *unless* it had extremely well-defined characters. For with such characters peopling the stage, certain relationships, animosities, attractions, revulsions, differences—situations—would of necessity begin to germinate and develop, and the result would have to be a kind of drama that might conceivably substitute for plot. If we are allowed to know the people, we would automatically be supplied with some sense of feeling, of caring. We would sense conflicts and affinities, struggles to associate or be rid of, efforts to charm, to repel, to love, or to hate. These are at least primitive foundations for or surrogates in lieu of a plot. They are at least situations. But characters defined sharply and identifiably would have to exist and with the greatest clarity.

Professor George Pierce Baker of Harvard published his famous *Dramatic Technique* in 1919. I would like to quote some lines that seem relevant here:

Some plays depend almost wholly upon mere bustle and rapidly shifting movement, much of it wholly unnecessary to the plot. Large portions of many recent musical comedies illustrate this.

Not a single one of these—many successful at the time—only 50 years later, is alive.

Characterization, preceding and accompanying action, creates sympathy or repulsion for the figure or figures involved. This sympathy or repulsion in turn converts mere interest into emotional response of the keenest kind... no higher form can develop till characterization appears to explain and interpret action.

While action is popularly held to be central in drama, emotion is really the essential....

Accurately conveyed emotion is the fundamental in all good drama.

It would seem, then, that a musical minus all of the elements of story, premise, characters, conflict, development would wind up as a revue, but the nonplot shows are *not* revues. There is no recognizable start or stop to the "happening" as a whole, no well-defined units, no sketches, no dance, no connecting thread. What is it then that such a theatrical "happening" has left? The complete answer usually can only be that it has "songs." No matter how good the songs are—and often they are excellent—they must lack the all-important theatrical ingredient of having been born of some recognizable situation and made for a specific identifiable character reacting in it. Without such motivations, the songs become generalized, will not arouse audience empathy, will occur in unconnected and therefore meaningless sequence. The audience may as well arrive and/or depart at will without having missed anything. This theatre is today's equivalent of vaudeville, or minstrel show or, at best, *Ziegfeld Follies*, although the latter nearly always contained literate amusing sketches which added up to a slight but complete denouement because characters within situations were developed swiftly to a (sometimes illogical) conclusion but with an ending which caused the audience to explode with laughter.

It is also true that the songs in most of the shows are (because of plotlessness) not going anywhere, not exposing anything or any-body. They are simply numbers which give themselves only a single opportunity of succeeding. Are they *that* interesting? Certainly these unmotivated separate songs can be equated to those very old non-working songs that occurred in the revues of the Twenties when the sudden restlessness and apathy of the audiences was all too embarrassingly apparent. Lastly, about the songs, for a reason which I cannot comprehend, they never end. They merely stop, or, as in many pop records, they fade away. That is as about as atheatri-cal as a theatre song can be.

The nonplot musicals have eschewed an important motivating theatrical element in being plotless and characterless because they have failed to furnish the audience with the sense of caring. They can no longer motivate any desire to see how anything will turn out since there is nothing to turn out, nothing impending-in fact, in this sense, nothing at all. There is nobody to root for because there is nobody, only (usually) a stage full of people, as full as the budget allows, one occasionally distinguishable from another physically by size, shape, or kind of hair. No one bears a clear-cut relationship to another so that there is no loving union to hope for, no mystery, lit-tle to laugh about unless generalized, naïve and already well-known puerile jokes fired at religion, family, the Establishment, draft eva-sion and the like are capable of provoking it.

Another thing. Since time and place occupy no part of the pro-ceedings there can be little if any sense of unified style. Costumes and scenery—if they exist at all—must be nonspecific, which is not the same as being abstract. In the good abstract there is recogniza-ble style and form. In the non-specific there is only negativism. We are careful to suggest nothing and to relate to nothing.

What remains is often considerable youthful vigor, ear splitting sound volume, sometimes mesmerizing rhythm, music composed of childishly simple and limited melody, narrowly prescribed har-mony, and the rhythm of incessant and unrelieved repetition. The latter two qualities also often apply to the lyrics.

On the other hand, the knowing use of nonplot recognizes spe-cial thinking on the part of the writers who have been steeped in tra-dition and in most cases have blasted off from such distinguished earlier writers as Chekhov, Ibsen, and even Büchner. However, the application of nonplot here refers to those inexperienced, immature, and thoughtless writers who merely suggest nonplot because of an inability to come up with a good, simple, and non-cliché plot. What residue remains suggests a story line that is derelict in being absent—a poor shaved-down plot in lieu of one that should be better defined and more original.

Certainly this kind of nonplot is due to three conditions: non-knowledge born of insufficient education and experience, an overwhelming desire particularly on the part of many young "creative" people to rush quickly into a situation in which they may (and frequently do) have a quick if temporary success, and very real reaction against the poor, threadbare, overused, non-creative librettos written and produced during the past two decades.

The latter condition has, I believe, corroded the judgment of many critics who have admittedly been bored with a large part of what they have had to tolerate during these some twenty years. They have obviously reacted favorably to almost everything that was different, that provided a change from their nearly unendurable nightly chores. But in being able to accept without the slightest queasiness the nonplot, directionless, characterless new musicals, these same critics have incubated a kind of kinetic non-musical which threatens to destroy and to a large extent discourage more serious, better based creativity. This nonplot, etc., musical is at most and at best a transitional groping toward something newer than anything which has existed for some time, but transitional it is and the eventual main event will unquestionably be spawned by more knowledgeable creative people who also eschew the threadbare trappings of the more recent past without disclaiming the very foundations of musical theatre. These foundations include, among other things, at least characters.

The more knowing and in many cases more talented writers have to contend with:

> Now the authors of the dowdy book—and brilliant lyrics—have done a very brave thing. They have in effect done away with it altogether. *Hair* is now a musical with a theme, not with a story.
> —Clive Barnes, *The New York Times*

The original, rather harmless plot [*Hair*] has been practically erased, and the music…carries the evening.
—John J. O'Connor, *The Wall Street Journal*

The story line of *Hair* is so attenuated that it would be merciful to label the piece a revue.
—Howard Taubman, *The New York Times*

It is fatuous for critics to look for narrative continuity and unity of style when the theatre has become a meeting-point for stylistic collisions and aesthetic jumble.
—Charles Marowitz, *Plays and Players*

There is a thread not exactly of plot (*Promenade*) but at least of continuity that runs through all the non sequiturs and monkeyshines.
—Edith Oliver, *The New Yorker*

In reviewing *Promenade* Clive Barnes wrote in *The New York Times*: "This is no book in any conventional sense. Indeed it comes close to being no book in any unconventional sense."

Walter Kerr in *The New York Times*, in speaking of *Salvation*, wrote:

Rock musicals have certainly arrived at one solution of the old musical comedy "book" problem. A forget-and-forgive policy has been worked out. The show forgets to have a book, and the audience forgives it for forgetting. Usually a minimal gesture is made toward a book, which is then mocked.… Peter Link and C.C. Courtney have written everything in *Salvation*, and while they are never going to grow up to become the librettists or lyricists for *Guys and Dolls*, they are already accomplished melodists, sunny and inventive and ripe for a cast album. The ear, having given in, is pleased throughout the evening. And the mind wanders, as mine has.

James Davis in the New York *Daily News* wrote:

> When the band is doing its thing and the performers
> are probably on stage and singing, *Salvation* is a pleasing
> if not exciting show. But when the band is mute and the
> players are being roguish, bantering with audience
> plants, running up and down the aisles and attempting to
> extract humor from the Bible and God one should close
> his eyes and turn a deaf ear to the dialogue. Otherwise,
> stay at home and buy the album.

In *Women's Wear Daily*, Martin Gottfried wrote:

> Between *Hair* and *Your Own Thing*, rock music finally
> made it into the theatre, no matter how painfully late,
> but the theatre still doesn't know what to do with it. Still
> not able to accept the music for all it's worth, the theatre
> insists on tying it to hippies and then making the hippies,
> drug references, sex equals love, frug dancing and light
> then—a concert, really—only in the sense that it lumps
> together everything that the older generation associates
> with rock music: hippies, drug references, sex equals
> love, frug dancing and light shows. It uses these ele-
> ments on only the most superficial of levels and even
> then it is behind the times in its devices (the light show,
> for example, uses stills instead of moving shapes and
> flashes the same old slides of race riots and sterile office
> buildings). Yet, for all of that, the energy of rock is there
> and with it the life of today. There are some tired things
> in *Salvation*, and a pretty silly narrative link drawing the
> old religion (God) toward a new one (sex).

How *can* you, Mr. Gottfried, have written such a silly, meaningless review, filled with contradictions and placing the blame for
obvious weaknesses, shortcomings, deficiencies, etc., on the *theatre?* The theatre did not write, produce, or direct any show—least
of all *Hair, Your Own Thing,* or *Salvation.* You say "the theatre still
doesn't know what to do with it." The theatre? The writers, direc-

tors and all those active in creating these noisy, thin, styleless pieces are the only ones who can be blamed. These are the people who succeed often, who reap the profits, and the elements which you find lacking can only be due to their lack of knowledge and experience.

Then you further accuse the theatre (four blank walls, will-less, innocuous) of lumping "together everything that the older generation associates with rock music: hippies, drug references, sex equals love, frug dancing and light shows." Did the theatre do these things or did the authors? The theatre has always known what to do with everything it has contained. Only too often writers and directors have not known what to do with what they have the temerity to put *inside* the theatre. The theatre itself has undergone many changes. The Greeks had one kind and its writers created in such a way that what their plays would require would fit into their surroundings. Shakespeare had a different stage without scenery, much lighting, and females. Sheridan, with other limitations, ditto. The theatre now has many kinds of stages. The writers ought to choose the kind they mean to write for. It is certainly not the fault of the theatre that the shows themselves are so lacking in basic elements which have never and will never really change.

You yourself, Mr. Gottfried, say in the same review: "It [the theatre still or the experienceless writer-directors] uses these elements on only the most superficial levels and even then it [?] is behind the times in its devices (the light show, for example, uses stills instead of moving shapes and flashes the same old slides of race riots and sterile office buildings.)"

The theatre uses what it is directed to use. If what you see is "superficial" and "behind the times" it is solely because nobody in charge of production ordered it or made it otherwise. You further say, "There are some tired things in *Salvation*, and a pretty silly narration link drawing the old religion (God) toward a new one (sex)."

Thank you, Mr. Gottfried, for those unkind but absolutely truthful words.

I think it is only fair to the existing theatre—those four mute walls with seats to accommodate an audience and a platform on which actors may disport in any way they are directed to—to say a word as to its innocence. Bach wrote his fantastic church cantatas (they are as dramatic as all hell because of the music and lyrics) for whatever resources he found available. He demanded nothing more. Mozart used the theatre as he found it, with its existing non-electric lights, its pit and stage for the production of fabulous operas beyond the conception of anyone preceding or following him—even now, two centuries later. So did Debussy and Berg, Gilbert and Sullivan, Strauss (Richard and Johann), and many others. The theatre which they inherited served them well because what they had to put into it was in every case now, vibrant, vital, and universal.

It was the seventeenth-century French school—Rameau and Lully—who demanded much more spectacle, lights, scenery, ballet, a larger orchestra, etc., than the world had ever previously known, and they today, like Ozymandias, are names rather than monuments. Two centuries later, Wagner went through a similar "development" of super music-drama with a much larger orchestra, some new instruments, a special kind of super-voice, and many other things which were difficult to come by and are rapidly receding today. All the while Verdi was giving us *Otello* and *Falstaff* for the traditional theatre, works of such freshness and genius that they live today as they did (perhaps even more so today) at the beginning. It is not new theatres that we are so drastically in need of, but creative people with roots and backgrounds and ideas and heads full of characters and situations who will make us scream welcomes, and music that is not so limited and untalented and styleless as we found, noisily if briefly, for instance, in *Salvation*.

God!

Richard Watts in the New York *Post* said: "…there isn't a book in any familiar sense." And Clive Barnes in the *Times* wrote:

> There are indications that *Salvation* wants to be loud, daring, adventurous and even outspoken. Well, it is loud all of the time—the performers carry microphones around as though they were rattles—and I suppose there are moments that are both daring and adventurous, and even, once in a while, outspoken. But most of all, this rock musical was fun and thoroughly endearing. Naughty, of course, but its naughtiness has the impertinence of youth rather than the slime of age.

William A. Raidy in the *Long Island Press* said:

> The music took care of my airline ears, but I didn't
> blow my mind over the simple-minded "book," if you
> want to call it that. I don't need a bunch of plastic flower
> kids (man, that cast is so fake!) to tell me sex is good, or
> maybe masturbation won't send you to the looney bin.
> Or that everything in the Bible's not true by the letter.
> There's something so dreadfully juvenile about
> *Salvation*'s "message." It's all hung together with rusty
> wire, a lot of slides (pulsating sperm and that sort of
> thing) that are definitely the year before last.

And again Edith Oliver in *The New Yorker* wrote:

> Mr. Courtney and Mr. Link are also given program
> credit for the "book," whatever that means; there is no
> plot and little continuity between numbers, although
> the revivalist theme is switched on and off throughout,
> and religion is the butt of all mockery.

Here and there among these reviews of *Hair, Promenade* and
Salvation—three non-book musicals—there are scattered sounds of
discontent. But the non-book aspect is never wholly faulted and for
whatever reason I cannot imagine since the libretto of a musical—
aside from the many positive attributes sighted earlier—forms at
the very least the functional space between the songs, creating a
theatre piece or musical as opposed to a disorganized song recital.

In the turn-of-the-century musical the book existed only to
string the songs together. I believe that this accurately describes the
"books" of the three above-mentioned "shows." However, there
were songs galore in those early musicals which were so good that
they exist and are reused today even by the most avant-garde singers
and electric combos. The books dropped dead in their own day.
Today the principal difference is that the music also drops dead
rather instantly.

The critics of our earlier shows—if I might digress for a
moment—wrote in essence that nobody expected a musical to have

a decent book and then they went on to praise the other elements: stars, costumes, scenery, and, lastly, music and lyrics.

It was after that period in the Twenties that our writers learned much about libretto-writing. Now today some people find it unnecessary to have books. To lay the blame on the foolish books of the past fifteen years and conclude that no book is better than a bad one seems somehow silly. Why don't the writers bother to learn their craft so that they can *extend* what has been accomplished and make it today's?

I said earlier that "the nonplot aspect is due to…non-knowledge born of insufficient education or experience." In precisely the same way the music in these shows, and most of the others in their category, is limited to a frozen, narrow, circumscribed bailiwick. The harmonies consist of three, four or five simple chords in any one song and in almost all songs of this style, and the melody seldom rises, falls, or cadences above or below a tiny limited range. Also most of the melodies are extremely old and predictable, while their harmonic welding was standard in turn-of-the-century hymnology. Does this non-book, narrow-gauge music seem to comprise a liberation? I doubt it. Rather it is like a corset the stays of which are only too clearly visible.

However, there is one thing that this movement may in the end accomplish. Not monumental or memorable shows or music that will become cherished either for their own quality or as a beacon to future writers. It is quite possible—possible—that just the breakaway in and of itself may constitute a revolution against what was and what was tenaciously holding on to its own superior progenitor as its only claim to being. If a non-book is to be considered superior to a poor book, this must be a fallacy and I strenuously object to it as a point of view. But a book has been an integral part of musical theatre, and the characters it has engendered (or vice versa), and the progress of a plot could be noted along the way, and the caring that these—plot and characters—bred in the audience. These constituted musical theatre at its best (*all* theatre, for that matter) along with music that stirred by its freshness and warmth—not its overnoisiness and its incessant, persistent percussive drive that would do credit to primitive man and was undoubtedly all that he had recourse to in his earliest stage.

Nonplot to me is a possibility in all kinds of theatre but at its best it is more sophisticated and requires more know-how than the old plot usage did. Nonplot does not exist successfully by default but is consciously made by design. Its creation has to be the work of knowledgeable craftsmen who know how to apply it and what to use as replacement for the plot, which, in non-existence, will leave a void.

Actually a more serious moral ought to be pointed out here. Musical theatre pieces from our past have evaporated—poof!—largely because they have been so tightly connected to their own times exclusively. *No, No, Nanette* (1925) by Vincent Youmans had some brilliant songs that lie around like those columns which once belonged to a majestic temple in ancient Delphi: nothing else remains. *This* was a flapper musical and once so very contemporary.[25] The first Pulitzer Prize for a musical went to the Gershwins' *Of Thee I Sing* (1931), a political lampoon. Today this work is a ruin because it was stapled into its own time and situations which nowadays we have to ask Great-grandpa or an archaeologist (nearly synonymous) to explain.

Think of the embarrassment that lies ahead. Vietnam, which is indeed a disgrace, will surely end in one way or another. "Pot" is almost certain to become legalized, and those who are extolling it now will be as amusing and then as interesting as Carry Nation. The discovery and freeing of sex is about as new as liquor was to me (I had French grandparents in Mississippi) when my college classmates to whom it had been denied first discovered it during—of course—Prohibition. And it's utter poppycock (I am anticipating a silly suggestion) to entertain any idea whatsoever that *Hair, Salvation* or any of the others will have exerted any pressures on our futures as once did *Uncle Tom's Cabin*. Think about it. The reasons for the failures of the first as a social force and the success of the latter are all too apparent.

The aforementioned Dr. Baker also wrote: "The permanent value of a play, however, rests on its characterization." I do agree, Dr. Baker, but suppose there are *no* characters, as in *Hair*; what then? And with no characters there can be no plot, and we are back where we started with nonplot. With no plot, the audience is cheated of any experiencing and are given in its place some "sensing." The first of these words suggests feeling, encounter, undergoing, actual living through an event, while the latter connects with sensuous perception, instinctive reactions, and many other things the precise effects of which cannot be calculated and require neither art, knowledge, discipline, or experience.

As Galsworthy suggested, "character is situation," and when characters are defined, set up, respond or react, they have to create some line which may very well involve the audience, even if this line is not, in essence, a plot. Among recent plays there are the very talented David Storey's two, *The Contractor* and *Home*, which, in lieu of plots, nevertheless have such clearly defined characters that the audience is made to care—plot or no plot.

However, *Hair*, the most successful of all the new nonplot rock shows, despite program assignments, lacks even characters. All the people are pretty much alike and indistinguishable, one from another.

The following is a fairly thorough summary of *Hair* based on its published libretto. It begins with a solo (joined by "others") which says that peace will guide the planets and love will steer the stars.

Hud—a black—introduces himself and proceeds to sing the cliches of 1910 re feeding blacks: watermelons, grits, etc. Whites and blacks in the South still enjoy this food. It is *Southern* food, not black food.

Woof introduces himself with a joke about refusing to join the YMCA because "all they have in the lobby are Protestant pansies."

The next song has lyrics, each line of which begins "Ain't got no" and each ends respectively with "home," "shoes," "money," "class," "scarf," "gloves," "bed," "pot," "faith," etc., for eighteen lines. Each line except the fifth in each of the two nine-line stanzas awaits an answer from another person. These begin "so," "poor," "honey," "common," "cold," "beat," "busted," "Catholic." Remarkably noncreative, easy and trite.

Claude and Mom begin an argument intended to show how foolish everyone is who is old enough to be Mom. There is the predictable argument of "find a job" and "your old man's not going to give you any more money," to which Claude replies: "Oh, I've got to get out of this flat and start Liverpoolin' it up with me mates." (Get it?)

> Mom: "What do you want to be?"
> Claude: "Kate Smith."

(Lots of laughs like that. N.B. It actually sounds like a minstrel show circa 1910.)

In answer to Mom's query "What have you got, 1968, that makes you so damn superior and gives me such a headache?" Claude replies in song in which "I got" begins each of fifty-seven lines and ends (each line) with a different pearl, "life mother," "laughs sister," "freedom brother," etc. After this section he begins a small section of "And I'm gonna," followed by a third series "Ain't got no" eighteen times (until the end of the song). These three words are followed by "smokes," "job," "work," "coins," and are answered with single words beginning "shit," "lazy," "hustler," "horny," etc.

This scene (?) proceeds into another between Berger and his father. Of course Berger (it says) answers quite predictably, "Screw *your* logic and reason. I'm tired of your brainwash education" and exits.

Dad is a school principal (it says), and in a long speech to students he objects to exactly what you'd expect a non-character in this situation (its really *Uncle Tom's Cabin*) to reject.

The Tribe reprises a part of the "Ain't go no's", but only nine lines this time.

Dad quotes, in turn, General Hershey, President Johnson, Governor Reagan and Pope Paul. (Get it?) The Tribe protests going to war and returns to the "Ain't got no's" for a reprise of sixteen lines, each (as before) ending with a different word: "earth," "fun," "bike," and other important items. The song evolves to only a series of single words beginning "city," "banjo," "toothpicks," and after fifteen of these and six "Bang, bang," etc., the list begins again with "A-bombs," "H-bombs," etc., for fourteen lines. Then there is another list of several dozen other words beginning "Vietnam," "Johnson," etc., etc., then goes into a solo, "Welcome, sulphur dioxide," and we're into a profound lecture on air pollution.

In a brief dialogue, it is mentioned that Jeannie (singer of the last song) is in love with Claude. (*There's* a plot for you.)

The Tribe has a short song made largely of initials such as "LBJ," "USA," "IRT," etc. Berger sings a song about Lucifer and me, celebrating his having been expelled from school.

After a brief scene[26] about drugs, Claude says he has been drafted and concludes, "I'll tell them I'm a faggot and hide out in Toronto."

He then begins a recitation in which every one of twenty-nine lines begins "My little," followed by "magic fellow," "block of gold," etc.

There is a conversation about Claude's *not* going into service in which the following exchange occurs

> CLAUDE: I'm not going in. I'll eat it first. I'm not.
> WOOF: Eat what?
> CLAUDE: My draft card.
> BERGER: I thought you burned it.
> CLAUDE: That was my driver's license.
> WOOF: Eat it on CBS television.

During the ensuing conversation, Claude ignites his library card.

The Tribe sings a song to "The Caissons Go Rolling Along" and "The Marine Hymn," beginning: "Lift your skirt, point your toe," etc., and peripherally discusses homosexuality as a possible "out."

Mom enters. (A sign appears saying "Ronald Reagan Is a Lesbian.") She asks Berger if he is a hippie. Berger: "Is the Pope Catholic?"

Another sign: "Jesus Was a Catholic." Another "Hair." There follows the title song beginning, "I'm just a hairy guy," extolling every kind of hair. Mom and Dad embrace the boys, and Mom ends a speech with: "Be free…no guilt…be whoever you are…do whatever you want…just so you don't hurt anyone…I am your friend."

Then there is a scene with Sheila in which she explains her having left home, husband and baby and now lives with a painter after she had had an affair with Berger. She announces: "I'm very social-injustice conscious."

The scene with Sheila continues. ("Berger grabs Woof and has him get on top of Sheila, screwing her.") ("She is fighting him off and reacts to his attack.") (It *says* so in the stage directions, but not a word following indicates either the rape or her reaction.)

Poster: "Legalize Abortion."

Claude announces he is writing a movie (after all, just anybody can write just anything) and as each one reads a fragment, Sheila says, "Your movie's about us!" Woof exclaims, "If I hear this Vietnam just one more time I'm leaving this theatre." (Won't you take me with you?)

Much bickering leading nowhere. No real subject ending with a speech of Sheila's. "No bicycling, no skating," and eleven more such catastrophes. Then a song beginning, "Dead End, Don't Walk," and fifty-five additional sign phrases, interrupted three times by longer lines like "Warning land mine," etc., and "Claude loves Sheila." Then a Hindu prayer beginning "Om Mane padme om," etc.

Woof and Berger begin a song about the flag, beginning "Don't put it down."

After a short interlude with Mom that goes nowhere Claude sings a song beginning, "The Flesh Failures,/ We starve-look at one another short of breath," etc., and ending with "Answer for Timothy Leary, dearie,/ and let the sunshine in."

Mom now is a ticket seller at a movie. Claude rejects Jeanie and says he's going to the movie. Jeanie: "Watch the fags don't get you." Claude: "Drop dead."

("The Tribe enters through the audience and pass out leaflets announcing the Be-In.")

Crissy-unintroduced-signs in one of the very best songs in the show, in which the lyrics begin: "I met a boy called Frank Mills," tells how she lost his address, describes him, and ends: "Tell him Angela and I don't want the two dollars back...just him."

The Be-In. Bells toll all around the audience. The Tribe enters from all directions with "bells, carrying candles and incense, enveloping the audience"-and going into "Hare Krishna," etc

"Dad and Mom participate. . .employing their rational, establishment, middle-class viewpoints and logic against all the music of the Be-In. . .which never ceases."

The lyrics are all repetitive: first eight "loves," four "drop-outs," four "Be-Ins," four "Hare Krishnas," four "Hare Ramas," etc.

Mom calls them a disgrace. Dad uses the predictable bromides, such as "use atomic weapons," "In two months my son will be in Vietnam and is going to be killed, and I'm proud of him."

The Tribe responds in song, "Hare Krishna," etc., then "Strip" thirty-three times. The famous nude scene follows briefly. Police-puppets close in for an arrest. (As I recall, actors dressed as police came down the aisle.)

The Tribe sings "We Love Cops" nine times, and against the middle section of this, some sing "Hare Krishna" three times and "Hare Rama" three times, ending "Hare Hare."

A 1776 flag is held aloft. Sheila enters holding a flaming Maxwell House coffee can and strikes a Statue of Liberty pose. Each guy lights his draft card and she gives each a daffodil. The flaming can is placed center stage, and the Tribe sits around it as though it were a campfire.

Claude, apart, sings, "Where do I go," etc. The song is taken up by the Tribe, and the act ends with antiphony between the Tribe and Claude: The Tribe: "Why?" Claude: "I live and die." End of Act One.

Cliché-ridden, repetitive, nonplot. All characters are indistinguishable—one from another—and predictable. No conflict and no surprise. Few lyrics. Little musical contrast. Act Two is blessedly shorter. Some entertainment. Some mesmerization with incessant rhythm and repetition. Nothing anywhere new and going nowhere slowly and loud.

What *Hair* gives is a sense of excitement. Most of this stems from the nearly continuous songs, which have heavy, unrelenting beats. The whole might be termed a "happening." It is not a musical because its almost non-existent book is too sketchy for it to qualify as one. In a nutshell the plot tells of a boy who is about to go off to war. That is all. The trimmings are so old that the present generation which extols the virtues of *Hair* are too young to have ever before seen anything else.

A large part of Act Two is a dream-the result of marijuana. It does not matter at all that it is caused by pot, because the same theatrical device has been used (dream ballets, etc.) since the days of Victor Herbert.

The evening is non-dramatic because of the sketchy relationships between people and poor identification of most of them.

Hair throbs and excites like a parade—any parade: circus, Labor Day, Nazi, St. Patrick's Day, or any other. It is noisier than any parade. It is less disciplined. It is not a theatre piece—neither "show" nor revue. Plotless, humorless, self-conscious, stale, largely lyricless in spite of many excellent tunes, characterless, and without development—except that Sheila will and won't and will and does go to bed with Claude, and the latter will and won't and will and must go to Vietnam. *Hair* is a *thing*, and it attempts to destroy what is, without a care, but fails to offer something new in its place.

I am glad that it has happened. It was inevitable. It may have opened an important door to something new. Hopefully that will be good—and good and interesting theatre with a shape and characters to care about. *Hair* itself is none of these things.

Surely we have progressed further along in history, in time. Surely it is abundantly clear to everyone that shows like *Henry, Sweet Henry, Minnie's Boys, Jimmy, George M!, Dear World, Coco, Her First Roman, Zorba, Maggie Flynn, Darling of the Day*, and many more like these with their impossibly bad books and music that is supposed to make us nostalgic are not indeed the progeny of *Carousel, West Side Story*, and *Fiddler on the Roof*. But by burning the bridges of our heritage, by not knowing what it emerged from, we will never build something worthily new. It is easy to negate, to destroy, to turn back on what was good, and very difficult on the other hand to pick up some connection and continue to build in a fresh new direction. But it can be done, and with all the pros and cons, the rantings and ravings, it *will* be done. But this interim vaccilation is not even a small part of doing it. Non-books, non-scores, and the endlessly reiterated narrow subject matter—pot, four-letter words, free sex, Vietnam, draft-card burnings, etc.—are all too tiresome. What existed in Greece, in the sixth century before Christ and then again and differently in the medieval music-plays, and later in new clothes in Shakespeare—love, hate, factional differences, ambition, and more—as they are eternal in life, so they are and always will be in the theatre.

I had no idea what the creators of *Hair* were doing. It is probable that they meant to experiment, but artists as well as scientists who try to find new paths base their trials on a profound knowledge of what already exists, combined with some precise wish as to what it is they are looking for. Their work then is a superorderly course of action leading hopefully in a new direction.

Experimentation ought to be characterized as a noble word. Webster says it is "a trial made to confirm or disprove something doubtful; an operation undertaken to discover some unknown principle or effect, or to test some suggested truth, or to demonstrate some known truth." Implicit in all parts of these definitions is some kind of knowledge or truth-finding from which or upon which some *orderly* test is to be made. Names in all fields of science or art tumble over one another: Pasteur, Einstein, Wassermann, Curie,

Euclid, Daguerre, the Wrights, Griffith, Lenin, Schönberg, da Vinci, Aristotle, Sophocles, Marconi, Stravinsky, Picasso, Nobel, Petrarch, Newton, Phidias, Edison, Pollock, and pages and pages of others. Every one covering many different fields, pointing the way to future development through their own achievements and themselves thoroughly knowledgeable about the past, self-disciplined, hard-working—these and the many others of their kind we honor and bend our knees to in gratitude.

Experimentation implies progress, a going from some specific place to another in an approach toward the future. It does not include harum-scarum.

In musical-theatre specifics it defined the road to Monteverdi, the first great composer for the lyric theatre. Many people worked on that road earlier, but it was Monteverdi who finally took it where it was always meant to go. Many microcosms through Buxtehude led to Bach, who finally pieced together all that they had experimented with, and it was he who amalgamated all of it into a new and complete art.

Because we are nearer in time we recall many people whose names fill in the transition from Johann Strauss to—let us say— Gershwin. These include Herbert, Friml, Romberg, and Kern. Arriving at the Gershwins and Rodgers with Hart, Porter, Berlin, we still had a long way to go before we could rightly claim that we had arrived. What we lacked then in the Twenties and Thirties were musical scores instead of many brilliant separate songs. More than that, our list of successful shows was enormous; they pleased many people but simultaneously they chased out of the theatre those thousands who could not continue to be interested in silly plots carried by pasteboard characters.

It was not until the turn of the fourth decade in our century that this was taken care of by the writers' discovery that it was not a hopeless task to create a good, interesting, and empathic book for musicals. When this was accomplished, songs began to characterize and to add up to scores. And the flown audience-bird returned.

This and much more in all fields has happened over thousands of years. The residue always hardened to provide another step forward for those who would follow. Always there was experiment because all creative people had the urge to advance in new directions, and they knew that they had to do so if only for themselves alone. However, the experiments began only after the mastery of earlier techniques and the working tools had been gathered firmly in their own hands. This was the most promising way to begin to build, and it was, at the same time, a short cut since the new young creators could avail themselves of what had already been tested. But they had to bother to do this. Then they went on from there.

Early Beethoven was Haydn and Mozart, but in time there was something new and strong and great on its own. Early Schonberg was pure Wagner. Early Picasso was Rousseau, Lautrec, and an entire gallery of others. This learning and copying never did any harm; it reinforced whatever it was that was to follow. Experimentation emerged bit by bit out of and because of and due to the past.

Today "experimentation" is so disorderly and unconnected that most of those who pride themselves on being a part of it are surely not going anywhere. They seize on popular trends, often achieve fame and fortune for a brief time, know nothing to begin with and end up really giving out nothing. Waste. And experimentation becomes a dirty word indicating a hodge-podge of ice cream, catsup, bean soup, and salt. No taste. No reason. All of the ingredients readily at hand but adding up to nothing when meaninglessly put together. Genuine laziness, foolishness, and a large amount of arrogance. *Promenade* and *Salvation* were theatre frauds. At least *Little Mary Sunshine* and *The Boy Friend* had the virtue of consistency when they employed the musical and stage style of the Twenties and stayed with it for a full evening of fun and games. *Promenade*, however, was not a score but a crazy quilt. It lacked sense of style. It was so ununified that it belonged to no one, no time, no place, and certainly to no theatre. The plot—as nearly as one could be discerned—was also a pretentious conglomeration. The lyrics grew in no direction and were largely meaningless. The many musical styles hashed together had to have been the work of an amateur.

Promenade, Salvation, and most of the others that claim to be "experimental" are unserious, immature, and undisciplined drivel. Experimentation is serious. Attending performances of these shows (and many others in the same category), I was appalled to find many—and especially young—people leaning forward in their seats, chin cupped in a knee-supported hand, behaving as though they were experiencing the Second Coming. They were in fact being duped and hadn't the background to recognize it.

Recently in the beautiful minuscule village of Taormina (Sicily) I was sitting at an outdoor café overlooking the sea one afternoon at sundown. An amateur pianist was obviously improvising. The general style was Mendelssohnesque. The harmonies were poppycock—conventional but eschewing all the rules of its own or our own or any other time. Everything was aimless meandering of what had been already achieved by knowledgeable and talented men a century ago. Yet when this amateur playing-by-ear, groping for some clichés that he could easily have learned correctly, finished, or mercifully stopped playing, time after time he received enthusiastic applause. My own reaction was one of disgust, not at the pathetic pianist, who was probably too poor to study and too far away from proper teachers and exposure to professional music to be any better than he was, but at the attentive listeners for whom this was actually an experience. I felt the same way at *Promenade* and its inexcusable, inexplicable so-called professional reception.

In the musical theatre of the Twenties and Thirties there was then (and there is today) a clearly detectable evolution at work. The new young men were broadening their harmonic palettes with more sophisticated colors, molding their melodies into shapes hitherto undreamed of in theatre and popular music although these had already been explored earlier in "serious" music. They were also beginning to use rhythmic patterns from the songs and dances of the folk art of the entire recently discovered world.

The lyricists were quickly going away from the clichés of the past toward original, particular images which they found our language to be filled with, images waiting only to be recognized and utilized. The librettists were finding that characters might be three-dimensional and that plots could be literate. All of these processes were proceeding simultaneously, and they erupted simultaneously from a number of different people into our universally respected and relished musical theatre of the Forties, Fifties, and early Sixties.

I believe that now again everyone recognizes the need for change, but in the meanwhile we have been jolted into many things that do not and will not fit into the musical theatre. None of these things are new, and they cannot develop because they have long ago been integrated as useful or bypassed as childish. The "new" theatre music is actually quite old. Basically it is rhythm 'n' blues, revivalist or a pale imitation of sixteenth-century madrigals. In writing of the beginnings of rock 'n' roll, Nik Cohn in his book *Rock* (Stein and Day) wrote that it "was very simple music. All that mattered was the noise it made, its drive, its aggression, its newness. All that was taboo was boredom. . . The lyrics were mostly non-existent, simply slogans one step away from gibberish.

Rock in its many guises has gone in many directions since the above-defined style of the Fifties, but it has not, thus far, really found a style that is for the theatre. Its tunes are too limited, the rhythms too unchanging. There are too few contrasts. It is meant for something abstract like records and large dollar earnings. It seldom characterizes the individual in either music or lyrics, and this latter-particularization—and the musical contrasts are essential musical-theatre concomitants.

At this same moment when Campbell Soup cans are being exhib-ited in art museums and studied seriously as *art nouveau*, there is true experimentation going on, minding its own business, truly aware of its own genesis ("honor thy father and thy mother: that thy days may be long upon the land which thy God giveth thee") and struggling sincerely to go somewhere. Until recently there were Ives and cummings and Joyce. Now there are Rauschenberg and Stockhausen, Babbitt and Dubuffet, and many more. They them-selves may (or may not) go where they surely want to go, but at the very least they will leave a heap of clean and thoughtful and orderly experimentation which is worthy of the name. Somehow, someday, this will all be used as part of a genuine and new and at once mature art.

Already the couturiers have made a fortune by digging up the past and stamping it "today." Look at the famous painting of Goethe (1749-1832) and of Lord Byron (1788-1824) and you will recognize the male hair-dos and the jackets and shirts which have recently been popularized. And the maxicoats worn by Elsie Janis (born 1889) during the early part of the century: today again. These, like the musical theatre of now, do not represent evolution or revolution but fad, and there will be nothing basically new until fad for its own sake, like the Golden Calf, stops being worshipped.

There is yet another angle and another element which has operated in this mélange of musical theatre. From early in the present century until the late Twenties the stage revue became the largest and most extravagant thing in our theatre. Then-on the stage-there was a very real revolt, and the public deserted the repetitious elephant in favor of the intimate, more intelligent small revue in which content superseded in importance and interest the size and extravagance expressed in costumes, scenery, and numbers of pretty girls.

However, the movies, which have usually been Johnny-come-latelies, in the Thirties and Forties continued the traditions of Ziegfeld and the others, with the even more elaborate Busby Berkeley musicals which entertained millions and then too faded away and are presently in for a limited revival in keeping with "contemporary" clothes.

None of their inauthentic hopscotch is going anywhere fast. It is for a moment and then it quietly fades away again.

Experimentation when it is real, when it takes advantage of history and quite rightly eschews the immediate past in favor of something new and authentic, will always be about to take our hands and help us up the steep, tortuous steps that lead on to what is solidly new. The rest is only a happening, a puny fireworks, a pale scream in the night which no one need worry about since it lacks credibility and direction. It will attract and it will also fade away.

How many readers recall *Chu Chin Chow*, even by reputation? Yet it was the most celebrated and successful musical of only half a century ago, having run in London from 1916, where it continued without a break for five years, played on Broadway in 1917 for 208 performances, and then toured the English provinces and the whole of the United States for many more seasons. Who remembers, and where is it now?

The libretto of the musical show is consistently two to three decades behind what has developed or evolved in the form and style of the non-musical drama. Of course the *strict* application of the non-musical form—new or old—is and always will be impossible for workable libretto since much of what does work is dependent on the functional inclusion of another and important element: the music. However, all forward-looking practices which take root in non-musical drama do eventually affect the progress of the libretto. And welcome.

Currently the nonplot revolution in "straight" theatre has found an echo—if only a hollow one at the moment—in musicals. *Hair* and several kindred spirits have wandered off in this direction, but with a rueful difference. The one element most importantly employed in nonplot dramas that work is the almost painful meticulous reliance on character development. This factor alone is enough to have created the interest, empathy, and deep concern in the plays of writers like Harold Pinter, David Storey, Eugène Ionesco, Doris Lessing, and many others.

Take, for example, Pinter's *The Homecoming*. The plot is of small consequence. What there is of one is brief and just enough to hold the characters together. The latter, however, are made so fascinating that watching the play unfold becomes an exciting, breathless experience. At the end when the husband takes leave of his wife, who has decided to stay on in London as a whore, abandoning in a somewhat cavalier way her husband and children who live in America, we must accept the wife's decision as basically characteristic of her true nature, but we are shocked by the husband's seemingly emotionless departure alone. We have become so involved that we are made to care, and under the conditions of this style of play with its limited, almost non-existent plot, such an effect is truly remarkable.

The same can be said of the various puzzling but emotionally stimulating situations in *The Birthday Party*. This is also due to the careful development of the characters even though or perhaps especially because each of them is surrounded by a thick shell of mystery. We are nevertheless fed just enough information about them, or we glean it from trivial things that they say or do or respond to, to whet our appetites. We are made to want more and more, and in the end we find ourselves starving for what we are not given. We leave the theatre still hungry for more.

This is a neat accomplishment. Actually it is not so very new if we had been able to observe the clues to this kind of writing as it had its genesis approximately a century and even longer ago.

Georg Büchner pointed in this direction with *Woyzeck* and *Danton's Death*. Ibsen and Chekhov employed minimal plots in their plays, leaning largely on highly developed characters. In this country the plots of the best plays of Williams, Miller, and Albee are of secondary importance and brief enough to be told in a single sentence. In musicals we have had at least the inconclusive ending in *My Fair Lady* as well as in Bock and Harnick's "The Lady or the Tiger?" from *The Apple Tree*.

Two contemporary musicals which came into being almost simultaneously provide sharp contrasts with regard to the forward direction of plays already described: *Applause* versus *Company*. *Applause* is a maze of plot, where *Company* is a succession of vignettes—storyless—pasted together by the presence of a single character and the employment of a single theme. In an absolute sense, *Applause*, which tries no uncharted path but sticks carefully to the techniques of the past, is the more successful of the two. However, there is no question that *Company*—forward-looking—is by far the more important. The problem here is that *Company* has one foot still stuck somewhat in the mud of the past while the other pulls ahead at what is likely to be. The past foot insists on the presence of a number of small plots, which are defined at the expense of extensive character development. The forward-looking foot tries to abandon all plot in the over-all but must wrestle with a "hero" who is insufficiently defined (we know only that he is unmarried and that his friends love him), with the result that the ending is disappointing. We are made to feel by the very nature of the show and its insistent theme that we are entitled to and will ultimately be supplied with some all-inclusive scoreboard with a precise total described in neon lights, and we are therefore frustrated when this does not happen. Not so with the endings of *Home, The Contractor, The Birthday Party, The Homecoming*, and *Who's Afraid of Virginia Woolf?*, to name only a few plays in this genre. And this is so because of the strong if mysterious (Bobby in *Company* is not quite big enough, too well if adequately defined, to be mysterious) character, and we have grown to expect that we shall be cut adrift at the end to work things out for ourselves. We are not disappointed when this happens. Also we are given *no* plot anywhere, and there is, as a result, no conclusion which the author is honor-bound (by tradition if nothing else) to spell out. The *style* of the writer dictates to a great extent what is and is not cricket.

What is perhaps of most importance here is that even with its single imperfection, *Company* is of greatest significance because it does look toward the future, and it is the first musical in our history to do so. In the plays which primarily develop characters and avoid plot, the compensatory characters are somewhat like certain chemical elements which, when thrown together, become disturbed. This conflict-in the case of characters-makes at the very least for a "situation," and this "situation" is at the very root of drama.

There is usually an unrecognized difference between identity and role which nevertheless does exist and is most important. Walter Kerr (*Thirty Plays Hath November*) has written:

> The gap between identity and role must be obvious to us all. We may indeed function as teachers or journalists or housewives but we are. . .all too painfully aware that our functions are dress suits, that they do not in the least contain all that we are or that we might be, and that in actuality we do not even fill the limited role properly. Role is inadequate to identity, certainly to potentiality.

Likewise, there is an important difference between plot and situation. The former occupies an over-all position in relation to a play or novel or other related storytelling media, while the latter is "a particular or striking complex of affairs at a stage in the action of a narrative or drama."[27] Plot will invariably *include* a number of situations, but the latter can exist without any life-giving permission from lot or narrative. Situation can exist apart from plot in a number of contrasting or even related capsules. This is what current playwrights have proven, and it is the absence of a detailed plot in today's best new plays that makes audience involvement more of a requisite than formerly when everything was spelled out.

In a large sense, drama of this style is governed by the same principles that all drama has always succeeded by. Feeling—the *sine qua non* of theatre—is still present in the new as well as the old, and usually for the same basic reasons. When the unaffected husband in *The Homecoming* leaves his wife without even a slight gesture or word of complaint, unhappiness, obfuscation, jealousy, or mystification, the author is throwing the husband's feeling into the laps of the stunned audience. The watchers *experience* what is not demonstrated on stage. This is in no way different from the mechanics of Mme. Ranevsky's final irrevocable departure from her old home, or Blanche DuBois' late speech describing in sunny terms her own death on a ship at noon, or Willy Loman's sudden happy recollection of his son Biff's football triumph immediately preceding his own suicide, or the bright singing of "You'll Never Walk Alone" by a group of starched high-school graduates in *Carousel*—meaningless to them. In all of these and many, many more examples the same mechanism of emotional transfer is at work.

One element invariably employed in musicals—at least until now—has been romance. As pointed out earlier, this element in one manifestation or another has always been of great importance to the singing theatre and all but disappeared from the plays of Ibsen, Chekhov, Ionesco, Albee, Williams, and Miller. It is still absent from *The Homecoming, The Birthday Party, Rhinoceros, Home, The Contractor*, and other leading works in today's non-musical drama.

As the relationship between prose drama and drama of the musical variety has always been fairly close—the latter trailing the former by two or three decades and never precisely becoming alike in the ways pointed out earlier in this book—it is possible that a duality will always need to remain, each proceeding in its own way. However, it also occurs to me that in the course of time each form— always undergoing alterations—must borrow from the other.

I have come to believe that the future of musicals may lie in the situation-identity practice as opposed to the past-present method of plot and role. This would necessitate a more gingerly, less fulsome definition of character. Provided that the latter were sufficiently interesting, I think this newer method would work. Songs, which grow out of character definition, would still come about in the same way but would become more elusive and less philanthropic.

On the drama side, it occurs to me to wonder about the future reintroduction of romance. I believe that this will be one logical potential course for the swinging pendulum.

If these suppositions should prove even partly accurate—and whether or not they do—the two aspects of theatre that we know (musical and non-musical) will, in the course of evolution, be drawn closer together as basic new practices always have. But at different times.

I firmly believe that the distance that separates, say, *The Birthday Party* as a style and method from *Company* will gradually be bridged, and each of the two styles—affecting each other—will in time-future be merged. The results will be richer on both sides. And in this milieu and the method which induces it there lurks the promise of the *new* musical.

COMMENTS ON NONPLOT

Much of the chapter on "nonplot" consists of an attack on *Hair*, which, when Engel wrote *Words with Music*, clearly seemed a greater threat to the future of the musical than it does now.

With the passage of thirty-five years *Hair* now seems surprisingly quaint, but that was true from very early on. I first saw *Hair* in the spring of 1971, when it had already been running on Broadway for three years. I'd missed it during its brief run at the New York Shakespeare Festival Public Theatre, when, I've been assured, it was a genuinely new and fresh show, almost totally different from the show I saw at the Biltmore. In those days I was a paying customer and would probably not have been able to wangle a ticket anyway to what was a sellout hit at the Public.

The reason I went to see it in 1971 was that the sister of a friend, who'd entered a convent in 1960, had recently left her order and was eager to see the show that had caused such a commotion during the years when she was theoretically cut off from the world. Apparently her order did subscribe to the weekly newsmagazines. So she'd read about *Hair* a lot. What struck me about seeing *Hair* in 1971 was that it was already extremely dated. Those years moved with such momentum that, while it told her where we'd been in 1968, we were already someplace else.

What gave *Hair* its three-year Broadway run was not its novelty or its score but its fifteen seconds of nudity at the end of the first act. Although disrobing was optional for the cast members, it hardly mattered, since they did so behind a scrim and in very dim light. But in those distant times any nudity—even in movies—was so provocative that it was a draw—needless to say, more for middle-aged customers than for young people.

For those of us who came of age in the Sixties, the score of *Hair* conjures up the spirit of the time as few other things do. Songs like "The Age of Aquarius" and "Let the Sun Shine" have a deep resonance. I find this curious since the hippie scene *Hair* describes had nothing to do with what interested me at that time.

In a similar vein, I saw *Promises, Promises*, the Burt Bacharach musical based on Billy Wilder's *The Apartment* in 1969, and hated it as much as I did *Hair* two years later. But in 1997, when City Center Encores! presented a concert version of *Promises, Promises* I found myself choking back tears on the way out. I had even less rapport with the "go-go years" Bacharach's music reflected than the hippie world of *Hair*, but it too was strangely moving. Perhaps it's just the music of one's youth that has so powerful an impact.

In 2002 City Center Encores! revived *Hair* and I found it as antipathetic as I had the first time. Its lack of a book—which had seemed novel, if not radical, in 1968—now simply made it tedious. As a number of the people Engel quotes noted even when it was new, *Hair* is a revue, but its sketches have not dated well. Their nostalgia value is great, their comedy limited, their dramatic value practically nil.

The songs from *Hair* (like the hit "I'll Never Fall In Love Again," from *Promises, Promises*) have a life apart from the show. The context of the show does not heighten their viability. The title song from *Cabaret*, both in its lyrics and its music, can be seen merely as an invitation to merrymaking. In the context of the show, set in a Berlin quickly succumbing to Nazism, it has much deeper implications.

Many of the standard songs in American pop music from the Twenties and Thirties came from shows whose titles now mean nothing to us. Some were book shows; some were revues. They take on a deeper meaning by the circumstances in which we first heard them. Many people, after all, have a great fondness for songs they're quite unaware come from the theatre.

What concerned Engel in *Words with Music* was not just the power of individual songs but how they fit into dramatic structures. His book was not about songwriting. It was about theatre. His outrage at *Hair* (few musicals in *Words with Music* are given as much space, even if it is negative) seems overdone now. In a sense, time has proved him right. What seemed so threatening then seems entirely marginal now. *Hair* has remained a significant work because of the way it came to symbolize an era. The other musicals Engel rails against (*Your Own Thing, Salvation*) have, in effect, been largely forgotten.

Rock itself is now an historic episode. It has been superseded by hip-hop, which the African-American cultural critic John McWhorter has described as "not a message from the streets but a histrionic pose." As discussed, the influence of rock on musicals has been surprisingly little, especially given its impact on entertainment in general. (At one point, unaccountably, Engel detects the influence of rock on Stephen Sondheim in *Company*. True, it had a cool, contemporary sound, but nowadays we see that its contemporary quality was hardly rock.)

Two rock musicals that did have an impact, interestingly, occurred in the Nineties, *Tommy*, based on The Who's work of several decades earlier, and a totally original piece, *Hedwig and the Angry Inch*. *Tommy* was a lavish visualization of a work that had been given a performance at the Metropolitan Opera in 1971. *Hedwig* is a performer-oriented piece that may indicate more than many splashy Broadway musicals the direction in which musical theatre is heading—it requires a minimum of production values and a maximum of talent.

Perhaps it's a sign of the theatre's apart-ness that it was able to resist rock so forcefully. Interestingly, few non-musical plays from that tumultuous era continue to interest us. Plays that seemed important at the time, like those of David Rabe, *Sticks and Bones* and *The Basic Training of Pavlo Hummel*, now seem merely period pieces. So does a more interesting play like Michael Weller's *Moonchildren*. These works capture the surface concerns of their time but have no deeper resonance. The same is true of *Hair*.

What all these works had in common—and it would have been considered a dramaturgical advance at that time—was that they were episodic. They didn't have the firm structure of plays of an earlier generation. *Death of a Salesman* is also episodic. It jumps back and forth in time, but it has a firm dramatic spine as it proceeds inexorably to Willy's suicide.

It might be argued that the economics of the theatre have dictated a smaller, quirkier kind of play. In the spring of 2002 Arthur

Miller's first play, *The Man Who Had All the Luck*, was revived. It had been such a flop in 1944 that Miller decided not to write any more plays. Happily, he changed his mind. What was striking about this work was that it was in three acts, had thirteen characters, only a few of which could be "doubled" by the same actor, and three sets. Even more interesting, when it was originally presented, it was a Broadway production—for a first time playwright. The playwright in those days had no limits on how many actors, or even how many sets, he required. The only limits were those of his imagination, though a play with a "nonplot" might not have been eagerly received by commercial producers.

Perhaps one of the reasons that few plays of the Sixties and early Seventies convey the concerns of those tumultuous times was precisely that they were not so much interested in content as they were in form. Creating new forms seemed more important to writers in the late Sixties and early Seventies than commenting on what was going on around them. In some sense there was validity to this view, since most attempts to comment (i.e., *Bones* and *Hummel*) were not particularly deep. Interestingly, even as politically involved a writer as Arthur Miller sidestepped addressing the issues of that moment in his plays.

In retrospect, even the experimentation with forms wasn't quite as radical as it once seemed. In the musical theatre, during the Eighties you heard a lot about "concept musicals." At one time there was some competition as to who'd actually come up with the phrase. Since you never hear it much any more, this seems fairly academic.

Essentially "concept musical" was a term applied to the shows of Stephen Sondheim. *Company*, after all, didn't really have a plot. It was about the concept of "company," what it means to be in a relationship with someone, what it means to be alone. Similarly, *Follies* played on the double meaning of its title—which implied both an outmoded form of entertainment and the foolish indiscretions of youth.

Even as lighthearted a work as *The Will Rogers Follies*, with book by Peter Stone and score by Betty Comden, Adolph Green and Cy Coleman, was developed as a "concept musical," the concept being that the life of Will Rogers would be presented not in a conventional biographical narrative but rather as a series of revue sketches, in the manner of the Ziegfeld Follies.

"Concept musical" seemed a useful way of categorizing shows that had a dominating idea rather than a standard plot. My own sense that the term still had cachet but had ceased to be meaningful came when I saw a television interview in which Marge Champion described a show her late husband, director-choreographer Gower Champion, had devised as a "concept musical." That show was *Hello, Dolly!*

Looking back, much of Engel's dour analysis has been borne out. Experimentation can be valuable, but often it was an excuse for self-indulgence. Moreover, a lot of what presented itself as experimentalism wasn't really all that experimental. One such work was *Dionysus in '69*, an attempt to update Euripides' *The Bacchae*. It was performed in a space surrounded by wooden structures that suggested the bunks in Nazi concentration camps. The audience was allowed into the space a few at a time, and they sat, lotus style, on these wooden structures.

As the play began, the actors moved around, asking members of the audience if they intended to participate. "I'll try," a brave soul near me declared. "You'll try, will you?" the actor responded, tauntingly. Clearly his question had been a form of intimidation, not an invitation.

The opportunities for "participation" were rather limited. At one point we were invited to join in a Bacchic dance. Since this was New York it was probably inevitable that the circle dance the audience performed bore a distinct resemblance to the hora, which is danced at Jewish weddings.

The action concerned the attempts of Pentheus to police the orgiastic activities of The Bacchae. A woman in the audience was asked to seduce Pentheus, the theory being he'd be more permissive if not so sexually "uptight," a very Sixties notion. The night I attended a young woman did attempt to offer herself to the handsome lad who played Pentheus. But her efforts were broken off when one of the actresses chided her for being too tentative. The actress then delivered a very graphic description of what she wanted Pentheus to do to her: "Spread open my legs, etc.," which now seems fairly routine, but in those days was quite startling.

(Amusingly, late in the run of *Dionysus in '69* an audience member who'd seen it before popped a similarly coarse invitation to him—the actors were outraged that she'd actually participated, and thus sabotaged their script.)

The one memorable thing about the production was a moment when, in the course of the climactic orgy, Pentheus crawled between the legs of the naked women, their bodies daubed in blood, recreating the traumatic journey through the birth canal. The moment was symptomatic of the period because its force was entirely visual. None of the words uttered that evening had comparable force.

Thinking back, the one play that did seem to find ways to dramatize the raging energies of the period was Jean-Claude van Itallie's *America Hurrah*, which, like the sophomoric *Macbird*, received ludicrously laudatory reviews. The final of the three sketches showed two huge puppet creatures entering a motel room and defacing it with graffiti. In 1967 this was considered a powerful indictment of American values. It's amusing to think that for the next few decades van Itallie's major activity was adapting—and very well—the plays of Anton Chekhov.

Much of the theatre of that time was important not for what it *was* but for what it was *not*. The absurdism of the Fifties and Sixties was a revolt against the well-made play that had dominated the stage for the previous century. The effect on the musical was to remove the solid underpinnings of character and event that were the hallmark of the musicals Engel was hoping could still be created.

Throughout the last century the avant-garde has been trying to relive a truly avant-garde triumph, the 1913 Paris debut of Stravinsky's *Rite of Spring*. As the savage music and the primitive dance steps began on the stage of the Théâtre des Champs Elysees, the audience began to howl in anger, and the performance had to be interrupted. It should be remembered that the opening night of Debussy's *Pelléas and Mélisande*, hardly a savage work, was equally obstreperous. So was the response to Alfred Jarry's turn-of-the-century play, *Ubu the King*, which begins with the word "Shit!"

These were occasions when the Parisian bourgeoisie was genuinely shocked, but in two cases the shock came from works of real substance; in the case of *Ubu*, as in much that followed, the shock was in response to something thoroughly adolescent. The nudity of *Hair* and the mock-audience participation of *Dionysus in '69* seem quite tame by comparison. As the great French poet Paul Valéry observed, "Everything changes, except the avant-garde."

It seems worth noting that in 1920, only seven years after *Rite of Spring*, Stravinsky embarked on an entirely new course in *Pulcinella*, a set of variations and tonal modifications of an 18th century piece by Paisiello. Stravinsky himself described his look backward at the 18th century as the resolution of an impasse in his creative work, but in a way it was as daring as *Rite of Spring*. After the romantic 19th century, in which composers were obliged to "push the envelope" as far as possible, it was quite unexpected for someone who'd pushed it as far as Stravinsky had to look back to the 18th century to find new approaches to form. In trying to embrace structure, Stravinsky consigned himself to decades of critical condescension, though his journey into the past was a very early foreshadowing of what came to be called post-modernism.

When Engel voiced his skepticism about "nonplot" it doubtless appeared as shortsighted, perhaps even provincial. In retrospect, we see that a lot of the nonmusical theatre attempting to point in new, important directions yielded little of significance. Not surprisingly, these paths were similarly unproductive for the musical.

In recent years, however, there have been a number of highly successful nonplot musicals that Engel might not have imagined. Although they were definitely related to music, they had only a tangential relationship to words. They were musicals based almost entirely on dance. Starting in the Sixties, there was a huge new interest in dance in America, sparked in part by the defections of spectacular dancers from Russia.

Dance had played a pivotal role in the creative life of New York for many decades. Martha Graham's iconoclastic work had found devoted adherents and disciples since the late Twenties. One of her students, Agnes de Mille, had had a revolutionary effect on theatre dance starting with her work on *Oklahoma!* in 1943. George Balanchine, who'd choreographed countless musicals in the Thirties and Forties, including the powerful *Slaughter on Tenth Avenue* in Rodgers and Hart's 1937 *On Your Toes*, was also quietly reinventing the vocabulary of classical dance in work he created for the New York City Ballet. Jerome Robbins brought a new electricity to Broadway dance beginning with his work on *On the Town* in 1944. His choreography for *West Side Story* reached a national audience through the movie version.

Nothing, however, did more to glamorize dance in America than the arrival of Rudolf Nureyev in 1961. Balletomanes may carp over his skills, but he brought an animal sensuality and passion to the stage that suddenly made dance sexy to people who'd hitherto regarded it as prissy. The Sixties and Seventies saw a proliferation of dance companies all across the country.

At the same time that the word was being devalued in favor of the picture there was a new interest in the language of the body, a new awareness of the ways movement could express things words might not. Several recent musicals have made both words and music ancillary to movement.

Bring in 'Da Noise, Bring in 'Da Funk was a celebration of black tap dancing. It grew out of a summer dance concert at the New York Shakespeare Festival Delacorte Theatre in Central Park, in which many legendary black tap dancers took part. The great dancers from the past were joined by a galvanizing figure from the present, Savion Glover, who'd created his own vocabulary, based partly on the break dancing you see on New York streets, partly on a funky reinterpretation of classical steps.

George C. Wolfe, the artistic director of the Shakespeare Festival, made Glover the focus of *Noise/Funk*, which had a cursory narrative about the history of blacks in America and how dance reflected their state over the last few centuries. The narrative took a decidedly secondary role to the steps.

In Robbins' theatre work the words were still paramount. Sheldon Harnick once recalled how often during rehearsals for *Fiddler on the Roof* Robbins badgered him and Joseph Stein, who wrote the book, "What is this about? Is it just the pre-adventures of The Goldbergs?" (Alluding to a once popular radio and TV show about Jews in a Bronx tenement.) At one point Stein spluttered, "It's about tradition," which not only led to the opening number but had an important effect on the choreography. The show begins with the cast doing a circle dance. In the final number, as the Jews leave Anatevka for America, the circle is broken.

Recent years have seen a divorce of words and dance. The hugely successful musical *Stomp* is based purely on percussive sounds, which helps explain its international appeal. In some of the British musicals, where the lyrics are, by our lights, substandard, foreign audiences could have a good time because their lack of English spared them the content. In *Stomp* there's nothing to overlook. It's based on the rhythms of everyday movements, like sweeping the floor, but it takes simple sounds and extrapolates them into something arresting, which serves as a background for highly acrobatic, equally arresting movement.

Luke Cresswell and Steve McNicholas, who created *Stomp*, were street performers, or buskers, in Brighton, England. The first thing buskers must do is catch the attention of passersby. One way was to use the striking of matches as a kind of "music" to which they moved, which is roughly comparable to a drummer using a "brush" on his drums. Soon they were employing pipes and cigarette lighters, brooms and garbage pail lids as the basis for their "choreography." Speech, dialogue and plot were all beside the point.

Two recent shows further confirm the increasing importance of nonverbal inspiration. In 1999 Susan Strohman created *Contact*, which was essentially three "scenarios" for dance, one set in the 18th century, making explicit the sexual implications in Fragonard's painting, *The Swing*. Another concerned an abusive husband and his long-suffering wife in a suburban Italian restaurant. The third, about a distraught advertising executive and his irritated neighbor, who meet inadvertently in a disco, is simply a pretext for explosive dancing.

These three comic scenarios are really pure ballet, except that the music for the second two, American pop standards, isn't likely to be heard in programs at, say, New York City Ballet (though Gershwin and Kern have figured in works created there, and Strohman created a new work based on songs by Irving Berlin and Walter Donaldson in 2004). *Contact* won the Tony for Best Musical in 2000, an unsettling precedent since there was no book and the music was from many years ago, not even performed live. In other years *Contact* might have been classified as a Special Event, but clearly that season there was no real competition.

In the case of *Movin' Out*, Twyla Tharp's musical based on the songs of Billy Joel, the music was performed live by an appealing young singer who gave the songs a lyrical quality they didn't have when the composer sang them, though he lost the composer's gritty quality. *Movin' Out* had a plot, about some young friends who go to Vietnam in the Sixties and what happened to them afterward. But the story was secondary to the spectacular dancing Tharp drew from her cast.

In these cases words have been upstaged by pure movement, but they remain the exception rather than the rule. "Nonplot" may play a far greater role than it did thirty years ago, but it remains a novelty.

14

The Original Musical

This is my letter to the World
That never wrote to Me—
The simple News that Nature told
With tender majesty

Her Message is committed
To Hands I cannot see—
For love of Her—Sweet—countrymen
Judge tenderly—of Me

Emily Dickinson

One of the great screams that all of us working in musical theatre are accustomed to hearing most often and from just everybody who has written or wants to write any part of a musical show is "I wish I could find a property." What is meant is "What film, play, or story can I adapt as a new show?" A pathetic few originals have succeeded at all.

Among potential adaptable material, *Virginia Woolf* and *Streetcar* are extreme cases, but there are many other plays today less extreme which might lend themselves to music. *Luv*, a comedy, might. The characters are naïve and romantic. *Rhinoceros* I think might make a certain kind of opera. The Kanin film *It Should Happen to You* is certainly a candidate for musicalization. I believe that none of the Pinter plays known to me—except possibly *The Basement*—would tolerate music. It is more conclusive than other Pinter plays, and it is romantic. *A Taste of Honey* might be made to work well provided its form were considerably altered. Among Peter Shaffer's plays *The Royal Hunt of the Sun* is a "natural" for opera and *Black Comedy* superb for a short musical comedy. Almost all of Noël Coward's plays would do well as musicals. Writers cry for ideas. Here are a few.

Actually the list of original productions is surprisingly long, but during the "best musicals" period (after 1940) only one show with an original book, *Lady in the Dark*, has survived. The length of the run of the others was usually due to the composer's reputation, the star, or the enterprising producer.

In point of fact, since 1940 there have been sixty-three musicals based on original book ideas. Of these, nineteen had runs of fewer than ten performances, sixteen ran fewer than fifty, five ran fewer than 100, thirteen ran under 200 times, and ten ran more than 200.

In addition to those sixty-three musicals between 1940 and the present which were based on original books, there were seventy-eight "adapted" musicals. Of these, eighteen ran fewer than 10 times, twenty-five ran fewer than fifty performances, eighteen ran under 100, twelve ran under 200 and five ran more than 200 performances.

Failure in most of these efforts does not indicate that such a job is impossible, but failure is chiefly due to lack of precise knowledge as to what the libretto of a musical is. In lieu of such technical understanding writers may feel that the employment of an already existent and once successful plot is an invaluable crutch as well as just any idea they themselves were not able to come up with. This latter attitude accounts for those oceans of musical shows, successful and un, which have been filched from every conceivable author, living and dead, and from all possible media. Almost *all* musicals also, living and dead, came about through this adaptive method.

It has been the custom or a long time now for writers to begin with a plot, or at least a theme. I am not certain—and here I am not referring to "nonplot"—that commencing with a plot is the *only* way or that truly comprehending composers and lyricists *need* to begin in this circumscribed and fairly limited manner. For it *is* a limiting way if writers must depend on existing material and the ideas of other creative people which have already appeared in some other form. It is also, or can too easily become, a bore for audiences.

"You've read the book and seen the movie, now see it all dressed up with songs and dances." This general idea, once almost the only one, has, by now, begun to pall. And meanwhile librettists, composers, and lyricists sit about unhappily, scanning the long-familiar bookcases in hopes of finding *the* idea. They reread Shakespeare because, after all, there were *West Side Story* and *The Boys from Syracuse*. They plow through shelves of Dickens because of *Oliver*, tear apart Shaw because of *My Fair Lady*, shred history because of *1776*, disinter the dead because of the biographical movie and stage essays (successes and failures) with *The Sound of Music* (the Trapp Family), *The Rothschilds, The King and I* (Anna Leonowens), *Ben Franklin in Paris, Song of Norway* (Grieg), and an entire library of many others.

I have for some time encouraged new composers and lyricists to make a scene-by-scene synopsis of the source material that interests them because I feel that it allows them the opportunity to shape up a libretto without actually filling it in. (No purple prose for distracting the attention from the basic faults.) The characters ought to be sketched into each scene together with a simple statement as to what they do. This process will make it possible for the writers (composer and lyricist at this point) to see the progress of the action so that each scene not only ends with strength but simultaneously points clearly ahead to what may happen. (This technique is as American as *The Perils of Pauline* or *Dick Tracy* or *Little Orphan Annie*. Nothing wrong with it. It works.)

With the characters and situations sketched in, it is possible for the song writers to create a large part of the score.

With a synopsis—in no other way any more than a skeleton—it is not only possible for the song writers to create but to audition a score; but what they may have achieved—assuming that they have done it well—is to provide their potential librettist with a jumping-off point: a shape, a plot meted out in scenes, a set of meshed characters, and in fact nearly everything except the dialogue itself. This synopsis can serve as a guide not only for the creation of a "book" in this strangest of all shapes but present the librettist in advance with the motivations for already existing songs.

This method may work well even if it is obviously subject to change, but if the synopsis plus the score are sufficiently beguiling to interest producer, director, and librettist, it ought to make a sub-

stantial contribution to the end product. In lieu of an experienced
librettist and one (since he is rarer than a day in June) who is probably not willing to work on "spec," the song writers are not compelled to sit around bemoaning helplessly what they cannot hope to
get. They can proceed in this other manner and can have accomplished a large part of their work, enough in fact—if even only a
part of it is reasonably good—to interest those who are needed to
complete and produce it. Action, then, replaces idleness.

It has occurred to me that beginning with a plot-original or not-
is by no means the only way for starting. After all, plots seem or
ought to seem as though they were created by the characters who
move them, motivate them, create the empathy for them, and are in
point of fact the core as well as the modus operandi of all stage
pieces.

In lieu of a plot it is possible for those who work in music and
lyrics to begin with a single character, perhaps nebulous at first but
becoming, as the idea progresses, more focused and specific. One
character may very well beget another, and when that happens each
will require sharper definition and they will in turn beget some
kind of situation. This, then, will suggest the need for other people,
and before long tensions and interplays will have to be growing. The
latter may eventually generate a subplot.

Meanwhile the characters will begin to sing. They will need to.
And out of the songs, situations and conflicts will radiate.

I should like to examine a musical, beginning—as it *might* have
been, but wasn't—with only one character. Let us assume that we
have an attractive young girl. Let's call her Nellie Forbush. She can
be just any girl, but we must pinpoint her. She might be a lady from
the American South. At once she will have other qualities. She is
polite and well mannered. She is also probably bigoted—an accident of birth. Let's say that she was born in the Twenties. Make
her—if she were actually born in 1920—about twenty-two, a
young woman ripe for romance and one whom the audience could
want to see happy.

At twenty-two the year would be 1942 and Nellie would just
have finished college. In 1942, also, the United States was heavily
involved in the war against the Fascist world. She would feel the
urge to "do her part."

Nellie enlists as a nurse in the Navy, is trained and assigned to duty on an island in the South Pacific. So far we have Nellie with a background, a specific job, and a special locale. It can be a physically beautiful place, but it is fraught with danger. There is now some hint of conflict even if it is as impersonal as war.

On her island Nellie would meet many people. Most of them would be service personnel. But it is inevitable that she would also meet upper-class local residents—one always does in time of war. The local residents have been lonely up till now and they will also want to be helpful.

Nellie, an attractive officer-nurse, meets a wealthy local male. He is known to the male officers through whom she has probably met him. He likes Nellie, and he, Emile, invites her to his plantation home for dinner. Natural and usual too. (Now we have a pair of people.)

Emile has to be an older man to afford such a charming house. He's not a "native," so let's say he's come from France and settled there on his island. What could he have done to earn the money? Well, he was a planter and sells his produce for export. Although he is older than Nellie, he is romantic and a proper age to interest our young heroine.

When we first see them together at his lavish place (by the time the first curtain rises) they are so in love that Nellie is the happy recipient of a marriage proposal. Where do we go from there? (It's only Act One, Scene 1.) As she is happy she may have a happy song about being a cockeyed optimist—remarkable because she is happy even in the middle of a bloody war.

Then comes Emile's turn, and, taking advantage of Nellie's happiness, he sings a romantic song about an enchanted evening and finding someone you love and never letting her go.

Meanwhile, Nellie wants to know something of Emile's background. What is more inevitable than her asking him why he left France and settled out here so far from home. Emile admits to having killed a man—a wicked man—and asks Nellie to understand. She does because she wants to, and this answers the question of Emile's presence just anywhere outside of France.

Nellie must get back to duty on the base. (Naturally the show cannot end here because it's too simple and there are no conflicts as yet.)

There should now be a contrast. The two main principals have been introduced, they are in love, but nothing else has begun.

Where should we look for contrast? Scene 1 has employed two people mainly. Now let's have a crowd—a gay, noisy crowd. Okay. Servicemen. They may sing a ballsy song. What *specific* subject will they sing about? It might introduce a different kind of character—another contrast. Okay. Let's make her comedic. (It's about time.) Let's make her a non-romantic female in contrast to these bawdy young men. Let's make her a native and this time a real one, not imported. What could be her reason to be with the Gis? Anyone who has traveled knows that there are souvenir vendors everywhere and especially where there are service personnel. Okay. We'll call her Bloody Mary. All we can do just now is introduce her and hear those good and loud male voices.

Having had a native character-woman, what would be more natural than to provide her with a comedic opposite—a funny man in service, poles apart and without any possible romantic connection. (Let's stick to comedy for a bit.) The man could be Joe or Jim, but as he is a con artist let's choose an outrageous name like Luther Billis, suggestive of nothing less than a professor, which he is nothing like.

Mary and Luther. As Mary is in business, perhaps Luther is also on to the tricks of the trade, and let's give him a job. What kind? Anybody who's been in service has encountered some money-mad fellow willing to do laundry if he is paid. (The Navy expects non-commissioned personnel to do its own laundry.) Okay. Billis is in the laundry business and Bloody Mary's kiosk is in the same vicinity because there isn't too much room on the island. Billis also needs to compete with the manufacturer of phony shrunken heads (Mary's chief stock-in-trade). As there is plenty of grass (in the old sense) about, Billis is ingenious enough to make grass skirts which all returning sailors will want to take back to Kokomo. This competition will make for fun in this part of the tale.

Now for these red-blooded fighting men, they need something other than souvenirs: sex. Someone will point to another distant island where it is commonly known that everything including sex and souvenirs can be had, but this place will be off limits to the military—except, of course, for officers.

Billis will try to envisage as another way of making money a way to get to the other island—Bali Ha'i. Tonight? Yes, there is some sort of boar's-tooth ceremonial, and Billis will need to get a friendly officer to go there and be willing to take some enlisted men along. Not for the ceremony, which wouldn't really interest the boys, but for the women. They would then sing a song something like "there is nothin' like a dame."

Now that we've had lots of men, let's also have lots of girls—another contrast. The nurses enter and with them Nellie, who has come for her laundry. The nurses and Nellie will be hustled off by their leader. (There can't be sex here. What would happen to Bali Ha'i?)

Now suppose we hear that Bloody Mary has a lovely daughter who lives on Bali Ha'i with Mary. In that case, we wouldn't want a mass rape, but some special young man—another but younger romantic. (Time now for a romantic return, but there seems to be such little mileage left in Nellie-Emile that we'd better have a *different* romance.) We need a young officer for getting to the other island, so let's invent a Lieutenant Cable—attractive, young, and romantic. Philadelphia. Mary finds Cable sexy and she will offer him her wares free. He will not accept a shrunken head but will want to know where Mary got it. Natch—it's Bali Ha'i, and Mary will sing about the mystery of the place because she will try to get the nice lieutenant to go there. The boys will want him to go also as a means of transporting them.

Now before anything new happens we'll need to tie together the elements (characters) we have already created.

A commanding officer (who has to exist) can enter ostensibly to break up Billis' and Mary's enterprises. He will really be introduced to the newly arrived Lieutenant Cable, who tells him that he is to embark on a dangerous mission—to go to another island to spy on Japanese shipping and to radio information so that the U.S. Navy can bomb enemy ships. Knowing nothing of the assigned place, Cable mentions that he will need some knowledgeable inhabitant to accompany him, and that man (he has been told) is our Emile!

For these purposes here it is not necessary to go any further. It all began not with a plot in this supposition but with a single young woman from the South. This illustrates what I mean by beginning with one person, evolving others as needed until finally an entire community exists and with it the conflicts which become the plot line. It can be done. One person and an implicit related theme arising from that person can create an entire holocaust.

Arthur Kober, the humorist and playwright, told me of a Screen Writers' show given in Hollywood during the lavish days of movie-making. In one sketch a writer calls the august chief executive at his studio to tell him excitedly that he had conceived a plot which he was eager to tell him. An appointment was immediately arranged, and the writer was off in a flash to confront his employer.

He began, "It's about this young guy who drives his girl friend nuts. One night in a dream his dead father appears to tell him that his own brother, now married to his former wife (the boy's mother), was his murderer and the dead father charges his son with avenging it. The son acts crazy, jumping into open graves, talking to skulls, etc.

"Get out, get out!" was all the boss had to say.

I think this illustrates clearly the dangers of a synopsis. *Hamlet* here (and of course quite intentionally) sounds nonsensical. The characters are not adequately represented, and in this case also the poetry of Shakespeare plays no part whatsoever. However, as there would be songs attached to a synopsis created for musical-show purposes, these could help considerably in defining character, plot, and style.

The start-with-a-single-character idea precludes such a dangerous potential pitfall since character definition is at the root.

If any writer doubts this method I have suggested let me assure him that it is a workable one and is capable of going in many new and original paths while still bringing to life people as we have always known them. The writer must have patience and the will to dream. He must dream a very great deal. The characters will haunt him, sometimes defy him, but the writer who has summoned them must in the end control them.

The late John Van Druten, in his charming book *Playwright at Work* (Harper & Brothers), writes:

> Do not worry over your character's apparent oddi-
> ties, if they seem real and truthful to you, and most cer-

> tainly do not worry over their interfering with the character's identification with the members of the audience. They will help it. . .Do not stick to the essentials. Do your best to avoid them, give [your character] thoughts that you think [he] might not have, interests that he might not have, daydreams that he might not have.

The stage is, after all, itself an unreality. What are seen and heard from it—when they are at their very best—are unreal. What matters is that they *appear* real. Shakespeare understood so well. "We are such stuff as dreams are made on. . . ."

Robert Edmond Jones also understood it from the scene designer's point of view. Once he told me that if he wanted the *effect* of cloth of gold on the stage and if he could manage to get the real thing, he would not use it because it would appear unreal. Instead, he would make costumes of burlap and spray them with gold paint!

This proposed method is best used by composers and lyricists who are themselves incapable of writing librettos. For them, the dream may begin with the character and the song which will eventually create the situation and the situation which the song can suggest. If so, the least that can finally come of a definition of characters and their emotions expressed in song would be their creators being able to pass along these living cells to a book writer or a truly knowledgeable director, who could then fill them out.

But aren't these two methods of work a great deal more than most writers now have to start off with, and don't they provide for the composer-lyricist escapes out of nothingness into a world of people and feeling and action?

For writers who proclaim loudly their inability to find on the shelf the ideal book at the necessary time, let them stop the fretting, sit down and dream for a while. Someone will appear, and in the end she may beckon all the others with her truly interesting problems that can end up as the *new* musical.

But it is people and not events which matter most because people make events. It is probable that without Adams, Jefferson, and Franklin, who were born to an intolerable situation, there might not have been a Declaration of Independence and a successful American Revolution. Without the personal excesses of King Louis

XVI and Marie Antoinette *plus* the American example there might have been no French Revolution. Ditto the one in Russia. History often creates men as leaders and articulators of causes—no matter, these men themselves become the *dei ex machinae* of them. And in life and therefore in theatre they are likewise the moving factors.

There is currently on Broadway a significant new musical built on an original idea—not an adaptation—which takes into account bookwise, lyrically, and musically what the past has had to offer and has successfully integrated with it meaningful present-day stylistic colorations. It is *Company*, with book by George Furth and music and lyrics by Stephen Sondheim.

It is a curious piece. It has created an enthusiastic cult—one which is better educated and more discriminating than the one that screams for *Hair*. *Company's* enthusiasts are also seasoned theatregoers, whereas many of *Hair's* are not and are therefore in no way able to discriminate between a bad and a good show; they are merely "turned on."

The critics of *Company* were nothing like in agreement with one another. Clive Barnes was "antagonized by the slickness, the obviousness. . . . But I stress that I really believe that a lot of people are going to love it. . . ." Walter Kerr in his weekly piece in the *Times* admired it tremendously and was disappointed. He ended, "Personally, I'm sorry-grateful." Douglas Watt in the *Daily News* loved it. Richard Watts in the *Post* found "*Company* disappointing." Most reviews admired the lyrics; there were differences about the music, and everyone loved Boris Aronson's set.

Before making my own comments I would like to describe this show. It is in two acts, each of which begins and ends with a surprise thirty-fifth birthday party for Robert, given in his apartment by his close friends—five married couples. The single set made of plexiglass is on two levels, with two elevators which allow the performers to go up and down with freedom. It is an abstract set that becomes—with light changes and some occasional furniture—anything desired: Robert's apartment, a park, a kitchen, a terrace, a discotheque, other living rooms, a bedroom, a garden apartment, etc. Due to the adaptability of the set and Harold Prince's direction, the action stops only at the one intermission; otherwise it remains fluid throughout.

Robert, the single leading man, appears in every scene. All of his friends love him. The question of his marrying is constantly being brought up by his friends, who themselves are constantly bickering in a variety of ways. Everyone feels that Robert is lonely. However, we do see him with each of three girls—with one of them sexually. He says he wants marriage but has never succumbed to it.

Robert's encounters with each of the married couples comprise almost the entire show—in fact, except for the encounters with the three girls, *all* of it. What he experiences are:

Couple A—husband on the wagon, wife dieting, both bickering. Wife is urged to demonstrate karate, which she is studying and now practices by overcoming her husband. (Both privately cheat; he drinks, she eats.)

Couple B are getting a divorce.

Couple C are high on marijuana.

Couple D are about to be married. The girl has changed her mind at the last minute, but when the disappointed groom leaves in the rain without his umbrella, she rushes after him and announces to Robert as she goes that she *will* get married. (Her objection to her groom is that he is "too sweet.") In every way, this scene is the most complete because the characters are more fully drawn.

In Act Two Robert encounters Couple B again. He is surprised to learn that they are actually divorced and the husband is living at home again with his former wife and "the kids" and they are happy.

Couple E are at a private discotheque with Robert. Wife is derisive of husband and propositions Robert, who is spared the embarrassment of an answer by the return of the husband from the men's room. Robert is not present at the final birthday party scene, but appears in it like a disembodied spirit.

The foregoing are the sum total of Robert's experiences with his five married-couple friends, all of whom love him and pity his loneliness. Between his encounters with Couples C and D, a girl, Marta, sitting on a park bench, begins to sing, "Another hundred people just got off of the train," etc. Robert enters and in front of the observant Marta encounters an airline stewardess, April, who thinks herself "dumb." As she exits, Marta continues: "And they find each other in the crowded streets and the guarded parks," etc.

Robert now encounters a third girl, Kathy. He says he wants to

marry her and she explains that she has wondered why he hadn't asked
her before. Her dialogue ties in with the theme of Marta's song:
"Some people have to know when to come to New York and some
people have to know when to leave." She is going to Vermont to marry.

Marta resumes her song. Robert sits on the bench with her, and
she tells him of her love for the city, especially 14th Street.

In the second act, between the first scene of the continuing birthday party and Robert's second encounter with Couple B, he goes to
bed with April, the stewardess, while his friends sing of his loneliness.

I think it is important to quote a line on marriage from each of
Robert's friends and his responses.

In Scene 1, at Robert's birthday party, Peter of Couple B says:
"And may this year bring you fame, fortune, and your first wife."

> ALL: Here, here.
> ROBERT: Listen, I'm fine without the three.
> JOANNA (Couple E): You bet your ass, baby.

In Scene 3 with Couple B:

> ROBERT: And, Peter, if you ever decide to leave her I
> want to be the first to know.
> SUSAN: Well. . .
> PETER: You're the first to know.
> ROBERT: What?
> SUSAN: We're getting divorced.
> PETER: We haven't told anyone yet.
> ROBERT: (pause—stunned): Oh, I'm. . .uh, so sur-
> prised. Maybe you'll work it out.

In Scene 4 with Couple C:

> ROBERT: Jenny, you're terrific. You're the girl I should
> have married.
> JENNY: Listen, I know a darling girl in this building
> you'll just love.
> ROBERT: What?
> JENNY: When are you going to get married?

DAVID: What?

JENNY: I mean it. To me a person's not complete until he's married.

ROBERT: Oh, I will. It's not like I'm avoiding marriage. It's avoiding me, if anything. I'm ready... But you know what bothers me... is, if you marry, then you've got another person *there* all the time. Plus you can't get out of it, whereas you just might want to get out of it. You are caught! See? And even if you do get out of it, what do you have to show for it? Not to mention the fact that...then...you've always been married. I mean, you can never not have been married again.

JENNY: I don't feel you're really ready. Do you think, just subconsciously...you might be resisting it?

ROBERT: No. Negative. Absolutely not! I meet girls all the time. All over the place. All you have to do is live in New York and you meet a girl a minute. Right now, I date this stewardess, cute, original....

Then he also refers to Kathy and Marta.

Robert ends that scene with a song, the first line of each stanza which I quote:

> Someone is waiting.
> Would I know her even if I met her?
> Someone will hold me,
> Did I know her? Have I waited too long?

In Scene 5 in the park during Robert's encounter with Kathy: "You wanted to marry me? And I wanted to marry you. Well then, how the hell did we end up such good friends?"

During Scene 6, when it looks as if Couple D is not going to get married, Robert tries to persuade Amy to go on with the wedding. Then Paul, the prospective groom, exits.

ROBERT: ...Amy, marry me.

AMY: What?

ROBERT: Marry me.

AMY: Huh? Isn't this some world? I'm afraid to get
married and you're afraid not to. Thank you, Robert.
I'm really. . .it's just that you have to want to marry
*some*body, not just some*body*.

In Act Two, Scene 2, April, the stewardess, comes to Robert's
apartment. After a brief scene they undress and go to bed. The
scene ends with an amusing duet (it's now morning and time to get
up).

ROBERT: Where you going?
APRIL: Barcelona.

In the course of the song Robert tries to persuade her to stay. The
duet ends:

APRIL: Oh well, I guess okay.
ROBERT: What?
APRIL: I'll stay.
ROBERT: But. . .[as she snuggles down] Oh, God![28]
(Blackout)

Scene 4 is in a private club. Robert is with Couple E.

JOANNA: Don't ever get married, Bobby. Never. Why
should you?
ROBERT: For company, I don't know. Like everybody
else.
JOANNA: Who else?
ROBERT: Everybody that fell in love and got married.
JOANNA: I know both couples and they're both
divorced. . .

Later in the same scene when Joanna's husband has gone to the
mens' room:

JOANNA: When are we going to make it?
ROBERT: (making light of it): What's wrong with now?

JOANNA: ...I'll take care of you.
ROBERT: But who will I take care of?

The husband returns.

In the final birthday party scene, Harry (Couple A) says: "It's all much better living it than looking at it, Robert."

Robert sings: "Being Alive."

It is my considered opinion that the score and lyrics of *Company* by Stephen Sondheim are the most satisfying, admirable, talented, polished, civilized, well-bred, knowledgeable, and attractive that I have found in any theatre for a very long time. They have quality and are thoroughly original.

In Douglas Watt's piece in the Sunday New York *Daily News* of May 3, 1970, he has summed up several things about the music with which I thoroughly agree:

> Sondheim has successfully bridged the gap between what we had become used to thinking of as show music and contemporary pop. There are rock elements in the *Company* score but they are introduced with skill and only at fitting places. Sondheim, as he has said in an interview, has welcomed the "freedom of form" rock allows but he is no slave to the idiom.
>
> He is, above all, always the theatre composer, always approaching each song situation in George Furth's book with intelligence and discrimination and, of course, with verve. There are Latin rhythms, which seem to be eminently suitable to the dreams that dance in the heads of a few of these people; there is a light-and-easy softshoe number, a march and—well, the variety you should expect in a musical.
>
> *Company*, then, points a way toward the future of our musical theatre. Sondheim accepts what was best in past musical devices and informs them with the expansiveness of today's.

I applaud this because I believe Watt has succeeded admirably in pointing out all that is most important in the music. The lyrics are

impeccably conceived as to character, situation, particularization, originality, variety, and cleverness of content as well as form.

The book might best be described in a musical term "Variations on a Theme." I believe that it would be possible to rearrange the sequence of most scenes in nearly any other order, and the impact of the show would be as about as effective as it is now. In other words, this kind of lackaday form therefore falls short of inevitability, which I cannot help feeling is a fault.

Also because we are presented with no fewer than five couples who are threaded together to comprise the whole, there is not time for any development in depth of any single character, including the principal one—Robert—who is a watcher, a casual participant, a person who does little and has very little done to him. (He is a great deal like Parsifal.) Much of his dialogue consists of monosyllabic reactions such as "Wow!" and workaday questions such as "Harry, could I have another bourbon?" Docile, non-active, non-interfering, adored, expressing few desires and no important ones and some studied apologies. What I have felt about the whole of the book— not the individual components, which are bright and witty—is that it does not quite add up. There is no conclusion. In the last song, Robert sings (ending):

> Someone to crowd you with love. . .
> I'll always be there as frightened as you,
> To help us survive. . .
> Being alive, being alive, being alive.

I feel that this is not a sufficient resolution to the theme of marriage: why or why not? What is more serious in my opinion is that the audience—even many other of *Company's* most enthusiastic admirers like myself—feel, at the end, cheated and unsatisfied. Sondheim tries heroically to create the wind-up in his final song, but that is insufficient.

I believe that this is due to several major factors: Robert is in all of it. Therefore he is the pivotal and leading character. In the end we have learned nothing about him other than the fact that his friends adore him and he is unmarried. Nothing more. He is an observer more than a doer in every scene. But most serious is the fact that

since he does not tell us what he does or doesn't want, we are deprived of any feeling of what we might or should or would like to want *for* him. In a sense we are deprived of feeling.

Henry Hewes in *Saturday Review* (May 9, 1970) says:

> . . .the end of the show suggests he [Robert] has abandoned the company of his friends to find such a person [defined in his last song] before it is too late.

Perhaps. But Mr. Hewes also calls "Barcelona"—a comedy song—"a dirge. . .the outcome. . .is romantic for her, but physically exhausting for him."

I feel strongly that this is not the point, but instead it is Robert's feeling that he wants something that—when he gets it—he no longer wants. Not at all unique in this world of sin and death.

Everyone has a different idea about the meaning of *Company*. Many of them are plausible. I have heard one which I was especially taken with: that Robert's friends feel their own needs to see Robert in their own situations—married—and that Robert never seems to be the leader in their discussions of his singleness. In other words, what bothers them in no way deeply concerns him. Perhaps.

But *Company* is always alive to everything else for us—the sound, the sight—and we are interested, but not quite satisfied by what to me is unresolved.

Still, this is the best new show since *West Side Story* and *Fiddler on the Roof*, and let us be eternally grateful for that and especially for Stephen Sondheim and for Harold Prince, who produced and directed it.

Without sounding like Pollyanna let me assure the reader that new good musical shows will be written. The very good older ones are by now permanent, and that is no small achievement. We also know that an era—an epoch probably—has reached not only its zenith but its end. That should not be a regrettable fact, because the best of what was made during it is universal, sturdy, and meaningful. Furthermore, it has become so definable that it now constitutes a model. Besides, that model is so identifiable that what follows now must do two things. The new shows must grow from those which have been best in the past, must profit by what was learned in their creation, their achievement, and secondly, what happens next must, like a grateful offspring, wave a fond farewell, then travel upward to the next plateau, finding the new, leaving the old behind without for a moment disclaiming it. By recognizing the shape that the old finally found for itself, the new can and must create its own based on acknowledgment as well as avoidance. Roots and discipline are both necessities and, most of all, feeling. The style and the shape will change. The fundamentals never do.

Whitman said it best:

> The past is the push of you, me, all, precisely the same,
> And what is yet untried and afterward is for you, me,
> all, precisely the same.

COMMENTS ON THE ORIGINAL MUSICAL

What better proof of the depth of Engel's understanding of the musical theatre than his devotion of the final chapter, a look forward, to an analysis of Stephen Sondheim's *Company*? Even though he has misgivings about it, he knows this is an important breakthrough, the most significant musical, he says, since *West Side Story* and *Fiddler on the Roof,* both, not so coincidentally, produced by Harold Prince.

Thirty years later *Company* remains the model for where the musical can go. There are a number of reasons for this. One is simply that no other composer has been allowed to experiment as much as Sondheim over the last few decades. These experiments have come at a cost. In the early years, creating such ambitious musicals as *Follies* and *Pacific Overtures,* Sondheim was able to rely on Prince's extraordinary track record as a producer. After the financial failure of *Pacific Overtures* and Prince's decision to retire from producing, that was no longer possible.

Even so, Sondheim created *Sweeney Todd* and *Merrily We Roll Along* within a commercial template. Starting with *Sunday in the Park With George*, he worked within the framework of not-for-profit theatres. Not-for-profit, of course, isn't entirely accurate, since many of the works these institutions produce are mounted in the hope there'll be a commercial transfer, which will indeed yield profit, enabling the theatre to continue.

With *Into the Woods*, the process was long and arduous. The production began at a theatre on the West Coast, moved to Playwrights

Horizons and then finally to Broadway, though that destination wasn't a certainty until shortly before it happened. In this respect Sondheim was treated no differently than a beginner might have been.

Nevertheless every Sondheim show represents a departure. Even the 1973 *A Little Night Music*, probably his most often revived show, was hardly guaranteed success. It was, after all, based on an Ingmar Bergman movie, admittedly one of his more accessible films but not necessarily the most surefire source.

Night Music contains Sondheim's most popular song, "Send in the Clowns," but it comes late in the evening, after a lot of musically subtle, quasi-operatic numbers. In this case the esthetic challenge Sondheim set himself—to do a show set in the 19th century in one of the predominant modes of that century, three-quarter time— was able to co-exist with material that was entirely entertaining.

Sondheim's daring has naturally been a magnet for young composers, though often they have a theoretical background rather than the Broadway orientation Sondheim had from the very beginning. It's often pointed out that Sondheim studied with Milton Babbitt, but his relationship with Babbitt (about whom it was once joked, while he had a residency at Princeton, that the university had built a computer to communicate with him) was not a formal student– teacher one. They were friends, and Babbitt, oddly enough, given the cerebral nature of his compositions, had started out as a Tin Pan Alley composer. The musical difficulties Sondheim presented grew out of the material he was wrestling with. He never construed difficulty with profundity.

Another reason *Company* remains a model for young composers is that it was the first musical to deal with the still troublesome issue of style. Several of the songs parody show business styles of earlier periods. ("You Could Drive a Person Crazy" mimics the harmonies of the Andrews Sisters; "Side by Side" sounds like a soft shoe number of decades earlier.) Sondheim would carry this parody technique even further in his next score, *Follies*.

In *Pacific Overtures* it was as if he were using the structures of Japanese art to give his own work a spine. One of the songs, for example, is based on haiku. But the most ambitious song in the score, "Someone in a Tree," has no Asian model. It has a repetiveness akin to the "iterative" music of Adams and Glass that was beginning to be heard in serious circles in the mid-Seventies. But the mounting tension that stems from the repetition wasn't an abstract choice. It's a musical representation of the conundrum in the lyrics—how baffling it is even for someone present at a historical moment to understand it.

Style had not been an issue for Sondheim's predecessors. Gershwin didn't have to decide what style he would compose *Of Thee I Sing* in; he could simply compose it in the style of Gershwin. (For *Porgy and Bess* he absorbed the African-based harmonies and rhythms of the Gullah people during a brief stay on an island off the coast of South Carolina, but the style of the opera is ultimately still Gershwin.)

Even Rodgers, working on *The King and I*, never considered writing it in some amalgam of Western and Eastern music (with the possible exception of the nonverbal "March of the Siamese Children," but its harmonies are adventurous in a Western manner rather than based on, say, the tonalities of gamelon music). Rodgers did use a Chinese form, the pantoum, for "I Am Going to Like It Here," a song in *Flower Drum Song*. But throughout his nearly sixty-year long career, working with a handful of collaborators, he wrote in a style that is always recognizably his own.

An early instance of a composer reaching to a foreign cultural idiom to build a score is Richard Adler's 1962 African-based musical *Kwamina*, which begins with a choral number in the fresh, dazzling harmonies of, say, Hugh Masakela, a name that wouldn't have been recognizable to an audience in 1962. Only now can we appreciate how superbly Adler absorbed his models.

As we've seen, until the Fifties, there was no disparity between the style of theatre music and that of popular music. They were essentially the same. As late as the early Fifties, for example, jazz trumpeter Miles Davis did a treatment of Leo Delibes' *The Maids of Cadiz*, a chestnut from 19th century French opera. In 1956, Frank Sinatra recorded one of his most haunting albums, *Close to You*, arranged, as most of his albums were, by Gordon Jenkins. This time, however, Jenkins didn't provide the usual backup, a full symphonic orchestra, but rather one of the pre-eminent classical chamber groups of the mid-20th century, the Hollywood String Quartet. On a TV variety show in the early '60s Dinah Shore, Ella Fitzgerald and

Joan Sutherland joined forces to sing "Three Little Girls From School Are We," from Gilbert and Sullivan's *The Mikado*.

What clearer illustrations of the unity of pop, classical and jazz could you find? By 1970, when *Company* opened, these varying strands had almost nothing in common, which explains why composers increasingly turned to styles of other periods, in part because it could be assumed the older musical forms were comprehensible, languages everyone understood,

Show business styles themselves became a form of shorthand to communicate to audiences (whose prime musical reference had become rock). Kander and Ebb's 1975 *Chicago* uses a witty, pungent version of Twenties jazz to frame its treatment of crime as a branch of show business. When the show originally opened, under the direction of Bob Fosse, it had an ominous quality to it. At one point an American flag filled the back wall, reminding the audience of its recently concluded misadventure in Vietnam. When City Center Encores! revived it in the spring of 1996, six months after the O.J. Simpson trial, *Chicago* projected a whole new set of references, and its artful playfulness was easier to perceive and appreciate.

Follies is based not only on musical genres that were old-fashioned in 1971 but also on theatrical models that had been outmoded. It was a way of suggesting, as he had in *Company*, how our understanding of relationships can be as mired in the past as our understanding of entertainment.

What this reliance on other styles reflects is a kind of breakdown in the lines of communication between the theatre and its audience. If you look at the opening night reviews of *Oklahoma!* in 1943, you see they were very good, but none suggesting that what happened at the St. James Theatre the night before was epochal. It was the audience, not the critics, who understood that *Oklahoma!* spoke to something deep in the American psyche. In March of 1943, Americans were embroiled in a world war far more trying than anything they'd ever known. But they understood that the title song spoke of the promise, the limitless possibilities of America, and they responded to it fervently.

There is also, in *Oklahoma!*, despite its patriotic underpinnings, a suggestion of a troubled world far from wartime optimism. It's the world of Jud, reflected both in the jagged edges of music and lyrics and even the unsettling orchestration of "Lonely Room." (In the late Seventies, Broadway wags used to remark that if Harold Prince had directed the original *Oklahoma!* it would have been titled *Jud!*)

By the time of *Company* we were preoccupied with the implications of The Lonely Room. Even the song "Barcelona," a duet, takes place in a Lonely Room. Laurey and Curley may spar in the love songs of *Oklahoma!* but we know they'll hit the hay together in the end. There's nothing quite so reassuring in any of Bobby's relationships in *Company*.

Company was based on a series of playlets playwright George Furth had written for Kim Stanley. It was Prince who suggested they be made into a musical. Interestingly, in the course of their work together, Sondheim and Furth shifted the focus from whatever female characters Stanley might have played to Robert, the single man with whom all the other characters are obsessed.

At the prompting of director Sam Mendes, who staged *Company* at the Donmar Warehouse in 1995, Sondheim and Furth restored some earlier discarded lines that referred to affairs Bobby had had with men. These lines suggested one reason he was having difficulties committing himself to one woman.

Oklahoma! was created in a world of near certainties. *Company* reflected a world in which the only certainty was that there were none.

One fascinating thing about *Company* is that Sondheim developed a mode for its non-parody numbers that seemed absolutely contemporary—edgy, frenetic, but also cool. Leonard Bernstein, who first explored contemporary idioms in his ballet *Fancy Free* and his orchestral piece *The Age of Anxiety*, not to mention the early musicals he wrote with Comden and Green, created a "modern" vocal style for his opera *Trouble in Tahiti*, but its tongue is always in its cheek. It lacks the directness or cutting quality of the music and lyrics of, say, "Barcelona."

Sondheim's style, which he began to develop in the 1964 *Anyone Can Whistle*, was perfect for the material. In the thirty succeeding years, with the exception of *Follies*, which jumps backward and forward in time, Sondheim did only one show that had a contemporary setting, *Merrily We Roll Along*, which started in about 1980 and worked its way back to the Fifties. That was the only time (except for some moments in *Sunday*) that he revisited the mode he'd created for *Company*. Most of the other shows are set in time frames and locales for which that style would be inappropriate.

If Sondheim has seldom revisited the style he brought to perfection in "Another 100 People" and "Not Getting Married," many others have. It's the style many young composers employ because it's virtually the only non-rock idiom they know that reflects the contemporary scene. Sondheim's work can be seen as a hybrid that grows out of plants with deep roots. His imitators are creating hybrids based on a hybrid.

Company is unquestionably musical comedy, but as Sondheim's career progressed he blurred the lines between musicals and opera. *A Little Night Music* is often done by opera companies. So is *Sweeney Todd*. In both cases many of the parts are well served by operatic voices. But Mrs. Lovett, the crafty baker in *Todd*, could be sabotaged if the voice were too pretty or if the singer has the common operatic practice of suppressing consonants. Mrs. Lovett comes alive when we hear Sondheim's brilliant lyrics; beauty of tone is irrelevant. In this case you absolutely want Angela Lansbury, not Joan Sutherland.

A potential candidate for the opera house is the 1994 *Passion*. By comparison to all the other Sondheim shows, this one, based on a film based in turn on a 19th century Italian novel, has a genuinely operatic theme—a soldier becoming obsessed with a sensitive, tragically ill and tragically ugly woman. It's the kind of material that might have attracted Verdi.

In some ways *Passion* is Sondheim's most economical score. The same themes, sometimes only six or seven notes in length, are recycled over and over. Even the grandest of its songs tends to have a simple melody that pivots back and forth over a few notes, sometimes building to moments of incandescent power, a reflection of the grotesque, harrowing but compelling love story. The dramatic scenes that link these musical numbers tend to be very short.

Whereas *Company* ends with a relatively young man singing ambiguously about "Being Alive," *Passion* ends with a woman on the point of death affirming life with a new fervor. Sondheim's is both a philosophical and musical journey that's remarkable and a testament to what was possible in the musical theatre in a period that overall seems undistinguished.

Traditional Broadway voices and vocal techniques might not be adequate for the demands of the music, technically or emotionally. The operatic structure of *Passion* is likely to inspire younger composers, but they lack Sondheim's ability to reduce technical complexities to emotionally involving themes.

The journey from *Company* to *Passion*, from a contemporary musical about the contemporary fear of commitment, to an operatic musical set in the 19th century and full of 19th century erotic sweep, couldn't have been foreseen when Engel wrote *Words With Music*. He would have been sympathetic to Sondheim's ambitions because he would have seen that musical theatre and opera have always been related.

In his perplexity over and disdain for the direction of contemporary pop music, Engel couldn't have foreseen that Sondheim, rather than succumbing to the surrounding culture's embrace of rock, would embark on a totally independent journey, in which he created his own musical language in the service of the theatre. At the beginning of Sondheim's journey it was feasible for other composers to follow his various leads. He has now reached a peak that doesn't permit easy imitation.

Engel wrote *Words With Music* at a moment that seemed bleak. What is now clear is that the period in which what we might call "iconic" musicals was over. With the exception of the Sondheim shows and a few others, the shows of the intervening thirty years are not "iconic" in the way that those of Rodgers and Hammerstein, Lerner and Loewe or Cole Porter, to cite a few examples, are.

That doesn't mean great shows have not nor will not be written. But we're no longer in an era when the musical is a pivotal form. When Engel wrote his book even he couldn't fully understand that that period was over. Throughout the 19th century, opera was a pivotal form. Operas continue to be written but they don't occupy the role they did when the form itself was central to the culture. The same is now true of musicals.

Whenever I grow pessimistic about the theatre, I force myself to remember a line from a guidebook to New York that runs close to 800 pages. Only two of those pages are devoted to the theatre, and the very brief chapter concludes with this sentence: "The era of sterling drama and talented actors is in the past, perhaps never to return."

That sentence was written in 1868, when, by our standards, the era of sterling drama was not even a speck on the horizon. There was little reason for Engel to be optimistic in 1971 when he wrote *Words With Music*. But he knew that you have to look beyond the present. Anticipation, after all, is the essence of drama.

POSTSCRIPT

Between the time I finished the manuscript for this book and the moment when it was about ready for publication the musically dismal Broadway season of 2004–05 occurred. As each musical opened, from the appalling *Dracula* to the slight *Spamalot*, I had the awful feeling that *Words With Music* was hopelessly irrelevant. The only conclusion to be drawn from this season was that the American musical had become a cartoon.

There were the so-called "juke box musicals," in which the flimsiest of plots were harnessed to the pop favorites of The Beach Boys (*Good Vibrations*) or Elvis Presley (*All Shook Up.*) All these shows were the spawn of the idiotic *Mamma Mia*, which wedded ABBA hits to a plot that was not sophisticated enough for a good sitcom. (The first such show was actually *Leader of the Pack* in 1984, based on the songs of Darlene Love, but this was clearly an idea too far ahead of its time.)

There was an uninspired adaptation of *Little Women*. There was the totally synthetic *Brooklyn*, with a clichéd plot leading to a singing contest between two caterwauling divas.

Then there were the adaptations of movies—*Dirty Rotten Scoundrels*, in which a film not without subtlety was turned into a series of obvious caricatures, and *Spamalot*, a version of *Monty Python and the Holy Grail*. It was, in its own way, a "juke-box musical," since it was essentially a series of stage versions of the 1975 film's sight gags, which at the performance I attended were greeted by the same applause as the Elvis standards in *All Shook Up*.

Mind you, I will defer to no one in my admiration for Monty Python, whose wit remains striking and powerful three decades later. A sketch like the "All England Proust Recitation Contest" still takes my breath away. It reflects the fierce intelligence and

OxBridge education of the Pythons. It demonstrates their refusal to condescend to their audience. Amazingly they found a huge and disparate audience in America, where educational standards are not as high as those in England (then.) Since we have the original *Holy Grail*, why do we need a diluted imitation?

Spamalot begins as a sendup of medievalism. But in its second act suddenly the writers decided they needed some plot. The show becomes yet another show biz story. Show biz stories sometimes seem the only kinds of narratives our writers are equipped to handle, perhaps because they have been involved in show business from such an early age they have no experience of the lives "real" people live. This was pointed up a few years ago in a revival of Rodgers and Hammerstein's *Flower Drum Song*. The poignant story of several generations of Chinese-Americans coping with each other in a new land, which reverberated for many immigrant groups, was transformed into a forced show biz narrative. In *Spamalot*, the song "You Won't Succeed on Broadway" (unless you have something to attract a Jewish audience) seems a blatant and lame parody of *The Producers*.

Then there was William Finn's *The 25th Annual Putnam County Spelling Bee*. Admittedly I came to it with unreasonable expectations, having been so taken with the film *Spellbound*, which dramatized the stories of the contestants in the national spelling bee, many of them immigrants, so artfully that one felt one was watching something epic. By contrast, there was nothing even dramatic about the musical. It had Finn's typical meandering melodies and strained rhymes. Its characters were, with one or two *possible* exceptions, not even deeply enough drawn for a TV after school special.

What had any of these shows to do with Engel's analysis of the principles of musical theatre? Worse, why should anyone bother trying to understand these principles if the extraordinary commercial appeal of *All Shook Up* or *Spamalot* had nothing whatsoever to do with them?

It was easy to lament that Broadway had become a gawdy, expensive recyclable bin.

Then, at the very end of the season, *The Light in the Piazza*, with a score by Adam Guettel, opened. I felt an enormous sense of relief. What Engel had understood about the musical still mattered. More important, a young composer saw the musical as a way to address serious human situations. In a time when the entire culture is ado-lescent, for a composer of any age to do so is no small thing.

Based on a story by Elizabeth Spencer that was filmed 40 years ago with Olivia de Havilland and Yvette Mimieux, *Piazza* is about Clara, a young American girl who has been kicked in the head by a pony, retarding her mental growth. Her mother, Margaret, takes her to Italy, where she and her husband, who has grown distant from her, spent their honeymoon just after World War II. There Clara falls in love. Her mother is nervous about how much she should tell her prospective in-laws about her daughter's condition. Other obstacles present themselves, but ultimately she senses it is better to let Clara risk life with someone who genuinely loves her than return to an overly protected, possibly institutionalized life back home.

Spencer's story is an American contribution to a genre that was very popular in the early 1960s. Its close kin are *Never on Sunday* and *Zorba the Greek*, both of which are about "uptight" Americans who discover how to embrace life while traveling in Europe. (A darker version of the story was also told in Dino Risi's now forgotten but brilliant *Il Sorpasso*, translated in English as *The Easy Life*, in which the life-loving Vittorio Gassmann liberates the shy, self-abnegating Jean-Louis Trintignant with unexpectedly tragic results. Come to think of it, this material might be worth singing about.)

As soon as the overture to *Piazza* begins, scored for strings, harp, piano and winds, a sound both traditional, romantic, and fresh, I knew this would not be a cartoon. The show, with a book by Craig Lucas, begins in the piazza in Florence where Margaret and her hus-band began their married life, which has not gone as smoothly as she had hoped. Clara's hat is swept off her head by the wind and caught by a young Italian, Fabrizio, who immediately falls in love with her.

Although Guettel's music and lyrics are not without complexity, there is never any doubt about the powerful emotions in play. Fabrizio's first solo is in Italian, but its swoony melody, as sung by Matthew Morrison, requires no subtitles. By contrast, Clara's first song has a jaunty quality to it. There is something jarringly American, for example, about the way she sings the three syllables in Italy. By the end of the show, of course, she is singing in the throbbing rhythms and melodies of the country where she will begin her new life. Kelli O'Hara's musical and emotional growth as Clara comes to terms with Fabrizio and his family were both impressive. As Margaret, Victoria Clark conveyed a poised American matron whose own growth was far more complicated than her daughter's. Her final "aria" was shattering.

It is a score that grows with repeated hearing but even at the first exposure, when I could not absorb all the lyrics, its emotional impact was undeniable.

The tears that welled in my eyes at the end were certainly a response to the first "adult" musical I had seen in a long time. But I think they were also a way of registering my intense pleasure that the musicals that have been at the center of my life were not the outmoded form I had feared they had become.

Light in the Piazza vindicated Lehman Engel's thinking. More important, it made me realize that great musicals may indeed follow rules such as he proposes but ultimately they depend on things that cannot be codified—great gifts, such as Guettel's.

Notes

1. John Van Druten, in *Playwright at Work* (Westport, Conn.: Greenwood Press, Inc., 1953), comments, "Working within limits is an easier thing than working with none."
2. Alan Dale, critic for the *New York American*, expressed a rather widely held view when, in his review of *Lady, Be Good!* (1924), he wrote: "[the characters] have been jellied [sic] into some sort of a plot, which eluded me, as such plots invariably do, and I never worry. Let 'em go, I say. Why worry with plots?"
3. T. S. Eliot, *Murder in the Cathedral*
4. *Company* will be discussed later. Its conclusion is not altogether definite.
5. Richard Strauss wrote in a letter to his librettist regarding *Der Rosenkavalier*, "Don't forget that the audience should also laugh! *Laugh*, not just smile or grin!"
6. The current *Company* has a single-character principal who, according to him has not yet found his own "someone."
7. The successful revival of *No, No, Nanette* is, strictly speaking, a reproduction of the songs and the plot. The book is almost an entirely new one by Burt Shevelove. Of course this "revival" is a delight, but it would very likely seem quite unfamiliar to Vincent Youmans.
8. In *Oklahoma!* Oscar Hammerstein II wrote, "The corn is as high as an elephant's eye," which makes the image real and unusual. Incidentally, Hammerstein first wrote "cow pony's eye," then found that the corn was higher than that and that it would be hard for the ear to catch.
9. Oscar Hammerstein II wrote: "The job of the poet is to find the right word in the right place, the word with the exact meaning and the highest quality of beauty or power. The lyric writer must

find this word too, but it must also be a word that is clear when sung and not too difficult for the singer to sing on that note which he hits when he sings it."

10. "When I see a play and understand it the first time, then I know it can't be much good."—T. S. Eliot, *New York Post,* September 22, 1963.

11. In a letter to Richard Strauss, Hugo von Hofmannsthal, the poet-librettist, wrote: "My special qualities as librettist are perhaps not so hard to define—I build on contrasts to discover, above these contrasts, the harmony of the whole...."

12. Clive Barnes, in writing of Neil Simon's *The Gingerbread Lady* (1971) in *The New York Times,* said, in part: "What mattered was the superb verbal fancy, the really incredibly funny jokes that were both at the same time truthful and artificial. Truthful because they had the edge of wit and were always based on common sense; artificial because they made everyone talk alike, act alike."

13. In J. D. Salinger's *Franny and Zooey* (Boston: Little, Brown and Company, 1961), in a letter from Buddy, the following is written: "Years ago, in my earliest and pastiest days as a would-be writer, I once read a new story aloud to S. and Boo Boo. When I was finished, Boo Boo said flatly (but looking over at Seymour) that the story was 'too clever.' S. shook his head, beaming away at me, and said cleverness was my permanent affliction, my wooden leg, and that it was in the worst possible taste to draw the group's attention to it."

14. "Comedy is an escape, not from truth but from despair; a narrow escape into faith."—Christopher Fry, *Time*, November 20, 1950.

15. In a letter from Hugo von Hoffmannsthal to Richard Strauss, the former wrote, "The public is never *altogether* wrong."

16. Strauss wrote to Von Hofmannsthal, "It is terrifying how short the libretto is for *Tristan*, for instance, and how long it takes to perform."

17. The late Oscar Hammerstein II, in his Foreword to *The Rodgers and Hart Song Book* (New York: Simon and Schuster, 1951), wrote: "Music is a difficult subject—anybody's music. Words are easier to analyze. Everyone speaks and writes words. Few

can write music. Its creation is a mystery. There are mathematical principles to guide its constructions, but no mere knowledge of these can produce the emotional eloquence some music attains. We are made sad or happy, romantic, thoughtful, disturbed or peaceful by someone else's singing heart. To me this is the most exciting and inexplicable phenomenon."

18. George R. Marek, in his book *Opera as Theatre* (Harper & Row), makes erudite and convincing arguments for the theatricality of ten well-known and distinguished operas. It is interesting that he points out dramatic defects in Puccini's *Tosca*, which is generally regarded as highly dramatic. Of the first act of *Tosca*, Marek says: "The compression of the whole exposition is extreme. It is no wonder that the audience is bewildered, having little idea of what the scurrying and the secrecy are about. . . . Sardou not only takes the opportunity to acquaint us fully and vividly with the man who is Tosca's lover, but he shows us what a careful craftsman he is by detailing the measures taken to effect Angelotti's escape." Later (also Act One): "How does Scarpia choose this very church in his search for the escaped prisoner? We are not given even the barest hint of the means by which so soon and so surely he has traced the beast to its lair."

19. Shaw wrote: ". . . the truth is that instead of *Otello* being an Italian opera written in the style of Shakespeare, *Othello* is a play written by Shakespeare in the style of Italian opera."

20. Late in 1954 Loewe and Lerner had tried to adapt *Pygmalion*. As Lerner has said: "We had decided that *Pygmalion* could not be made into a musical because we just didn't know how to enlarge the play into a big musical without hurting the content. But when we went through the play again. . . we had a great surprise. We realized that we didn't have to enlarge the plot at all. We just had to add what Shaw had happening offstage." (From *The American Musical Theatre* by David Ewen)

21. "Most picaresque novels, novels of adventure, and plays adapted from them, have little or no plot. The hero wanders; he meets a man in this place, an old woman in that; he falls in love with a girl and leaves her; he falls in love with another girl, and she leaves him. In the end, he meets another girl, and marries her. This is a story. There is no 'why' to be answered. The

only answer would be that he kept on moving." John van Druten, *Playwright at Work*.

22. There are four "A" scenes in the show. These are transitional scenes during which the scenery "carries" the characters from one place to another.

23. "...it is not the plots of great novels that can be learned from or transposed to a new medium, but their language, their vision, their inner relationships and pressures."—Richard Gilman, writing in *Common and Uncommon Masks*.

24. John Buchan, in a much documented biography of Caesar, wrote: "He had an affair with Cleopatra. . . She had a son during the year whom she fathered upon him. . . ."

25. The 1971 successful revival of *No, No, Nanette* does not invalidate the above statement. In fact, it has nothing to do with it. The recent revival has a nearly 90 percent new book by Burt Shevelove, and it not only works well as a tasteful "entertainment," but as the characters are left two-dimensional as originally drawn, their songs—though enormously charming—are also two-dimensional and could therefore easily be inserted into a new book. Also as this musical comedy has no pretensions to emotional depth (who ever thought of such a thing in 1925?), character depth and situation depth are not even to be considered.

26. In *Hair*, "scene" refers to a subject or a group of people (as in Molière).

27. Webster's Third New International Dictionary, Unabridged.

28. "In this world there are only two tragedies. One is not getting what one wants, and the other is getting it. The last is much the worst; the last is a real tragedy!"—Oscar Wilde, *Lady Windermere's Fan*.

Bibliography

Baker, George Pierce, *Dramatic Technique*. Boston: Houghton Mifflin Co., 1919.

Belz, Carl, *The Story of Rock*. New York: Oxford University Press, 1969.

Brustein, Robert, *Seasons of Discontent*. New York: Simon and Schuster, 1965.

Burton, Jack, *Blue Book of Broadway Musicals*. New York: Century House, 1952.

Capote, Truman, *House of Flowers*. New York: Random House, 1968.

Cohn, Nik, *Rock*. New York: Stein and Day, 1969.

Correspondence between Richard Strauss and Hugo Von Hofmannsthal, The. London: Collins, 1961.

cummings, e.e., *Collected Poems*. New York: Harcourt, Brace & Co., 1938.

Dickinson, Emily. *Poems*. Cambridge: Harvard University Press, 1955.

Druten, John Van, *Playwright at Work*. New York: Harper & Brothers, 1953.

Ewen, David, *American Musical Theatre*. New York: Henry Holt & Co., 1958.

Fields, Joseph A., and Chodorov, Jerome, *My Sister Eileen*. New York: Dramatists Play Service, Inc., 1946.

Fields, Joseph A, *Wonderful Town*. New York: Random House, 1953.

Gassner, John, editor, *Best Plays* (7 volumes). New York: Crown.

Gershwin, Ira, *Lyrics on Several Occasions*. New York: Alfred A. Knopf, 1959.

Gilman, Richard, *Common and Uncommon Masks*. New York: Random House, 1971.

Gottfried, Martin, *Opening Nights*. New York: G.P. Putnam's Sons, 1969.

Green, Stanley, *The World of Musical Comedy*. New York: Ziff-Davis, 1960.

Grove's Dictionary of Music and Musicians. New York: The Macmillan Company, 1935.

Guernsey, Otis L., Jr., *Broadway Song & Story*. New York: Dodd, Mead, 1985.

Hammerstein, Oscar, II, *Lyrics*. New York: Simon and Schuster, 1949.

Hellman, Lillian, *Candide*. New York: Avon, 1970.

Ionesco, Eugene, *Notes and Counter Notes*. London: John Calder, 1964.

Kantor, Michael and Maslon, Laurence, *Broadway: The American Musical*. New York: Bulfinch, 2004.

Kerr, Walter, *Thirty Plays Hath November*. New York: Simon and Schuster, 1968.

Kerr, Walter, *Tragedy and Comedy*. New York: Simon and Schuster, 1967.

Kissel, Howard, *The Abominable Showman*. New York: Applause Books, 1997.

Laurents, Arthur, *West Side Story*. New York: Random House, 1957.

Lawrence, Jerome, and Lee, Robert E., *Mame*. New York: Random House, 1967.

Lerner, Alan Jay, *My Fair Lady*. New York: Coward-McCann, Inc., 1956.

Lerner, Alan Jay, *The Musical Theatre: A Celebration*. New York: McGraw-Hill, 1986.

Mandelbaum, Ken, *A Chorus Line and the Musicals of Michael Bennett*. New York: St. Martin's, 1990.

Marek, George R., *Opera as Theatre*. New York: Harper and Row, 1970.

Masteroff, Joe, *Cabaret*. New York: Random House, 1967.

Melville, Herman, *Billy Budd*. New York: A Signet Classic, 1961.

Michener, James A., *Tales of the South Pacific*. New York: Pocket Books, 1948.

Molnár, Ferenc, *Lilliom*. New York: Samuel French, 1945.

Mordden, Ethan, *The Happiest Corpse I've Ever Seen*. New York: Palgrave, 2004.

Oates, Whitney, and O'Neill, Eugene, Jr., editors, *The Complete Greek Drama*. New York: Random House, 1938.

Peyser, Joan, *The Memory of All That*. New York: Simon & Schuster, 1993.

Pinter, Harold, *The Birthday Party*. New York: Grove Press, Inc., 1959.

Pinter, Harold, *The Homecoming*. London: Methuen and Company Ltd., 1965.

Portantiere, Michael, editor, *The TheaterMania Guide to Musical Theater Recordings*. New York: Backstage, 2004.

Prince, Hal, *Contradictions: Notes on Twenty-six Years in the Theatre*. New York: Dodd, Mead, 1974.

Rado, James, and Ragni, Gerome, *Hair*. New York: Pocket Books, 1969.

Rigdon, Walter, editor, *Who's Who in the American Theatre*. New York James H. Heineman, Inc., 1965.

Riggs, Lynn, *Green Grow the Lilacs*. New York: Samuel French, 1931.

Rodgers and Hammerstein, 6 Plays of. New York: The Modern Library, 1942–1953.

Rodgers and Hart Song Book, The. New York: Simon and Schuster, 1951.

Scholes, Percy, editor, *The Oxford Companion to Music*. New York: Oxford University Press, 1960.

Shakespeare, William, *Plays*.

Shaw on Music. New York: Doubleday, 1955.

Shaw on Theatre. New York: Hill and Wang, 1958.

Shaw, George Bernard, *Pygmalion*. New York: Penguin Books, 1951.

Shevelove, Burt, and Gelbart, Larry. *A Funny Thing Happened on the Way to the Forum*. New York: Dodd, Mead and Company, 1963.

Singer, Barry, *Ever After*. New York: Applause, 2004.

Stein, Joseph, *Fiddler on the Roof*. New York: Pocket Books, 1965.

Thompson, Oscar, *Debussy, Man and Artist*. New York: Dover Publications, Inc., 1967.

Voltaire, *Candide*.

Wasserman, Dale, *Man of La Mancha*. New York: Random House, 1966.

Zadan, Craig, *Sondheim & Co*. Second Edition, New York: Harper & Row, 1989.

Index